Workplace Reform in the Healthcare Industry

Workplace Reform in the Healthcare Industry

The Australian Experience

Edited by
Pauline Stanton
Graduate School of Management
La Trobe University
Victoria

Eileen Willis
School of Medicine
Flinders University
South Australia
and

Suzanne Young
Graduate School of Management
La Trobe University
Victoria

palgrave
macmillan

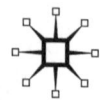

© Selection and editorial matter © Pauline Stanton, Eileen Willis and Suzanne Young Individual chapter © Contributors 2005

All rights reserved. No reproduction, copy or transmission of this publication may be made without written permission.

No paragraph of this publication may be reproduced, copied or transmitted save with written permission or in accordance with the provisions of the Copyright, Designs and Patents Act 1988, or under the terms of any licence permitting limited copying issued by the Copyright Licensing Agency, 90 Tottenham Court Road, London W1T 4LP.

Any person who does any unauthorised act in relation to this publication may be liable to criminal prosecution and civil claims for damages.

The authors have asserted their rights to be identified as the authors of this work in accordance with the Copyright, Designs and Patents Act 1988.

First published 2005 by
PALGRAVE MACMILLAN
Houndmills, Basingstoke, Hampshire RG21 6XS and
175 Fifth Avenue, New York, N. Y. 10010
Companies and representatives throughout the world

PALGRAVE MACMILLAN is the global academic imprint of the Palgrave Macmillan division of St. Martin's Press, LLC and of Palgrave Macmillan Ltd. Macmillan® is a registered trademark in the United States, United Kingdom and other countries. Palgrave is a registered trademark in the European Union and other countries.

ISBN-13: 978–1–4039–3571–7   hardback
ISBN-10: 1–4039–3571–8   hardback

This book is printed on paper suitable for recycling and made from fully managed and sustained forest sources.

A catalogue record for this book is available from the British Library.

Library of Congress Cataloging-in-Publication Data
Workplace reform in the healthcare industry : the Australian
  experience / edited by Pauline Stanton, Eileen Willis, &
  Suzanne Young.
     p. cm.
Includes bibliographical references and index.
  ISBN 1–4039–3571–8 (cloth)
   1. Health care reform–Australia. 2. Medical policy–Australia.
3. Public health administration–Australia. 4. Health services administration–Australia. 5. Health facilities–Australia–Personnel management. 6. Industrial relations–Australia. 7. Medical personnel–Australia. I. Stanton, Pauline, 1953– II. Willis, Eileen, 1946– III. Young, Suzanne, 1957–

RA395.A8W67 2005
362.1'0994–dc22   2005047310

10 9 8 7 6 5 4 3 2 1
14 13 12 11 10 09 08 07 06 05

Printed and bound in Great Britain by
Antony Rowe Ltd, Chippenham and Eastbourne

Contents

Foreword by Kerryn Phelps	vii
Acknowledgements	xi
List of Tables	xii
List of Figures	xiv
List of Abbreviations	xv
Notes on Contributors	xviii
Introduction	1
Pauline Stanton, Eileen Willis and Suzanne Young	

Part I The Australian Healthcare Sector

1. **Health Sector and Industrial Reform in Australia** — 13
   Eileen Willis, Suzanne Young and Pauline Stanton

2. **The Australian Healthcare Workforce** — 30
   Stephen Duckett

Part II Case Studies in Healthcare Reform and Workplace Change

3. **The Structure of Bargaining in Public Hospitals in Three Australian States** — 63
   Mark Bray, Pauline Stanton, Nadine White and Eileen Willis

4. **Outsourcing and Structural Change** — 91
   Suzanne Young

5. **Casual and Temporary Employment in NSW Regional Hospitals** — 112
   Alex de Ruyter

6. **The Processes of Workplace Change for Nurses in NSW Public Hospitals** — 131
   Nadine White and Mark Bray

vi Contents

7	**Work Intensification for Personal Care Attendants and Medical Scientists** *Eileen Willis and Kerryn Weekes*	150
8	**Emotional Labour and Aged Care Work** *Sue Stack*	170
9	**Flexibility at a Cost: Responding to a Skilled Labour Shortage** *Keith Townsend and Cameron Allan*	187

Part III   Future Challenges in Healthcare Reform and Workplace Change

10	**Inspiring Innovation** *Sandra G. Leggat and Judith Dwyer*	209
11	**Developing a Strategic Approach to People Management in Healthcare** *Tim Bartram, Pauline Stanton and Raymond Harbridge*	232
12	**Clinical Governance: Complexities and Promises** *Rick Iedema, Jeffrey Braithwaite, Christine Jorm, Peter Nugus and Anna Whelan*	253
13	**E-Health Services: Is the Future of Australia's Health Service in Offshore Outsourcing?** *Jan Sinclair-Jones*	279
14	**Conclusion: Reflections on Past Healthcare Reform and Future Directions** *Suzanne Young, Eileen Willis and Pauline Stanton*	298

Index — 307

Foreword

The healthcare system is multidimensional and complex. With shifting demographics, a constantly evolving workforce, increases in technology and rising expectations of consumers, healthcare reformists need to be cognisant that the consequences of change in one area may well reverberate throughout the entire system.

Depending on the political climate of the day, the perceived need for healthcare reform ebbs and flows. For many in the community, specifically people who find themselves in need of timely and excellent health care, and those of us who work within the system day to day, the desirability of health care reform is chronic and apparent.

In my role as President of the Australian Medical Association, I quickly realized that a prerequisite to any constructive involvement in reform of the Australian health care system is a detailed understanding of the territory, including the major players, the various levels of political responsibility, the interaction between the various medical groups and the politics between different types of health care providers. Not to mention the influence of the media and the expectations of consumers.

Given the intractable inertia that traditionally besieges the process of change in the health system, I admit I had to throw a few political grenades to provoke much needed action in areas like workforce planning, medical indemnity, and public hospital funding.

Sometimes, reform is part of an ideological master plan, but all too often it comes as a response to a media or lobbying 'blitzkrieg'. This in turn can result in piecemeal measures, populist announcements or, worse still, massive but poorly managed reform which leaves workers at the coalface struggling with the consequences of change.

Reform comes up against seemingly impenetrable obstacles, the most glaring example being the nature of health system administration between Federal, State and Territory governments. When I coined the phrase 'blame-shifting', it was in response to the frustration I was feeling about the endemic 'cost-shifting' between the different levels of government, who would then sit back and point the finger at each other as the perpetrator of the problems being faced by people within the system.

The division of responsibilities in the system also leads to groups of people, most notably the aged and indigenous communities who fall between the cracks. For example, a (Federal) under-resourcing of aged care places would leave a frail elderly patient in a far more expensive and less appropriate State-funded acute hospital bed.

Every five years the State and Federal health ministers would get together to argue about the size of the Federal funding pie, and who gets what share of it. This meeting is always preceded by posturing, media conferences, pronouncements of political positioning, the meeting goes ahead and, given that the States have no choice but to accept what is on offer, they all go back to their respective capital cities to reformulate their budgets.

The Federal-State system of health care administration and funding also means there is a much greater focus on tertiary care to the neglect of other healthcare sectors. This is largely because of the immediacy of need for acute hospital beds, and the very public exposure of deficiencies. Hence the stories of ambulances doing rounds of the city to find an emergency department open, sick neonates being airlifted all over the countryside, long waiting times for elective surgery and so on.

The longer term focus on health promotion and prevention strategies, or chronic community-based care just isn't top-of-mind and is in need of far greater attention. An issue emerging in the area of social justice is the problem of providing adequate medical care in rural and remote regions of Australia. Economic rationalists argument simply do not apply when it comes to providing quality healthcare to rural and remote populations, and a 'one size fit all' model cannot apply to all Australian communities. Local regional planning needs to be a precursor to healthcare delivery, taking into account the special needs of those populations.

This book looks at the impact of so-called 'New Public Management' on healthcare workers, and its sometimes unpredictable and perhaps unintended impact on medical scientists, nurses, or doctors in the early stages of their careers. The ultimate impact of a demoralized and undervalued healthcare workforce will be on patient care as good people are lost to the system because their concerns have not been addressed, or because 'efficiency' measures failed to take into account the impact they might have on professionals' work environment. In a health system with private and publicly operated workplaces functioning side by side, workers have choices. Industrial issues such as the piecemeal approach to enterprise bargaining across the country, sometimes complicated by the draconian presence of the ACCC, create inconsistencies and unrest.

In 2000 when I assumed the role of AMA President, I was confronted with a series of government workforce measures which began with the assumption that there was an 'oversupply' of GPs. This was repeated like a mantra throughout Health department documents and Health Ministers' statements. However, the word from the trenches told us that, far from being an oversupply, GPs were becoming scarcer by the day and those who remained were just keeping their heads above water. The workforce planning data had not taken into consideration the shifting gender balance in general practice, the move by many GPs to reduce their consulting hours in favour of other pursuits, how long they intended to keep working in general practice and so forth. An independent study commissioned by the AMA analyzed these trends and more, and the 'oversupply' became a drastic undersupply.

Looking to the future, planning of the Australian healthcare workforce will become increasingly complex following labour market flexibility initiatives such as part-time work and demands for a better work-life balance.

No view of the future would be complete without a discussion of e-medicine, which is on an exponential trajectory. There are very real concerns around possible negative impacts such as invasion of an individual's privacy. It has long been my view that advances in e-medicine, despite technical readiness, must be preceded by a careful consideration and public debate about the ethical and privacy implications of new information technology, and appropriate safeguards put in place.

And where do consumers fit into all of this? Certainly the various 'disease related support groups' do a magnificent job in rallying volunteers and raising awareness. A strong, single unified voice for consumers is lacking though and much of the advocacy for patient care falls to the healthcare professions who are exposed to the difficulties encountered by patients, and immersed in the deficiencies of the administration of healthcare on a daily basis.

Just as evidence-based medicine has become the trend in clinical practice, so should evidence-based principles be the gold standard in healthcare reform.

This book draws together some of Australia's foremost experts in the areas of healthcare reform and related industrial relations to examine the principles of healthcare reform and its implications for the people working within the public system. The authors also examine some of the lessons of the past, both in Australia and internationally.

Future healthcare reform must be informed by history. It must also be based on evidence and research, and a deep understanding of the complexity of this vitally important community sector.

I believe this book will be of tremendous value to anyone involved in the administration of healthcare and I would certainly recommend it to any aspiring future Health Minister.

Planning for future reforms must always bear in mind the bottom line...not just the financial implications of proposed changes in terms of costs or savings to governments, but the effects on people...people as healthcare workers, and most importantly, the quality of care delivered to people as patients.

Professor Kerryn Phelps
Adjunct Professor
School of Public Health and Discipline of General Practice
Faculty of Medicine
University of Sydney
President, Australian Medical Association 2000–2003

Acknowledgements

No text arrives on the bookshelves without the assistance of a number of people. This is especially so for edited collections such as this text that report on original research. We wish to extend our thanks to each of the contributors; all of whom worked patiently with us producing draft chapters on time and responding with good will to our various editorial demands. Many of the authors in this book have drawn on their original research done with health professionals around the country. Our thanks are also extended to these anonymous nurses, doctors, allied health professionals, managers, medical scientists, cleaners, orderlies and personal carers who gave of their time during what for many were turbulent times. Thanks are also extended to the many union officials and government bureaucrats and administrators who responded with candor to the probing research questions revealed in the chapters of this book. We are also grateful to our families; husbands, partners and children who provide the nurture so necessary for creative and productive work. Special thanks is also extended to Associate Professor Heather Gardner who gave us valuable advice and direction in the planning stages of this book. A final note our thanks is extended to the staff at Palgrave, particularly to Jackie Kippenberger and Shirley Tan from EXPO Holdings. Jackie showed the initial interest in the project, worked with us over the eighteen months the book came together and continued her support through to final production. Shirley displayed wonderful good naturedness and politeness that characterizes proof editors. It was a joy to work with her.

List of Tables

Table 2.1	Australia: number of persons in health occupations in health and other industries, 2001	32
Table 2.2	Costs of workforce imbalance	35
Table 2.3	Options for addressing workforce imbalances (shortage)	39
Table 2.4	Medical workforce policy recommendations	48
Table 5.1	The standard and non-standard workforce in Australia 1988–2000	113
Table 5.2	Public hospital, temporary and casual workforce, August 1999	117
Table 5.3	Public hospital: temporary and casual workers by occupational group (cohort), August 1999	118
Table 5.4	Private hospital: temporary and casual workers by occupational group (cohort), May 2000	123
Table 5.5	Private hospital, temporary and casual workforce by gender, May 2000	123
Table 5.6	Length of service, casual nurses, private hospital, May 2000	124
Table 6.1	The responsibilities of nursing unit managers	136
Table 6.2	Activity and performance data, NSW public hospitals, 1995/96–1998/9	140
Table 6.3	Activity data, division of medicine, hospital, 2000–2001	141
Table 7.1	Activity data and staffing numbers 1994–2000 Westernvale Hospital	157
Table 9.1	Pressure at work compared to employees in other industries (percentage)	195
Table 9.2	Employee perceptions of management and unions between Sympathy Hospital nurses and workers from other industries (percentage)	201
Table 9.3	Control over working time for nurses at Sympathy Hospital compared to employees in other industries (percentage)	203
Table 11.1	ANOVA of strategic human resource management for CEOs	242

List of Tables   xiii

Table 11.2	ANOVA of strategic human resource management for general managers	243
Table 11.3	ANOVA of strategic human resource management for human resource directors	244
Table 11.4	Aspects of HRM that your organization does particularly well at	245
Table 11.5	Barriers to practicing HRM in your organization	246
Table 11.6	Which areas of HRM could be improved?	246

List of Figures

Figure 2.1	Factors affecting health workforce supply	36
Figure 2.2	Australia: trends in nurses per 100,000 population, by state or territory, 1993–99	40
Figure 2.3	The Australian medical workforce, 2000	45
Figure 2.4	Australia: general practitioners per 100,000 population, 1984–85 to 2000	47
Figure 2.5	Australia: allied health workforce per 100,000 population, 1998–99	51
Figure 12.1	Collaborative and Inspectorial Concepts associated with Clinical Governance	259

List of Abbreviations

Abbreviation	Full title
AAMT	American Association for Medical Transcription
ABS	Australian Bureau of Statistics
ACHS	Australian Council of Health Care Standards
ACQSHC	The Australian Council for Quality and Safety in Health Care
ACTU	Australian Council of Trade Unions
AGPAL	Australian General Practice Accreditation Limited
AGREE	Appraisal of Guidelines for Research & Evaluation
AHIMA	American Health Information Management Association
AHMAC	Australian Health Ministers' Advisory Council
AHWAC	The Australian Health Workforce Advisory Committee
AHWOC	The Australian Health Workforce Officials Committee
AIHW	Australian Institute of Health and Welfare
AIMS	Adverse (or Advanced) Incident Monitoring Scheme
AIRAANZ	Association of Industrial Relations Academics of Australia and New Zealand
AIRC	Australian Industrial Relations Commission
ALP	Australian Labor Party
AMWAC	The Australian Medical Workforce Advisory Committee
AMA	Australian Medical Association
ANF	Australian Nursing Federation
ANOVA	Analysis of Variance
ASU	Australian Services Union
AWAs	Australian Workplace Agreements
AWIRS95	Australian Work and Industrial Relations Survey 1995
AWU	Australian Workers' Union
BLS	Bureau of Labor Statistics
BPO	Business Process Outsourcing
CEC	Clinical Excellence Commission
CEO	Chief Executive Officer
CFO	Chief Financial Officer
CHI	Centre for Health Improvement
CIAP	Clinical Information Access Project
CPSU	Community and Public Sector Union
DAIS	Department of Administrative Services

DEWRSB	Department of Employment, Workplace Relations and Small Business
DHHS	Department of Health and Human Services
DHS	Department of Human Services
DON	Director of Nursing
DOSA	Day of Surgery Admissions
DRG	Diagnosis Related Groups
EB	Enterprise Bargaining
EBA	Enterprise Bargaining Agreement
EBM	Evidence-Based Medicine
EFT	Equivalent Full-time
EN	Enrolled Nurse
EQuIP	Evaluation of Quality Improvement Program
GDP	Gross Domestic Product
GFM	General Functional Manager
GP	General Practitioner
HACC	Home and Community Care Program
HAREA	Health and Research Employees' Association
HCA	Health Care Assistants
HCCC	Health Care Complaints Commission
HCSU	Health and Community Services Union
HCSSA	Health and Community Services Staffs Association
HECS	Higher Education Contribution Scheme
HIC	Health Insurance Commission
HIPAA	Health Insurance Portability and Accountability Act
HIRSAC	Health Industrial Relations Strategic Advisory Committee
HITH	Hospital in the Home
HPA	Health Professionals Association
HR	Human Resources
HRD	Human Resource Director
HRM	Human Resource Management
HSUA	Health Service Union of Australia
ICE	Institute for Clinical Excellence (now CEC)
IBM GSA	IBM Global Services Australia
ICTs	Information Communications Technologies
ICU	Intensive Care Unit
IR	Industrial Relations
IT	Information Technology
ITES-BPO	Information Technology Enabled Services-Business Process Outsourcing
IVF	in-vitro fertilization
LHMU	Liquor, Hospitality & Miscellaneous Worker's Union

LOS	Length of Stay
MBS	Medical Benefit Schedule
MCOs	Managed Care Organizations
MDCs	Medical diagnosis categories
MHPB	Metropolitan Health Planning Board
MSAV	Medical Scientists Association of Victoria
NCA	National Commission of Audit
NCP	National Competition Policy
NDHP	National Demonstration Hospitals Program
NHS	National Health Service
NICS	National Institute of Clinical Studies
NPACC	National Pathology Accreditation Advisory Council
NPM	New Public Management
NRB	Nurses' Registration Board
NSW	New South Wales
NUMs	Nurse Unit Managers
OECD	Organization of Economic Collaboration and Development
OH and S	Occupational Health and Safety
PCAs	Personal Care Assistants
PSA	Personal Service Attendants
QIC	Quality Improvement Council
QNU	Queensland Nurses Union
RACGP	Royal Australian College of General Practitioners
RACN	Royal Australian College of Nursing
RCA	Root Cause Analysis
RCS	Resident Classification Scale
RN	Registered Nurse
SA	South Australia
SAC	Severity Assessment Code
SASMOA	South Australian Salaried Medical Officers Association
SHRM	Strategic Human Resource Management
TQM	Total Quality Management
UAP	Unlicensed Assistive Personnel
UK	United Kingdom
USA	United States of America
VA	USA Veterans Health Administration
VDP	Voluntary Departure Package
VHA	Victorian Hospitals Association
VHIA	Victorian Hospitals Industrial Association
VIRC	Victorian Industrial Relations Commission
VMO	Visiting Medical Officer
VPA	Victorian Psychologists Association

Notes on Contributors

Cameron Allan is a Senior Lecturer with the Department of Industrial Relations, Griffith University. His interests include employment relations in health and fast food, non-standard employment, working time, teaching and learning in higher education, and child labour.

Timothy Bartram is a Senior Lecturer in Human Resource Management in the School of Business at La Trobe University. He has a Bachelor's degree and Masters degree in Commerce from the University of Melbourne and a Phd from La Trobe University. His current research interests include human resource management in a unionized environment and linking people management practices to performance.

Mark Bray is Professor of Employment Studies and Head, Newcastle Business School, University of Newcastle. He has published on industrial relations and human resource management in a number of industries, including road transport, airlines, manufacturing and health care, while he has also published extensively on comparative industrial relations. He is the new lead author of the latest edition of the popular textbook Industrial Relations: A Contemporary Approach.

Jeffrey Braithwaite is Director of the Centre for Clinical Governance Research and Associate Professor in the School of Public Health and Community Medicine, Faculty of Medicine, The University of New South Wales. He has published widely on health sector policy and organizational issues. He has twenty-five years' experience in managing, researching and consulting in healthcare settings. His major current research interest is the multi-dimensional and politically rich organizational field we label 'the teaching hospital' and its status in various health sector and managerial policies.

Stephen Duckett is Professor of Health Policy and Dean of the Faculty of Health Sciences at La Trobe University. From 1994 to March 1996 he was Secretary of the Commonwealth Department of Human Services and Health. From 1983 to 1993, Professor Duckett held various operational and policy positions in the Victorian Department of Health and

Community Services and its predecessors, including Director of Acute Health Services, in which position he was responsible for designing and implementing Victoria's Casemix funding policy. He is currently Chair of the Board of Directors of Bayside Health (the metropolitan health service responsible for The Alfred, Caulfield and Sandringham hospitals), Chair of the Board of Directors of the Brotherhood of St Laurence and Convenor of the Council of Deans of Health Sciences. He was elected a Fellow of the Academy of the Social Sciences in Australia in 2004.

Judith Dwyer is Associate Professor and Head of the Department of Health Policy and Management at La Trobe University. She is a former CEO of Southern Health Care Network in Melbourne, and of Flinders Medical Centre in Adelaide. Her research interests are in health system governance and indigenous health care management.

Raymond Harbridge is Dean, Faculty of Law and Management, La Trobe University, Australia. He has written extensively about employment relations, human resource management and public sector forms over the past two decades.

Rick Iedema is Senior Researcher at the Centre for Clinical Governance Research and Senior Lecturer at the School of Public Health and Community Medicine, The University of New South Wales. He researches the organization of healthcare provision from a performative perspective. He has published over forty papers in the areas of discourse analysis and organization theory. His book, *Discourses of Post-Bureaucratic Organization*, was published in 2003. He is Co-Chief Investigator on a 4-year *Australian Research Council Linkage* project and Chief Investigator on a 3-year *ARC Discovery* project.

Christine Jorm is the Lead Medical Clinician for Quality at St George Hospital, Sydney. After 15 years as an anaesthetist she now works fulltime in the area of patient safety and quality. While involved in root cause analysis of serious incidents; implementation of evidence and change management are her preferred work roles. Her research interest is specialty medical culture and its interaction with the patient safety and quality agenda, and she is enrolled in a PhD at the Centre of Clinical Governance Research.

Sandra G. Leggat is with La Trobe University School of Public Health and has international and Australian experience in healthcare. She was a consultant with PricewaterhouseCoopers and the HayGroup, and has had a number of senior management roles, as Chief Planning Officer of the Inner & Eastern Health Care Network and in Canada, at The Toronto Hospital, Baycrest Centre for Geriatric Care and the Health Station. Sandra is co-editor of *Australian Health Review* and is a member of the Board of Northern Health in Melbourne.

Peter Nugus holds a BA (Hons) in Politics, an MA (Hons) in Sociology (University of New England) and a Graduate Diploma in Adult Education (University of Technology Sydney). Peter is a doctoral candidate in the Centre for Clinical Governance Research UNSW, using interviews, focus groups and observation to examine the talk and situated practices of cardiologists around issues of clinical safety.

Jan Sinclair-Jones is a Senior Lecturer in sociology in the Faculty of Media, Society and Culture at Curtin University of Technology. She has had a long-standing teaching interest in technology and work. Her research is currently focussed upon the telemediated relocation of service sector work from the advanced economies to India.

Sue Stack has many years' experience in human resource management and industrial relations in both the public and private sectors. Currently a contract researcher at the University of South Australia and principal training consultant for St. Paul's Ethics Services, her continuing research interests focus on issues affecting the health and aged care workforce.

Alex de Ruyter is a Lecturer in the Birmingham Business School, University of Birmingham, United Kingdom. His research interests are in non-standard employment, health sector restructuring and employee participation.

Pauline Stanton is an Associate Professor in the Graduate School of Management at La Trobe University, Melbourne. She has a background in industrial relations, healthcare management and project management in Australia and the United Kingdom. Her present research areas include health sector employment relations and human resource management effectiveness.

Keith Townsend is a Lecturer in the Department of Industrial Relations, Griffith University. He has previously published in the areas of working time, employee resistance and managerial control, work intensification and work teams.

Kerryn Weekes is a practising medical scientist in the fields of haematology and genetics and has worked in both diagnostic and research laboratories in Australia and overseas. Her interest in work related stress evolved from her time as an industrial representative during the early 1990's, which led her to postgraduate studies in this area.

Anna Whelan is Senior Lecturer at the School of Public Health and Community Medicine, Faculty of Medicine, The University of New South Wales. Her research interests include the organization and management of public health services (especially multicultural health services, refugee health services and Aboriginal health services), international health systems (especially human resource management), diversity management and leadership (ways of working with diverse groups, communities and workforces), and reproductive health services.

Nadine White is a Lecturer in the School of Business and Government at the University of Canberra, and a PhD candidate in the Newcastle Business School at the University of Newcastle.

Eileen Willis is Senior Lecturer in the School of Medicine at Flinders University, South Australia. Her research interests include theoretical approaches to working time, workload measuring tools, enterprise bargaining and the impact of workplace innovation and reform on nurses and early career doctors.

Suzanne Young is Senior Lecturer in the Graduate School of Management at La Trobe University Victoria. She has taught in both undergraduate and postgraduate programs and specializes in organizational theory, organizational behaviour, industrial relations and strategic management. Her research areas include; the public sector, organizational structures and industrial relations.

Introduction

Pauline Stanton, Eileen Willis and Suzanne Young

Background to the collection

This book is the culmination of the research of a number of Australian scholars in the fields of employment relations, health policy, health sociology, health economics and health services management. In the first instance it arises from the three editors' doctoral studies, carried out between 1994 and 2004. We began our PhD research at a time when healthcare reform was high on the agenda in Australia; we were concerned with the impact of these reforms on the work of various health professionals and on the quality of care extended to patients. During this period we found ourselves presenting work-in-progress papers at the Association of Industrial Relations Academics of Australia and New Zealand (AIRAANZ) annual conferences and other related conferences. Sometimes the conference organizers would program us in the same session, for example making *health* a case study in employment relations, at other times we were separated by themes such as *human resource management, enterprise bargaining, casualization, labour flexibility* or *working time*. Through this process we discovered other academics with similar interests and it became clear that while there were many similarities in our investigations, there were also differences in our research approach, discipline orientation or theoretical explanations. It is this that has provided the underlying challenge to this research collection and we believe it is this that makes the text unique. The questions raised in this Introduction, the framework outlined in Chapter 1 and responded to in Chapter 14, recognize the tensions and synergies created in bringing these disciplines together to explore the impact of health and industrial relations reform on the work of health professionals and the quality of care delivered to those who are sick.

Some of the authors contributing to this collection are situated within generalist management or business schools and their work appears in the traditional management and employment relations literature (For example, the Journal of Industrial Relations, Labour and Industry and the New Zealand Journal of Employment Relations.) Other authors are situated within schools of medicine or departments of public health and their work has appeared in other texts on healthcare reform and change in Australia, usually textbooks with a focus on politics or economics (For example, Palmer and Short, 1994; Gardner, 1997; Mooney and Scotton, 1998; Bloom, 2000; Barraclough and Gardner, 2002). The challenge in organizing this book has been to use the strengths of the disciplines in order to provide both a descriptive account as well as a set of broad theoretical arguments addressing the impact of both healthcare and industrial relations reform on the work of health professionals.

British and USA research on healthcare reform

Our underlying rationale for this book is that despite a decade of reform within the health sector and in industrial relations in Australia there had been little work published that has attempted to systematically or theoretically explain the way in which both reform processes act as a set of coherent strategies in the management of health workers. A number of scholars within the sector are recording the changes, but few are incorporating industrial relations reform into their analysis. Given the proliferation of published work coming out of the United States of America and Britain this seemed strange and in need of rectifying. In our own research we were reading British work by Harrison and Pollitt (1994), Bach (2000), Ham (1994), Ham and Øvretveit (1998), Dent (1998), Harrison and Ahmad (2000) and North American commentaries by Leicht and Fennell (2001). These social and political commentators were not just recording events, but were analyzing the outcomes in terms of the impact the changes had on major sociological, economic, political, industrial and professional themes. These included the impact of New Public Management (NPM) and industrial relations strategies on professional relationships and work, shifts in the understanding of medical dominance and professional autonomy, and the incorporation of some doctors into the state's agenda through the reform processes. From the perspective of health sociology this is very much a critical *Sociology of health* (Cockerham, 1978). From the perspective of health policy and employment relations these researchers were also using *health* as a case study to illustrate the impact of the new managerialism and industrial relations on the public sector.

While there is considerable commentary in Australia, mainly by political scientists, but also economist, sociologists, public health advocates and epidemiologist on health reform, these accounts tend to incorporate explanations derived from political and economic theory such as neo-liberalism and the associated economic rationalism (Bloom, 2000). They rarely explore the impact of industrial relations changes or the way in which industrial relations policy acts in concert with NPM practices and impacts on the delivery of health care from the perspective of the employee. Further, on the other side of the disciplinary fence few researchers in employment relations appear interested in the health sector, and within the discipline of sociology, scholars appear to have retreated to explorations of the corporal body, rather than the body politic. Within industrial relations literature there are exceptions, for example Braithwaite's work in the early 1990s (1997) and Buchanan and Considine's recent studies of work intensification in nursing in New South Wales (2002) and Victoria (1999). Within sociology, exceptions include; Collyer (1997), White and Collyer (1998) and Grbich's (2002) studies on privatization of public hospitals and White's (2001) study of the corporatization of general practice. However, none of these accounts provide a systematic approach that deals directly with the industrial relations implications. There are a number of possible explanations for this apparent lack of interest in the intersection of microeconomic health and industrial relations reform and the NPM. For example there are often difficulties in accessing health professionals, particularly doctors; difficulties of understanding the language of healthcare; and that hospitals deal with vulnerable humans in intimate contexts where ethical issues loom large. Also that most of the events outlined in this book occur in the public sector which perhaps is not of interest to industrial relations researchers with their focus on the manufacturing, factories, mining and call centres. It is also possible that there are gender issues here as the health sector is largely female dominated and that there is a general belief that women do not join and participate in trade unions to the extent that men do. However, if as Bryan Turner (1987) has argued *health* and *healthism* have replaced religion as the means of salvation for many citizens in western industrialized secular societies, this neglect is indeed intriguing, particularly as the sector is labour intensive and a number of the professional unions are increasing their union membership against a background of international decline. This book attempts to redress some of the gaps by bringing together the work of a number of researchers across the disciplines.

The organization of this book

This text is divided into three discreet parts. In the first part the reader is introduced to the Australian healthcare sector, key factors in the reform process and the issues surrounding workforce planning and development. In Chapter 1 we provide an overview of the Australian healthcare system in terms of its structure, funding arrangements and breadth. This discussion is situated within a broader framework that argues that the reform processes of the last decade can be understood as a highly organized and systematized set of strategies instituted by the state. These strategies include broad-based industrial relations reform, specifically enterprise bargaining and the introduction of the principles of the NPM into the public sector. Neither of these strategies is peculiar to the healthcare industry, but is system wide, with some variations that are explored throughout this text.

An important point alluded to in Chapter 1, is the shared funding relationships between the Commonwealth and states. Healthcare in Australia is funded by all three levels of government; federal, state and local. While local government is usually defined as a cluster of suburbs headed by a mayor and councillors who may or may not have links or allegiances to the major political parties, this is not so for the states and territories. The major political parties operate at both federal and state level. As a consequence it is possible to have a conservative party; such as the Liberal Party in coalition with the National Party in power at the federal level, and the Australian Labor Party in power in any number of states, and of course vice versa. The consequences of this for funding and policy direction can make for considerable conflict and gamesmanship. A further complexity is the two tiered system of elected representation, or upper and lower houses that characterize the federal and state systems of government. At the federal level, policies and laws are introduced by the party in power via the lower house, or House of Representatives, which is made up of directly elected members of either party. This legislation must pass through the upper house or Senate. However, it is not unusual for the Senate to have a majority of members from the parties in opposition making it difficult for the government of the day to enact legislation.

In Chapter 2, Stephen Duckett takes a similar approach to that taken in Chapter 1 by first describing the health workforce and the processes used by the state, various government agencies and committees, along with professional associations in planning for an adequate supply of doctors, nurses, allied health professionals and other health-related occupational groups. The second thrust of Duckett's chapter is to outline the political and logistical complexities of this task. These include the impact of the feminization of the medical workforce, the difficulties of providing adequate health cover for people in rural and remote regions of Australia, where few doctors wish to practise, and the political squabbles that loom over the division of labour in healthcare; the most prominent being the role of the Nurse Practitioner as a substitute doctor. As a final point, Duckett explores the lack of human resource policy and training for all health professionals, including the challenges in multi-disciplinary teamwork and the impact of the various reforms on the quality of care. This is a tantalizing hint to content that makes up Part 2 of the book.

In Part 2 of this book seven case studies illustrate the nexus between the neo-liberal strategy of the NPM, industrial relations and healthcare reform. In Chapter 3 Bray, Stanton, White and Willis provide a series of examples of the way in which broadly-based industrial relations reform has been introduced in different states. We read that decentralization of industrial relations through enterprise bargaining (EB) was a core reform strategy in the states of Victoria and South Australia, but not in New South Wales. This raises questions about the role EB played in achieving productivity and efficiency improvements in the sector and whether decentralization really took place. In Chapter 4 Young moves away from industrial relations reform to outline the impact of the implementation of the National Competition Policy and NPM strategies during an era of budget constraint on two public hospitals in the state of Victoria during the 1992–99 Liberal–National Government. As she demonstrates, the process of outsourcing non-core health services of public pathology, radiology and various maintenance functions, down-sizing and redundancies was not uniform across the sector. Individual managers and decision makers, including health professionals, did exercise agency in this process based on their understanding of the broader political and social environment and the needs of patients.

In Chapter 5 de Ruyter continues the commentary on the rural-urban divide when he notes that the impact of casualization on nurses is not uniformly negative. When proponents of workforce flexibility pushed for non-standard hours and employment arrangements in the 1990s they argued that these arrangements could facilitate family friendly workplaces (Mathews, 1989). However, de Ruyter introduces another dimension into the equation of significant relevance to the Australian context; this is the divide between metropolitan and inner city, regional, rural and remote health services. Consistent with Duckett's comments on the difficulties facing policy makers in coming up with a workable rural workforce strategy, and Young's point that differences occurred across the rural-urban divide in implementing the government's competition policy, de Ruyter shows that a policy of casualization impacts differently on different segments of the population. Attitudes to casualization are shaped by the age, gender, life-style and aspirations of workers, along with the social and physical environment and economic cost of living and working in a large sprawling megametropolis such as Sydney.

Chapter 6, by White and Bray provide both a theoretical framework and case study on work intensification for nurse unit managers in a large public hospital in regional New South Wales. We see in this chapter evidence of work intensification independently of the industrial relations mechanisms of enterprise bargaining. The authors also provide evidence of increasing workload and work intensification for middle managers within the profession of nursing that resonates with Willis and Weekes account of medical scientists and personal service attendants outlined in Chapter 7. The theme of work intensification is picked up by Willis and Weekes through an exploration of two very different occupational groups; personal service attendants (PSAs) and medical scientists. In making their argument, Willis and Weekes demonstrate the synergies that occur in a complex organization when a range of workers experience significant workplace change.

Chapters 8 and 9 can be read as cautionary commentaries on the case studies discussed to date. Chapter 8 and 9 present two case studies that outline the dangers inherent in any attempt to intensify or overly control the work of health professionals. In Chapter 8 Stack uses the sociological theory of emotional labour and work to illustrate the impact on the personal sense of professionalism and vocation of care workers. She shows clearly that the economic constraints built into managed care impact on health workers' sense of themselves as caring humans. Read in conjunction with Chapter 9, by Townsend and Allan, readers will not be surprised to learn that some health units are now finding it difficult to recruit adequate nursing staff. As Townsend and Allan indicate this is a national and global problem, particularly in western nations that have engaged in a process of healthcare reform with a focus on budget constraint, with little thought of the impact these policies might have on professional commitment. Coupled with the feminist movement, which has encouraged women to think beyond the traditional careers of nursing and teaching, recruitment and retention are now serious issues being addressed at global, national, state and local hospital level.

Part 3 of this book brings together the responses of the state, health professionals, human resource managers and the private for-profit sector in the design of 21st century strategies to curtail healthcare costs and increase productivity and efficiency. In Chapter 10, Leggat and Dwyer note that both federal and state governments funded a range of innovation programs during the 1990s alongside the industrial relations and funding-related reforms. Examples include the Coordinated Care Trials, the National Hospital Demonstration Program, and the Clinical Support System Program under the auspices of the Royal Australian College of Physicians. Innovations instigated under these programs took two forms; one focusing on managerial and system-based change, the other on evidence-based medicine (EBM). Leggat and Dwyer direct their attention to the human resource and managerial qualities needed to facilitate innovation in healthcare, rather than medically controlled evidence-based care innovations. They note that organizations and agencies are now encouraged to amalgamate into larger units where economies of scale can be optimized; and to encourage inspirational leaders, work teams and organizations.

These shifts and the subsequent tensions created are explored in detail by Bartram, Stanton and Harbridge in Chapter 11. They suggest that the challenge now facing human resource managers is a cultural change from control of, to commitment by, individuals to the organization's goals. Strategic human resource management could seek to capture the hearts and minds of professionals to the degree that these workers themselves assiduously seek better ways of working that can contribute to organizational outcomes. However, they also highlight the complex web of powerful stakeholders and the vested interests in which healthcare managers operate. These include governments who set direction and often control and monitor through funding policy, and professional associations and trade unions who act on behalf of their members. Such an environment presents enormous challenges for the practice of strategic human resource management at the organizational level.

Chapter 12 by Iedema, Braithwaite, Jorm, Nugus and Whelan can be read as a discourse analysis of Evidence-based Medicine (EBM) and clinical governance. This research team based at the Centre for Clinical Governance within a school of Public Health and Community Medicine state categorically that models of clinical governance are a choice between improved productivity defined as the reduction of risk and adverse events that works in a collaborative way with clinicians or one that operates as a technology for surveillance and blame. The direction taken by the state at the level of policy and bureaucratic prescription will, to a large extent, determine how the profession of medicine and other health professionals cooperate amongst themselves and with management. However, it should be noted that these authors do not reduce clinical governance simply to a more sophisticated strategy instigated by the state in the interests of efficiency; they argue that doctors also wish to improve practice.

In the final case study in Chapter 13, Sinclair-Jones alerts the reader to a future where electronic records and diagnosis may very well cross the continent in search of cheaper or more efficient labour. In this scenario the old divisions between north and south, core and periphery, primary and secondary labour markets may well collapse. As Sinclair-Jones illustrates, the future of e-medicine is off shore in countries like India where highly educated and trained middle class health professionals perform transcription or diagnostic work at a reduced cost to the attending specialist. This is outsourcing on a grand scale.

Concluding comments: what this book does not do

It is also true that the 1990s was characterized by a number of significant technological advances in medical and related technology that would surely have changed the nature of healthcare work independently of industrial or health policy reform. These technological advances have certainly strained capped budgets in both welfare and for-profit healthcare systems across the globe. During this period we have witnessed the completion of the Human Genome Project (Willis, 1998) and made considerable progress since the 1970s in the ethical debates around stem cell and embryo research or how many transplants an individual may reject before heroic medicine gives up (Fox and Swazey, 1974). Coupled with this, the advances in information technology have spurned new bio and e-technologies previously beyond our imagination; key-hole surgery is now mundane and some individuals now boast of having several cardiac bypass grafts or their own private, at home dialysis machine. While these advances in medical science offer the possibilities of relieving the suffering of many thousands of people, they also highlight the high cost of publicly funded healthcare and the need for some mechanism for rationalization.

In this book we do not raise the ethical issues of healthcare funding, nor do we explore the possibilities for consumers to be engaged in rationing such as that conducted in the 1980s in the now famous Oregon Experiment. Like Bloom (2000) we do not believe consumers played much of a significant role in the 1990 reforms, despite the rhetoric. Nor do the various researchers writing for this book deal with community-based healthcare such as the de-institutionalization of patients with mental illnesses and those with a disability, although it is recognized that outsourcing, privatization and contracting out have resulted in increased community or out-reach care. A text bringing together the impact of ideologies of normalization, economic rationalism and industrial relations reform is waiting to be written. However, in Chapter 14 we do offer some comment on future directions. We bring together the main issues arising from each of the chapters; we highlight key questions and suggest further areas of research. We also comment on what we learnt through the process of writing this book.

References

Bach, S. (2000) 'Health Sector Reform and Human Resource Management: Britain in Comparative Perspective' *International Journal of Human Resource Management*, 11, pp. 925–42.
Barraclough, S. and Gardner, H. (eds) (2002) *Health Policy in Australia* (South Melbourne: Oxford University Press).
Bloom, A. (2000) *Health Reform in Australia and New Zealand* (Australia: Oxford University Press).
Braithwaite, J. (1997) *Workplace Industrial Relations in the Australian Hospital Sector* (Sydney: University of New South Wales; Health Services Management).
Buchanan J. and Considine G. (2002) *Stop telling us to Cope: New South Wales Nurses Explain why they are Leaving the Profession* (Sydney: ACRITT).
Cockerham, W. (1978) *Medical Sociology* (Englewood Cliffs: Prentice-Hall).
Collyer, F. (1997) 'Privatisation and the Public Purse: The Port Macquarie Base Hospital' *Just Policy*, 10, pp. 27–35.
Considine, G. and Buchanan, J. (1999) *The Hidden Cost of Understaffing* (Melbourne Report prepared for the Australian Nursing Federation: Victorian Branch).
Dent, M. (1998) 'Hospitals and New Ways of Organising; Medical Work in Europe: Standardization of Medicine in the Public Sector and the Future of Medical Autonomy', in P. Thompson and C. Warhurst (eds) *Workplaces of the Future*, (London: MacMillan Press Ltd) pp. 204–24.
Fox, R. and Swazey, J. (1974) *The Courage to Fail: A Social View of Organ Transplant and Dialysis* (Chicago: University of Chicago Press).
Gardner, H. (ed.) (1997) *Health Policy in Australia* (Melbourne: Oxford University Press).
Grbich, C. (2002) 'Moving Away from the Welfare State: Privatisation of the Health Care System' in S. Barraclough and H. Gardner (eds) *Health Policy in Australia* (South Melbourne: Oxford University Press) pp. 79–99.
Ham, C. (1994) *Management and Competition in the New NHS* (Oxford: Radcliffe Medical Press).
Ham, C. and Øvretveit, J. (eds) (1998) *The Background to Health Care Reform: Learning from International Experience* (Philadelphia: Open University Press).
Harrison, S. and Ahmad, W. (2000) 'Medical Autonomy and the UK State 1975 to 2025' *Sociology*, 34, pp. 129–46.

Harrison, S. and Pollitt, C. (1994) *Controlling Health Professionals: The Future of Work and Organization in the National Health Service* (Buckingham: Open University Press).

Leicht, K. and Fennell, M. (2001) *Professional Work: A Sociological Approach* (Massachusetts: Blackwell Publishing).

Mathews, J. (1989) 'From Post-Industrialism to Post-Fordism' *Meanjin*, 48, pp. 139–52.

Mooney J. and Scotton R. (eds) (1998) *Economics and Australian Health Care Policy*, (Sydney: Allen and Unwin).

Palmer, G. and Short S. (1994) *Health Care and Public Policy: An Australian Analysis* (Melbourne: Macmillian).

Turner, B. (1987) *Medical Power and Social Knowledge* (London: Sage).

White, K. and Collyer, F. (1998) 'Health Care Markets in Australia: Ownership of the Private Hospital Sector' *International Journal of Health Services*, 28, pp. 487–510.

White, K. (2001) 'What's Happening in General Practice: Capitalist Monopolisation and State Administrative Control: A Profession Bailing Out' *Annual Review of Health Social Science*, 10, pp. 15–18.

Willis, E. (1998) 'The Human Genome Project: A Sociology of Medical Technology' in Germov, J. *Second Opinion* (ed.) (Melbourne: Oxford University Press) pp. 174–88.

Part I
The Australian Healthcare Sector

1
Health Sector and Industrial Reform in Australia

Eileen Willis, Suzanne Young and Pauline Stanton

Introduction: reform and the Australian healthcare sector

This chapter introduces the reader to the Australian health sector under three main headings in order to provide background to subsequent chapters. The first section describes the Australian healthcare sector and outlines key features in relation to finance, organization, employment and control of health professionals. The second section examines the health sector reform process, exploring the main drivers for reform and the policy and management initiatives that were incorporated within a New Public Management approach. The third section outlines the industrial relation reform strategies and their impact on the healthcare sector.

The Australian healthcare industry
Finance, organization and control

Although the Australian healthcare system is a complex mix of public and private providers, Medicare is at the heart of the system. Medicare is a universal, health insurance scheme based on the principles of equity and equal access (Australian Institute of Health and Welfare {AIHW}, 1998). Medicare is funded largely through a taxation levy of 1.5 per cent of income collected by the federal government.

In the public sector, organization, control and finance are divided between state and federal governments. The federal government is directly responsible for the funding of medical and pharmaceutical benefits and residential aged care. The state governments, through financial assistance from the Commonwealth, via the five-yearly Medicare Agreements (now called the Australian Healthcare Agreements), are largely responsible for the funding and support of public hospitals, community health and support services, women and children's programs and mental health. However, over the last decade the federal government has increased its involvement in the funding of public hospital services. The effect of this has meant that even though the federal government has left the detailed control of hospital policy to the states (Duckett, 1998, p. 102), in 2001–02, for example, it provided 46.1 per cent of total government outlays for services in public state based hospitals (AIHW, 2004, p. 3). This relationship is often contentious and in recent times some of the state governments have called for the Federal government to take over complete financial responsibility for health services.

Under the Medicare Agreement all Australians are entitled to free public hospital services and financial support for primary medical care from general practitioners, medical specialists, optometrists, and in the case of the chronically ill, limited access, via a referral from their general practitioner, to allied health professionals such as psychologists, chiropractors, physiotherapists and podiatrists. However, the Medicare Levy does not fully cover the costs of these services and healthcare is the second highest expenditure of the Australian federal government, and one of the highest costs for state governments. The Australian Institute of Health and Welfare (2004, p. 1) reported in 2001–02 that total health expenditure in Australia was in the order of $66.6 billion, or 9.3 per cent of Gross Domestic Product (GDP). This amount is similar in proportion to that expended on healthcare in Canada and France, more than is allocated in Japan, New Zealand and the United Kingdom (UK), but considerably less than the United States (AIHW, 2004, p. 1). Government spending on healthcare in terms of GDP has been relatively stable since 1991–92, however, it has doubled over the last four decades, with health expenditure per person increasing from $65 to $3397 between 1960–61 and 2001–02 (AIHW, 2004, pp. 2–3). Successive Australia governments, like their counterparts in many other countries, see the rising costs as unsustainable and the sector as a target for reform (Twaddle, 1996). This is part of a worldwide emphasis on achieving better value for the health dollar and more effectiveness through greater accountability from service providers (Evans, 1995).

A secondary problem in the healthcare industry is the fact that the major share of the health budget is expended on hospital-based services. Public hospitals receive one-third of all government health expenditure (AIHW, 1998, p. 167). In 1994–95, 80 per cent of all healthcare funding went to public hospitals who are also the largest employers of staff within the sector (Duckett, 1998). In 2001–02, state and territory governments spent 55 per cent of their total health expenditure on public hospitals as well as a large proportion of capital expenditure on public hospital infrastructure (AIHW, 2004, p. 2).

In Australia, the private sector also plays an important role and private medical care is available through private health insurance and privately-owned hospitals or charitable organizations. Around 36 per cent of Australians have private health insurance to cover the cost of private hospital care and allied health services (Grbich, 2002). The numbers of Australians with private insurance has been recently boosted through a Federal Liberal–National government financial incentive that includes rebates for individuals and families with private insurance and penalties for individuals on incomes above $50,000 per annum, or families on $100,000, who do not take out insurance. This includes an additional Medicare levy, and in the case of those entering private insurance after the age of 30 years, added premiums.

The private sector operates alongside the public sector creating a complex mix of public and private services. For example, general practitioners and specialists, including radiology and pathology services operate private practices, with the federal government providing either the full fee or a co-payment to the patient. In the 1990s a small number of general practices were fully corporatized, in some cases being purchased by multi-national companies (White, 2001) however, this trend seems to have abated in the last three years. In areas such as disability services, almost the entire community-based sector is outsourced to private providers who must compete for contracts to provide services to welfare recipients. Increasingly aged care is shifting away from government owned or charitable not for-profit services to private providers.

One of the difficulties of achieving reform in the Australian healthcare sector is its complexity, which in no small part is due to the various levels of government involvement – local, state and federal – with increasing power to set the policy agenda being accorded to the federal government. Indeed, Duckett (1999, p. 71) has commented that 'The Commonwealth [federal] government's domination of health policy in Australia prevails despite the fact that its formal constitutional powers with respect to hospitals is limited'. Such differing responsibilities and funding sources point to a problematic relationship between the federal government and states in healthcare which manifests in discussion over escalating costs, cost-shifting between the two parties, and the states' responsibilities in implementing federal government policy (Duckett, 1998, pp. 73–6). As patterns of service delivery also vary between different states (Donato and Scotton, 1998) such fragmentation in delivery and responsibility produces competition between the public and private sectors, between service delivery agencies and between different professionals (Draper, 1999, p. 133).

The five-yearly negotiations over federal funding allocations to the states for Medicare, produce months of public and behind-the-scenes wrangling independently of whether or not individual states are governed by the same political party or not. Duckett has referred to these five-yearly negotiations as 'the elephant dance of Commonwealth/ State relations' (Bloom, 2000, p. 20).

The healthcare workforce

The professional bio-medical health workforce is made up of doctors, nurses, allied health workers and others such as paramedics and dentists. The most powerful group of workers is the doctors, although there is a high level of stratification within the medical workforce especially between general practitioners and the 14 Specialties. While each specialty has a professional college, the interests of doctors are also served by the Australian Medical Association (AMA); a professional association which also has an industrial function, and various state-based unions such as the Salaried Medical Officers Association who negotiate enterprise bargaining agreements between salaried medical staff and employers. The largest group of workers is nurses. There are two grades of nurses; registered and enrolled nurses. Their professional interests are met by the Royal Australian College of Nursing (RACN) with competition from the Australian Nursing Federation (ANF) which serves both the professional and industrial interests of nurses. The ANF is a national federation with autonomous state branches.

Allied health professionals include physiotherapists, occupational therapists, speech pathologists, social workers, podiatrists, dieticians, psychologists, pharmacists, medical scientists, health information managers, radiographers, audiologists, dental therapists, health librarians, nuclear medicine technologists, medical illustrators, and the professions of orthoptics, orthotics and prosthetics (DHHS Tasmania, 2003). Allied health professionals work in public and private hospitals and health centres, but also in some instances in private practice. A number of private health insurers reimburse the services of dentists and some allied health professionals, such as speech pathologists, dieticians and psychologists, as well as chiropractors. As a consequence allied health professionals can be further divided between those that diagnose and engage in private practice and those that perform procedures directly under the control of medicine such as radiologists. Each of the professional groups has their own professional associations and within some states there are a number of union branches that serve the interests of allied health professionals that are affiliated nationally to the Health Services Union of Australia (HSUA).

All medical, nursing and allied health groups are educated within the university sector, with nursing and paramedics being the last two to come into the tertiary sector. Paramedics are an emerging profession with a number of states moving to tertiary education for this group, but this is not uniform with some services maintaining in-house training. The health workforce also includes a number of managers whose education and training may or may not have a health focus. A number of universities have moved to introduce health-related commerce and human resource programs in order to better prepare managers for the health sector. Other skilled occupational groups include cleaners, personal service and care attendants, ward clerks and technicians. Training for these categories of workers tends to be in the vocational education sector or in-house. In some states they are members of branches of the HSUA.

A major feature of the health sector is its highly feminized nature with women accounting for 77.4 per cent of employees. Women predominate in nursing and the allied health professions although the higher income professions such as medical specialists and dentists are largely male (Duckett, 2000). Nursing has had a long and, at times, bitter struggle over wages and professional recognition. This has included conflict with the medical profession over establishing separate domains of practice, and with the state over access to tertiary education (McCoppin and Gardner, 1994).

The female proportion of the medical professions has stabilized at just under 50 per cent. Recent evidence also shows that the percentage of women in general practice has increased to over 50 per cent, although these women tend towards part-time work (AIHW, 1998, p. 181). The health sector is also characterized by a higher percentage of part-time employees. In 1998 over 39.1 per cent of workers in this sector worked part-time compared to 25.8 per cent in the overall workforce (Australian Bureau of Statistics, 1999, p. 13). Between 1993 and 1998 female part-time employment in the health sector increased by 14 per cent; a much faster rate than the full time increase of 4.4 per cent (AIHW, 2000, p. 258). These figures are probably a reflection women's dual role and family responsibilities and account for the fact that while women predominate in the sector their numbers are not represented in higher management positions.

The health sector is also subject to constant innovation and changes which impact on both the skills and numbers of workers in the industry. Over the last two decades there have been major advances in, and increased use of, medical diagnostic and treatment technology and services, and the development of new systems and processes including information systems. There has been a growth in the numbers of specialist medical practitioners and increasing nursing specialization, including, now that paramedic education is in the tertiary sector, moves to establish physician, assistants or dual-trained registered nurse-paramedics, to work in rural and remote towns given the failure of the national rural health strategy to recruit sufficient doctors to these positions. The contraction of hospital employment (partly due to the reduction in psychiatric hospitals) has been associated with increased community care and a growth in community health services. The medical workforce growth has slowed, although the federal government has funded three more schools of medicine in the last five years, including a first for a private university. Allied health numbers have increased by 20 per cent between 1996 and 2001 and there has been a significant restructuring in nursing (AIHW, 2001). The AIHW reports that in 1996 the health workforce was more efficient and more productive with fewer staff treating significantly more people at a much higher rate of patient turnover and a declining rate of stay, than in the previous decade (AIHW, 1998, p. 181).

The nature of professionalism in the sector has an impact on the introduction of work practice reform, and is often seen to be a barrier to reform, especially in the case of doctors. It is not possible to force doctors into salaried positions in Australia as can occur under the National Health Service in Britain. A ruling by the High Court in 1946 following a Labor Government attempt to create a national health service deemed this a form of conscription and unconstitutional (Daniel, 1990). However, while the majority of doctors in Australia work in private practice on a fee-for-service basis those working in the public hospital sector are salaried medical officers or private consultants paid on a sessional basis, often referred to as visiting medical officers or VMOs. Like their colleagues in private practice these doctors are trained to be independent and self-reliant. They are taught to rely on their own judgement, to be accountable to their profession, with limited sharing of their decision-making processes with other professional groups. In effect, doctors control the production process in hospitals. They are at the apex of a hierarchical division of labour (Freidson, 1970), they decide who is admitted, who is discharged and what treatment patients receive. Scrutiny of their practice is often seen as a challenge to their clinical judgement, yet if employers are to have some control over labour utilization they need to have some control over the production process – over doctors. Such challenges by the state and third parties insurers have invariable led to conflict with organized medicine and at the local level to confusion over allegiances (Harrison and Pollitt, 1994).

Enter workplace reform: the New Public Management and health policy initiatives

Workplace reform has become a major goal of successive Australian governments since the early eighties. The current endeavours have their origins in the Federal Labor Government's National Health Strategy begun in 1989 although prior to this date previous governments had attempted a range of reforms (Daniel, 1990). The fact that the public health sector is a large employer and labour intensive means that policies that include cost containment strategies targeting the workforce are attractive for governments. Often this has been expressed through industrial relations policy. However, as O'Brien has argued (1997), public sector industrial relations is as much a political process as it is an industrial process as governments are fiscal guardians and policy generators as well as service providers and employers. Governments fund public services such as health and are therefore the effective employer if not the legal employer. Governments control the policy framework in which health institutions operate and therefore can 'steer' organizations in the direction they wish them to go. They have a range of mechanisms open to them to encourage workplace reform such as funding mechanisms, budgetary control and accountability processes. They do not have to rely solely on industrial strategies to achieve reform of work practices. One such mechanism utilized in the last decade has been the strategies of the New Public Management (NPM), sometimes referred to as *managerialism*.

Cairney (2002) argues that there is no accepted definition of the NPM except to suggest that the principles of the market are applied to public institutions and, as a consequence, to the working conditions of those employed in these institutions, such as salaried medical officers, nurses and allied health professionals. Alternatively Ferlie (1998, p. 2) lists six features of the New Public Management. These are (1) privatization of public utilities; (2) the introduction of market-like mechanisms into the public sector; (3) separating core (policy) from peripheral (service delivery) tasks and (4) outsourcing the service delivery, while maintaining government control over policy; (5) more active management such as performance management systems; and (6) labour market flexibility. Added to these are the emphasis on outputs over inputs and the break-up of large, uniform organizations into smaller business units (Bach, 2000, p. 928).

A number of the above strategies have been part of healthcare reform in the public sector in Australia. This was especially true of privatization and the introduction of market-like mechanisms into the sector throughout the 1980s and 1990s. It involved the sale of government assets to private enterprises, contracting out of service provisions (outsourcing), repeal of monopolistic licenses, deregulation of government enterprises, devolution of authority to public sector managers, greater reliance placed on user pay services and franchising (Deery, Plowman and Walsh, 1997, p. 4). This was fuelled by the introduction in 1995 of the National Competition Policy (NCP) by the Federal government. The government's rationale was based on a belief that the public sector would become more efficient if subject to private sector competition (Young, 2004).

The support for such propositions was widespread. For example, in 1996, the National Commission of Audit (NCA, p. 7 as cited in Faircheallaigh, Wanna and Weller, 1999, p. 54), argued that in a market-based economy controlled by a democratically elected government there were only two reasons for government involvement in the activities of the community. The first was social equity, where the market is incapable of delivering outcomes demanded by society. The second was market failure, which is associated with monopolistic situations, undue influence or power of the parties producing negative outcomes, or excessive or inadequate supply of the good or service. The fact that market failure was regarded as a risk in the health sector and that the linkage between the provision of healthcare and improved health were not always direct, was dismissed. The 'past wisdom' was reversed with the [neo-liberal] argument in the 1990s based on the proposition that 'the individual was not in need of protection from the market' (White and Collyer, 1998, p. 499).

Industry analysts (Duckett and Hunter, 1999, p. 8) argued that NCP was not a crusade founded on a belief that competition should be elevated above the public good, nor did the policy equate competition with the public good. Rather, it required a rational articulation of the objectives of anti-competitive measures and, if they were still thought to be worthwhile, an analysis of alternative means of achieving those objectives. As such, decision-makers in Australian health networks and hospitals were left to make their own decisions about how to implement NCP and New Public Management, whilst keeping in mind that health provision is a 'public good' (Young, 2004). Whatever local hospital managers decided, they could not escape the fact that at the national level, competition policy was built into the various Medicare Agreements through a series of benchmarks and best practice incentives that state governments were required to attain on order to be eligible for funding. These benchmarks forced public hospitals to engage in workplace change.

Competitive benchmarks and incentives to change

As already noted, funding for public hospitals in Australia is through a mix of federal and state grants. Since the introduction of Medicare in February 1984, the federal government has entered into six, five-year cycle agreements with the states and territories. One of the most successful ways both the Labor and Liberal–National Governments have coerced the state governments and hospital-based health professionals into engaging in the 'reform' process is through the creation of performance management strategies. This has been achieved by reducing the Medicare base funding, and tying additional funding to targets and benchmarks. Incentive based funding remains a contentious aspect of the Medicare Agreements (Willis, 2004).

However, the overall direction of block grants and incentive funding, while requiring clinicians to speed up the delivery of services, does not demand changes to the way the work is organized or to clinical decision-making. Change in the pace of work or in its organization is more readily achieved through the variety of Casemix systems of funding. The introduction of Casemix diagnoses related groups (DRGs) into the Australian public acute hospital system was first mooted in the National Health Strategy (1989–92). The 1988–93 Medicare Agreement established the Casemix Development Project and in the following Medicare Agreement (1993–98) the Federal Labor Government indicated that it intended to build into the next agreement a nationally unified Casemix system (Reid, Palmer and Aisbett, 2000). Given this, states and individual public hospitals had no choice but to comply. Indeed Victoria had introduced Casemix funding in 1993, well before the 1998–2003 Medicare Agreements were struck.

The underlying motivation of Casemix is to encourage hospitals to treat patients within the average cost structure, which is seen to be best measured by length of stay (LOS) as a predictor of resource intensity. This then becomes the benchmark and determiner of best practice. Where costs exceed the national or state determined cost weights, the assumption is that inefficient clinical work processes, or population factors are present. Hospitals can respond to this through changing clinical practices, reorganizing the production process or arguing that their Casemix deserves special pleading. Much of the workplace reform, including redundancies, outsourcing and contracting out, are a result of state governments and their hospitals attempting to operate within the Casemix model of funding in either acute hospitals, using DRGs, or community based settings using other Casemix models, although it is also true that for the states of Victoria and South Australia the introduction of Casemix was accompanied by severe budget cuts.

Diagnosis related group and the creation of a managerial class

Diagnosis related groups also provided the clinical framework for the reorganization of professional governance in public hospitals in Australia, as they did in the United States of America (USA) and the UK. DRGs measure an episode of care defined by the date and hour of admission and discharge. The original Yale system had 23 medical diagnosis categories based on body systems, usually linked to a medical specialty or major diagnosis category (MDC). Diagnosis Related Groups are then further divided into several hundred surgical and medical diagnoses and procedures, classified according to anatomy. This classification of patients into surgical or medical categories is the rationale behind the reorganization of hospitals away from separate medical and nursing divisions with their own budgets, into medical and surgical divisional directorates made up of multidisciplinary teams, often referred to as the Johns Hopkins (USA) or Guy Hospital (UK) model of devolved management (Willis, 2004).

Some commentators believe that the reorganization of the various professions according to clinical rather than occupational categories has been a strategy of incorporation of health professionals, mainly doctors, into the state's agenda (Harrison and Pollitt, 1994; Willis, 2004). It is also been a strategy used to consolidate quasi-markets within the public hospitals whereby the medical and surgical divisions become departments with their own budgets with the capacity to purchase and provide services to other parts of the hospital or healthcare sector. On a positive note the reorganization of hospitals into clinical divisions has allowed the development of separate allied health divisions in Australian public acute hospitals, bringing this group of health professionals out from under direct control by medical directors (Boyce, 1998).

Achieving workplace reform through industrial strategies

For those western countries bent on a political agenda of lower taxation and reduced government service provision, the control of labour costs has become an important goal and a number of strategies to encourage health professionals to work more productively and efficiently have been utilized. Thornley (1998) has described how the British government introduced a number of industrial strategies to curtail labour costs. These included direct suppression of pay aspirations through funding constraints, a divide and rule approach of treating the professions differently in relation to the payment of wages, and the continuous reformulation of pay determination mechanisms. A further strategy employed in Britain was substitution by cheaper labour. This was the creation of a new grade of staff, the personal healthcare attendants whose pay was determined outside of national arrangements (Thornley, 1998).

These labour market mechanisms do not operate independently of the NPM strategies. Outsourcing, competitive tendering and redundancies also facilitate labour market flexibility. For example, a Labour Research Department study on the impact of competitive tendering in the British public sector during the mid 1990s reported that the reduction in wages and conditions was linked to outsourcing, and resulted from an increased trend towards the use of part-time labour by contractors (Industry Commission, 1995, p. 160).

In Australia, similar trends and patterns have emerged. The Industry Commission (1995, p. E28) found that outsourcing could be used to change the composition of the workforce to one where lower wages and conditions were payable, whilst retaining the same labour input. The extensive review of work practices that outsourcing has initiated in government services has also been cited as a reason behind the privatization policy of governments (Industry Commission, 1995, pp. E27–8). In this instance, it is suggested that the mere threat of contracting out in-house services can lead to improvements in efficiency and productivity (Industry Commission, 1995). In this regard, workers are spurred by the threat of outsourcing to adopt more flexible work practices and improve productivity to ensure that their jobs are secure, however, this does not mean these practices are just, safe or conducive to quality healthcare. Similarly some hospitals have sought to substitute nursing labour through the introduction of personal care/service attendants and a number of states have used funding constraints and budget cuts to alter work practices or to move to casualization and agency labour.

Governments have also used the industrial relations system itself to achieve labour market flexibility. In Australia this has been achieved through a move away from centralized wage determination through compulsory conciliation and arbitration processes to locally-based or enterprise bargaining. From 1906, and with the establishment of the Commonwealth Court of Conciliation and Arbitration, until the mid eighties, Australia had developed a system of industrial relations where the processes of compulsory conciliation and arbitration were the main features of the federal and most state jurisdictions (Fox, Howard and Pittard, 1995, p. 474). The process was carried out by a public official whose decision was legally enforceable and either party could enforce arbitration on the other. Terms and conditions of employment were formalized into legally binding industrial awards largely set by third parties, such as federal and state industrial relations tribunals and usually involving national or state trade union officials and employer representatives (Fox, Howard and Pittard, 1995, p. 474). Also national wage cases were used to establish minimum wages and conditions and centralized wage rises.

By the 1980s the desire of successive governments for increased competitiveness and productivity due to the impact of globalization on the economy led to the Australian system increasingly being seen as inflexible and rigid (Rimmer, 1995). Much of the early advocacy for this way of thinking came from the employer groups such as the Business Council of Australia (Macdonald, Campbell and Burgess, 2001). However, the Australian Council of Trade Unions also played a role in advocating this view as they were having difficulty keeping all their affiliated unions committed to centralized wage determination (Briggs, 2001). In 1988 the Commission introduced the 'Structural Efficiency Principle' which was a two-tiered approach to wage determination. While the first tier involved a straight forward wage increase, the second tier depended on award restructuring in an attempt to encourage work practice reform. There has been controversy on the outcomes and the success of this approach (Dabscheck, 1995, pp. 51–2).

The Federal Labor government also introduced legislation in 1988 and 1993 which broadened the powers of the AIRC to encourage and promote the development of an enterprise bargaining system (Keenoy and Kelly, 1996, p. 105). The Labor government and trade unions saw enterprise bargaining as a way of making the tribunal system more flexible while at the same time keeping a central role for trade unions (Keenoy and Kelly, 1996, p. 183). The election of a Federal Liberal–National government in 1996 hastened the process of moving to workplace bargaining. The emphasis of the *1996 Workplace Relations Act* was away from a gradual managed approach to decentralization, which had largely operated as an extension of existing awards and structures, to a greater shift and more responsibility at the level of the enterprise. The legislation emphasized bargaining at the enterprise level both collectively through the introduction of certified agreements and individually through the introduction of Australian Workplace Agreements (AWAs) and excluded trade unions from much of the process, thus attempting to weaken their power.

The legislation also led to a process of award simplification whereby awards are viewed as safety nets with minimum terms and conditions; indeed awards were reduced to 19 minimum conditions (MacDermott, 1997). The Act established a new body called the Office of the Employment Advocate whose role was to approve and monitor the new individual Australian Workplace Agreements. The role of the Australian Industrial Relations Commission was curtailed through limiting its powers in matters of arbitration and new bargaining arrangements (MacDermott, 1997).

Enterprise bargaining in the health sector

Throughout this process there was discussion on the impact and suitability of enterprise bargaining on essential services such as the public health industry. Some argued that the emphasis on productivity achievements was not possible in healthcare because of the difficulties of measuring output (AHA, 1993). Others argued that workplace reform was already taking place in the health sector in other guises, for example, through the incentives built into Medicare and the benchmarks underpinning DRGs (Willis, 2004).

Up until recently there was little research into enterprise bargaining specifically in the health sector (Stanton, 2002; Willis, 2002), although. Braithwaite (1997, p. 91) did research the industrial relations of Australian hospitals in the early 1990s. Examining the 1991 Australian Workplace Industrial Relations Survey followed up by case study research he concluded that 'the health sector's relatively inflexible and award bound working conditions and compensation structures need alteration' and that enterprise bargaining had had limited impact on the sector yet substantial workplace change had already taken place for many of the reasons already outlined.

Health is a very complex industry to change industrially. The health sector is one of the more highly unionized industrial sectors in Australia. The Australian Bureau of Statistics figures from 1999 indicate that trade union density in the health and community services sector was 30.7 per cent compared to 25.7 per cent for all industries (Australian Bureau of Statistics, 1999) and for the profession of nursing, Stanton (2002) estimates it as high as 60–70 per cent in some large, tertiary public hospitals. The health sector trade unions have resisted strongly the decentralization of wages and conditions. As well as this, healthcare is often a very emotive issue and decision makers can be influenced not only by their own political objectives but also by lobbying of pressure groups, including those with commercial interests, trade unions, professional associations and consumer groups. The Australian Medical Association and the Australian Nursing Federation are particularly skilled at appealing directly to the public via the media through raising the spectra of ever-increasing waiting lists, when they are agitating for more resources. Any attempt at workplace reform in the health sector runs the risk of an electoral backlash for a government (Harkness, 1999).

Conclusion

The chapter has presented a more detailed account of the factors impacting on healthcare reform as well as giving an overview of the Australian healthcare system. In this book we argue that healthcare reform has been achieved through a process of changes within the health portfolio, but that this has also been accompanied by changes in the industrial relations system, along with fundamental changes in ideologies about citizen rights to healthcare. The original ideals of Medicare as a universal health insurance scheme based on the principles of social justice and equity, rather than ability to pay, have been tempered with new ideas of economic rationalism. From this has spurned the idea that public, especially welfare state-based services, are inefficient and the most productive way to reform them is to introduce market-like mechanisms. As a consequence the idea of New Public Management became part of the reform processes of the 1990s in healthcare across Australia. Many of the strategies drew on reforms from other Western nations. Casemix emerged out of the United States, but politicians have also kept a close eye on the change processes in Britain, New Zealand and Canada. The results of this reform process have met with mixed success. While these strategies for the most part remain in place, federal and state governments have moved to refine their endeavours to curtail healthcare spending and increase productivity. Some of these newer developments are outlined in part 3, but they should not all be read as state-led strategies for reform; some such as those directed towards risk-management have the full backing of the professions. As Iedema *et al.* note in Chapter 11, the area of contention is over the processes, not the aim or outcome.

References

Australian Bureau of Statistics (1999) *Employee Earnings and Benefits and Trade Union Membership* Catalogue no 6310.1 (Canberra: Australian Bureau of Statistics).

Australian Health Association [AHA] (1993) 'Reform in the Health Workplace', *Proceedings from the AHA Industrial Relations Seminar* 23 September (Canberra: Australian Hospital Association).

Australian Institute of Health and Welfare (AIHW) (1998) *Australia's Health 1998* (Canberra: Australian Institute of Health and Welfare).

Australian Institute of Health and Welfare (AIHW) (2000) *Australia's Health 2000* (Canberra: Australian Institute of Health and Welfare).

Australian Institute of Health and Welfare (AIHW) (2001) *Health and Community Services Labour Force 2001* Catalogue 27/ABS. No. 8936.0 (Canberra: Commonwealth Government Printer).

Australian Institute of Health and Welfare (AIHW) (2004) *Australia's Health 2000* (Canberra: Australian Institute of Health and Welfare).

Bach, S. (2000) 'Health Sector Reform and Human Resource Management: Britain in Comparative Perspective' *International Journal of Human Resource Management*, 11, pp. 925–42.

Bloom, A. (2000) *Health Reform in Australia and New Zealand* (Oxford: Oxford University Press).

Boyce, R. (1998) 'The Allied Health Professions' in Clinton M. and Scheiwe D. (eds) *Management in the Australian Health Care Industry* (2nd edition) (Sydney: Addison Wesley Longman Australia).

Braithwaite, J. (1997) *Workplace Industrial Relations in the Australian Hospital Sector* (Sydney: School of Health Services Management University of New South Wales).

Briggs, C. (2001) 'Australian Exceptionalism: The Role of Trade Unions in the Emergence of Enterprise Bargaining' *The Journal of Industrial Relations*, 43(1), pp. 27–43.

Cairney, P. (2002) 'New Public Management and the Thatcher Healthcare Legacy: Enough of the Theory: What about the Implementation?' *British Journal of Politics and International Relations*, 4, pp. 375–98.

Dabscheck, B. (1995) *The Struggle for Australian Industrial Relations* (Melbourne: Oxford University Press).

Daniel, A. (1990) *Medicine and the State* (Sydney: Allen and Unwin).

Deery, S., Plowman, D. and Walsh, J. (1997) *Industrial Relations: A Contemporary Analysis* (NSW: McGraw Hill).

Department of Health and Human Service (2003) *Allied Health Professional Workforce Planning Project Workforce Mapping Report* (Tasmania: Department of Health and Human Services).

Donato, R. and Scotton, R. (1998) 'The Australian Healthcare System' in G. Mooney and R. Scotton (eds) *Economics and Australian Health Policy* (St Leonards: Allen and Unwin).

Draper, M. (1999) 'Casemix: Financing Hospital Services' in L. Hancock (ed.) *Health Policy in the Market State* (NSW: Allen & Unwin) Ch. 7, pp. 131–48.

Duckett, S. (1998) 'Economics of Hospital Care' in Mooney, G. and Scotton, R. (eds), *Economics and Australian Health Policy* (St Leonards: Allen and Unwin).

Duckett, S. (1999) 'Commonwealth/State Relations in Health' in L. Hancock (ed.) *Health Policy in the Market State* (NSW: Allen and Unwin) Ch. 4, pp. 71–86.

Duckett, S. (2000) 'The Australian Health Workforce: Facts and Futures' *Australian Health Review*, 23(4), pp. 60–77.

Duckett, S. and Hunter, L. (1999) *Health Services Policy Review: Final Report* Victorian Government Department of Human Services, November, http://www.dhs.vic.gov.au/ahs/servrev/index.htm (Accessed 2nd April 2001).

Evans, R. G. (1995) 'Healthy Populations or Healthy Institutions: The Dilemma of Healthcare Management' *The Journal of Health Administration Education*, 13(3), pp. 453–72.

Faircheallaigh, C., Wanna, J. and Weller, P. (1999) *Public Sector Management in Australia: New Challenges, New Directions* (2nd edn) (Sth Yarra: Macmillan Education).

Ferlie, E. (1998) 'The New Public Management in the United Kingdom, Origins and Implementation', *Paper given at the Managerial Reform of the State. International seminar*, Brasilia, November, {Online} http://www.tce.sc.gov.br/biblioteca/artigos/newpubmanagement.html (Accessed 10th November 2001).

Fox, C., Howard, W. and Pittard, M. (1995) *Industrial Relations in Australia: Development, Law and Operation* (Melbourne: Longman).

Freidson, E. (1970) *Profession of Medicine* (New York: Harper and Row).

Grbich, C. (2002) 'Moving away from the Welfare State: Privatisation of the Health Care System' in S. Barraclough and H. Gardner (eds) *Health Policy in Australia* (South Melbourne: Oxford University Press).

Harkness, A. (1999) 'Prognosis Negative: Healthcare Economics and the Kennett Government' in B. Costar and N. Economou, N. (eds) *The Kennett Revolution* (Sydney: NSW Press) pp. 203–13.

Harrison, S. and Pollitt, C. (1994) *Controlling Health Professionals* (Buckingham: Open University Press).

Industry Commission (1995) *Competitive Tendering and Contracting by Public Sector Agencies* (Melbourne: Australian Government Printing Services).

Keenoy, T. and Kelly, D. (1996) The Employment Relationship in Australia (Marrickville NSW: Harcourt Brace).

MacDermott, T. (1997) 'Industrial Legislation in 1996: The Reform Agenda' *The Journal of Industrial Relations*, 39(1), pp. 52–76.

Macdonald, D., Campbell, I. and Burgess, J. (2001) 'Ten Years of Enterprise Bargaining in Australia: An Introduction' *Labour and Industry*, 12(1), pp. 1–25.

McCoppin, B. and Gardner, H. (1994) *Tradition and Reality: Nursing and Politics in Australia* (Melbourne: Churchill Livingstone).

O'Brien, J. (1997) 'Occupational and Professional Identity as an Industrial Strategy in the New Zealand State Sector' *The Journal of Industrial Relations*, 39(4), pp. 499–517.

Reid, B., Palmer, G. and Aisbett, C. (2000) 'The Performance of Australian DRGs' *Australian Health Review*, 23, pp. 20–31.

Rimmer, S. (1995) *Australian Labour Market and Microeconomic Reform*, La Trobe University Press, Melbourne.

Stanton, P. (2002) *Employment Relations in Victorian Public Hospitals: 1992–1999* Unpublished PhD thesis (School of Public Health, La Trobe University).

Thornley, C. (1998) 'Contesting Local Pay: The Decentralisation of Collective Bargaining in the NHS' *British Journal of Industrial Relations*, 36(3), pp. 413–34.

Twaddle, A. (1996) "Health Systems Reforms: Toward a Framework for International Comparisons' *Social Science and Medicine*, 43(5), pp. 637–54.

White, K. and Collyer, F. (1998) 'Health Care Markets in Australia: Ownership of the Private Hospital Sector' *International Journal of Health Services*, 28, pp. 487–510.

White, K. (2001) 'What's happening in General Practice: Capitalist Monopolisation and State Administrative Control: A Profession Bailing out' *Annual Review of Health Social Science*, 10, pp. 5–18.

Willis, E. (2002) 'Enterprise bargaining and Work Intensification: An Atypical Case Study from the South Australian Public Hospital Sector' *New Zealand Journal of Industrial Relations* 27(2), pp. 221–32.

Willis, E. (2004) *Accelerating Control: An Ethnographic Account of the Impact of Micro-economic Reform on the Work of Health Professionals* Unpublished PhD thesis (School of Social Inquiry, University of Adelaide).

Young, S. (2004) *An Analysis of Outsourcing in the Victorian Public Health Sector* Unpublished PhD thesis (Bowater School of Management and Marketing, Deakin University).

2
The Australian Healthcare Workforce
Stephen Duckett

Introduction

Healthcare reform and industrial change impact directly on the health workforce in a number of ways. The structure of the workforce and the number of people employed can often be the subject of government action and policy change, and industrial issues are quintessentially about payment and employment arrangements for the health workforce. This chapter is a scene-setting chapter for the other chapters of this book, providing information about the size and composition of the health workforce, with particular attention to nursing, medical and allied health personnel, as well as identifying contemporary issues affecting those professions.

The structure and functioning of the health workforce is critical to the structure and functioning of the health system overall. The significance of the health workforce is also highlighted by the fact that, as is typical of most service industries, labour costs account for a large proportion of health costs (around 70 to 80 per cent).

Although this chapter focuses on the Australian healthcare workforce, many of the problems and issues associated with workforce policy are global in nature. Health professionals are increasingly mobile, and recruitment of health professionals trained in developing countries to work in the developed world is further impoverishing the healthcare system of the former.

Workforce roles and educational preparation are often regulated on a supra-national scale. For example, occupational therapy programs need to meet standards prescribed by the World Federation of Occupational Therapists. As with other areas of the economy, globalization is impacting on the shape of the current workforce and affecting planning for the future.

There are two ways of looking at the health workforce. First, in terms of the health professions, that is, groups that have specific training related to diagnosis and treatment of patients or consumers, and/or the organization of healthcare delivery. The second way of looking at the health workforce is in terms of those people who work in the health industry, be they health professionals, other professionals (such as accountants) or people without a professional qualification. Table 2.1 shows information on the place of the health workforce (using both approaches) in terms of the Australian labour market.

Table 2.1 shows that the health industry accounts for 6.72 per cent of the employed workforce, smaller than the health share of Gross Domestic Product. Health professionals account for 43 per cent of employment in the health industry (other groups include managers, cleaners, social welfare professionals, people in trades, and so on). Nurses comprise the single largest health profession, accounting for just over one-quarter of all health industry employment.

Many industry sectors have a role in promoting or protecting health, for example local government, water supply authorities. However, over 90 per cent of medical practitioners and over 85 per cent of nurses are employed in the health industry, with the remainder being employed across a range of industries including tertiary education and the government sector. About two-thirds (65 per cent) of nurses are employed in hospitals and nursing homes.

Nurses represent two-thirds of the health professional workforce with medical practitioners being the second largest group (14 per cent of the health workforce). The next major health professional groups are radiographers ('medical imaging technologists'), pharmacists, physiotherapists and dentists, together accounting for a further one-ninth (11.7 per cent) of the health workforce (Duckett, 2004).

The health workforce is predominantly female (77.4 per cent) although the higher income professions tend to be male dominated (79 per cent of specialist medical practitioners are male; males make up 59 per cent of generalist medical practitioners, compared with eight per cent of registered nurses and 18 per cent of physiotherapists). Specialist medical practitioners earn substantially more than other professionals. The overall pattern is that groups with a larger proportion of women tend to have lower earnings. In addition health professionals generally have higher earnings than people in other occupations.

Table 2.1 Australia: number of persons in health occupations in health and other industries, 2001

Industry	Medical Practitioners	Nursing Professionals	Other Health Professionals	Total Health Professionals	Other Occupations	Total
Hospitals and nursing homes	12,725	111,359	11,370	135,454	145,955	281,409
Medical and dental services	28,711	9242	10,974	48,927	69,850	118,777
Other health services	3994	27,597	25,395	56,986	100,490	157,476
Total health industry	45,430	148,198	47,739	241,367	316,295	557,662
All other industries	2781	23,409	24,047	50,237	7,690,707	7,740,944
Total	**48,211**	**171,607**	**71,786**	**291,604**	**8,007,002**	**8,298,606**

Source: ABS unpublished Census cross-tabulations

The health workforce has grown substantially over the last 40 years. The number of health professionals per head of population increased from 6.9 per 1000 population in 1961 to 15.4 per 1000 population in 2001 (Duckett, 2004).

Table 2.1 shows that over half of all people who work in the health industry are not health professionals but are from other professions, such as accountants or managers, or from non-professional backgrounds, such as cleaners and clerical workers. The proportion drawn from these other occupations is slightly lower in hospitals and nursing homes and in medical and dental practices than in other parts of the health sector. The number employed and the employment relationships for these other occupations have been the subject of significant change in the health sector over recent years. Change in these occupations, especially unskilled or semi-skilled, has often been a focus of drives to improve efficiency through reductions in employment and improved productivity, or through outsourcing. Cleaning and catering services, for example, have often not been seen as core business of hospitals. Health authorities have attempted to reduce employment and costs through a wide range of outsourcing strategies, ranging from outsourcing management to outsourcing all aspects of service provision. The support workforce has also suffered from increased casualization as employers attempt to align job demands more clearly with labour supply.

Issues in health workforce supply and demand

An important and regularly recurring policy issue relating to the health workforce is the adequacy of supply to meet demand: do we have enough doctors; are we facing a nursing shortage crisis? Increasingly, governments are concerned with ensuring that there is an adequate supply of skilled labour in all areas of the economy, usually implemented through education and training policy. In Australia, government has historically been active in health workforce issues, particularly relating to the medical workforce, because of the government's role as both a funder and provider in the health sector. Health workforce policy has usually been driven by health (rather than education and training) portfolios and policy levers applied to influence the supply and distribution of the health workforce have been a mix of 'health' and 'education' instruments.

There are three main committees that have been established to co-ordinate health workforce planning in Australia:

- The Australian Health Workforce Officials Committee (AHWOC) consists of senior staff from each of the state health authorities, and from the Commonwealth education and health departments. This committee aims to provide national oversight and coordination across all health workforce planning activities.

- The Australian Medical Workforce Advisory Committee (AMWAC) has membership drawn from medical associations and colleges, representatives of universities and consumers, experts (for example in health economics), as well as nominees from state and Commonwealth departments and agencies.
- The Australian Health Workforce Advisory Committee (AHWAC) is responsible for providing advice on the non-medical workforce: nursing, midwifery, and allied health. Its membership includes representatives of the professions, universities, and bureaucratic agencies.

All three committees report to the meeting of heads of health authorities/departments (Australian Health Ministers' Advisory Council, AHMAC) and all are serviced by a secretariat based in Sydney.

Health workforce policy attention is directed to whether the workforce is in balance at a state or national level as well as whether segments of the market (specialty, location) are in balance (Zurn et al., 2004). Ensuring a balance of supply and demand in the health workforce is difficult for a number of reasons:

- low mobility of health professionals means that there can be oversupply in some areas and undersupply in others, thus reducing the likely success of training additional professionals as a means of redressing imbalances;
- long lead times for education and training of health professionals, especially specialists; and
- long-term predictions must also take account of changes in technology in the health industry (and hence demand) and yet technological change is quite rapid, possibly invalidating even recent predictions.

Health workforce policy is further confounded by the existence of real costs associated with an imbalance, both in terms of undersupply and oversupply (see Table 2.2).

Typically, health workforce policy attempts to influence supply, viewing demand as exogenous. This is not the case, however, as changes in broad policy settings or the labour force may in turn affect demand for consultations with health professionals. There can also be

Table 2.2   Costs of workforce imbalance

Costs of Undersupply	Costs of Oversupply
Poor access, unmet need, potentially poorer outcomes	Unnecessary costs incurred in education sector in training workforce
Overworked and stressed workforce (which may make the profession/area unattractive and further reduce supply)	Unnecessary services provided where workforce can create own demand
Increased costs of alternative provision (for example travel costs)	Workforce may not maintain skills because of insufficient consultation rate

Source: AMWAC and AIHW 1998

policies to affect demand for health consultations; for example, providing additional information to consumers may increase their ability to self-manage a particular condition.

The starting place for health workforce planning should be the role of the professional. Planning should be for meeting community needs for *services*, with consideration then given to what professionals (and associate professionals) are required to meet these needs. This approach focuses attention to the possibility that needs can be met in a variety of ways, by a variety of professionals who can provide substitute services.

A second critical factor relates to the productivity of the professional (and their substitutes). Planning for workforce supply needs to be preceded by clarifying decisions, assumptions and policies about roles and expected productivity.

Figure 2.1 summarizes the key flows that affect the size of the health workforce.

The key inflows are new graduates, internationally trained health professionals, and people returning to the workforce. Major outflows are retirement and death, and other exits including emigration. A key focus of policy attention is the flow of new graduates into the health workforce. Here, there are three major factors:

- the number of entrants into educational programs, that is, the size of the intakes into university and other training programs;
- the proportion of intakes who graduate (flow A) and who then enter the workforce. The dropout rate from universities in the higher

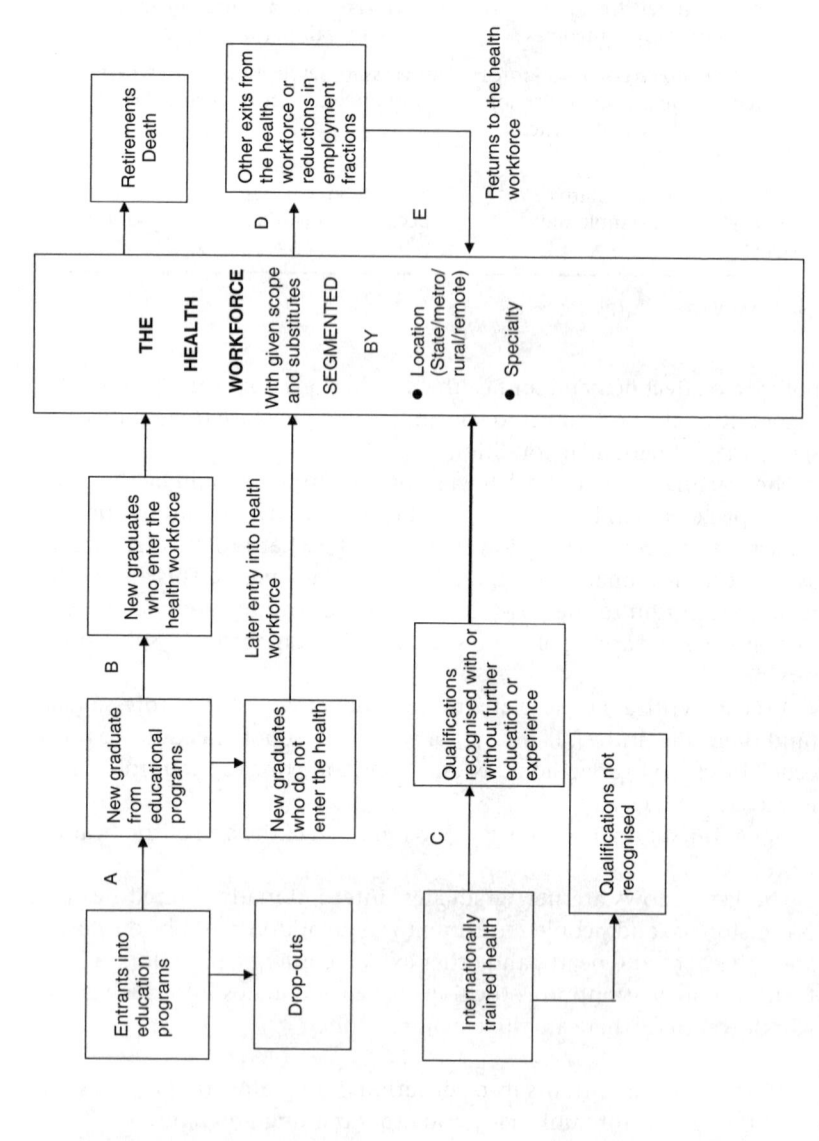

Figure 2.1 Factors affecting health workforce supply

status health professions (such as medicine or physiotherapy) is quite low but there is significant dropout from other professions, such as nursing; and
- the number of graduates who eventually enter the workforce.

Most graduates of health professional programs enter the workforce immediately after graduation (around 90 per cent of 1996 graduates (Johnson, 1997)). However, that leaves a significant number who do not immediately enter the workforce because of an interest in further training (in postgraduate programs, including research programs), who defer entry into the Australian workforce to travel, or who decide that, having obtained a professional qualification, they do not propose to enter that profession.

A second major flow relates to the number of internationally trained health professionals who enter the workforce. Given the long lead times involved in adjusting workforce supply by increasing student intakes, the flow of internationally trained workers is critical to workforce planning (Walker and Maynard, 2003). Australia is a relatively attractive country for internationally trained health professionals and a significant number of professionals seek to migrate to this country. Australian immigration rules tend to discourage migration from professional groups seen to be in oversupply through allocation of priorities for migration work permits. A further barrier to immigration comes from the processes for recognition of education or experience (Kunz, 1975).

Decisions about standards of entry into the professions are controversial. The health professions themselves often have an economic incentive to reduce competition in the marketplace, and hence may place tight restrictions on entry of overseas graduates. This situation has also applied where the Commonwealth government has attempted to reduce the supply of overseas medical graduates in order to reduce pressure on its expenditure under the Medicare Benefits Scheme. The flow of internationally trained professionals into the workforce can be a significant reason for growth in workforce supply. The economic incentive to reduce competition is often argued by the professions on the grounds of the need to maintain 'standards'.

The effect on overseas-trained health professionals who cannot obtain registration to practise in Australia can be quite traumatic (Kunz, 1975; Kidd and Braun, 1992). In some professions, internationally trained professionals may be restricted to practise in rural and remote areas in order to address the perceived shortages of professionals in those areas.

The health workforce is obviously reduced by retirements and deaths. Although there is no requirement for persons to retire at a particular age, there is a tendency for most health professionals to retire between 60 and 65 years of age, with some reducing their practice involvement on a graduated basis starting some years earlier. This is especially the case for those professionals whose work requires a high level of physical activity or manual dexterity.

Professionals might also leave the health workforce (either temporarily or permanently) for a host of other reasons including overseas travel, child rearing, pursuing other opportunities, and so on (flow D in Figure 2.1). This flow is particularly influenced by the broader economic situation, including the relative attractiveness of working in the health professions (relative wages and conditions). Those health professions that have a higher proportion of females are particularly affected by temporary and permanent exits from the workforce associated with family formation (Kanagarajah et al., 1996).

Depending on the length of time absent from the workforce, the professional may need to undergo retraining prior to re-entry. Again, the flow back into the health workforce (flow E) of those who temporarily exit is affected by opportunities within the workforce for retraining, support arrangements such as child care, and flexible work arrangements which make return to employment easier. It is also affected by the general economic situation, including relative wages and employment prospects in the health sector versus other sectors, by employment opportunities for spouses, and by broad societal trends such as attitudes to women's employment.

The health workforce for any profession is highly segmented in terms of both location at state level (persons who trained in one state tend to work in that state) and also within state in terms of metropolitan, rural, and remote practice. There are different market conditions applying in metropolitan and rural areas, both in terms of the nature of the profession and also the remuneration.

As indicated earlier, many of the professions now involve specialization in a particular skill area and this further segments the workforce. The effect of this segmentation is that workforce planning normally needs to be undertaken at a specialty level (for the example of specialist physicians, see Dent and Goulston, 1999).

Identifying whether there are shortages or surpluses of a particular profession requires analysis of both workforce supply and demand. As indicated above, there can be interactions between supply and demand; for example, if there is a severe workforce shortage, this may create queues and waiting lists which in turn may reduce demand. Table 2.3 shows several options for addressing an imbalance between workforce supply and demand, focussing on the effects of shortages. For ease of presentation Table 2.3 has been structured in terms of addressing a workforce shortage; addressing a workforce oversupply involves symmetrical strategies. Each of the strategies in the table needs to be assessed in terms of the general criteria for assessing health systems: efficiency, equity, quality, and acceptability. In terms of equity, the co-payment strategies, for example, will have an adverse effect on equity; other strategies may have adverse effects on acceptability (for example, encourage self-management of care needs) or efficiency. The strategies also need to be assessed in terms of their cost-effectiveness and whether they will establish precedents that would result in increased expenditure for professions or specializations that are not subject to a workforce imbalance.

Table 2.3   Options for addressing workforce imbalances (shortage)

	Demand Side	Supply Side
Price	Increase/introduce consumer co-payments	Increase relative wages/fees for health professionals Increase/introduce recruitment/retention bonuses (flows D and E) Introduce retraining incentives to reskill professionals to skill area of short supply Introduce mobility incentives to encourage relocation of professionals to geographic area of short supply
Volume	Encourage use of substitute professionals Encourage self-management of care needs through information provision or other strategies Support informal carers Reduce demand through changing consumer expectations	Increase educational intakes (flow A) Reduce program dropouts Increase flow of internationally trained professionals into the workforce (flow C) Facilitate re-entry (flow E) through retraining programs, job redesign Increase use of technology to expand available provision (for example e-health)

The nursing workforce

In 2001 there were 268,873 nurses in Australia, 80 per cent of whom were registered nurses. Nursing represents the largest component of the health professional workforce. The most recent source of nursing workforce data (Australian Institute of Health and Welfare (AIHW), 2003a) provides a range of data on nurses and most of the data in this section are taken from that publication. Updates of nursing labour force data are available on the AIHW web site (www.aihw.gov.au).

Figure 2.2 shows that in Australia in 1999, there was an average of around 1200 nurses per 100,000 population. There is about a 15 per cent variation in the number of nurses per 100,000 population between the highest provision state (Victoria, 1297; the AIHW views the Northern Territory data as being less reliable than the other states and territories) and the lowest provision state (New South Wales, 1093). Despite increased demand for hospital and other healthcare services, the number of nurses per capita has declined about four per cent over the period 1993 to 1999, with larger declines in some states (for example Tasmania, 12 per cent).

A review of nursing education in Australian universities in 1994 (Commonwealth Department of Human Services and Health, 1994) identified a range of policy issues affecting the nursing workforce including issues of labour force planning, career pathways, and educational preparation. In its report, the review made a large number of recommendations for change and development that received little policy attention. National policy interest in nursing was reawakened in 2001 with two inquiries being established, one by the Senate (Senate

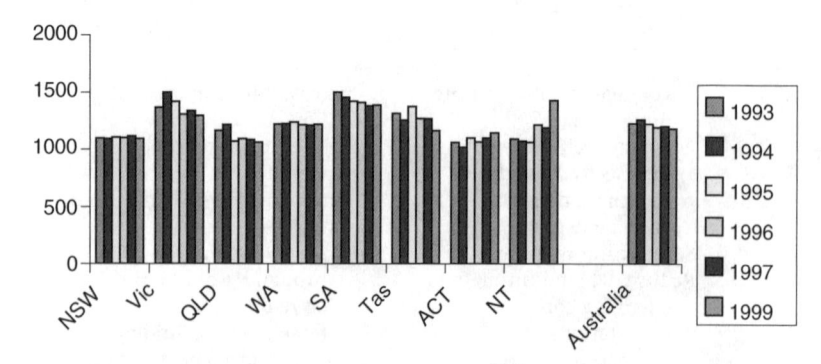

Figure 2.2 Australia: trends in nurses per 100,000 population, by state or territory, 1993–99

Community Affairs References Committee, 2002) and one by the Commonwealth government (National Review of Nursing Education, 2002). In addition there had been a number of state-based reviews of nursing (see listing in Senate Community Affairs References Committee, 2002, p. 3). Both national reviews recognized there were significant problems in workforce planning for the nursing profession. The 2002 National Review, for example, highlighted:

- the lack of long-term planning for the health workforce and nursing specifically; and
- the fragmentation of responsibilities for different aspects of nursing and nursing education combined with the different contexts in which nurses work (p. 107).

Fragmentation of responsibility means that there are four parties who need to be involved in addressing issues relating to the nursing workforce: universities that make decisions about intakes and curriculum design and development (which affect retention in courses); health agencies that have responsibility for employment practices (which affect retention); states and territories that make decisions about award pay and conditions; and the Commonwealth government which funds universities and regulates migration intakes. Unfortunately there are no structures that bring these parties together to ensure a coherent and combined response to nursing workforce issues.

Both recent reviews of nursing identified critical shortages of nurses (see pp. 14–17 and 48–52 of the Senate report and pp. 188–9 of the 2002 National Review). The extent of the shortage of general nurses has been estimated at 40,000 by 2010 (see National Review, 2002, p. 188). Shortages of nurses are also reported in the USA (for example see Coile, 2002; Sochalski, 2002) and in other countries. Given the international migration of nurses, recruitment of Australian nurses to work overseas might exacerbate the forecast shortage. Although the response to a shortage of the magnitude forecast must include provision of additional nursing places in universities, restructure of the workplace and changing demand patterns for nurses must also be considered.

A major issue for nursing workforce policy in the medium term therefore relates to the role of the professional (registered) nurse. Without clarification of the role of the nurse, there cannot be clarity about how many nurses are needed in the workforce, and educational institutions will find it difficult to make coordinated decisions about design of curricula and appropriate number of nurses that ought to be enrolled in nursing education programs.

The role of the nurse is the subject of a number of pressures, posing both threats and opportunities to the profession. In the first instance, the educational preparation of all nurses is improving, associated with the move to university-based education and the continuing refinement of university curricula. This broader educational preparation of nurses provides a foundation for nurses to undertake more complex roles and tasks. Failure to provide challenges in the workplace may lead to dissatisfaction among nurses with contemporary levels of educational preparation and affect retention. Further, as the postgraduate preparation of nurses is also now largely university-based, this provides further opportunities for developing highly skilled nurses. There is now a developing literature about the potential for nurses to undertake roles that were previously the sole preserve of doctors, with some studies suggesting that up to 30 per cent of the work of doctors could be undertaken by nurses (Richardson and Maynard, 1995; Sakr *et al.*, 1999; see also Sergison *et al.*, 1999 for a comprehensive bibliography on skill mix in primary care). Whether this substitution is cost-effective depends not only on the relative pay rates of nurses and doctors but also the relative time taken to complete the tasks.

New South Wales was the first state to consider the potential for nurses taking broader roles through a series of pilot programs under the general rubric of 'nurse practitioner'. This is an unfortunate term as it is poorly defined. The New South Wales nurse practitioner pilot programs initially focused on practice in rural and remote areas where there is said to be a shortage of medical practitioners. Developing the nurse practitioner model in the other states has not been limited to rural and remote practice (Offredy, 2000).

Nurses can substitute for general practitioners in many primary care tasks, for junior doctors in intensive care units, and can undertake high level triage functions in hospital emergency departments. Midwives also play a significant role in maternity care. In Australia, most experience in substitution has occurred in areas that are relatively unattractive to medical practitioners (for example rural areas, aged care, services for Aboriginal people and Torres Strait Islanders) and hence substitution strategies have not caused conflict with the medical profession.

The Australian experience with nurses substituting for the work of general practitioners is relatively recent. In contrast, there is an extensive experience in the United States of nurses and other professionals (especially 'physicians' assistants') substituting for the work of medical practitioners (Reinhardt, 1975; Reinhardt and Smith, 1974). The payment arrangements for medical practice in the United States has facilitated the emergence of physicians' assistants and nurse practitioners who have contributed to significant increases in physicians' productivity over many decades (Sloan, 1974). In some circumstances these professionals have been able to establish independent practice providing primary care.

The basis for independent nursing practice is a sound educational base to make diagnosis and treatment judgments. Opportunities for substitution would be substantially greater if nurses had independent prescribing rights (for either a limited range of drugs, or according to specific protocols). The extent to which nurses should have independent prescribing and practice rights is thus a critical issue for determining the future role of the nurse. It is also likely to be a contentious one, attracting opposition from the medical profession, as did the transfer of nursing education to universities in the 1980s (Hazelton, 1990).

The economic viability of substitution and enhanced nursing roles must also take account of the effects on treatment thresholds. If nurses become the first point of contact with the healthcare system, this may change the perception of consumers about whether or not they should initiate a health consultation. Conditions that might have previously been self-managed may, in the new environment, lead to a professional consultation, with consequent increases in the volume of consultations and total costs.

Policies on substitution should also involve consideration of whether all the tasks currently undertaken by professional nurses should continue to be undertaken by those nurses, or whether they can be delegated to other personnel, either associate professionals (enrolled nurses) or persons with shorter, more generic training.

Finally, resolution of legal, economic, and organizational issues relating to broader nursing roles will not necessarily mean that implementation of the new roles is easy. Opposition to broader roles may well derive from ideological/value differences or opposition to a perceived market competitor. Broader roles for nurses may eventually lead to increased power for nurses in policy debates, to the detriment of those, especially the medical profession, who occupy that policy space at present.

Responsibility for initial preparation of nurses rests with the universities, loosely coordinated by the Commonwealth government. Each university makes an independent decision about course design, postgraduate course offerings, and so on, although the changes to university accountability arrangements following the Nelson review have reduced university flexibility to vary enrolment levels (Duckett, 2003). University decisions have critical consequences for the health and community service sectors in terms of the numbers of entering registered nurses, and yet there are no mechanisms at national level and few mechanisms at state level to ensure that these decisions have a positive impact on future workforce requirements. The need for national coordination in this area is self-evident but sadly lacking.

Unless issues of the appropriate role and composition of the nursing workforce can be resolved, nurse workforce planning cannot be undertaken in any meaningful way.

Medical workforce

The medical workforce accounts for about 13 per cent of the entire health workforce. The most recent source of data on the medical workforce is for 2000 (AIHW, 2003b). Figure 2.3 summarizes the overall medical workforce situation.

There are approximately 50,000 individual medical practitioners working in Australia. There are approximately 62,000 medical practitioners on state and territory registers, but this includes multiple state registrations as well as medical practitioners currently working overseas. Of the individual practitioners registered, 94 per cent are in the medical workforce, most of these being clinicians (90 per cent).

The clinical workforce is divided into primary care practitioners (about 45 per cent of the medical workforce), hospital-based non-specialists (11 per cent), specialists (34 per cent), and specialists in training (11 per cent). The proportion of women in each of these areas differs remarkably, with 32 per cent of primary care practitioners being female compared with 14 per cent of specialists. It is interesting to note that there are a larger proportion of female specialists in training relative to the female specialist workforce, which may suggest that, over time, the proportion of women in the specialist workforce will increase to that found in the primary care practitioner workforce, subject to similar attrition patterns.

The female proportion of medical graduates increased from 40 per cent in 1988 to 47 per cent in 1994 and has stabilized since then. Females therefore comprise a significantly higher proportion of entrants into the medical workforce as a whole than they do of the current medical workforce. Females have a different work pattern from

```
┌─────────────────────────────────┐
│  Registered medical practitioners at │
│         December 2000           │
│           64,203                │
│ (56,115 individuals working in Australia) │
└─────────────────────────────────┘
                │
      ┌─────────┴──────────┐
┌──────────────┐    ┌──────────────────┐
│In medical labour│  │ Not in employed  │
│    force     │    │medical labour force│
│   51,748     │    │      4367        │
└──────────────┘    └──────────────────┘
```

- **Clinicians**
  - **46,619**
  - 27% female
  - 4.5% growth 1995–2000

- **All other**
  - **5129**

- **Primary care practitioners**
  - **20,815**
  - 31.6% female
  - 4.4% growth 1995–2000

- **Age (1999 data)**
  - 22%, <35
  - 29%, 35–44
  - 25%, 45–54
  - 15%, 55–64
  - 7%, 65–74
  - 2%, 75+

- **Hospital non-specialists**
  - **5052**
  - 42.0% female
  - 0.5% growth 1995–2000

- **Specialists**
  - **15,684**
  - 14.0% female
  - 0.5% growth 1995–2000

- **Specialists in training**
  - **5068**
  - 31.6% female
  - 18.6% growth 1995–2000

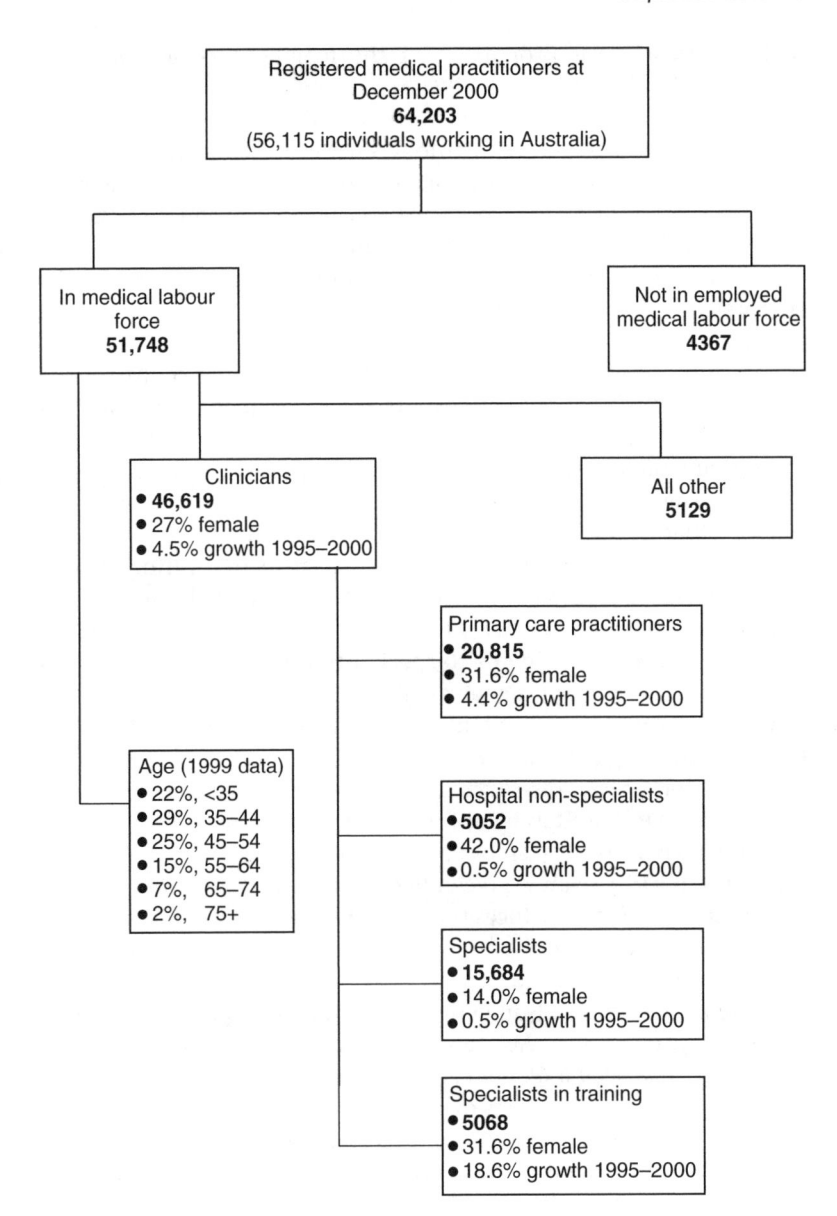

Figure 2.3 The Australian medical workforce, 2000

males, with a lower proportion of the female workforce working full-time (AIHW, 2003).

'Feminization' of the medical workforce therefore results in fewer effective full-time medical practitioners being available. Although the proportion of female medical practitioners working full-time may increase as family-friendly workplace policies are introduced, the relative proportion of female practitioners in the workforce will remain a significant variable to be taken into account in workforce planning (for comprehensive reviews of this issue see AMWAC and AIHW, 1996 and 1998).

The clinician workforce has grown by about 4.5 per cent over the period 1995–2000, but with almost no growth occurring in the specialist workforce (that is, those working in specialty (or sub-specialty) areas of medicine such as surgery, radiology, cardiology). It is interesting to note that the number of specialists in training is growing rapidly. This suggests that as the trainees graduate, the specialist growth rate will begin to increase. The rapid growth in specialists in training may be driven by 1996 government policy to limit access to Medicare provider numbers – the right to bill Medicare, Australia's national health insurer, for service provided – to specialists and general practitioners with advanced training (or equivalent).

A rapidly growing component of the clinician workforce is hospital-based medical practitioners who do not have specialty recognition. This growth is a result of specific policies to change the composition of the workforce in hospitals by using career medical officers to undertake work previously undertaken by specialists in training or junior doctors (Mason *et al.*, 1993; van Konkelenberg and McAlindon, 1993). Use of career medical officers reduces the overtime hours of trainees and also provides experienced personnel in a range of specialty areas, albeit without specialist qualifications.

Figure 2.4 shows trends in general practitioner: population ratios in urban and rural areas in Australia. Over the 15-year period 1984–5 to 2000, there has been a 66 per cent increase in the number of general practitioners per capita. Rates of growth were fairly evenly distributed across all geographic classifications, although there were particularly high rates of growth in remote areas where the provision doubled on a per capita basis. The pattern of lower provision in smaller rural communities relative to larger rural centres is consistent with a previous study (Richardson *et al.*, 1991) that found that the likelihood of general practitioner presence increased with town size and a threshold effect for presence of other medical specialists. Brasure *et al.* (1999), in

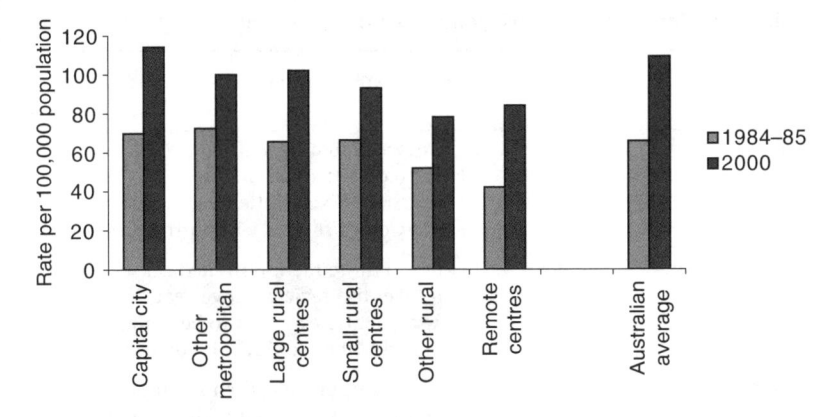

Figure 2.4 Australia: general practitioners per 100,000 population, 1984–85 to 2000
Source: AIHW (1998) Medical Labour Force 1996. Cat. No. HWL 10, Canberra: Ausinfo – Table 1

a US study, found a similar threshold effect, and noted that the population increment needed to attract a second medical practitioner was less than required to attract the first. There has been a significant increase in general practitioner provision in both metropolitan and rural areas, with a higher ratio in capital cities relative to rural and remote areas. What is remarkable about this is that, although there is a perception of under provision of general practitioners in rural areas, and a significant focus of policy attention on access in rural and remote areas (Humphreys et al., 1997) and factors affecting medical practitioners choosing rural practice (Laven et al., 2003), the contemporary level of rural access is above the metropolitan level in 1984–5. As Figure 2.4 shows, the general practitioner: population ratio has increased over the period 1984–5 to 2000.

Contemporary issues in medical workforce planning

Policy on the development and management of the medical workforce has changed dramatically since the 1970s. There have been a series of government reports and budget decisions which have resulted in a complete reversal of policy over this period from recommending expansion of the medical workforce, to contraction, to expansion again (see Table 2.4).

Development of policies on the medical workforce is confounded by two conflicting objectives of government. On the one hand, govern-

Table 2.4 Medical workforce policy recommendations

Report Year and/or Budget	Direction	Key Recommendations
Karmel Report 1973	Expansion	Increase graduates by about 300 per annum New medical schools at: University of Newcastle James Cook University in north Queensland
Doherty Report 1988	Stable	No need for reduction in medical school intakes but review in five years New graduates expected to be around 1160 in early 1990s and this is adequate
Federal Government Budget 1995	Contraction	Aim to reduce medical school intakes from around 1200 to around 1000 per annum
Federal Government Budget 2000	Expansion	Funded expansion of medical school intakes of 100 per annum, targeted at rural students
Federal Government Budget 2003	Expansion	An additional 234 medical school places, to be filled by students 'bonded' to work in rural areas New medical schools at: Notre Dame University in Western Australia Griffith University on the Gold Coast in Queensland Australian National University (announced March 2001)
Medicare Plus/Federal Government Budget 2004/ Federal pre-election commitments 2004	Expansion	12 additional medical school places at James Cook University New Medical Schools at University of Western Sydney (subject to State funds matching); Notre Dame University in Sydney and University of Wollongong

ment, through Medicare, is the major funder of medical services in Australia. Viewed from that perspective, government objectives are associated with minimizing growth in medical expenditure. On the other hand, government also has objectives about ensuring adequate access to medical services as part of its health policies. During the mid to late 1990s, government pursued two strategies with respect to restraining expenditure. The first, implemented by the Labor Federal government in 1995, was an attempt to reduce the number of medical graduates produced in the country by limiting intakes into medical schools (flow A in

Figure 2.1). Although some temporary reductions were achieved and there was some redistribution of intakes from South Australia to the Northern Territory, this strategy failed to effect any long-term reduction in medical school intakes. The second strategy, implemented by the 1996 Liberal–National Federal government, separated medical registration from entitlement to bill Medicare for medical services. The government introduced a policy of restricting new Medicare provider numbers to people who had achieved specialist, including the College of General Practitioners, recognition. Simultaneously, the government also introduced steps to address the perceived relative shortage of services for medical services in rural Australia.

A critical issue in medical workforce planning relates to the future role and place of the medical profession. There can be considerable overlap in the role of nursing and medical practitioners in primary care and in major hospitals (see also Dowling *et al.*, 1995). Nurses, especially if granted limited prescribing rights, can undertake many of the contemporary functions of medical practitioners in primary care without any reduction in quality of care (Sergison *et al.*, 1999). Given the difficulty of attracting medical practitioners to rural areas, a nurse-led strategy would seem to form a key part of addressing rural medical workforce shortages. Similar strategies could also be applied in metropolitan areas.

There are also potential overlaps in some areas of the specialist workforce. For example, in the USA, nurse anaesthetists play a significant role in the provision of anaesthetic services, complementing and substituting for medically qualified anaesthetists. In the USA and the United Kingdom, podiatric surgeons undertake some orthopaedic surgery which in Australia tends to be the preserve of orthopaedic surgeons. These issues of substitution and role clarification are going to become increasingly important as the cost of educating nurses, podiatrists, and others is substantially less than educating general practitioners, and the average earnings of these groups are lower than for the general practitioners or specialists for which they substitute. It would appear cost-effective for there to be wider use of alternative personnel in provision of healthcare, subject to ensuring that the time taken to perform similar tasks is around the same and that the quality of care is not affected. In the long run, however, wage creep might change the salary relativities. Identifying what is the unique role of medical practitioners then becomes an important issue for policy.

Workforce supply is determined by multiplying two variables: the number of professionals and the hours each professional works. The increase in feminization of the medical workforce will impact on the average hours worked of medical personnel and hence will reduce the effective supply. The extent to which a given level of workforce supply can meet demand is affected by a further variable: the consultation rate per professional per hour. This latter variable is particularly amenable to short-term change through financial incentives to change the average length of consultation, and by improving efficiency through better organization of a practice. For example, increased productivity in medical practice could be achieved by consolidating medical practices into larger practice groups and using auxiliary personnel. This may also have benefits in terms of increasing quality by improving patient access to practitioners with a different set of skills in the health team (such as nurses or physiotherapists). Policy change on length of consultation time is quite complex, as very short consultation times are often perceived to be associated with poorer quality care. Workforce policy thus needs to be clear with respect to the trade-offs it is trying to achieve.

As already discussed, the medical workforce is segmented both by a series of specialties and by location. Medical workforce policy needs to be quite sophisticated to ensure that relative shortages in labour market segments are addressed without creating excess supply in other segments of the market. This suggests that financial incentives, when used, need to be carefully targeted. Workforce segmentation also highlights the importance of training (and retraining) programs.

Globalization of the international economy will also have an impact on the medical workforce, with pathology and radiology services probably the first to be affected with the dissemination of technology for the digital transmission of views of specimens and medical images. This will mean that a specialist pathologist or radiologist, located remotely from the patient, will be able to provide a report on the examination. Internationalization of the ownership structure of pathology and radiology practices is already occurring.

Policy on 'e-health' has typically focused on the potential to improve services in remote Australia by telecommunication connection to metropolitan areas. However, there is no technological reason why the communication cannot be to a pathologist or radiologist in another country. The extent to which this occurs will in part depend on financial incentives (Medicare may not pay for these services), and legal constraints (Is the pathologist or radiologist providing a medical service in Australia? Are they registered? Do they need to be registered for this purpose? Can another doctor rely on a pathology or radiology reported by a practitioner who may not be registered in Australia? Who is legally liable for negligence and how is that enforced?). Nevertheless, inevitably there will be increased emphasis on e-health that will have an impact on labour force requirements.

Other health professionals

About one-fifth of the health professional workforce consists of people trained in a wide variety of professions including pharmacists, dentists, chiropractors, therapists (for example, physiotherapists, occupational therapists, speech pathologists), and non-medical professionals trained to assist in diagnostic techniques (for example, medical imaging technologists). Some of these groups are able to diagnose and treat patients independently (dentists, podiatrists, chiropractors). Others may not have direct interactions with patients (for example, health information managers and those supporting diagnostic modalities). These health professionals are involved in a range of employment locations. Unlike nursing staff, the vast majority of whom are employed in hospitals, only a minority of these other health professionals (around 20 per cent) are employed in institutional locations with the majority employed in non-institutional settings, including private practice.

The AIHW collects and publishes data on a number of the allied health professions including physiotherapists (AIHW, 2001b), podiatrists (AIHW, 2002), optometrists (AIHW, 2000), pharmacists (AIHW, 2003c), and, for selected states, occupational therapists (AIHW, 2001a). It's Dental Statistics and Research Unit publishes data on dentists (Brennan and Spencer, 2002). Figure 2.5 shows the number of allied health personnel per 100,000 population derived from these publica-

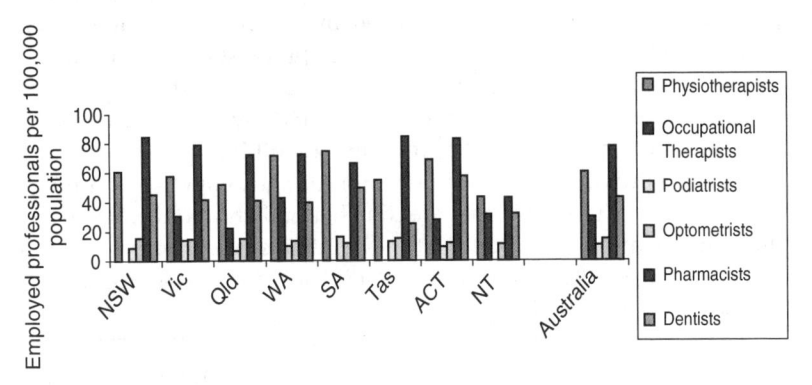

Figure 2.5 Australia: Allied health workforce per 100,000 population, 1998–99

tions. (Note: data were not available for occupational therapists in some states)

Obviously, the professions are not of equal size: there are about 11,000 physiotherapists in employment in Australia (60 per 100,000 population), compared with only 2800 optometrists (15 per 100,000) and 2000 podiatrists (11 per 100,000). There is also significant variation in provision across states in all professions, with close to twofold variations occurring in provision in occupational therapy (Western Australia at 43 per 100,000 versus Queensland at 22.2), podiatry (South Australia at 16.4 versus Queensland at 7.0), and dentistry (Tasmania at 25.2 versus South Australia at 49.7). This variation cannot be explained by demographic characteristics and 'need' for services (for example, differences in the age profile of the population). The variation can in part be explained by availability to education programs (for example, there is no dental school in Tasmania). Most of these professions are growing rapidly. For example, in 1999 128 students completed podiatry programs in Australia, a ratio of about one for every 16 employed podiatrists. In contrast, in medicine the graduating to employed ratio is 1:40.

Although the Medicare Benefits Schedule is principally focused on rebates for the work of medical practitioners, it includes a number of items that do not require the direct personal provision by the medical practitioner. These items can be rendered 'on behalf of' a medical practitioner where another professional, either employed by the medical practitioner or 'acting under the supervision of the medical practitioner', renders the service. In either case the service must be billed in the name of the medical practitioner who accepts full responsibility for the service. Typically, where the other health professional is not directly employed by the medical practitioner, there would need to be quality assurance processes for data acquisition and the medical practitioner would sign off on the report, presumably after analyzing the data reported by the other health professional. The most widespread use of billing for services not 'personally provided' is in the provision of pathology services but it also applies in a range of other areas such as radiation oncology where imaging technologists administer the treatment, audiology, and orthoptics. The MBS also provides for a subsidy for dental services, but only in the area of oral surgery.

The Medicare Plus implemented from February 2004, introduced Commonwealth reimbursement for the work of nurses and allied health professionals for the first time. These changes provide rebates for the work of allied health professionals which is provided under a multi-disciplinary care plan developed in conjunction with a GP, for services billed in the name of the GP. The level of the rebate is significantly lower than contemporary prevailing fees, but nevertheless it marks a significant change in Commonwealth policy in this area. Data on the take-up of the rebate was not available at the time of writing this chapter (August 2004).

Challenges facing health professionals

The working environment for other health professionals in the public sector has been significantly affected by the financial squeeze in that area (Ferguson, 1998). The non-medical, non-nursing health professionals have been traditionally relatively weak in hospital power structures as they do not have the status and role in attracting and treating patients directly as medical practitioners do, nor the numerical dominance of nurses. As a result, these health professionals have felt excluded from the decision-making processes of hospitals. The strategy of the mid to late 1980s to counteract this was the creation of 'allied health divisions', to parallel similar structures for the medical profession, and the creation of senior allied health leadership positions in hospitals to head the division. However, these leadership positions were often removed with the funding reductions of the mid to late 1990s (Boyce, 2001).

The increased use of Casemix funding in hospitals has called into question the contribution of the health professions to the treatment process. The evidence about the extent to which therapy services contribute to improved outcomes or improved efficiency is somewhat mixed (Liang et al., 1987; Haas, 1993; Cherkin et al., 1998). This may in part be due to the fact that most of these professions were relative latecomers to university education and so do not have a long tradition of research to determine their effectiveness. This is changing, and for the last decade all of these professions have been educated in university settings and there has been a parallel development of research into these areas.

Although many of the professions are educated in faculties with a multidisciplinary focus, only a small proportion of the undergraduate curriculum is designed to foster the teamwork necessary in these professions post-graduation. As a result there is some disjunction between the expectations of therapists on graduation and the nature of the work that is undertaken. This means that, as with medicine, people graduating in other health professions require consolidation of their professional training through a formal (or informal) internship arrangement. Unfortunately, the funding reductions in the hospital sector have tended to reduce these learning opportunities.

The increased use of multidisciplinary care plans (Tallis and Balla, 1995; Wang et al., 1997) which systematized the treatment and care processes in hospitals has provided increased opportunities for the various health professions to articulate and demonstrate the contributions they can make to improving outcomes or increasing efficiency in hospitals. Although care plans cover a minority of the care provided in hospitals, they at least provide a framework of ensuring that the role of all the health professions is clearly recognized.

As relative latecomers to university-based education, the non-medical professions do not have as strong a research base as the medical profession, nor do the university-based health professional schools have the generous funding that medical schools have been able to garner. However, university-based education and the development of clinical academics in the non-medical professions means that the scientific base of these professions is increasing, as is their visibility in the workplace and in policy formation. In the long term, these changes may begin to address some of the power imbalances in the health sector and provide a sounder basis for more equitable teamwork in healthcare. This will be to the long-term benefit of patients and other consumers.

Conclusion

The health sector is at a critical juncture, requiring a major rethink of the way its workforce is organized. Significant shortages are foreshadowed in nursing, the largest of the health professions. Changes in the organization of medical work in hospitals, and the reduction in average hours worked of medical practitioners, also presage further workforce change. The health workforce is an input into provision of health services and therefore health workforce planning should not simply be concerned with planning the numbers required in each profession but rather should focus on planning the provision of professionals with the mix of skills necessary to ensure adequate provision of services. Further, expanding intakes into health professional courses will not be sufficient to meet the emerging needs. New roles and new patterns of working will be required. At present the health sector does not have the right structures to facilitate a rethink of workforce roles, let alone implement them.

Workforce redesign is complex. It can involve four types of changes:

- moving a task up or down a traditional uni-disciplinary ladder (for example, senior medical staff doing work previously done by junior staff);
- expanding the breadth of a job (for example, rehabilitation practitioner working across traditionally determined boundaries);
- increasing the depth of a job (for example, nurse practitioners); and
- creating new roles formed by combining tasks in a new way (National Health Service [NHS] Modernization Agency, 2003).

Workforce substitution may involve conflict between the health professions. The interests of the professions are not coincident because substitution affects the professions differentially. Nursing staff may substitute for medical staff in rural communities; similarly, substitution can also occur in major teaching hospitals where nursing staff could appropriately substitute for some medical staff in intensive care units, cancer treatment, emergency departments, and patient admissions. In some states, hospital funding design militates against such substitution, for example by providing a significant subsidy for employing hospital-based registrars. There are similar possibilities for substitution of allied health for nursing staff (and vice versa) and other non-medical disciplines for medical practitioners (Brooks, 2003). Workforce substitution will initially be facilitated by specifying protocols for performance of the new roles outside traditional professional boundaries. Protocol-based care might improve quality of care by ensuring a sounder evidence base for provision.

The health professions themselves are also facing a range of problems. Some of the problems being faced by the professions are similar: during the 1990s all hospital-based staff have been subject to reduced funding and organizational restructuring. The reduced funding has often been associated with increased accountability through Casemix funding and calls for a greater emphasis on evidence-based practice.

The political environment in the institutional sector means that the professions have not been equally affected by these changes. Medical staff have traditionally had greater power in the sector and, although they have not escaped unscathed, their power has ensured that the medical profession has not been challenged to the same extent as the two other main groups of professionals – nurses and 'allied health staff'. The impact on these two other groups has principally come through reduction in the number of staff and increased intensity of the workplace (reduced staffing per patient and increased acuity or complexity of patients). These changes are often short-sighted because of the role of professions such as occupational therapy and social work in facilitating discharge. Indeed, expansion of these services may be a cost-effective use of institutional funds.

Workforce policies, as in other areas of health policy, should be informed by research and evidence. However, the track record of health workforce planning studies in getting projections 'right' is not good (Walker and Maynard, 2003). Although there have been methodological improvements in workforce studies in recent years (Antonazzo *et al.*, 2003), workforce planning in Australia and many other countries is still weak. Bloor and Maynard (2003) present this damning indictment:

> The basis of current physician workforce planning is incomplete and mechanistic, using fixed ratio relationships that have no empirical validity.
> They argued this situation has continued because of a combination of the ignorance of policy makers ... and the failure of economists and other researchers to convince policy makers that different methods may be productive.

There is an urgent need to address workforce issues. Creative policy development, underpinned by sound evidence and research, is clearly long overdue. Although health professionals take between four and six years to enter the workforce, change to employment patterns and roles could occur rapidly. Hopefully, the health workforce of 2020 might thus be quite different from that which new graduates entered a decade earlier.

References

Antonazzo, E., Scott, A., Skatun, D. and Elliott, R. F. (2003) 'The Labour Market for Nursing: A Review of the Labour Supply Literature' *Health Economics*, 12, pp. 465–478.

Australian Institute of Health and Welfare (2000) *Optometrist Labour Force 1999* (Canberra: AIHW, National Labour Force Series No. 18, Cat. No. HWL17).

Australian Institute of Health and Welfare (2001a) *Occupational Therapy Labour Force 1998* (Canberra: AIHW, HWL21).

Australian Institute of Health and Welfare (2001b) *Physiotherapy Labour Force 1998* (Canberra: AIHW, Cat. No. HWL22).

Australian Institute of Health and Welfare (2002) *Podiatry Labour Force 1999* (Canberra: AIHW, Cat. No. HWL23).

Australian Institute of Health and Welfare (2003a) *Nursing Labour Force to 2001* (Canberra: AIHW, National Health Labour Force Series No. 26, Cat. No. HWL 26).

Australian Institute of Health and Welfare (2003b) *Medical Labour Force 2000* (Canberra: AIHW, Bulletin No. 5).

Australian Institute of Health and Welfare (2003c) *Pharmacy Labour Force to 2001* (Canberra: AIHW, Cat. No. HWL25).

Australian Medical Workforce Advisory Committee and Australian Institute of Health and Welfare (1998) *Medical Workforce Supply and Demand in Australia: A Discussion Paper* (Sydney: AIHW, AMWAC Report 1998.8, AIHW Cat. No. HWL12).

Australian Medical Workforce Advisory Committee and Australian Institute of Health and Welfare (1996) *Female Participation in the Australian Medical Workforce* (North Sydney: AMWAC, Report 1996.7).

Australian Medical Workforce Advisory Committee (1998) *Influences on Participation in the Australian Medical Workforce* (North Sydney: AMWAC, Report No. 1998.4).

Bloor, K. and Maynard, A. (2003) *Planning Human Resources in Health Care: Towards an Economic Approach. An International Comparative Review* (Ottawa: Canadian Health Services Research Foundation).

Boyce, R. A. (2001) 'Organisational Governance Structures in Allied Health Services: A Decade of Change' *Australian Health Review*, 24(1), pp. 22–36.

Brasure, M., Stearns, S. C., Norton, E. C. and Ricketts III, T. (1999) 'Competitive Behavior in Local Physician Markets', *Medical Care Research and Review* 56(4), pp. 395–414.

Brennan, D. S. and Spencer, A. J. (2002) 'Practice Activity Trends among Australian Private General Dental Practitioners: 1983–84 to 1998–99', *International Dental Journal*, 52(2), pp. 61–6.

Brooks, P. M. (2003) 'The Impact Of Chronic Illness: Partnerships with other Healthcare Professionals' *Medical Journal of Australia*, 179, pp. 260–2.

Cherkin, D. C., Deyo, R. A., Battie, M., Street, J. and Barlow, W. (1998) 'A Comparison of Physical Therapy, Chiropractic Manipulation, and Provision of an Educational Booklet for the Treatment of Patients with Low Back Pain' *New England Journal of Medicine*, 339(15), pp. 1021–9.

Coile Jr, R. C. (2002) *Futurescan 2002: A Forecast Of Healthcare Trends 2002–2006* (Chicago: Health Administration Press, American College of Healthcare Executives).

Commonwealth Department of Human Services and Health (1994) *Nursing Education in Australian Universities: Report of the National Review Of Nurse Education in the Higher Education Sector – 1994 and Beyond* (Canberra: Australian Government Publishing Services).

Dent, O. F. and Goulston, K. J. (1999) 'Trends in the Specialist Workforce in Internal Medicine in Australia, 1981–1995' *Medical Journal of Australia*, January, 170(4), pp. 32–5.

Dowling, S., Barrett, S. and West, R. (1995) 'With Nurse Practitioners, Who Needs House Officers?' *British Medical Journal*, 311, pp. 309–13.

Duckett, S. J. (2003) 'Making A Difference in Health Care' in S. Ryan and T. Bramston (eds) *The Hawke Government: A Critical Perspective* (North Melbourne: Pluto Press).

Duckett, S. J. (2004) 'Turning Right at the Crossroads: The Nelson Report's Proposals to Transform Australia's Universities' *Higher Education*, 47, pp. 211–40.

Ferguson, K. (1998) 'The Nexus of Health Reform and Health Professional Practice: Narratives of Health Professionals in Times of Change', (La Trobe University: EdD thesis).

Haas, M. (1993) 'Evaluation Of Physiotherapy using Cost-Utility Analysis', *Australian Physiotherapy*, 39(3), pp. 211–16.

Hazelton, M. (1990) 'Medical Discourse on Contemporary Nurse Education: An Ideological Analysis' *Australian and New Zealand Journal of Sociology*, 26(1), pp. 107–25.

Humphreys, J. S., Mathews-Cowey, S. and Weinand, H. C. (1997) 'Factors in Accessibility of General Practice in Rural Australia' *Medical Journal of Australia*, 166, pp. 577–80.

Johnson, T. (1997) *The 1996 Course Experience Questionnaire* (Melbourne: Graduate Careers Council of Australia).

Kanagarajah, S., Page, J. H. and Heller, R. F. (1996) 'Changes in Job Aspirations During Physician Training in Australia' *Australian and New Zealand Journal of Medicine*, 26(5), pp. 652–57.

Kidd, M. and Braun, F. (1992) *Problems Encountered by Overseas-Trained Doctors Migrating to Australia* (Canberra: Australian Government Publishing Services).

Kunz, E. F. (1975) *The Intruder: Refugee Doctors in Australia* (Canberra: Australian National University Press).

Laven, G. A., Beilby, J. J., Wilkinson, D. and McElroy, H. J. (2003) 'Factors Associated with Rural Practice among Australian-Trained General Practitioners' *Medical Journal of Australia*, July, 179(21), pp. 75–9.

Liang, M. H., Cullen, K. E., Larson, M. G., Schwartz, J. A., Robb-Nicholson, C., Fossel, A. H., Roberge, N. and Poss, R. (1987) 'Effects of Reducing Physical Therapy Services on Outcomes in Total Joint Arthroplasty' *Medical Care*, 25(4), pp. 276–85.

Mason, C., Adamson, L., Cotton, R., Reid, M., Lapsley, H., Barrett, E. and Rotem, A. (1993) *General Practitioners in Hospitals* (Sydney: School of Medical Education, University of New South Wales).

NHS Modernization Agency (2003) Changing Workforce Programme Pilot Sites Progress Report – Spring 2003. Available at: http://www.portal.modern.nhs.uk/sites/workforce/usingstaffskillseffectively/CWP%20Publications/1/Pilot%20Sites%20Progress%20Report.pdf

National Review of Nursing Education (2002) *Our Duty of Care: Final Report of National Review of Nursing Education* (Canberra: Ausinfo).

Offredy, M. (2000) 'Advanced Nursing Practice: The Case of Nurse Practitioners in Three Australian States' *Journal of Advanced Nursing*, 31(20), pp. 274–81.

Reinhardt, U. E. (1975) *Physician Productivity and the Demand for Health Manpower* (Cambridge: Ballinger Publishing Company).

Reinhardt, U. E. and Smith, K. R. (1974) 'Manpower Substitution in Ambulatory Care' in J. Rafferty (ed.) *Health Manpower and Productivity* (Lexington: D. C. Heath & Company).

Richardson, G. and Maynard, A. (1995) *Fewer Doctors? More Nurses? A Review of the Knowledge Base of Doctor-Nurse Substitution* (York: The University of York).

Richardson, J., Macarounas, K., Milthorpe, F., Ryan, J. and Smith, N. (1991) *An Evaluation of the Effect of Increasing Doctor Numbers in their Geographic Distribution* (Melbourne: NHMRC National Centre for Health Program Evaluation, Technical Report No. 2).

Sakr, M., Angus, J., Perrin, J., Nixon, C., Nicholl, J. and Wardrope, J. (1999) 'Care of Minor Injuries by Emergency Nurse Practitioners or Junior Doctors: A Randomized Control Trial' *The Lancet*, 354(9187), pp. 1321–6.

Senate Community Affairs References Committee (2002) *The Patient Profession: Time For Action. Report on the Inquiry into Nursing* (Canberra: Senate Printing Unit).

Sergison, M., Sibbald, B. and Rose, S. (1999) *Skill Mix in Primary Care: A Bibliography* (Manchester: National Primary Care Research and Development Centre, University of Manchester).

Sloan, F. A. (1974) 'Effects of Incentives on Physician Performance' in J. Rafferty (ed.) *Health Manpower and Productivity* (Lexington: D. C. Heath & Company).

Sochalski, J. (2002) 'Nursing Shortage Redux: Turning The Corner on an Enduring Problem [Comment]' *Health Affairs*, 21(5), pp. 157–64.

Tallis, G. and Balla, J. I. (1995) 'Critical Path Analysis for the Management of Fractured Neck or Femur' *Australian Journal of Public Health*, 19(2), pp. 155–9.

van Konkelenberg, R. V., and McAlindon, A. (1993) *Hospital Non-Specialist Medical Workforce Survey 1993 [report]* (Canberra).

Walker, A. and Maynard, A. (2003) 'Managing Medical Workforces: From Relative Stability to Disequilibrium in the UK NHS', *Applied Health Economics and Health Policy*, 2(1), pp. 25–36.

Wang, A., Hall, S., Gilbey, H. and Ackland, T. (1997) 'Patient Variability and The Design of Clinical Pathways after Primary Total Hip Replacement Surgery' *Journal of Quality Clinical Practice*, 17, pp. 123–9.

Zurn, P., Dal Poz, M. R., Stilwell, B. and Adams, O. (2004) 'Imbalance in the Health Workforce' *Human Resources for Health*, 2(13), Available at: www.human-resources-health.com/content/2/1/13

Part II

Case Studies in Healthcare Reform and Workplace Change

3
The Structure of Bargaining in Public Hospitals in Three Australian States

Mark Bray, Pauline Stanton, Nadine White and Eileen Willis

Introduction

This chapter concerns employment relations in the public hospitals of New South Wales, Victoria and South Australia. The main aim of the chapter is to describe and then compare trends in the structure of bargaining in the public hospitals of three Australian states; the 'structure of bargaining' being defined as 'the institutionalized arrangements by which employers and employees determine the terms and conditions of the employment relationship' (Bray and Waring, 1998). In this context, the focus is mostly on union-management relations and collective bargaining, but at the same time there is a broader subject because these collective forms of regulation in which employees are represented by unions operate alongside individual bargaining, managerial prerogative and state regulation to determine the conditions of employment of public hospital workers.

Different types of bargaining structures are generally distinguished by a number of 'dimensions'. Although they vary slightly among authors, there are generally five such dimensions that are utilized to categorize bargaining structures:

- The *level of bargaining* refers to the location of bargaining in terms of production units within the economy and corresponds to the degree of centralization of bargaining.
- The *bargaining agent* is the representative body, either organization or individual, that engages in bargaining on behalf of employers or employees.
- The *scope of bargaining* describes the issues that are being bargained and thereby addressed in the resulting agreements.

- The *status of bargaining* relates to the legal standing of procedures and outcomes of the bargaining process.
- The *coverage of bargaining* is the proportion of the determined workforce whose terms and conditions of employment are established by the bargaining process (Bray and Waring, 1998, pp. 62–3).

These dimensions underlie the analysis of bargaining in the public hospitals that is presented in this chapter, but they are not applied rigidly or mechanistically. Rather, they provide a valuable reminder that bargaining structures are complex and encompass many issues beyond the centralization or decentralization of wage bargaining.

Each of the three state-specific accounts is presented separately in section two of the chapter. Section three compares the three stories and speculates on the factors that might explain the similarities and differences and briefly draws together the main themes.

To anticipate these themes, the picture that broadly emerges is that the three public hospital sectors have generally not experienced the rapid and savage changes in bargaining structures, and employment relations generally, that have been seen in other Australian industries. Union membership has remained high across most occupations and the extensive coverage of bargaining has been consistent; the tribunals have retained a presence; and despite flirtations with more decentralized bargaining, each of the three states has largely stuck with centralized bargaining structures. In this way, the experiences of the three states bear remarkable similarities that appear to be related to the public ownership of the sector, the desire of most governments to retain control of wage costs and the strength of unions, which in turn is associated with the large workplaces that characterize the sector and the professional nature of the workforce. Some differences are also identified between the states, but it is the similarities that dominate.

The Structure of Bargaining in Three States

(i) New South Wales

The public health sector in New South Wales is managed by the NSW Health Department, a government agency that reports directly to the NSW Minister for Health. Public hospitals consume approximately 57 per cent of state government health expenditure (NSW Health Council, 2000). In 1998–9, those employed by the NSW Health Department accounted for around 100,000 employees (NSW Department of Health Annual Report, 1998–9).

Since the enactment of the *Area Health Services Act (NSW)* in 1986, the central NSW Health Department has devolved much of the management of public health care facilities within specified geographical regions to Area Health Services and their Chief Executive Officers (NSW Health Department, 1998, p. 15). The apparent thrust of this regionalization was the decentralization of decision-making to the Area Health Services, which acquired their own one-line budgets and greater autonomy in the way they allocated their budgeted resources within their region. The reality, however, was rather more complex because the Department of Health, and through it the NSW government, continued to retain considerable centralized control (O'Donnell, 1994). Human resource policy is one area where this central control is most conspicuous (Bray and White, 2002).

Union membership in the NSW public hospital sector is high compared to most other industries. For example, by 2000 union membership across all industries in Australia had fallen to about 25 per cent of the workforce, while the corresponding figure for the industry category 'Health and Community Services' in New South Wales was 32 per cent (ABS, 2001). These broad industry data, however, included the private and public sectors as well as both hospitals and the lowly-unionized community services sector. Unpublished desegregated ABS data for the health and community services sector for NSW reveals that after 1994, union membership declined from 63 per cent to approximately 50 per cent in 2000 for 'public sector hospitals and nursing homes' (ABS Unpublished data, 1994, 1996, 1998, 2000). As this data covers all employees, it is possible to assume that union membership is higher than 50 per cent in some occupations, especially nursing or medical professions. These high levels of union membership and public ownership generally explain the virtually universal coverage of bargaining in the sector – in other words, almost all workers have their wages and working conditions collectively regulated by either awards or, in some periods, collective agreements.

The public hospital workforce in NSW – as elsewhere – is highly segregated by occupation, which is reflected in the structure of union representation – almost every distinct occupational and professional group has its own union. Many of the unions (such as the NSW Nurses Association and the Health and Research Employees Association) are state-wide occupationally-based health-sector-specific unions, which are state branches of federal unions (such as the Australian Nursing Federation and the Health Services Union respectively). There was considerable stability in these union structures during the 1990s and 2000s, with only two minor exceptions (Bray and White, 2002). Firstly, there was an amalgamation of the Health Officers Association with the Health and Research Employees Association in 1995. Secondly, the Health and Research Employees Association later took over the representation of allied health, clinical support services and junior medical officers from the Public Service Association/Professional Officers Association. All of the unions are recognized by the NSW Health Department for bargaining purposes and occupational segmentation is a strong characteristic of bargaining structures in the sector. In other words, almost all awards and collective agreements are occupation-specific, or they cover a group of occupations.

In terms of the scope of bargaining, the range of issues addressed in the occupational awards (and collective agreements) that dominated the sector for most of the period was broad. Most occupational groups had a general award, referred to as a 'conditions award', which contained all of the generic substantive and procedural provisions of employment for that group. For example, the most recent *Health Employees Conditions of Employment (State) Award*, which covered all the generic issues for the group of employees represented by the Health and Research Employees Association, included provisions on the status of employment and loadings, various forms of leave, hours of work and rosters, allowances, association representatives, subscriptions and trade union leave, dispute resolution mechanisms and termination of employment. In addition to the 'conditions award', there were occupation-specific awards or 'occupationally-streamed' awards, which contained the terms and conditions of employment that were peculiar to the particular occupational groups. Examples of these specific occupational awards were the *Health Managers (State) Award* and the *Health Employees Pharmacists (State) Award*. The issues included in these awards focused more on professional registration, clinical skills and grading systems. There were, however, some exceptions in which both generic and specific issues were combined into a single award for some occupational groupings; generally those with fewer job classifications, such as the *NSW Nurses' (State) Award* and the *Public Hospitals Medical Officers (State) Award*.

Not only was the range of issues incorporated in the various awards and collective agreements broad, but the scope of regulation actually increased, especially in the late 1990s. For example, provisions relating to payment for non-clinical staff who were on-call were inserted into the relevant awards. Additionally, some existing NSW Health Department policies covering specific conditions of employment were imported into awards; instances include family and community service leave and parental and adoption leave provisions. This too was the case for the training, education and study leave, and funding provisions for senior medical practitioners, which were also inserted into the relevant award. This trend was in stark contrast to many awards in the federal jurisdiction, where the scope of bargaining was narrowed significantly through the 'award simplification' process, which reduced the content of awards to just 20 'allowable matters' (Community and Public Sector Union, 1997)

Despite this broad scope of bargaining, some very important issues continued to lie outside the formal bargaining system. Many aspects of work allocation and workload, for example, remained largely the prerogative of management to determine unilaterally rather than being regulated through either awards or enterprise agreements. This gap, which contrasts with the situation in several other states of Australia (for South Australian nurses, see Willis, 2002), seems to have contributed to growing conflict over work intensification in New South Wales hospitals (Bray and White, 2002; White and Bray, 2003).

There were, thus, a number of continuities in the structure of bargaining in New South Wales public hospitals between the late 1980s and early 2000s; in particular, the coverage and scope of bargaining remained largely unchanged. There were, however, some dimensions of bargaining that changed and these fall into three main periods. First, in the years before 1993, the bargaining structure was dominated by state-wide, occupationally-based and sector-specific awards negotiated within the public sector framework. This was the traditional pattern in the sector and reflected the strong occupational structure of the workforce and its unions. The second period commenced in April 1993 when John Hannaford, Minister of Industrial Relations in the Liberal–National government, announced a new public sector wage policy in which funded wage increases were contingent on the negotiation of enterprise agreements that delivered productivity improvements. This second period covered 1993–94 to 1996–97, during which one round of enterprise bargaining was undertaken by local Area Health Services, in accordance with the state government wages policy. The third 'post-enterprise bargaining' period commenced at the cessation of the enterprise agreements, when a new round of state-wide occupational awards for the industry was negotiated.

1980s–1993

In the first period before 1993, bargaining in the NSW public hospital sector was dominated by occupational awards determined at an industry-wide level across the state. These awards were negotiated centrally between the agents for the respective parties, with the occasional involvement of the Industrial Relations Commission. On the one hand, the NSW Health Department established bargaining committees to represent 'employers'. This committee had representation from Area Health Services, but the central NSW Health Department drove their agendas and decisions. Like other parts of the public sector, however, the Health Department was constrained by the NSW Treasury, which determined the capacity for wage negotiations by establishing a funding agreement for the wage increases for the particular round of bargaining. On the other hand, individual unions that were party to each award were normally represented by state-level full-time officials and branch secretaries. Despite the increasing trend in the early 1990s towards decentralization and deregulation, both federally and in NSW, the level of bargaining in the NSW public hospital sector remained largely unchanged until the introduction of the Liberal–National government's new approach to public sector wage increases in April 1993.

1993–1996

During the second period, bargaining was apparently decentralized to the Area Health Services, which represented the 'enterprise' level.[1] Local bargaining units were established within each Area Health Service, based around existing occupational structures. Within each of these units, negotiations were conducted by a bargaining committee comprising equal numbers representing management and unions. The management side generally included an Area Health Service human resource representative and several line managers from the clinical or occupational group in question, while union representatives usually included the local union delegate and several rank and file union members with special interest or expertise. Only occasionally were full-time union officials directly involved. With government funding of wage increases being contingent on successfully negotiated and completed enterprise agreements, the bargaining units pragmatically accepted the decentralization of bargaining to the enterprise level and, by necessity, the additional workload this entailed for management and unions alike.

These apparently decentralized bargaining processes, however, were subject to centralized co-ordination. A state-wide NSW Health Department committee, the Health Industrial Relations Strategic Advisory Committee (HIRSAC), was established to provide strategic direction and to monitor the progress and reforms of the enterprise bargaining period. HIRSAC also negotiated state-wide framework agreements with individual unions and the NSW Labour Council, which set the parameters of local bargaining (Public Health System Heads of Agreement, 1994). Once local agreements were agreed, they were referred to the Health Department and to union state secretaries for approval, while the agreements did not become binding until they had been signed off by the Director General of the Health Department. Finally, the Department established a process whereby the funding supplementation for the wage increases was not forwarded to Area Health Services until they demonstrated that the productivity improvements anticipated in agreements had been achieved. In this way, the NSW Health Department and state-level union officials continued to be active participants in the bargaining process.

The bargaining process also saw a heavy reliance on 'pattern bargaining'. The first Area Health Service to successfully complete negotiations and gain approval from the Department was the Hunter Area Health Service (based around the city of Newcastle) and the majority of subsequent enterprise agreements across the state mirrored the Hunter agreements. For the unions, especially the Health and Research Employees Association, there was a high priority on maintaining consistent conditions for members across the state. However, for Area Health Service managers there was the need to successfully complete negotiations and have Department approval of the agreements within the established timeframes to ensure government funding. There was some room in these arrangements for Area Health Services to negotiate over truly local (and mostly minor) enterprise issues, but such concessions to localism were limited.

The enterprise agreements during this second period continued to be occupationally-based and they were negotiated by occupationally-based union representatives, as awards had been in the previous period. The only discernible change was a reduction in the number of agreements by grouping similar or comparable occupations into 'streamed' agreements. For example, in the Hunter region, the clinical support staff (such as Radiographers and Pharmacists), who were represented by the Health and Research Association, were grouped under one enterprise agreement, whereas there had previously been two separate awards.

As the expiry date of the enterprise agreements approached, in mid-1996, local Area Health Services began to prepare for a second round of enterprise bargaining, with a view to rationalising the number of agreements and, in the longer-term, moving towards one agreement per Area Health Service. The second round of enterprise bargaining, however, never really commenced because the Labor Party had won government in the April 1995 NSW election.

1996–2000s

The third period brought a return to industry-wide occupational awards that operated across the state. The Health Department established bargaining 'working parties' in each occupational area, with some representation from local Area Health Services, whose activities were overseen by HIRSAC. The strategic direction and monitoring role of HIRSAC, however, became more ad-hoc during this period. These management working parties negotiated with the respective state union representatives to determine the content of the state-based occupational awards.

In summary, in terms of the remaining dimensions of bargaining, there were two consistent themes running through the three bargaining periods. First, there was a strong centralization in the level of bargaining and in the bargaining agents. Even in the mid-1990s, when government rhetoric and policy most strongly emphasized decentralization and enterprise bargaining, the Health Department and the state-wide unions maintained effective central controls over local bargaining. Second, while the status of bargaining changed according to the legal regime sponsored by the alternate governments – in particular, the changing legal emphasis on enterprise bargaining – these changes had little practical effect. The one round of enterprise bargaining did not break away significantly from the old awards and any new content in the enterprise agreements was subsequently incorporated back into the awards after 1996.

(ii) Victoria

In Victoria, the State government funds and administers public hospitals through the Department of Human Services, which has been restructured and renamed a number of times since 1990. In 2003–4 the Department of Human Services (DHS) had an annual budget in excess of $9 billion, which amounts to approximately 32 per cent of recurrent expenditure making it the largest department in the government. Unlike NSW, public hospitals in Victoria historically are largely independent bodies run by semi-autonomous boards of management. These boards of management have had substantial autonomy from government and, in effect, the Victorian government has never directly managed hospitals but has 'steered' their direction largely through funding policies and procedures (Lin and Duckett, 1997,

p. 48). Public hospitals also have two strong industry groups, the Victorian Healthcare Association and the Victorian Hospitals Industrial Association, which have played key roles in the funding process. Like NSW, the level of unionization in the Victorian health sector is high, with disaggregated ABS statistics suggesting 43 per cent union density in 'public hospitals and nursing homes' in 2000, declining from 55 per cent in 1994 (ABS Unpublished data, 1994, 1996, 1998, 2000). These figures mask the fact that some unions, such as the Australian Nursing Federation, have been increasing their union membership over these years and some hospital managers suggest that union density amongst nurses in their hospitals as high as 70 per cent (Bartram and Stanton, 2004). The major unions are:

- the Victorian branch of the Australian Nursing Federation;
- the Australian Medical Association (AMA); and
- the Health Service Union of Australia (HSUA).

The HSUA in Victoria is organized into five branches each with their own decision-making processes and officials:

- the Health Services Union of Australia (Number One branch), representing hotel services;
- the Health and Community Services Union (HCSU) (Number Two branch), representing workers in the disability and psychiatric areas;
- the Health Professionals Association (HPA) (Number Three branch), representing allied health professionals;
- the Medical Scientists Association of Victoria (MSAV) (Number Four branch); and
- the Health and Community Services Staffs Association (HCSSA) (Number Five branch) representing managers and administrators.

Some of these branches have a history of conflict with each other and Lin and Duckett (1997, p. 49) argue that the health trade unions have traditionally had strong links with the Australian Labor Party (ALP), making them powerful players in the industrial process and able to resist any real reform of work practices.

There have been three different government approaches to the management of the healthcare sector and employment relations in Victoria over the past twenty years and these have directly influenced the level and scope of bargaining: the Cain/Kirner Labor government (1983–92) presided over a centralized industrial relations framework, the Kennett

Liberal–National government (1992–99) heralded a move to decentralization and the Bracks Labor government (1999–present) has seen a return to a more centralized system. However, as the following section demonstrates, in practice it can be argued that it has led to little real change.

1980s–1992

Under the Cain/Kirner Labor government, hospital staff were employed by the individual hospital on state awards under the jurisdiction of the Victorian Industrial Relations Commission (VIRC). The VIRC was modelled on its federal counterpart and incorporated conciliation and arbitration principles (Creighton and Stewart, 2000, p. 38). The state awards were based on occupational groupings such as nursing, allied health, medical, hotel services and medical scientists, with these groupings negotiating separately from each other through their respective trade unions. Bargaining processes were largely conducted centrally with direct state government involvement. The Victorian government often played a principal employer role, even though it was not actually the employer and often excluded hospital employers from the award-making process, meaning that hospital managers had to implement the decisions of these players despite little input into their deliberations. The Victorian Hospitals Association (VHA) was critical of this situation (Fox, 1991, p. 58) and employers also argued that there was little room for flexibility at the local level leading to inefficient work practices (Stanton, 2002b).

Up until 1992, public hospitals were block funded retrospectively on an annual basis. The public hospitals, along with the VHA, were adept at media manipulation and the funding process was extremely political. Critics argued that there were few incentives for efficiency in this process and a number of reports had suggested that Victorian public hospitals were inefficient compared to hospitals in other states (Lin and Duckett, 1997). Also, in common with other areas of the public sector, middle (and sometimes senior) management in the public hospital sector was highly unionized. Many medical managers were likely to be members of the Australian Medical Association, directors of nursing were often members of the Australian Nursing Federation and middle managers belonged to the then Hospital Administrative Officers Association (Fox, 1991, p. 23). Any attempts to make hospital managers more responsible for resource allocation and cost control had to deal with this industrial context.

Despite the fact that the government did not directly control public hospitals, Health Department Victoria (later renamed and reorganized into Department of Human Services) had been attempting to exert more control over the directions and efficiency of hospitals through the introduction of Health Service Agreements. Health Service Agreements were supposedly quasi-contracts entered into by two parties, hospital and government. They were an attempt to move away from line-by-line budgetary accountability to agreement over broad directions and productivity. However, they were often seen more as a mechanism of control, leading to resentment from some hospital employers who saw this as interference in their business (Stoelwinder and Viney, 2000).

1992–1999

The Liberal–National government under Premier Kennett was elected on a platform which included a commitment to small government through outsourcing and privatization, the introduction of private sector managerial practices through the development of performance reviews, audits, and contractual relationships, and a 'steering not rowing' approach to service delivery (Alford and O'Neil, 1994). The government was also committed to industrial reform, including the decentralization of industrial relations through enterprise bargaining and controlling the power of unions (Teicher and Gramberg, 1998).

Fears of rising costs in the public hospital sector and its strong trade union base made it a logical target for reform and the government moved quickly to implement its health reform agenda, including stringent budget cuts, with the availability of voluntary departure packages, and the encouragement of outsourcing. At the same time, Victoria became the first Australian state to introduce Casemix funding (based on throughput) in 1993. According to unpublished data from the Australian Bureau of Statistics, 12,000 jobs disappeared from the health and community services sector between February 1992 and February 1994 (Stanton, 2002b). The Victorian Hospitals Association saw some benefits in the cuts, arguing that they enabled hospitals not only to make massive reductions in staff numbers but also to make substantial changes to work practices (Hughes, 1993, p. 1).

In 1995, the state government established the Metropolitan Network Boards, which contained a number of previously independent hospitals within their jurisdiction. Individual hospital boards of management were abolished and the new network boards were governed by directors who were more commercially oriented (MHPB, 1995, p. iv). These new structures introduced a concept of governance that, although originating from the private sector, was being increasingly used in public sector management (Perkins *et al.*, 2000; Ferlie *et al.*,

1995). They were also a conscious expression of a purchaser-provider relationship in which government would step back from the direct provision of services, instead purchasing services from others who would carry out the 'hands on' management (MHPB, 1995, p. 72).

The government's industrial relations strategy mirrored its 'arms length' health management strategy. It was committed to a decentralized industrial relations system and introduced its industrial relations reforms early in its term. The *Employee Relations Act 1992* came into effect in March 1993 (Teicher and Gramberg, 1998). The Act abolished the VIRC and existing state awards and introduced individual and collective agreements with basic minimum conditions. However, the federal Labor government in December 1992 introduced amendments to federal legislation to allow the transfer of state employees, who had no recourse to compulsory conciliation and arbitration, to the federal arena (Creighton and Stewart, 2000, p. 38). The health sector unions immediately acted on this. The Kennett government fought through the courts to prevent the transfer of Victorian awards to the federal jurisdiction but, after a series of challenges, they lost (Gardner, 1995). All formal regulation of employment conditions in Victorian public hospitals was thereby transferred to the federal system. In 1997, the Kennett government handed over its whole industrial relations jurisdiction to the federal arena, but this had no impact on public hospitals because of the transfer had already occurred.

Unions did not, however, escape industrial reform as the federal Labor government was also committed to enterprise bargaining and the Kennett government sought to use new bargaining arrangements to initiate change, as well as trying to weaken the power of the trade unions through abolishing union payments at source and by publicly excluding unions from consultation processes. There were three major enterprise bargaining rounds in the public hospital sector during the period: one in 1995, the next in 1997 and the last in 1999. As a result, there was a large increase after 1994 in the numbers of enterprise agreements in the broader public health and community services sector in Victoria (Stanton, 2002b). One reason for the growth in agreements was that during this time there was an increase in separate bargaining units with agreements being struck with each of the different employers, at the hospital and/or network level, rather than a single central agreement covering a range of separate employers.

The first round of bargaining in 1995 was highly centralized and carried out by the Victorian Hospitals Industrial Association (VHIA) on behalf of the hospitals, as the government was determined to appear uninvolved. Most assessments of the first round of bargaining agreed that it was largely a wages round, with little in the actual agreements that specified productivity gains or changes to award provisions. The productivity gains made later were essentially due to further budget cuts outside of the bargaining process (Stanton, 2002b).

By 1997, the Metropolitan Network Boards were fully established and adamant that no centralized negotiations occur in the second round of bargaining. The DHS was also determined not to be part of any negotiations, although they did consult with the employers regarding wages and funding policy (VHIA, 1997). There was a new federal government, the *Workplace Relations Act* was in place and the Kennett government had handed over jurisdiction of industrial relations to the Australian Industrial Relations Commission (AIRC), so the process of enterprise bargaining was ostensibly simpler.

Despite the government's intentions, however, the major health unions launched industrial campaigns that eventually drew an unwilling government to the bargaining table, forcing centralized bargaining. The unions managed to roll over most of their award conditions into the new enterprise agreements thereby thwarting the award simplification process of *Workplace Relations Act*. The final agreements were centralized in outcomes with some marginal differences (Stanton, 2002b).

In the final round of bargaining in 1999, the employers did not wish to repeat the experience of 1997. There was a view that formal enterprise bargaining in the public health sector was not favourable for employers, with little productivity savings from enterprise bargaining as few agreements had yielded changes in work practices. Instead, all significant change had been brought about outside the enterprise bargaining process through outsourcing, Casemix funding and budget cuts (Djoneff, 1999).

The agreements up for renegotiation included the HSUA, the HCSU, the HPA, the HCSSA and the AMA. The government had already announced its policy of only funding a wage increase of nine per cent over three years (or three per cent per annum). The winter of 1999 saw a long and bitter dispute with the HPA, culminating in arbitration before the AIRC, plus a less intense dispute with the HSUA No. 1 branch. Yet, for the first time, the employers and the government were more coordinated and the employers managed to achieve the government's wages objective of nine per cent over three years with the HSUA and the HCSSA. The AMA had also accepted nine per cent over three years, plus an agreement to establish a Medical Remuneration Review to examine the competitiveness of medical remuneration in Victoria by comparison with other states. Only the HPA managed to achieve a greater result, interestingly enough through arbitration.

Stanton's (2002b) study into employment relations in the Liberal–National years in public hospitals found that much of the promised autonomy for local employers did not eventuate and health organizations were still controlled by government directions. The actual number of enterprise agreements grew during these years, but the level of wage bargaining was still centralized; at best, the process could be described as a type of pattern bargaining with some flexibility around the edges. In terms of the scope of bargaining, especially the regulation of non-wage issues, employers had hoped to use enterprise bargaining to increase flexibility. However, this rarely happened and other studies showed that the focus on cost invariably led to non-bargained workplace changes that had a negative impact on work intensification, labour shortages, staff commitment and morale (Considine and Buchanan, 1999; Weekes et al., 2001). There was also inadequate long-term human resource planning within the health sector and no proactive support for investment in local HRM during this period (Stanton, 2002a).

1999–2000s

In 1999, the Australian Labor Party came to power in Victoria under Premier Bracks. The new government inherited a public health industry that was in poor shape financially because of years of budget cuts. Its response was to put more money into the sector, to re-emphasis planning, to put a greater focus on quality rather than just efficiency and to encourage collaboration rather than competition (Stanton, 2002a).

There was also a return to centralized industrial relations processes in the health sector and the government was keen to involve the AIRC in decision-making. Early in the government's term of office the 2000 enterprise bargaining round with the Australian Nursing Federation (ANF) developed into a major industrial dispute, in which the ANF's industrial strategy of closing beds rather than taking strike action succeeded in placing great pressure on hospital management and government (Stanton, 2002a).

As enterprise agreements were due to be re-negotiated with other groups of workers, both in the health sector and in the public sector at large, the government was nervous about agreeing to high wage increases and quickly passed the issue on to the AIRC for arbitration.

As well as significant wage rises, the final arbitrated award included a nurse-patient ratio (four patients to one nurse) welcomed by the union but criticized by employers. For many employers this judgment represented a return to a centralized industrial response linking employment issues with service delivery issues with no flexibility at the local level. The ratio formula was also handed down at the same time as a government review was taking place addressing nurse shortages. There was little consultation with industry by the commission and the question of how to fund the ratios and manage the process of implementation proved contentious (Stanton, 2002a). In the negotiations for the 2004 EBA with the ANF, the government attempted to remove the nurse-patient ratio and replace it with a more flexible tool. However, the ANF rallied their membership into taking industrial action and eventually the government backed away from this proposal.

In summary, the structure of bargaining in Victorian public hospitals changed much less than might be expected given the major political shifts that occurred during the period after the late 1980s. The coverage of collective regulation was complete throughout. The status of the various bargaining forms evolved with the legislative changes and switches in jurisdiction, but the practical effects were not profound, apart from a great deal of activity around the EBA process. The introduction of enterprise bargaining by the Kennett government appeared to dramatically lower the level of bargaining to the enterprise level, but the real effect was considerably less State-wide action by unions which led to apparently autonomous enterprise agreements containing uniform wages, an outcome that was not strongly opposed by employers. At the same time, employers were less impressed with the modest variations across agreements in non-wage issues. The return to formal centralization under the Bracks government was strengthened by the introduction of the nurse-patient ratio. The scope of bargaining also remained wide throughout. The transfer of formal regulation from the state to the federal system brought the possibility of reduced scope of regulation through the 'simplification' of awards, but the unions were able to ensure that enterprise agreements replicated the content of awards. The formal regulation of nurse workloads actually expanded the scope of regulation.

(iii) South Australia

As is the case in Victoria and New South Wales, in South Australia the state government funds the public health care sector from revenue received from the federal government through the Australian Health

Care Agreements. Overall management of the sector rests with the South Australian health department, although it underwent a number of changes in nomenclature and structure in the period under discussion: the South Australian Health Commission was established in 1976 as a body corporate (Brooker, 1997), changing to a section within the Department of Human Services under the Liberal government (1993–2001), and shifting back to a separate department in 2004 under the Labor government. The most recent reforms under the Generational Health Review implemented by the state Labor government in July 2004 moved the organization and funding of healthcare towards a regional model closely based on the New South Wales approach, where Area Health Boards have been in place since 1986 (Menadue, 2003).

Under the 1993 *Public Sector Management Act*, local hospitals and health care units are common law employees able to directly employ their own staff, but conditions of employment must be sanctioned by the Department of Health and the Department of Administrative Services (DAIS). This arrangement allows for the Commissioner of Public Employment, Treasury, the Department of Industrial Affairs and state Cabinet to keep a close watching brief on any agreements or changes to awards in the public sector with a view to ensuring consistency in standards.

Like its counterparts in other states, the level of unionization in the South Australian health sector is higher than the state all-industry average percentage of 24.6. Union density in public hospitals, community health centres and nursing homes in 1994 was around 55 per cent (Brooker, 1997). In line with the other states, these figures mask the fact that some unions, such as the Australian Nursing Federation, have increased union membership over this time with national membership at around 60 per cent (ANF, 2003). The major unions are:

- the ANF, which represents nurses and Personal Care Workers employed in nursing homes.
- the South Australian Salaried Medical Officers Association (SASMOA), which represents interns, Resident Medical Officers, Registrars and Visiting Medical Officers (VMOs), who are in private practice but do sessional shifts in public hospitals (SASMOA, 2004). Union density ranges from around 60 per cent for salaried doctors to 45 per cent for VMOs (SASMOA, 2004).
- the Community and Public Service Union (CPSU) that represents the interests of ward clerks and a number of allied health professionals, such as social workers, physiotherapists and psychologists.

- the Australian Liquor, Hospitality & Miscellaneous Worker's Union (LHMU), which represents Personal Service Attendants, hospital cleaners, kitchen and maintenance staff employed in both the public and private sector.

The structure of bargaining in the South Australian public health sector is complicated by different occupational groups being covered by different jurisdictions. Prior to 1993, for example, all workers in the sector were covered by industrial awards, but nurses came under a federal award, while ancillary staff, allied health, trades and salaried medical officers were under state awards. After the introduction of enterprise bargaining, only the nurses and those from the metal trades had federal coverage under the 1996 *Workplace Relations Act*, while all other health professionals and occupational groups employed in hospitals were covered by the state-based *Industrial and Employee Relations Act* of 1993. The evolution of these bargaining arrangements, however, is best revealed in three time periods.

1993-1998

The approach of the Brown Liberal government, elected in December 1993, to bargaining in the public health sector was affected by two key contextual factors. First, it came to office during a major fiscal crisis associated with the collapse of the State Bank. In 1994 in an endeavour to deal with this situation the state Liberal government cut 15 million dollars from the public acute hospital sector, instituted competitive tendering for non-core services across the entire sector and provided funding for a round of redundancies that focused initially on the professions of medicine, nursing, allied health and lower level workers such as cleaners, porters, and maintenance staff (Willis, 2004).

Second, the trend towards enterprise bargaining was underway at federal level and within the state. The previous Labor government had largely followed the lead of its federal Labor counterpart, but the new Brown government's *Industrial and Employee Relations Act* of 1994 was closer to the more radical approach of the Kennett government in Victoria in moving against unions and jettisoning awards in favour of enterprise bargaining (Ronfeldt and McCallum, 1995).

Ironically, however, there were significant limits to the decentralization of bargaining in the South Australian public sector, which came to be covered by a single enterprise agreement, within which different occupational and industry groups were regulated by different sections. The net effect of these arrangements in public health was that the

Department of Human Services represented a single bargaining unit within which there was considerable standardization in matters such as rates of pay, hours of work and job classifications.

The first two rounds of enterprise bargaining for nurses and doctors, in 1996 and 1998, were overshadowed by workplace reforms occurring as a result of state government budget cuts. At the same time, the federal government also implemented a range of reforms and benchmark exercise that linked budgets to productivity and efficiency measures. Productivity was, however, not dependent on enterprise bargaining agreements; it occurred through the funding mechanisms and the processes put into place by management to deal with budget shortfalls (Willis, 2004).

1999–2001

By the third round in 2000 the situation changed considerably, at least for nurses and doctors. Nurses were not prepared to enter into an agreement without workloads being part of the negotiating package and the shortage of nurses became a source of bargaining power. Capitalizing on a similar situation that had arisen in Victoria between the ANF and the Victorian DHS the previous year, where the newly elected Labor government was forced to agree to staff public acute hospitals on a ratio of one nurse to four patients, the South Australian branch of the ANF brokered an agreement with the DHS to provide 200 extra nurses for the public hospital sector and to staff all public hospitals according to a computerized workload product (Australian Industrial Relations Commission {AIRC}, 2001).

What the DHS did not take into account at the time of these negotiations, despite advice from the metropolitan directors of nursing, was that hospital managers had been consistently undercutting staff levels on wards. Had the process of negotiations been conducted at the level of each hospital enterprise, rather than centrally, or had the hospitals had representation on the team, this would have been more forcefully stated. When the third EB agreement came into effect in 2001, a number of the public acute hospitals were unable to staff wards according to the agreement because of budget cuts. As a consequence, the ANF imposed industrial bans and closed a number of beds across the sector. In the world-wide climate of nursing shortages, the state government had few options but to acquiesce to union demands.

The introduction of Casemix, the establishment of incentive and benchmark funding, and the state Liberal government demand for outsourcing also resulted in a radical shift in the organization of hospitals in the 1990s. Much of this impacted on day-to-day life on the wards and the work of base level grades of registered and enrolled nurses who saw their work become more complex, but opportunities for promotion diminish. The union met this with successful demands for a revised career structure that recognized the complexity of work for base level nurses. Advanced promotional positions and salaries could be achieved independently of hospital established quotas for promotion. The ANF also worked to bring the salaries of nurses in the aged care sector into line with the acute sector through the enterprise bargaining processes. These gains have also carried over into the private sector although they have taken longer and been less attractive (AIRC, 1999).

The situation is not as positive for allied health professionals and hospital scientists. In the public sector both groups of professionals are represented by CPSU through its Professional Officers stream. However, the CPSU has been unable to negotiate enterprise bargaining agreements for these groups that have kept pace with nurses. This is partly explained by the fact that the CPSU negotiates for several categories of workers during each round of bargaining, but also, because allied health professionals and medical scientists do not have the political clout of nurses and doctors who are in a position to seriously disrupt waiting lists for elective surgery and accident and emergency departments. In effect these workers are non-core and the gains they have made reflect this.

Finally, for doctors, federal government reform in the provision of Medicare provider numbers has limited the number able to enter into private practice and increased the numbers seeking on-going employment in the public hospital sector. Workloads are high, but their numbers have steadily increased in the public sector. In the agreement made in 2000 the state Liberal government attempted to limit the salary sacrificing provisions, as well as the salary increases, to three per cent annually. With the base salary of doctors some $10,000 below other Australian states, it became difficult to staff public hospitals. As a consequence by the time negotiations began for the 2004 EB round parity of salaries rates with other states was on the agenda.

2002–2004

Agreements negotiated with the newly elected Labor government have once again demonstrated the uniqueness of the centralized nature of bargaining under the *Public Sector Management Act 1993*. However, where the Liberal government tended to construct the single bargaining unit as the Department of Human Services and the unions, the

Labor government has sidelined the health portfolio making the Industrial Relations portfolio the centre for negotiations. For example in the 2004 EB round between the ANF and the government, the Minister for Health and the relevant public servants sat at the table, but negotiations were conducted directly with the industrial relations portfolio. Initially the ANF found this frustrating as the two departments – health and industrial relations – attempted to wrest control of the processes from each other. In the end the ANF and IR Minister negotiated directly and health was sidelined. Comments from ANF negotiators indicate that this proved to be more effective, although initially ANF had assumed that the Health Department/DHS would be more understanding of the issues in the sector and therefore easier to deal with.

Negotiations in 2004 over the fourth EB round between the ANF and the Department of Human Services (now the Department of Health) and DAIS initially attempted to get nurses to abandon the previous agreement to staff wards according to a computerized formula. This was an interesting approach given that at the same time the DHS in Victoria was attempting to get nurses to abandon ratio staffing in favour of a computerized workload product. Despite what initially looked like being a protracted bargaining period the agreement was signed in record time. Overall the union achieved 90 per cent of what they requested, moving wages for nurses in the public sector into the top three in the country, second only to NSW and significantly reducing work intensification through provision for additional staffing.

The ANF has also been able to progress the professionalization agenda of nursing through the process of enterprise bargaining. South Australia now has the highest ratio of Nurse Practitioners in the country. In the 2001 agreement, midwives moved to the more professional caseload model of work productivity. This was maintained in the 2004 agreement with agreement to extend it to community health and mental health nurses over the life of the agreement. The ANF believes these gains reflect the fact that the state Labor government knew that the public health system was highly efficient and engaged in continuous quality improvement. In the previous decade budget restraint had meant that the system was run down, particularly in terms of capital works and equipment. However, the most significant factor in providing nurses with positive EB outcomes is the continuing difficulties in the recruitment and retention of nurses. A stated aim of all EB agreements for nurses and a focus of many of the conditions is to 'attach nurses/midwives to, and retain nurses/midwives in full-time or part-time employment in the South Australian public health sector and to reduce reliance on casual and/or agency employment to meet planned labour force requirements' (AIRC, 2004, p. 3).

Significant gains have also been made by PSAs, cleaners, plumbers, disability workers and maintenance crews in the public system under the Labor government. In 2003 the government agreed to a separate EB agreement for these workers. Previously they were part of a single bargaining unit that also included hospital managers, administrators and technicians. The LHMU believed the focus was on the needs of professionals rather than waged staff, many of whom are employed part-time, on split shifts and as casuals. The case for allied health is not as positive. They remain within the CPSU generic 'professional officer' category, along with engineers and others working across the entire public sector. The agreements take little account of the nature of hospital work and are limited in their capacity to incorporate the gains made by nursing and medicine. Allied health have used RN salaries to bolster their claims, but unfortunately the ANF claim is part of a recruitment and retention claim, which is not seen as an issue for allied health professionals except in rural and remote regions.

In summary, prior to the introduction of enterprise bargaining into the health sector in South Australia, the various professional and occupational groups were subject to awards. Salary and wage increases were achieved through national wage cases. Individual unions attempted standardization of rates across the country or pattern bargaining. With EB, significant discrepancies in rates of pay and conditions have developed within each professional group depending on whether they work in the public or private sector, as well as between professional and occupational groups. Those professions able to mobilize public opinion or, like nurses, where there is a shortage of staff, have made significant gains. The phrase now employed eschews terms such as 'pattern bargaining', arguing that workers achieve what the 'market will bear'. The ANF in South Australia often looks to the Victorian ANF experience to see 'what the market will bear'.

Union officials from the ANF agree with Stanton's (2002b) hypothesis that EB has had little to do with increased productivity and efficiency. Enterprise Bargaining is perhaps best described as a vehicle for compensating the more draconian workplace changes that have resulted from both federal and state budget constraints and policies that tie funding to workplace reform or efficiency measures such as outsourcing non-essential services. Initially EB agreements were limited to achieving salary and wage increases or penalty rates for shift work.

Unions sought little in the way of agreements that might reduce work intensification or long hours, both of which are seen by health professionals to impact on patient quality of care. In more recent years some unions have been able to shift the focus and use the EB process to capitalize on the perceived staff shortages and to further the groups' professional aspirations or achieve separate coverage based on the uniqueness of the work.

Comments and comparisons

The picture that emerges from these three case studies is of an industry in which the structure of bargaining has changed far less than in most other industries in Australia. First of all, the coverage of bargaining has remained almost universal in all three states. In other words, despite the significant deregulation of the employment relationship and the rise in individual bargaining in many industries (Waring and Bray, 2003), virtually all employees in the public health sector have continued to be covered by collective forms of regulation.

Second, despite the rhetoric of decentralization and the introduction of potentially radical reforms by many state governments (such as New South Wales between 1989 and 1995, Victoria between 1992 and 1999, and South Australia between 1993 and 2002), the level of bargaining has changed little. In reality, even during the periods of apparently radical reform focused on enterprise bargaining, collective bargaining in all three states has remained remarkably centralized. Similarly, the parties involved in bargaining – the agents of bargaining – have changed little, with governments continuing to dominate health sector managers, and state-level union officials retaining control of employee representation.

Third, in line with reforms to the broader industrial relations legislation in all three states, the status of bargaining has changed. Except perhaps in NSW, where the state system after 1995 has remained most faithful to tradition, both enterprise collective bargaining and individual bargaining have assumed far greater legitimacy and prominence than before. And yet, the new status of these bargaining forms does not seem to have affected industrial relations in the public hospital systems at all.

Finally, again in contrast to the experience in many other industries, the scope of bargaining remained broad. Indeed, the range of issues bargained and agreed in the public health sector has in some cases increased, the best example being the introduction of nurse-patient ratios in Victoria, South Australia and, most recently and most cautiously, in New South Wales. A key to understanding these unusual bargaining arrangements is the role of governments. As Fox (1998) argues, 'he who pays the player calls the tune', and at the end of the day in the public health sector it is government who provides the funds and is keen to control labour costs. Even those governments that have been most ideologically committed to labour market deregulation and the decentralization of bargaining have refused to give up decision-making responsibility on wages. The sector is also a highly political arena, industrial disputes quickly make front page headlines and governments are susceptible to bad publicity and generally act quickly to 'fix' problems that can influence public opinion.

The role of trade unions within the sector is also central. A number of health sector unions, contrary to national and international trends, have been increasing their union membership and density. Examining the Victorian branch of the ANF, Bartram and Stanton (2004) argued that the union had been able to increase its membership through a combination of strategies including appeals to employees' professional and occupational identity at times of insecurity, taking advantage of the enterprise bargaining process to recruit and organize members, and providing specific services such as professional indemnity insurance to its members. The success of these strategies, aided undoubtedly by labour shortages, deepened the ANF's bargaining power, allowing it to maintain its preferred bargaining structure and advance the substantive interests of its members. The best illustration is the insertion of nurse-patient ratio into enterprise agreements in Victoria, a development that was followed in other the other two states with some variation. Other health sector unions may not have been quite as successful as the nurses, but their memberships have survived and their bargaining activities have yielded better outcomes than in many other industries.

The apparent success of public health sector unions aside, there is also evidence in all three states that employers have made a number of efficiency and productivity gains over the past decade. These gains, however, have been achieved largely outside of the enterprise bargaining process. Budget cutbacks, new forms of funding and increasing non-labour costs have placed great pressures on health sector managers to reduce labour costs and improve efficiency. Workplace change has consequently been widespread, including outsourcing, changes in work practices, new shift patterns and other changes to working hours, but they have been introduced largely through managerial prerogative rather than through collective bargaining. In turn, these developments have often led to increased work intensification and greater dissatisfaction with working conditions leading to increased labour turnover, increased levels of workplace stress and union attempts (sometimes successful) to 'claw back' some of these managerial gains through the enterprise bargaining process.

These observations so far have emphasized the similarities between the three states, which are significant. There are, however, also some differences between the states, albeit mostly in legal and institutional detail rather than substance – differences of degree rather than kind. Given the importance of governments in affecting the complexion of public health sector industrial relations, the timing of elections in the three states and their political outcomes produced differences. Clearly, the different state governments chose different legislative vehicles for the pursuit of their policies and different frameworks and processes. In Victoria, the Kennett government's more radical industrial relations agenda in 1992–6 was largely thwarted and resulted in the hand over of the industrial relations function to the federal government and the dominance of federal awards/agreements in the Victorian public health sector; the Bracks Labor government has not sought to reverse this. The election of the Carr Labor government in New South Wales in 1995 saw a return to a more traditional industrial relations arrangements and an entrenchment of state awards. In industrial relations policy, the Labor government in South Australia before 1993 largely followed the lead of its federal counterpart, but the election of a Liberal government in late 1993 saw the beginning of a more conservative trend that was subsequently reinforced by the election of the Howard federal government in 1996. The mixture of federal and state regulation of public health sector employment in South Australia made both these developments important.

With respect to employers, public health managers are powerful key stakeholders in Victoria through their industry associations and they have the ear of government. These associations developed largely because of the relative independence of the Victoria public hospitals compared to their interstate counterparts. Also in Victoria, staff are employed by the individual hospital or network and the human resource management function is very much situated at the local level. The state government plays little role apart from initiatives through its Workforce Planning Branch. Under the Kennett administration very little workforce data was collected; the government believing that such data was not its business rather the business of the individual hospitals. The state's Office of Public Employment plays an influencing role rather than a regulatory role with organizations in the public sector. There are differences between union strategies. In NSW, unlike Victoria and South Australian (SA), the NSW Nurses Association was slower in prioritising work intensification as an industrial issues, preferring to seek wage increases to compensate for changes in 'work value' rather than directly regulating workload. At the same time, the NSW union eventually achieved workload reform, and while the various branches of the ANF carefully scrutinize wage deals made with the various state governments to ascertain the 'market wage' they all operate independently.

Conclusion

The federal system of government in Australia has clearly made the funding and administration of the public health sector extremely complex, with both state and federal governments retaining key roles in both health and industrial relations policies. This constitutional situation suggests great potential for diverse bargaining structures across the states of Australia and the three case studies presented in this chapter reveal some realization of this potential. However, it is the similarities between the bargaining arrangements of the three states that remain the key finding. Each of the three states in its own way has maintained a comprehensive, highly regulated and largely centralized bargaining structure despite the trend towards deregulation and decentralization in other industries around the country, particularly in the private healthcare sector.

Note

1   There is clearly some room for ambiguity in this case as to what constitutes 'the enterprise', just as Kelly (1990) argued there was ambiguity in the meaning of 'workplace'. Depending on legal and operational issues, it is possible that either individual hospitals and services (such as pathology units) or even the entire Health Department could be defined as an 'enterprise'. The most common practice in the sector, which is repeated here, was to define the Area Health Service as the enterprise.

References

Alford, J. and O'Neil, D. (eds) (1994) *The Contract State: Public Management and the Kennett Government* (Melbourne: Centre for Applied Social Research Deakin University).

Australian Bureau of Statistics (2001) *Employee Earnings, Benefits and Trade Union Membership*, Catalogue 6310.0 (Canberra: Australian Government Printer).

Australian Industrial Relations Commission (1999) *Nurses' (South Australian Private Sector) Enterprise Agreement 1999* (Adelaide: Commonwealth Government Printer).

Australian Industrial Relations Commission (2001) *Nurses' (South Australian Public Sector) Enterprise Agreement 2001* (Adelaide: Commonwealth Government Printer).

Australian Industrial Relations Commission (2004) *Nurses' (South Australian Public Sector) Enterprise Agreement 2001* (Adelaide: Commonwealth Government Printer).

Australian Nursing Federation (2003) *Time to Reflect: The ANF Federal Secretary's End of Term Report 1999-2003, ANF Home Page* {Online} http:www.anf.org.au (Accessed 20th October 2004).

Bartram, T. and Stanton, P. (2004) 'How to Make your Union Grow: The Case of the Victorian Branch of the ANF' *New Economies: New Industrial Relations - Volume 1*, pp. 42-52, Association of Industrial Relations Academics of Australia and New Zealand, 3rd-6th February 2004 (Queensland).

Bray, M. and White, N. (2002) 'A System under Pressure: Industrial Relations in New South Wales Public Hospitals', *New Zealand Journal of Industrial Relations*, June 27, 2, pp. 193-220.

Bray, M., and Waring, P. (1998) 'The Rhetoric and Reality of Bargaining Structures under the Howard Government' *Labour and Industry*, December, 9(2), pp. 61-79.

Brooker, J. (1997) *An Evaluation of Casemix Funding in South Australia 1994-95* (Adelaide: Casemix Development Program; Commonwealth Department of Health and Family Services and the South Australian Health Commission).

Community and Public Sector Union (1997) *Workplace Relations Act- Section 89A List of Allowable Award Matters* {Online} http://www.cpsu.org/ir_allow20htlm (Accessed November 2nd 2002).

Considine, G. and Buchanan, J. (1999) *The Hidden Costs of Understaffing: An Analysis of Contemporary Nurses' Working Conditions in Victoria* (Sydney: Australian Centre for Industrial Relations Research and Training University of Sydney).

Creighton, B. and Stewart, A. (2000) *Labour Law: An Introduction* (Sydney: The Federation Press).

Djoneff, A. (1999) *Industrial Relations Briefing* 26th February (Melbourne: Monash Medical Centre).

Ferlie, E., Ashburner, L. and Fitzgerald, L. (1995) 'Corporate Governance and the Public Sector: Some Issues and Evidence from the NHS' *Public Administration*, 73(3), pp. 375-392.

Fox, C. (1991) *Enough is Enough: The 1986 Victorian Nurses Strike* (Sydney: University of New South Wales).

Fox, C. (1998) 'Collective Bargaining and Essential Services: The Australian Case', *The Journal of Industrial Relations*, June, 40(2), pp. 277-303.

Gardner, P. (1995) 'High Court Rejects Award Challenge' *Australian Nursing Journal* May 2(10), p. 12.

Hughes, A. (1993) 'Budget Strain – the Pressure Increases', *Victorian Hospitals' Association Report*, April, no. 90.

Kelly, D. (1990) 'Defining the 'Workplace' in Workplace Industrial Relations', *ACIRRT Working Paper No. 4*, July (University of Sydney).

Lin, V. and Duckett, S. (1997) 'Structural Interests and Organisational Dimensions of System Reform' in H. Gardner (ed.) *Health Policy in Australia* (Melbourne: Oxford University Press) pp. 46–62.
Liquor, Hospitality & Miscellaneous Union (2004) *Home Page*. {Online} http://www.lhmu.org.au (Accessed 29th October 2004).
Menadue, J. (2003) *Better Choices, Better Health: Final Report of the Generational Health Review* (Adelaide: Department of Human Services).
MHPB (1995) *Developing Melbourne's Hospital Network: Phase 1 Report* (Melbourne: Metropolitan Hospitals Planning Board).
New South Wales Health Council (2000) *A Better Health System for New South Wales* (Sydney: NSW Government).
New South Wales Health Department (1998) *Annual Report 1997/98* (Sydney: New South Wales Health Department).
New South Wales Minister for Industrial Relations, John Hannaford (1993) *New Public Sector Wage Policy for NSW*, Press Release 5 April 1993 (ref 033/92).
O'Donnell, M. (1994) 'Up the Garden Path? Enterprise Bargaining and Decentralisation in the New South Wales Public Sector' in D. Morgan (ed.) *Dimensions of Enterprise Bargaining and Organizational Relations* (UNSW Studies in Australian Industrial Relations) pp. 203–217.
Perkins, R., Barnett, P. and Powell, M. (2000) 'Corporate Governance of Public Health Services: Lessons from New Zealand from the State Sector' *Australian Health Review*, 23(1), pp. 9–21.
Public Health System Heads of Agreement (1994) *Collective Agreement*.
Ronfeldt, P. and McCallum, R. (eds) (1995) *Enterprise Bargaining: Trade Unions and the Law* (Sydney: The Federation Press).
South Australian Salaried Medical Officers Association (SASMOA) (2004) *Home Page* {Online} http:www.sasmoa.org.au (Accessed 29th October 2004).
Stanton, P. (2002a) 'Managing the Healthcare Workforce: Cost Reduction or Innovation' *Australian Health Review*, 25(4), pp. 92–98.
Stanton, P. (2002b) *Changing Employment Relationships in Victorian Public Hospitals: The Kennett Years 1992–1999*, Unpublished PhD thesis (La Trobe University, School of Public Health).
Stoelwinder, J. and Viney, R. (2000), 'A Tale of Two States: New South Wales and Victoria' in A. Bloom (ed.) *Health Reform in Australia and New Zealand* (Sydney: Oxford University Press) pp. 201–222.
Teicher, J. and Van Gramberg, B. (1998) 'Industrial Relations and Public Sector Reform: The Victorian Case' *Australian Journal of Public Administration*, 57(20), pp. 60–67.
VHIA (1997) '"New" Enterprise Bargaining' *Journal of the Victorian Hospitals' Industrial Association*, 3(1), p. 3.
Waring P. and Bray M. (2003) 'Human Resource Management and the Individualisation of the Employment Relationship' in R. Weisner and B. Millett (eds) *Human Resource Management: Challenges and Future Directions* (Sydney: Jacaranda Wiley) pp. 117–34.
Weekes, K., Peterson, C. and Stanton, P. (2001) 'Stress and the Workplace: the Medical Scientists' Experience' *Labour and Industry*, 11(3), pp. 95–120.
White, N. and Bray, M. (2003) 'The Changing Role of Nurse Unit Managers: A Case of Work Intensification?', *Labour & Industry*, 14(2), December, pp. 1–20.

Willis, E. (2002) 'Enterprise Bargaining and Work Intensification: An Atypical Case Study from the South Australian Public Hospital Sector', *New Zealand Journal of Industrial Relations*, June, 27(2), pp. 221–232.

Willis, E. (2004) *Accelerating Control* Unpublished PhD Thesis (University of Adelaide, Department of Social Inquiry).

4
Outsourcing and Structural Change

Suzanne Young

Introduction

In Victoria throughout the late 1990s structural change in the public hospital system was immense as hospitals embarked on a range of market-testing and benchmarking exercises accompanied by downsizing and, in some cases, outsourcing. The clinical services which were subjected to these processes included radiology, pharmacy and pathology, and the non-clinical services included car parking, catering and cleaning, engineering and supply. In Victoria with the election of the Liberal–National government in 1992, outsourcing became a key part of the public management program (Stockdale, 1995, p. 29). This occurred alongside considerable decreases in state government funding, the implementation of industrial reform and the aggregation of metropolitan public hospitals into networks. The introduction of the Federal Liberal–National government's National Competition Policy (NCP) in 1995 with its rationale that private sector pressures and competition would make the public sector more efficient, saw widespread changes to the provision of structure of all public sector services.

National Competition Policy was introduced in Australia within the auspices of what is commonly referred to as the neo-liberal agenda, or New Public Management. Although each country's reforms had their own characteristics, certain common patterns emerged in the United States, the United Kingdom, Australia and New Zealand (Dunford, Bramble and Littler, 1998, p. 386). These objectives were to reduce the size of government, improve the effectiveness and efficiency of the public sector, improve the responsiveness of government agencies to their customers, decrease expenditure and improve managers' accountability (Dunford, Bramble and Littler, 1998, p. 386). The Australian government, in reshaping relationships in and between the nation and the states, sought to recompose and reconstitute the public sector, whilst deregulating the economy, introducing competition policies and changing the focus of industrial relations (Fairbrother, Paddon and Teicher, 2002, pp. 1–2).

In applying NCP, Victorian state and local government agencies were encouraged or required to market test their services by exposing them to competitive tender although in-house bids were allowed (State Government of Victoria, 1996, p. 7). The Liberal–National State Government stated that the primary consideration was the selection of a supplier best able to deliver the service, whether internal or external, to the organization. The assessment was to be made on the basis 'that the expected benefits to economic efficiency and better resource allocation would outweigh the expected costs of implementation' (State Government of Victoria, 1996, p. 36). The application of NCP was expected to result in the activity being kept in-house, or becoming outsourced, commercialized or administratively reorganized (State Government of Victoria, 1996, p. 35).

It is worth noting that NCP did not require services to be outsourced, but, rather, required governments to introduce procedures to increase competition. Even though all states were subject to the policy, Victoria was the most pro-active of all the states, linking its restructuring and privatization processes to NCP and was the only state which made competitive tendering compulsory for local government (Fairbrother, Paddon and Teicher, 2002, pp. 11, 14).

But even before the introduction of NCP, since 1993 the Liberal–National State government had encouraged public health organizations to investigate the use of outsourcing. Subsequently, with the implementation of NCP the State Victorian Government Policy (1996, p. 21) specifically stated that significant business activities undertaken within public hospitals, such as non-clinical services of car parking, computing, laundry services, engineering, cleaning and catering, and clinical services, including radiology, pathology, pharmacy, allied health services and general practitioner services, were to be subject to the policy. The process included benchmarking against private sector practices, with the result that in some instances the service was to be outsourced. Nursing and medical services, however, were classified as core activities, and were consequently exempted from examination.

Through a case study approach, this chapter discusses how two public health organizations implemented this policy. It investigates how outsourcing market-testing, benchmarking, and downsizing have been used to bring about workplace change. Whilst the resultant structural arrangements may differ, implications for the workplace have been similar.

Reasons for outsourcing

Generally, six reasons can be gleaned from the theoretical and empirical outsourcing literature to account for, or justify, its adoption (See Young, 2002 for a fuller discussion of these reasons).

The first reason for outsourcing is that managers have wanted to reduce costs and increase efficiency. Based on Transaction Cost (Williamson, 1979, 1986) and Agency theories (Eisenhardt, 1989) it is proposed that the 'firm' is the optimal structure when it can accomplish exchanges at a cost lower than any other form (Borland and Garvey, 1994). In contrast, the outside provision of services introduces economic efficiencies through the outsourcing vendor's ability to utilize specialist human resources, technologies and physical infrastructure.

Focusing on core competitive advantage is a second reason discussed in the outsourcing literature. Based on Porter's (1980) Corporate Strategic theory, researchers have proposed that outsourcing peripheral functions where excellence is not achievable enables organizations to concentrate on their core competencies (Cannon, 1989; Smith, 1991; Morkel, 1993; Quinn, 1992, p. 51).

Introducing workforce flexibility is a third reason cited in the literature and is based on Atkinson's (1984) 'flexible firm' model. Outsourced labour forms part of the peripheral labour group whose labour can be manipulated in accordance with changes in demand.

The labour market and political literature (Burgess and Macdonald, 1990, p. 32; Campbell, 1993) suggest a fourth reason for outsourcing is the management of industrial relations problems. The associated increase in the power of management over labour and weakening of the power of trade unions have been put forward as reasons for contracting out.

The satisfaction of decision-makers' personal objectives is a fifth reason and is primarily found in the political literature (Pfeffer, 1994). Public Choice theory (Hanke and Walters, 1990) asserts that public sector decision makers are motivated by self-interest which Downs (1967) maintains is divided into self-interest, through a desire for power, money and prestige as well as more broader interests of maintaining loyalty to work groups, agencies, government or nation.

In this vein, a sixth reason is the shaping of public sector agencies to align with the ideology of the government providing the funding. The reasoning here assumes that decision makers are motivated by a desire for power and see this desire being fulfilled by acting in the interests of the government. The neo-liberal government agenda advocates outsourcing, alongside private sector competition, a reduction in the size of the public sector, and a decrease in the power of labour.

Effects of outsourcing

A number of effects have been reported in the empirical literature (see Young, 2000 for a fuller discussion of these effects). For instance, Domberger and Rimmer (1994, p. 446) asserted that 'a review of the [international] literature illustrates a broad consensus that competitive tendering and contracting usually leads to substantial reduction in service costs, [with] average reductions of 20 per cent', with similar findings in Australia (Carver, 1989; Cubbin, Domberger and Meadowcroft, 1987; Donald, 1995; Domberger, 1994; Domberger, Meadowcroft and Thompson, 1986, 1987, 1988; Ferris, 1984, 1986; Hodge, 1996; Sharp, 1995).

Labour savings from outsourcing were the result of increased flexibility of the labour force. For example, in Britain, a Labour Research Department study stated that the reduction in wages and conditions linked to outsourcing resulted from an increased trend towards the use of part-time labour by contractors (Industry Commission, 1995, p. 160). Other studies into outsourcing in Britain reported significant evidence suggesting that contractors were able to reduce labour costs by utilizing more flexible labour practices (Ascher, 1987; Walsh, 1991; Walsh and Davis, 1993), and specifically in terms of pay, promotions and conditions (Willcocks and Currie, 1997).

Other research found that outsourcing increased the expertise of core staff and injected professionalism and skilled personnel, whilst improving access to technology (Rimmer, 1993; Industry Commission, 1995). The outsourcing process also engaged the public sector organization in setting specifications and monitoring of performance which were previously lacking (Domberger and Rimmer, 1994, p. 84). But even so, questions were raised with regard to the effect of outsourcing on quality (Industry Commission, 1995, p. 102).

Rimmer (1993) and the Evatt Research Centre (1990) reported that the use of contractors by local government councils did not always lower costs. Willcocks (1994) also found that as staff moved to private sector conditions, cost increases resulted. Rimmer (1993) furthermore contended that a lack of competition in bidding for contracts may have caused cost increases, especially in rural communities due to the lack of vendor numbers.

Other researchers found that contracting out produced switching costs that lock in the use of the existing supplier. Willcocks and Currie (1997, p. 45) reported that the contracting out of projects with huge infrastructure capabilities often resulted in a monopoly situation as very few suppliers have the capabilities to service the contract. Rimmer (1993) and the Evatt Research Centre (1990) also argued that as contracts are awarded to the same service vendor more than once, costs of in-house and contracted provision converged.

The management of contract staff, morale of internal staff, equity between contract and internal staff, and trust, motivation and commitment of both internal and contract staff have been highlighted as complex issues by numerous researchers. For instance, Pfeffer (1994, pp. 22–4) contended that contract staff lack loyalty, dedication and firm-specific knowledge and introduce problems of reduced productivity and motivation. Similarly, Young (2002) cited research highlighting the relationship between downsizing and outsourcing, with a reduction in trust and co-operation between management and staff.

Method

To investigate these issues, this chapter turns to two case studies which describe these processes in more detail. Interviews were conducted with organization managers, staff, union representatives and private sector proprietors between 1999 and 2001. The organization names are disguised and interviewees were granted confidentiality. The interviewer first contacted and interviewed the Chief Executive Officer, and then arranged interviews with subsequent personnel. All interviews were conducted face-to-face with the interviewee alone at the health organization location. All interviews began with the interviewee asked to talk generally about the workplace changes since the early 1990s, with subsequent semi-structured questions focusing on the reasons, processes and effects of market-testing, benchmarking and outsourcing. Interviews were taped and later transcribed. Annual reports, newspaper articles, consultants' reports and other published and unpublished material were used to supplement the interview material.

Case study one: Rural hospital

This hospital performs a variety of health activities for a large rural area in Victoria, with a population of around 60,000. Since the early 1990s, it has amalgamated with a number of smaller hospitals and health services and, as such, increased its coverage and bed numbers so that by 1 July 1999 the latter amounted to 246. Alongside this, it has been subjected to budget reductions and decreased government funding. The hospital provides medical, nursing, psychiatric, allied health and health promotion services to inpatients, outpatients, domiciliary care clients and the general public. Between 1991–2 and 1994–5, at the time when outsourcing was being contemplated across a variety of services, staff numbers (equivalent full-time (EFT)) in the acute section of the hospital fell from 701 to 573. In 1994–5, 11,623 inpatients were treated, 5901 operations were performed and 343,832 meals were served.

Pathology and radiology were outsourced prior to NCP, in 1994–95 and 1995–96 respectively, and the non-clinical services of dental technician and gardens and grounds were outsourced under the auspices of NCP. The services of engineering and maintenance and food were benchmarked but not outsourced.

All of the decisions were implemented within an environment of decreased government funding and hospital amalgamations, and NCP's introduction in 1996 added political factors to the decision-making. Furthermore, the financial environment put pressure on the hospital's ability to provide funding for capital replacement, whilst the characteristics of the rural labour market added demands on the hospital's ability to obtain professional staff. Boards and executive management drove the changes, with information being provided to staff about the rationale and progress of the process. Once outsourcing was considered viable, negotiation between management, unions and employees tended to focus on the transfer process. Not to be confused with consultation, this was patriarchical in nature, with management telling the workers that change was needed and outlining the method of implementation.

Economic reasons for outsourcing, namely to reduce costs, focus on core competencies and increase labour flexibility, were apparent in the decision-making. Evidence was given of decreased costs from using more flexible work practices in contracting out gardens and grounds, dental technician services, pathology and radiology. For example, the outsourcing of pathology saved approximately $200,000–$300,000 per annum. Escalating rates of pay and resistance to flexible rostering, both being subject to industrial negotiation at the time of outsourcing, were regarded as direct causes of outsourcing of pathology right across the Victorian health industry.

In addition, the hospital's use of private contractors provided updated equipment in both radiology and pathology, which amounted to $3 million in radiology alone. However, in gardens and grounds a reduced scope of service was integral to the savings made.

Even without outsourcing, costs were also reduced by changing conditions of work and reducing employment numbers, For example, the staff numbers in engineering and maintenance services fell from 25 EFT in 1992 to 11.4 in 1997, and in food services were reduced by half from 72 to 35 EFT. Consultants then argued that outsourcing these services would further reduce costs, but there was a lack of concrete evidence that this would eventuate, considering that changes to work practices and downsizing had already occurred.

The prospect of reduced quality from outsourcing was raised particularly in maintenance activities. The line manager explained that the nature of hospital work necessitated that contractors perform each job perfectly, not quickly and cheaply in the manner commonly found in the private sector. So instead of outsourcing, changes were made to work practices based on consultation and accountability. The line manager stated that the threat of outsourcing had decreased staff morale, but 'once that idea was "put to bed" and staff were given more responsibilities and changed their work practices, productivity increased'.

The idiosyncrasies of the rural labour market were a factor in the choice between outsourcing and internal production, especially in relation to engineering and maintenance services. The lack of expertise in the rural area made it impossible to use local labour. Also shortages of labour which, in some instances, led to high wages being earned external to the hospital, rendered the use of contract labour a necessity. In other cases, where the contractors' locations were remote from the hospital site, this raised impracticalities in using a contractor on an on-call basis.

In radiology the use of a private contractor also allowed the hospital to gain expertise that was not available locally, hence reducing management problems of recruitment. In general, rural areas suffer from both a distance and expertise disadvantage. The distance to major cities, and thus other sources of labour, makes it difficult to gain numerical flexibility at short notice by using contract labour. Furthermore, it is often problematic to attract skilled expertise in rural areas, especially if the complexity of the task is not consistently high.

The objective measurement of transaction costs was found to be a problem in both engineering and maintenance and food services, where managers and union officials questioned the external consultants' benchmarks, the nature of the key performance indicators and the non-inclusion of transaction costs. Also, in radiology, there were questions raised concerning whether the analysis included redundancy and superannuation payments, and whether performance was monitored prior to outsourcing.

Environmental uncertainty was apparent in pathology with increasing competition and a decline in fee-paying patients. The Director of Medical Services indicated that the impetus of an existing private hospital opening a competing laboratory produced fear of a reduction in market share. In radiology, it was manifested with decreased government fees payable for public provision and a lack of funds available for upgrades in technology. In both of these clinical services the acquisition of skilled staff was also problematic. Using contracts to lock in costs, staffing and technology over the long-term in order to reduce environmental uncertainty was evident at this hospital. Hospital managers' indicated that all incumbents were likely to regain the contracts upon termination, providing for continuity of relationships, capital equipment and stability of employment for staff who had simply transferred from hospital employment to the private contractor.

In addition, as no further cost/benefit analyses had been conducted since the initial contracts were awarded it was improbable that the services would be transferred back in-house. The continuing cost advantages of the contract situations were difficult to ascertain due to a lack of data. The renegotiation of both pathology and radiology contracts would be subject to sunk costs and small numbers bargaining, which economic theorists (see Williamson, 1979) believe would increase the contract costs in subsequent negotiation. Specifically, in radiology the costs of capital equipment provided by the contractor would make it highly improbable that the contractor would be changed.

In addition, broader reasoning was apparent and included self-interest, or opportunism, the power of the union movement and government ideology. For example, throughout the early 1990s the incumbent radiologists had not been supportive of the hospital and had opened a private practice in competition with the public hospital service, with the effect being that all private outpatients were referred to the radiologists' private clinic. The outsourcing of the radiology service negated the power of the radiology incumbents and stopped their manipulation of the hospital processes to benefit themselves, which had often occurred at the expense of the hospital service. In pathology, the ability to decrease the power of the Health Services Union Association (HSUA) No. 4 Branch, representing the medical scientists was raised as a reason for outsourcing.

Political and economic reasons overlapped, and political reasons produced economic effects and vice versa. The use of contractors in radiology was not simply used to solve the problematic relationship between the incumbents and management, as the contractor's provision of new capital equipment allowed gains to be made in revenue through increasing patient numbers from 35 to 100 per day. Even though political reasons were raised in outsourcing pathology, equally the changes to funding rendered it highly likely that economic benefits would be gained through the private provision of pathology. Loss-leading practices were also used by the private sector to break into the pathology market, as the change to funding rendered it more profitable. Increased competition in the pathology and radiology market minimized the ability of contractors to engage in opportunistic behavior, thereby decreasing hospital risk, leading to reduced costs. So even if the decision was pushed by political imperatives, economic benefits resulted and vice versa.

A cultural perspective was also apparent with decision makers taking the values and relationships between the parties into account. In food, and engineering and maintenance services, although management employed consultants to benchmark these services, they then insisted that internal staff retain their jobs to repay loyalty and maintain quality.

This case also showed that clans and relationships could be beneficial to the organization in external arrangements. In outsourcing radiology, the relationship between management and operating staff improved, staff morale raised and on-going long-term relationships benefited all parties. The sharing of culture and values was enhanced with the transfer of employees from internal employment to the contractor, as in radiology and pathology. A staff member explained: 'The private proprietors did the right thing; they were genuine people; they were well-liked by everyone; and it was a relief because the previous radiologists' relationship with the departmental staff and the hospital management was poor'.

But in the non-clinical areas public perception was important and the managers believed that the local community would view the replacement of low skilled blue-collar workers by those from outside the region unfavorably.

The ideological predilections of the Liberal–National federal and state governments have also been demonstrated as important in the outsourcing decision. Transferring services from the public to the private sphere was an aim of the federal government in altering the payment for pathology services, which alongside decreased state government funding gave the hospitals no choice but to privatize pathology. The state government's lack of funding for upgrades to capital equipment meant that, especially in rural hospitals where there was also a lack of community funds and donations, the introduction of the private sector into public provision of radiology was imperative.

There are many examples of the use of power and political tactics in this case. For example, in the operation of the radiology service there were conflicts of interest, criticisms of hospital equipment by the radiologists to patients and staff, and incompatible personalities, attitudes and values between the staff and the radiologists. Self-interest was also evident in a number of cases where workers accepted change more readily once outsourcing had been used at the hospital, or when it was threatened. In this regard, employees were willing to become multi skilled and change work practices to retain their jobs. Managers referred to this as staff adopting a 'change culture'. The Chief Executive Officer (CEO) stated that across all areas of the hospital the staff realized that the hospital would examine outsourcing, so it was better to work with the organization to provide a better and efficient service. The power of line and departmental managers was also an important consideration, as managers within the Food, and Engineering and Maintenance Departments displayed hierarchical authority and an ability to alter the Board of Management's perceptions. Their selective use of decision criteria and information was a factor in keeping some functions in-house. Manipulating figures, selecting appropriate key performance indicators, and discrediting consultants' reports were all examples of political tactics used to sway opinions. In doing so, self-interest may also have played a part, as once the function was outsourced it was likely that the manager concerned may have lost their position. In addition, the use of outside experts to provide legitimacy to a decision already made may have been a tactic used in the decision to outsource radiology. It was interesting that consultants' reports were accepted more readily in some areas than others.

Managers often give prominence to the view that reducing costs is the primary reason for outsourcing however, on the basis of the case it is clear that other factors impact on the decision-making. These can typically be service quality, relationships, loyalty, power, culture and the idiosyncrasies of the rural labour market. Notwithstanding this, whether benchmarking and outsourcing was used or benchmarking alone, the consequences were decreased staff numbers, increased productivity, altered work practices, and increased numerical and functional flexibility, alongside increased staff vulnerability and decreased staff morale.

Case study two: City network

In 1995 the Victorian Liberal–National state government introduced a network structure for the metropolitan public health service whereby hospitals, which had been autonomous with their own boards of management, were subjected to numerous changes to their structures, systems and work operations. As state governments changed, two subsequent changes to the composition of networks were made. The first network administered from this site was comprised of four metropolitan hospitals. In November 1997, a larger conglomeration was formed, comprised of ten hospitals and health services.

The current health network serves a population of nearly 1,000,000 people predominantly living in two areas of the metropolitan city, as well as offering a range of specialist services for the whole state. Support services are also provided to two adjoining networks, which were disaggregated from this network on 30 June 2000. It operates 1200 beds and the major hospital of the network is the State's leading teaching and research hospital. In 1995–6 at the time when outsourcing was being considered the network serviced 112,910 acute inpatients and 568,530 acute outpatients. It also treated 3459 psychiatric inpatients, 83,170 psychiatric outpatients and 2125 aged care inpatients.

The hospital network, within the auspices of NCP, embarked on a review of services in the Infrastructure Division, plus pathology and pharmacy services. It was conducted within an environment of turbulent network amalgamations and restructures, continuing operating losses and numerous benchmarking exercises. A review of the on-going structural changes since 1995 found that they had an adverse impact on staff morale and standards. Continual leadership instability led staff to comment that there was a lack of accountability, a lack of consultation, a lack of vision and too great a focus on fiscal matters.

Specifically, the result of the review process was that car parking, gardens and grounds and supply management were outsourced to external contractors. Internal teams won the contracts for food services and engineering, whilst pharmacy, pathology and cleaning services continued operating within the internal hierarchical structure.

The Infrastructure Division was the first area subjected to the process due to its peripheral nature with regard to patient care and the financial savings which it was believed could be made through changing work processes and downsizing. Network management displayed mixed adherence to the private sector ideological perspective. Although they market-tested those services recommended by the state government and used the word 'mandate' as an explanation to staff for involvement in the process, they did not seem to be completely focused on the introduction of outsourcing per se. Outsourcing was considered but a variety of other arrangements were used, both before and after the implementation of NCP.

The contract for the provision of food services was awarded to the internal team based on increasing efficiency through changing work practices and introducing new technology. A manager explained that there was a perception that mass production of food was going to be cheaper and better. The line manager also claimed the evaluating committee looked favourably on the changes the in-house team had already made in reducing staff numbers from 320 to 160 upon aggregation into the network structure and transforming work practices. On awarding of the contract 'wholesale workplace reform' again occurred in relation to rosters, work practices and bringing into line the payment of allowances with industrial agreements.

Pathology was not outsourced due to the high costs of each of the bids and the realization that costs could not be reduced through outsourcing. Due to the nature of the network's pathology service and it teaching and research components, the bids were uncompetitive. It was claimed by the Director that the benchmarking process got lost in the process, with the total bid cost being based on forward estimates of services that were not being currently provided, whilst there was a lack of infrastructure and knowledge within the existing system to costs the service reliably. Hence, management, prior to market-testing had been unaware of the service's cost of operation and looked to the private sector to 'fix' the problem and, although work practices had been altered prior to the bidding process, there was inadequate investigation of how the service could be operated more efficiently.

The outsourcing of gardens and grounds was due to its peripheral nature which it was believed would produce cost savings on outsourcing through the ability of the contractor to specialize. By transferring internal staff to the contractor the benefits of using staff with corporate knowledge would be retained. The contract cost of $160,000 per annum was less than half of the internal staffing cost of $350,000 per annum. However, the outsourcing was unsuccessful and after two years the service was brought back in-house due to problems with quality and excessive monitoring. A director explained: 'We couldn't find the contractor and we spent so much time going around to check if he'd done what he should have done in accordance with the contract, it cost money'. It could be argued that management did not understand the nature of the contract's complete transaction costs or that the costs were simply ignored in the haste to outsource.

The introduction of specialization and expertise were also seen as advantages in outsourcing supply management to a multi-national logistic contract organization, but the overarching aim was still to increase efficiency through changes to management and work practices, and downsizing. The aim was always to bring the management of the service back in-house once the contract time was expired. A director explained: 'At the end of the contract the internal staff would be trained, and the people that went to work for the contractor could be bought back whilst retaining the knowledge'.

In regard to engineering services, prior to aggregation into the network structure staff numbers were 160 EFT. Within 12 months, the network had contracted out 30 selected specialist services, including fire, lighting and generators, with accompanying savings of over 30 per cent. So that by July 1996 and with a flatter management structure staff numbers had fallen to 63. The contract for engineering services was then awarded to the internal team to increase efficiency, decrease costs and promote workforce flexibility in the belief they had the capabilities to downsize, using contractors for specialist tasks, whilst the use of internal staff provided for the retention of corporate knowledge. The line manager claimed: 'We had all the knowledge of critical areas and the person walking off the street was not familiar with the operation at the depth that the in-house team had'. Staff numbers continued to fall so that by 2000 they were reduced to 35. A director argued that such workplace reform would not have eventuated in a 'normal' workplace due to union obstruction. It is interesting to note that contract staff earned higher wages than internal staff, but provided more flexibility.

In outsourcing car parking to a private contractor the network was aiming to reduce costs, increase efficiency and reduce risk, through introducing expertise in systems, technology and management. Low trust existed between management and internal staff with perceived problems of pilfering. Once the service was outsourced, external audits paid for by the network reduced the opportunity of the contractor to engage in opportunistic behavior, whilst the contractor introduced expertise to counter internal problems. Fraud was an apparent risk in both internal and outsourced arrangements, although external audits were not considered as an option to minimize risk in the former.

In contrast, pharmacy services were retained internally after market-testing due to lack of provable benefits in efficiency and the heightened risk factors associated with private sector involvement. The patient contact, teaching and research components involved utilizing specialist knowledge, which management felt was not available to the same extent in the private market.

The relationship between food services staff and the network was one of the reasons given for outsourcing food services to the internal team, rather then outsourcing to an external contractor. A manager of a receiver hospital in the network explained that network managers showed loyalty to the internal team as they believed that the service was sustainable, in terms of it being long-term with low risk, compared to the service offered by some external contractors. Although loyalty could be hardly be said to be pervasive, taking into account the downsizing which had occurred prior to outsourcing. The lack of trust between internal staff and management was an impetus in outsourcing car parking to an external organization. The gardens and grounds service suffered from a problematic relationship between the network and the contractor, although the lack of political problems with internal provision was not considered to be an advantage of the previous internal arrangement. Hence, similar to car parking, there was a risk of opportunistic behavior on the part of the contractor, although the difference in costs between the internal and outsourced service was so great that the risk was not considered pervasive. On re-awarding the contract to a previously employed staff member, expertise was retained whilst relationships were improved, thus ridding the network of the political problems.

Goal conflict and power struggles were evident in the internal management of the supply department with outsourcing used to change the management style. Similarly, in regard to food services there was evidence of goal conflict, changing power structures and lack of trust, but the contract was awarded to the internal team, thus allowing for the relationship between upper management and operating staff to be maintained. The major difference between supply and food was that in the former, the outsourcing process was used to remove middle managers, downsize, and alter work practices, whereas with the latter, downsizing had already occurred. In addition, there was a lack of management expertise in supply and outsourcing was used to introduce a learning environment. Furthermore, the outsourcing of food services was claimed to be partly due to a lack of power of middle managers to influence the decision, particularly having proved adaptability through introducing and overseeing change.

One of the rationales in the market-testing of pharmacy services was the removal of department management, and the market-testing of pathology services resulted in the exiting of the manager. In relation to the latter, a director claimed, 'he felt he didn't want to be part of the change...thought it was all too hard'.

In regard to the pathology service, the changing funding arrangements and industrial relations environment also provided political and ideological impetuses for the investigation of outsourcing. Moreover, both directors and union officials claimed that staff at the affiliated university and medical staff used political tactics in lobbying for maintaining the status quo.

Even though the industrial relations environment was generally not referred to in the interviews, the process was used to alter work practices and downsize employee numbers. A director explained to the internal staff:

> You can win it, but you're going to have to change your work practices...As management had the opportunity to set the specifications, it was a way to change work practices without necessarily having to go down the track with the unions.

In addition, the director claimed that the process resulted in an effective bargaining tool in conducting enterprise bargaining negotiations.

> I'm saying to them...we kept you in-house, one of the few to have done that and we're working well, so just go easy with your work bans. Because, guys, if you're really going to give me a hard time ... I'll test the market place because the contract's up – five years, so legally I can do that.

Across the State, changing structures from hospitals to networks, accompanied by centralization of services, downsizing of employee numbers, geographical re-locations, hospital closures and financial difficulties saw the union movement reeling from the immense changes to the environment in which they were operating. In this instance, the network had greater power than the HSUA No. 1 Branch, who staffed the non-clinical areas. Outsourcing was only one of many pressures the union was facing, and hence contracts awarded to internal teams were seen as the lesser of many evils. In relation to the contracts awarded to external teams, minimal industrial relations problems eventuated, partly explained by factors, such as the nature of the labour force and the use of internal labour by the contractor. For example, car parking was staffed by casual workers who had minimal power; gardens and ground's internal staff moved to the contractor; and the supply contract was a management contract only, notwithstanding staff numbers decreased by half through voluntary redundancies. Industrial activity only occurred in pathology where the external conditions provided the impetus for statewide stop work activity. The wholesale changes imposed on the health organizations rendered staff very unsure of the future and pressured them into taking voluntary redundancy packages rather than stay and 'fight'.

So even though increased efficiency and reduced costs were the stated rationale for testing all services, it was only in the non-clinical services where management believed they were achievable by outsourcing. Outsourcing was rejected in the clinical areas of pathology and pharmacy as it would have produced a heightened risk to patient care, alongside minimal capabilities in changing work practices and downsizing to bring about large cost reductions. In the non-clinical areas, the use of specialists, who could introduce expertise into internal departments, was a factor which management believed would assist in cost reduction and work practice changes. The network also used downsizing and changes to work practices to achieve cost reduction, in both outsourced and internal arrangements.

In conclusion, economic reasons were numerous in the network's decision-making, whether outsourcing was proceeded with or not. The availability of specialists and introduction of expertise, both operational and management, were a high priority and tended to sway the decisions between an internal and an outsourced arrangement. In addition, the power of middle managers was a factor that impacted on the decision-making. When they were seen to be capable of making change the departments were generally outsourced to the internal team, but when management lacked skills or power, external outsourcing occurred. The effect of these different processes, however, were similar. Departments were downsized, working conditions were altered, middle managers were removed, numerical flexibility was increased, staff became multiskilled, costs were reduced and morale was reduced. And in outsourced departments problems of contract management and 'cost creep' on re-awarding of the contract were spoken of. By awarding contracts to internal teams, the power of management increased through the continual threat of outsourcing to external organizations being considered at the contracts' termination date. Furthermore managers expected employees to repay them by minimizing industrial relations activity.

Conclusion

The six reasons for outsourcing initially focused, in economic terms, on the desire to reduce costs, focus on competitive advantage and introduce workforce flexibility, and, in political terms, on the desire to adhere to government ideology, satisfy decision makers' personal objectives and improve industrial relations problems. From the evidence of the above case studies, another reason seems apparent, namely a desire to improve departmental management. Although management/staff relations have figured in the literature as a reason for outsourcing (Reilly and Tamkin, 1996; Burgess and Macdonald, 1990), it has tended to focus on the industrial relations imperatives or problems associated with changing work processes. This chapter has highlighted the problematic relationship between upper and middle management and the use of outsourcing to change or improve the relationship between the two. In some decisions this was achieved by removing the managers in question, and in others by removing the middle management layer altogether. In still others the threat of outsourcing induced managers to introduce change or, by threatening their power bases, induced them to leave. But the lack of middle management skills, their unwillingness to change, their use of political tactics to stop change and the difficult relationship with upper management have certainly been highlighted as factors leading to the outsourcing decision (See Young, 2005).

The reasons for outsourcing varied both within and between the health organizations. The lack of consistency in reasons for, and the processes of outsourcing show the autonomy of individual boards of management and managers operating in the health sector. There was a general view that, in adhering to government ideology, costs could be reduced through changing management practices, introducing more flexible work practices and downsizing. However, specific decisions about which services were to be outsourced were made on other bases, which included the characteristics of the labour market, employee skill levels and the nature of industrial relations, the perception of what was core in relation to patient care, the level of internal management skills, the ability of internal teams to implement change and the relationship between management and staff. Moreover, managers were of the opinion that, in some instances due to minimal sunk capital costs, the outsourced services could be brought back in-house if the contracts were unsuccessful, if circumstances changed or once objectives, such as downsizing or increases in expertise, were obtained. However, in other circumstances where sunk costs were high, especially in instances where the contractor provided capital equipment as in pathology and radiology services, such change was not thought capable of being accommodated.

The effects of outsourcing did not always align with managers' expectations, and unintended outcomes were apparent at the two health organizations. The rural hospital experienced deterioration in quality with the use of sub-contractors in engineering and maintenance. The risk of increased costs on subsequent contracting out of clinical services at the rural hospital was also apparent. The city network also experienced unintended outcomes in gardens and grounds with deterioration in quality, as well as conflict between the network management and the contractor which had not been evident with the use of internal staff. Fewer unintended outcomes were experienced at the city network in outsourcing food and engineering and maintenance, as the internal teams provided advantages in retaining corporate knowledge and scope for management to monitor behavior as well as contractual outcomes.

The termination of contracts was due to poor quality, the excessive cost of monitoring, and the contractors' inability to meet the specifications. In this regard, problems arose as excessive measurement was costly, especially where the writing of specifications was not adequately developed.

The interplay of political reasoning and economic effects was also evident. Even though management problems were an impetus in considering outsourcing in radiology at the rural hospital, in practice outsourcing led to reduced costs and changed work practices. Similarly, the use of outsourcing to solve industrial relations issues and/or take up government funding opportunities also produced financial benefits, through the injection of private sector capital funds, higher rates of pay and changes to work practices. Hence, the health sector's fiscal environment was linked to the political nature of the decision-making. Indeed, the industry's public sector characteristics were crucial to the political nature of the decision-making, as the bureaucracy were able to affect the decision-making at individual organizations through board composition, and changes to network structures and budgets. The attainment of personal objectives was relevant in the context that managers' could exert power to obtain a decision that reflected their needs, such as maintaining staff levels, retaining their own position, using new technology, restraining change or fostering change.

When outsourcing was used, cost savings and increases in efficiency generally resulted. But even when it did not proceed the results were similar to the use of other change mechanisms, such as introducing new technology, changing departmental structures and promoting workforce flexibility. In some cases, not all transaction costs were included in the analysis. For instance, at the rural hopital management costs, voluntary departure packages and the risk of increased contract costs on subsequent tenders were not generally taken into account. Often managers did not have a clear understanding of internal processes and required outcomes, and outsourcing was used to develop these through writing the contract specifications. Furthermore, the use of outsourcing to solve problems of managing staff was not effective where contract managers were unaware of the specific requirements of hospital services. In cases where problematic relationships existed between upper and middle management, the process, whether outsourcing eventuated or not, generally improved relationships and staff morale and changed department management. Hence, a variety of arrangements such as outsourcing benchmarking and downsizing were used to achieve similar outcomes.

References

Ascher, K. (1987) *The Politics of Privatisation: Contracting Out Public Services* (London: Macmillan Education).

Atkinson, J. (1984) 'Manpower Strategies for Flexible Organisations' *Personnel Management*, August, pp. 28–31.

Borland, J. and Garvey, G. (1994) 'Recent Developments in the Theory of the Firm' *Australian Economic Review*, First Quarter, pp. 60–82.

Burgess, J. and Macdonald, D. (1990) 'The Labour Flexibility Imperative' *Journal of Australian Political Economy*, 27, pp. 15–35.

Campbell, I. (1993) 'Labour Market Flexibility in Australia; Enhancing Management Prerogative?' *Labour and Industry*, October, 5(3), pp. 1–32.

Cannon, D. (1989) 'Keeping Outsourcing in Hand' *Chief Executive Magazine*, Nov–Dec, pp. 38–41.

Carver, R. (1989) 'Examining the Premises of Contracting Out' *Public Productivity and Management Review*, 13(1), pp. 27–40.

Cubbin, J., Domberger, S. and Meadowcroft, S. (1987) 'Competitive Tendering and Refuse Collection: Identifying the Sources of Efficiency Gains' *Fiscal Studies*, 8(3), pp. 49–58.

Domberger, S. (1994) 'Public Sector Contracting: Does It Work?' *The Australian Economic Review*, Third Quarter, pp. 91–6.

Domberger, S., Meadowcroft, S. A. and Thompson, D. J. (1986) 'Competitive Tendering and Efficiency: The Case of Refuse Collection' *Fiscal Studies*, Nov, 7(4), pp. 69–87.

Domberger, S., Meadowcroft, S. A. and Thompson, D. J. (1987) 'The Impact of Competitive Tendering on the Costs of Hospital Domestic Services' *Fiscal Studies*, 8(4), pp. 39–54.

Domberger, S., Meadowcroft, S. A. and Thompson, D. J. (1988) 'Competition and Efficiency in Refuse Collection: A Reply' *Fiscal Studies*, 9(1), pp. 80–90.

Domberger, S. and Rimmer, S. (1994) 'Competitive Tendering and Contracting Out in the Public Sector: A Survey' *International Journal of Economics and Business*, 1(3), pp. 439–53.

Donald, P. (1995) 'Leading Public Sector Management at the City of Melbourne' in *How to Run a Business within Government* (Sydney: IIR Conferences Pty Ltd).

Downs, A. (1967) *Inside Bureaucracy* (Boston: Little Brown).

Dunford, R., Bramble, T. and Littler, C. (1998) 'Gain and Pain: The Effects of Australian Public Sector Restructuring' *Public Productivity and Management Review*, 21(4), pp. 386–402.

Eisenhardt, K. M. (1989) 'Agency Theory: An Assessment and Review' *Academy of Management Review*, 14(1), pp. 57–74.

Evatt Research Centre (1990) *Breach of Contract: Privatisation and Management of Australian Local Government* (Leichhardt New South Wales: Pluto Press/Evatt Research Centre).

Fairbrother, P., Paddon, M. and Teicher, J. (2002) 'Introduction: Corporatisation and Privatisation in Australia' in P. Fairbrother, M. Paddon, M. and J. Teicher (eds) *Privatisation, Globalisation and Labour: Studies from Australia* (Sydney: The Federation Press) Ch. 1, pp. 1–24.

Ferris, J. (1984) 'Co-Provision: Citizen Time and Money Donations in Public Service Provision' *Public Administration Review*, 44(4), pp. 324–33.

Ferris, J. (1986) 'The Decision to Contract Out: An Empirical Analysis' *Urban Affairs Quarterly*, 22(2), pp. 28–31.

Fraser, L. (1997) *Impact of Contracting Out on Female NESB Workers: Case Study of the NSW Government Cleaning Service* (Canberra: Research and Statistics Branch, Department of Immigration and Multicultural Affairs).

Hanke, S. H. and Walters, S. J. K. (1990) 'Privatization and Public Choice: Lessons for the LDC's' in V. Wright and L. Perrotti (eds) *Privatization and Public Policy Vol I*, 2000 (USA: The International Library of Comparative Public Policy Elgar) pp. 331–42.

Hodge, G. (1996) *Contracting out Government Services: A Review of International Evidence* (Melbourne: Monash University).

Industry Commission (1995) *Competitive Tendering and Contracting by Public Sector Agencies*, Draft Report, October (Australia: Industry Commission).
Morkel, A. (1993) 'Industry Clusters and Value-System Strategies for Australia' in G. Lewis, A. Morkel and G. Hubbard (eds) *Australian Strategic Management Concepts, Contexts and Cases* (Sydney: Prentice-Hall) pp. 389–99.
Pfeffer, J. (1994) 'Competitive Advantage through People' *California Management Review*, 36(2), pp. 9–28.
Porter, M. E. (1980) *Competitive Strategy: Techniques for Analyzing Industries and Competitors* (New York: The Free Press).
Quinn, J. (1992) 'The Intelligent Enterprise a New Paradigm' *Academy of Management Executive*, 6(4), pp. 48–63.
Reilly, P. and Tamkin, P. (1996) *Outsourcing: A Flexible Option for the Future?* IES Report 320 (Brighton UK: The Institute for Employment Studies).
Rimmer, S. (1993) *Aspects of Competitive Tendering and Contracting in Local Government Administration*, PhD thesis, University of New England.
Sharp, P. (1995) 'Competition as Opposed to Outsourcing: The Commercial Support Program in the Defence Science and Technology Organisation' in *How to Run a Business within Government* (Sydney: IIR Conferences Pty Ltd).
Smith, J. (1991) 'Corporate Little Helpers' *Australian Business*, Aug 7, pp. 44–6.
State Government of Victoria (1996) *Competitive Neutrality A Statement of Victorian Government Policy* (Melbourne: Department of Premier and Cabinet).
Stockdale, A. (1995) 'Contracting Out: A Victorian Perspective' in J. Guthrie (ed.) *Making the Australian Public Sector Count in the 1990s* (Sydney: IIR Conferences Pty Ltd) pp. 26–9.
Walsh, K. (1991) *Competitive Tendering of Local Authority Services: Initial Experience* (United Kingdom: Dept. of Environment, HMSO).
Walsh, K. and Davis, H. (1993) *Competition and Services: The Impact of the Local Government Act 1988* (United Kingdom: Dept. of Environment, HMSO).
Williamson, O. (1979) 'Transaction-Cost Economics: The Governance of Contractual Relations' *Journal of Law and Economics*, 22, pp. 233–61.
Williamson, O. (1986) 'Transaction-Cost Economics: The Governance of Contractual Relations' in J. Barney and W. Ouchi (eds) *Organizational Economics* (San Francisco: Jossey-Bass), pp. 98–129.
Willcocks, L. (1994) 'Managing Information Systems in UK Public Administration: Issues and Prospects' *Public Administration*, 72(1), pp. 13–32.
Willcocks, L. and Currie, W. (1997) 'Contracting Out Information Technology in Public Sector Contexts: Research and Critique' *Journal of the Australian and New Zealand Academy of Management*, 3(2), pp. 34–49.
Young, S. (2000) 'Outsourcing: Lessons from the Literature' *Labour and Industry*, April, 10(3), pp. 97–118.
Young, S. (2002) 'Outsourcing and Downsizing: Processes of Workplace Change in Public Health' *The Economic and Labour Relations Review*, December, 13(2), pp. 244–69.
Young, S. (2005) 'Outsourcing in the Australian Health Sector: The Interplay of Economics and Politics' *International Journal of Public Sector Management*, 18(1), pp. 25–36.

5
Casual and Temporary Employment in NSW Regional Hospitals

Alex de Ruyter

Introduction

The hospital industry in Australia has been subjected to widespread change in the last 20 years. Previous chapters of this book have demonstrated that significant workplace change has taken place in the hospital industry, as evidenced by the introduction of new management practices such as benchmarking and enterprise bargaining. These have been initiated as a response to public sector fiscal austerity and the introduction of private-sector practices under the auspices of New Public Management. There has been an overall increase in per capita health expenditure in Australia in the last 25 years (AIHW, 1998, p. 163). However, it has not kept pace with increased demand for services due to an ageing population. It is here that demand-side pressures have contributed. Evident is an increasing role for the private sector, and a diminishing public sector share of health expenditure. This has been encouraged by a federal government, keen to promote private treatment through tax rebates for private health insurance as a means of reducing public sector waiting lists. One consequence of fiscal austerity has been work intensification, compounded by the 'caring work ethic' displayed by health sector professionals.

However, a significant aspect of workplace change in the last 20 years has been the increased use of non-standard employment in the hospital industry. Non-standard employment is any form of employment that is not salaried, permanent full-time. This chapter examines the use of temporary and casual employment in two NSW regional hospitals.

Background: the growth of non-standard employment

The growth of non-standard employment has been evident both in Australia, and internationally, and has occurred across industries, occupations, and gender (Standing, 1997). Table 5.1 provides a breakdown of the standard (permanent full-time) and non-standard share (%) of the workforce between 1988 and 2000; with the non-standard share in turn disaggregated into permanent part-time, casual and self-employment (non employee). From Table 5.1, it is evident that the standard employment share of the Australian workforce has declined. To a certain extent, growth in non-standard employment is associated with structural developments in the Australian economy, including growing feminization of the workforce and the growth in service sector employment. However, the important point is that the incidence of non-standard employment is increasing across the workforce irrespective of gender, industry, sector or firm size (Burgess and Campbell, 1998).

Table 5.1 The standard and non-standard workforce in Australia 1988–2000

Year	Standard Workforce (%)	Non-std Workforce (%)	Permanent Part-time (%)	Casual (%)	Non *Employee* (%)
1988	64	36	5	15	16
1989	63	37	5	16	16
1990	62	38	5	16	17
1991	60	40	6	17	17
1992	59	41	7	17	17
1993	58	42	7	19	16
1994	56	44	7	20	17
1995	56	44	7	21	16
1996	55	45	7	22	16
1997	54	46	8	22	16
1998	54	46	8	21	17
1999	53	47	9	22	16
2000	53	47	9	23	15

Source: Burgess and Strachan, 1999; Burgess and de Ruyter, 2000; ABS, The Labour Force, Catalogue 6203.0; ABS, Employee Earnings, Benefits and Trade Union Membership, Catalogue 6310.0. Columns 4–6 sum to give column 3.

Casual employment has been the dominant component of employment growth during the 1980s and 1990s (de Ruyter, 2002). In the "new economy" the vast majority of the additional jobs being generated are part-time and/or casual. Indeed, it can be said that non-standard jobs are rapidly becoming standard in Australia. This does not include the extensive growth in fixed-term contract jobs, subcontract employment arrangements and multiple job holdings (Burgess and de Ruyter, 2000). Casual and fixed-term employees have considerable advantages in terms of the flexibility they provide to management. However, the use of casual and agency workers in particular raises issues pertaining to the continuity of patient care and in turn poses issues of integration into the workplace and career development for the employees concerned. It has been argued that non-regular employees impose an added cost in terms of making them familiar with unit procedures and continuity of patient care (Lumley, 2001). Contracting out was increasingly utilized during the 1990s, with the states initially introducing competitive tendering in gardening and maintenance, catering and even some medical and nursing services for which demand is irregular (Patrickson and Maddern, 1996, p. 108; Young, 2003, 2002). Indeed it could be said that

> governments at both federal and State levels are no longer seeking to achieve efficiencies by introducing incremental types of change which leave the hospital structure and decision processes basically untouched. Rather they are moving towards a more radical outcome whereby health activities, including many of those once thought to be havens of secure job tenure, are now being contracted out to private providers (Patrickson and Maddern, 1996, p. 105).

There has been some research published on the uses of non-standard employees in hospital workplaces. In metropolitan areas, it has often been difficult to fill permanent positions (Allan, 1996; Gough and Fitzpatrick, 2000), and hospitals have had to recourse to utilizing casuals and agency workers – an example of supply-side factors driving the growth of non-standard employment (de Ruyter, 2002). However, there is a paucity of research on to what extent the use of non-standard employment can be integrated within wards and departments. This is an important issue as it raises implications for occupational health and safety, training, and most importantly, continuity of patient care. Traditionally, casual employment in particular, has been conceived of as being short-term and intermittent (see Burgess and Campbell, 1998 for a discussion). However, hospitals generally express a preference for regular, permanent employees (de Ruyter, 2002). There is thus a manifest tension between the need to meet budgetary requirements, as depicted by the use of part-timers and casuals, and the need for providing ongoing quality care.

However, what research there is has tended to focus on the rationales of using *permanent* part-time employment, and the advantages and disadvantages of doing so (Short, 1993; Allan, 1996; Bailey and Hocking, 1997; Reeves, 1999; and internationally see Arrowsmith and Mosse, 2000; Hiscott, 1994; Kemp, 1994). There is also the predictable slant towards examining the labour use practices of the nursing workforce, whilst the work practices for ancillary employees and allied health employees have remained relatively unexplored. Similarly, the uses of casual and temporary employees have received less attention (Allan, 1996; Lumley, 2001 being notable exceptions). In part, this reflects the highly feminized nature of the industry itself and the numerical dominance of the nursing cohort, with the result that most attention is focused on whether female part-time employees attain an adequate career-life balance; as typified in the debate surrounding the integrative capacity of part-time employment (Short, 1993; Bailey and Hocking, 1997).

Whilst not seeking to deride the importance of research into the dynamics of permanent part-time employment, the fact remains that many permanent part-time employees are in the mid-stage of their careers, and typically are constrained to working part-time because of family/child-rearing duties (Allan, 1996; de Ruyter, 2002). Such research therefore is of less use in highlighting how potential employees are drawn into the workplace, particularly younger workers, who are more likely to gain a foothold in the hospital workforce through casual/ agency or fixed-term appointments (de Ruyter, 2002).

Thus, there is a need to further explore how casual workers, agency workers, and fixed-term workers in particular are utilized within the workplace. Allan (1996) found that in the public sector, casual employment and agency employment was used to cover for short-term absences such as sick leave, while temporary/fixed-term employment was used virtually to cover only for extended absences such as maternity leave. Where non-standard employment was more extensively used, it was more for supply-side reasons. In medicine a chronic shortage of staff led to the widespread use of casual and part-time Visiting Medical Officers (VMOs). In contrast, Allan (1996) found that the use of non-standard employment was greater in the private sector hospitals studied ('Privcare' being a for-profit private hospital). Privcare had the greatest incidence of non-standard employment: only 18 per cent of its employees were permanent full-time. Casual employees comprised 44 per cent of the workforce and permanent part-timers 38 per cent during 1994. Privcare had an overriding imperative to minimize costs, and thus utilized casuals, although they faced a relatively stable demand for services. Allan's study emphasizes demand-side factors as driving the use of casual and temporary employment. How widespread are these trends? Evidence from metropolitan areas (Lumley, 2001; Gough and Fitzpatrick, 2000) for nursing in particular indicates that permanent positions often cannot be filled, and that nurses are choosing to work on a casual or agency basis. The nation-wide shortage of nurses has been recognized by governments, with the NSW State government, for example, trying to attract more people into nursing courses and encourage former nurses to return to practice (Sub-Regional Newspaper, 2000, p. 56). Evidence suggests that casuals and temporary employees display less commitment to the workplace, and can be less-skilled (de Ruyter, 2002). This in turn poses implications for quality and continuity of patient care. It is thus of importance to ascertain the factors contributing to the uses of casual and temporary employees in the workplace.

Method

Case studies on two hospitals in a region of New South Wales were conducted between 2000 and 2001. The selected region offered a number of distinct features, which increases the merit of case studies conducted within it. There is a long tradition of formalized industrial relations practices, and the commitment of the regional union movement to 'constructive' workplace change. This was evidenced through the development of highly effective site agreements, and placing priority on regional issues over national trade union issues. The region also contains a significant proportion of disadvantaged people, and a higher proportion of elderly people than the NSW state average, which reinforces the requirement for comprehensive health services to meet their specific needs. Most importantly, the region is perceived as having an attractive lifestyle and is located near Sydney. This serves to potentially increase the number of individuals attempting to obtain work at the hospitals within it, and higher average tenure levels as individuals stay in the area.

One case study was conducted in the public sector: this was conducted within the regional Area Health Service, here designated as 'Regional Health' at a hospital designated as 'Public Hospital'. Another case study was conducted in the private sector, in a hospital that is owned by an operator that runs private hospitals throughout Australia: 'Private Hospital'. Pseudonyms were used for privacy and confidentiality reasons. All privately collected information was subject to ethics clearance procedures enforced by the local health authorities. The case studies followed the method used by Allan (1996), in which employment information was used to construct cohorts for which employment composition could be identified, followed by interviews with managers and employees. This approach can overcome the restrictions of using self-administered questionnaires and enables a greater understanding of the idiosyncrasies and undercurrents in each enterprise.

Temporary and casual work in public hospital

Public Hospital is one of the oldest hospitals in Australia. It provides a number of specialist services, including orthopedics; rheumatology; rehabilitation medicine; and a range of outpatient services (1997–8 Annual Report). Allied health services such as physiotherapy, occupational therapy, speech therapy, and social work are also available at the hospital. The hospital also had a collaborative venture with a church welfare group that provided 'transitional care to elderly patients who have been discharged from acute hospitals and are awaiting permanent residential care placement' (Establishment Profile). As at 30 June 1998, it had a yearly average full-time equivalent of 464.7 staff employed; 119.7 average available beds; and 95.8 daily average inpatients. Apparent from Table 5.2 is that the non-permanent workforce, while not insignificant, is still only a minority of the workforce. Table 5.2 gives a breakdown of casual and temporary employees in Public Hospital, as at August 1999, in terms of numbers, and as a percentage of the total hospital workforce. Temporary employees (full-time plus part-time) and casual employees comprised about 13 per cent and 11 per cent of the workforce respectively.

Table 5.2 Public hospital, temporary and casual workforce, August 1999

Employment type	Females #	Females %	Males #	Males %	Total #	Total %
TFT	21	4.9	18	12.0	39	6.8
TPT	27	6.4	13	8.6	40	7
Casual	51	12.1	11	7.2	62	10.8

Source: *Regional Health*, Payroll database
Notes: TFT = temporary full-time (fixed-term) TPT = temporary part-time (could be fixed-term or paid by the hour; 'casual')

The restructuring of NSW public hospitals into area health services in 1988 (de Ruyter, 2002) resulted in employees of NSW Health being designated as employees of the area health services for payroll and personnel purposes. However, employees were still attached to their individual hospitals when it comes to the allocation of work and determination of rosters. Thus, an employee at one hospital conducted all their work at that hospital. Very rarely were staff pooled or shared. In extreme cases it is possible to seconde staff from one hospital to another, say in the case of a severe shortage of staff within a ward. Even casual employees tended to work for the one hospital, as unit managers (who determine the allocation of shifts) preferred employees to demonstrate loyalty to, and familiarity with, the establishment. This however, did not preclude the possibility of promotion or transfer to another hospital (within a health service, or to another health service) should positions become available. Indeed, progression could occur between hospitals in an area health service and into other area health services, via horizontal job ladders.

Examining employment in Public Hospital indicated a significant use of casual and temporary employment across occupational groups, as shown in Table 5.3, ranging from 29 per cent of the nursing cohort, to less than 11 per cent of the administrative and clerical cohort. There was a high use of casual employment particularly in the nursing cohort. Casuals were often recruited through an agency. Often the agency was the first port-of-call for Public Hospital to obtain casuals, rather than incurring the costs of advertising directly – the agency then served as a

Table 5.3 Public hospital: temporary and casual workers by occupational group (cohort), August 1999

Staff type	TFT (#)	TPT (#)	Casual (#)	Total* (#)	% of cohort
Administrative and clerical	1	6	–	7	10.4
Allied health and diagnostic	6	10	–	16	20.8
Medical	8	–	2	10	22.2
Nursing	14	–	60	74	28.5
Support and domestic	10	24	–	34	27.9
Total	39	40	62	141	

Source: Regional Health, Payroll database
Notes: TFT = temporary full-time (fixed-term), TPT = temporary part-time
* total temporary and casual

screening device, for which a small commission was paid.[1] Thus, casuals were considered as employees, under the guise of a casual contract of employment (Interview: HR Officer #1, 25 October 1999). Hence, they are classed under casuals in this chapter (nursing was the only occupational cohort for which agencies were regularly used). Not all casuals are recruited through agencies –some were 'recruited' directly by Regional Health. At the time of the research, only the medical and nursing awards stipulated a distinct category of casual employment. Other awards referred to the looser category of 'temporary' employment (which could be fixed-term or effectively casual). The following section examines the use of the different types of non-permanent employment at Public Hospital.

Fixed-term employees tend to be used for two reasons: to cover for extended absences; and as a probationary and a training device. In maintenance, four employees were apprentices on fixed-term contracts at the time of writing. In nursing, a major consequence of the increased use of casual and fixed-term (temporary) work is that direct entry into permanent entry-level positions no longer occurs. Graduates enter into a 12-month fixed-term internship. The graduate placements are full-time and consist of nurses who undertake rotation between inner city establishments and other regional health establishments for the year. At the completion of their contract they might or might not be offered permanent work. Generally they go onto an eligibility list for permanent employment however in practice this usually means working as a casual. As one manager explained,

> at the end of the year, if there's any permanent positions – in my recollection I don't think a lot of them got permanent positions – if there's a position they can get one, but most of them go onto casual positions, and they go onto an eligibility list in HR (Manager 4).

A number of employees were on temporary contracts at the time of the research. These were primarily low-skilled hospital assistants in the support and domestic divisions. The Support Services and Catering units displayed a high usage of non-standard employees. In Support Services (cleaning and laundry) there were ten temporary employees as at November 1999 (Manager six), of which six were regular fixed-term employees who were working 40 hours a week and thus were full-time, and four were 'casual'/irregular. Cost was a primary factor in using these employees, allowing the hospital to better adjust staff numbers to demand and hence make budgetary savings. Temporary full-time and temporary part-time employees were also used to fill in for absences, and for positions where a permanent appointment had not been made, for example during a staff freeze.

A major disadvantage as perceived by managers of using temporary part-timers was that they were 'sectorized', in that they could work for more than one hospital within Regional Health. Hence, a temporary part-timer might not be 'available' when a unit manager required them as they might have already taken a more 'choice' shift at another establishment (Manager 22). On some occasions this impeded their acceptance by the permanent workforce. In Support Services though, the six temporary employees who have been employed on an ongoing basis had experienced multiple contract renewals, generally on a three-month basis – giving them a high degree of familiarity with the units (in effect regular employees). Furthermore, it was notable that as these employees had worked more than 13 weeks continuously, they were viewed by the Health and Research Employees' Association (HAREA) as warranting permanent jobs. This subsequently occurred following the negotiation of a new Health Employees' Award later in 2001, with the emergence of a new specific *short-term* category of employment designated as *casual*.

In contrast, as the overwhelming majority of casuals were in nursing, the following discussion will pertain to nursing employees only. The casual workforce was not homogeneous and comprised two distinct groups. There were those who wanted to work casually; usually women, who were constrained by child-rearing duties. Other casuals expressed a preference for being able to 'choose' when they did their work and avoiding getting involved in 'office politics' and administrative duties. It is of interest to compare this to metropolitan hospitals. In many hospitals, permanent positions cannot be filled. Rather, there is evidence to suggest that many nurses choose to work on a casual basis for the flexibility and freedom from administrative responsibilities it entails (Lumley, 2001). However, a distinct feature of casual employment in hospitals in the region was the phenomenon of individuals working casually because they could not obtain a permanent position, and thus were trying to use casual work as a bridge to permanent employment. Managers suggested that the lifestyle attractions of the region were a prominent reason for nurses taking on casual positions, in the hope of subsequently obtaining permanent employment. While casuals were seen as necessary to cover short-term absences, some were also perceived as less loyal to the area where they work and less skilled:

> a problem with some casuals is lack of loyalty to the ward – they only work their hours and that's it. Some are double-booked on

other hospitals' pools which causes problems in availability, and some have slapdash practices and they get away with it because they're not being supervised day after day–it seems that they can be less-skilled even though they're presented as skilled (Manager 14).

When we need a casual, we just contact the nursing office and they send us whoever. However it doesn't always mean that they know what they're doing when they come in when they get to the ward (Manager 16).

Casuals could specify their hours, unlike permanent part-timers who had to work at least 20 hours per week. The use of casuals for covering short-term absences thus presented a distinct advantage over permanent part-timers in that there effectively was no minimum to the hours they must work. However, it was those casuals who readily made themselves available/on-call that were more likely to get permanent work–they were around more often and were more able to become part of a ward and acquire new skills through on the job training. Indeed, casuals were less likely to get access to staff training. There was a perception from management that it was not worth investing in someone who might not be around for long (see also Lumley, 2001: 96). If casuals wanted to attend courses they generally had to pay for it themselves (Manager 14), and attend in their own time (Manager 16). There was also evidence that some tension existed between casuals and permanent employees:

> life as a casual can be very hard because they don't have a home to go to. They'll tell you that sometimes it can be hard because some of the permanent staff sometimes look down on them. This happens because they don't think they're going to get the same amount of work out of the casual, even though we've got some very good casuals. The casual isn't used to the routine, so casuals can be alienated from permanent staff. You get some casuals coming down to the roster office saying 'I don't want to work in that area again; the nursing staff are awful.' (Manager four).

The use of a casual to a ward was also perceived to result in extra paperwork for regular ward staff (Manager 16). How widespread such tensions were is difficult to determine. The same manager (16) suggested that tension between permanent and casual employees was not widespread. Rather, it was suggested that the lack of ward knowledge and skills exhibited by some casuals provided an opportunity for permanent staff to 'demonstrate' their knowledge to such casuals. Indeed, 'it makes them [regular staff] feel important because they know something someone else doesn't' (Manager 16). The potential for tension could also be reduced because of the hospital's relatively small size – meaning that it would be more likely that the casual was already known to regular staff, and hence having some type of social connection with them.

Though not official hospital policy, both casual employment and fixed-term employment could fulfill a probationary function – when the individual concerned was able to obtain permanent work afterwards.

Temporary and casual work in private hospital

Private Hospital provides a number of services, including medical, surgical, oncology, psychiatric, in-vitro fertilization (IVF), pathology, radiology, and rehabilitation services. The hospital is also able to accommodate patients of considerable acuity, with a four bed intensive care unit (primarily coronary care patients), and provides specialist services in orthopedics, urology, ophthalmology, plastic surgery, and cardiology. Private Hospital however, focuses on elective surgery (some minor procedures can be conducted in the acute injuries area). The number of services has diversified in recent years, as the establishment of an oncology unit demonstrates. Private Hospital, then, is providing services that are also found in public hospitals. It operates on a for-profit basis (generally through health insurance funds).

In contrast to Public Hospital, the non-permanent workforce represents a significant proportion of the total, at some 45 per cent of the workforce during May 2000. This is a reflection of deliberate company policy to recruit people into casual (and permanent part-time) positions.[2] Table 5.4 provides a breakdown of casual and temporary employment compared to total employment for Private Hospital. In contrast to Public Hospital, (at the time of the research) private sector awards allowed for the use of casuals across all occupational groups. From Table 5.4 it is apparent that casualization was particularly evident in the nursing and allied health cohorts, where slightly over 50 per cent of employees worked (or were on the books) as casuals. In contrast, the administrative and clerical cohort was the least casualized, with fewer than 17 per cent of employees employed on a casual basis. Some 13 per cent of males and 35 per cent of females across the hospital worked on a permanent part-time basis. Thus, it was notable that casual employment comprised the largest single category of employment for both males and females, as demonstrated in Table 5.5.

Table 5.4 Private hospital: temporary and casual workers by occupational group (cohort), May 2000

Staff type	TFT (#)	TPT (#)	Casual (#)	Total * (#)	% of cohort
Administrative and clerical	–	–	8	8	16.67
Allied health and diagnostic	2	–	30	32	52.46
Medical	–	–	6	6	75
Nursing	1	1	136	138	51.49
Support and domestic	–	–	13	13	27.08
Total	3	1	193	197	45.4

Notes: TFT = temporary full-time, TPT = temporary part-time
* total temporary and casual.

Table 5.5 Private hospital, temporary and casual workforce by gender, May 2000

Employment type	Females #	%	Males #	%	Total #	%
TFT	2	0.5	1	1.3	3	0.6
TPT	1	0.5	–	–	1	0.2
Casual	158	44.0	36	47.0	194 *	44.7

Source: *Private Hospital*, Payroll database
Notes: TFT = temporary full-time (fixed-term) TPT = temporary part-time (analogous to casual)
* includes one employee of unknown occupational status

However, temporary employees (full-time or part-time) could only be employed on that basis for up to 13 weeks. Employment beyond 13 weeks required conversion to permanent full-time or permanent part-time status under the relevant awards. It is not surprising then that there were only four temporary workers at the Hospital as at May 2000. Labour variability to match demand was achieved through casuals and permanent part-timers. Where temporary employees were used, it was typically to cover for medium-term absences, such as that brought about by a permanent employee being on maternity leave for example. Thus the discussion in this section will focus on casual employees only.

Table 5.6 Length of service, casual nurses, private hospital, May 2000

Unit	0–<1	1–<2	2–<3	3–<4	4–<5	5–<10	10+	Total
Casual pool	13	21	6	–	2	5	–	47
CD	–	1	–	1	–	–	–	2
IC	1	3	1	–	–	–	–	5
IVF Unit	–	1	–	–	–	–	–	1
Oncology	1	–	1	–	–	–	–	2
Theatre	2	5	1	–	–	–	2	10
Psych ward	1	1	–	1	–	1	–	4
Other wards	21	20	9	10	4	1	–	65
Total	39	52	18	12	6	7	2	136

Source: Private Hospital, Payroll data.
Notes: CD = Central Sterile Supply Department; IC = Intensive Care Unit.

The need to balance quality service with bottom line considerations was attempted through the extensive use of casual employees. In nursing, casual employees formed the largest cohort, with slightly over 50 per cent of employees working (or at least available to work) on a casual basis. Recruitment in nursing was usually directly into the casual pool. From the casual pool, casuals seeking permanent employment could apply for permanent part-time positions. Thus, casual employment served as an entry point and as a screen. The casual pool nurses were recruited through an agency, but were on the payroll and thus could be considered employees of the hospital. A majority of casuals had employment duration of less than two years (approx. 67 per cent), as seen in Table 5.6.

This provided a contrast to permanent employees, of whom only 10 per cent had less than two years' service. This suggested that casuals who wanted permanent work either obtained it relatively quickly, or did not and then left the organization. Notable were two casuals in theatre with more than ten years service (both females). The data however did not reveal changes in employment status, thus it should not be automatically assumed that a casual with, for example, ten years service had been casual for the whole period of employment. Casuals were also less likely to be reimbursed for non-essential staff training, as they were perceived by management to have fewer ties to the organization. As one manager explained,

> they might be busy, they might go to Japan, you never know. They have to do their traditional courses, the manual handling, and the OH and S. But no, I couldn't say to one of them 'I'll pay for you to go to the pain course for a day' (Manager 31).

There was a perception from some managers that the amount of funding devoted to training was small. This was ascribed to pressures to cut costs: 'they're funny with their budgets here – they say they want to offer training, but they give you a thousand dollars a year, which is hardly anything' (Manager 37). In this context, training was seen as something that could be externalized onto the employee.

Across support units such as catering and housekeeping, casual employment was widely used – providing distinct advantages to the Hospital in being able to adjust hours worked to patient demand, thereby driving down costs. Labour adjustment in the kitchen could take place within two hours, with the availability of casuals on-call (Manager 40). In housekeeping, with cleaning shifts mostly commencing in the early morning to work around peak levels of activity (principally the operating theatres), there is little need for full-time employees (Manager 44). In these low-skill occupations, opportunities for promotion appeared to be minimal. In the kitchen, job ladders constituted only three levels of incremental progression before reaching the promotional position of Manager. Hence, career structures in these areas appeared to be minimal, though employees could be multiskilled across a number of areas: cleaners being given work in catering for example. This practice further served to enable the Hospital to adjust labour use in the face of varying demand by shifting employees between units (Manager 40).

It is evident that changes in work practices have taken place in Private Hospital with the advent of the current owner. However, there was little evidence to suggest that Private Hospital had pursued strategies of segmenting its workforce. In common with Allan's (1996) findings, non-standard employees across all occupational groups could perform essentially the same range of functions as standard employees. Some degree of occupational segregation is evident, with males dominating managerial and medical positions, and females predominate in nursing and clerical positions. However, it is difficult to assess whether this is a persistent trait. The medical cohort is quite small and not particularly representative of the hospital as a whole. With males being heavily represented at managerial level, there is some evidence to indicate that women are largely confined to lower levels of the job ladder.

Discussion

Evident from the two case studies is that casual and fixed-term employees were extensively used in the hospitals studied. However, there was very little use of outsourcing in either hospital. Furthermore, the presence of *involuntary* casual (and temporary/fixed-term) employment was a distinct phenomenon in the hospitals studied. Indeed, there was a considerable excess of labour supply over labour demand for nursing within the region. This is evident in casuals wanting permanent work but being unable to obtain it. In contrast, in metropolitan areas, hospitals are offering permanent full-time positions that cannot be filled (Gough and Fitzpatrick, 2000; Lumley, 2001).

Both Public Hospital and Private Hospital displayed the same excess of labour supply, suggesting the need to consider local variations in labour supply and demand, rather than a narrow focus on public versus private. When interviewed on the reasons for working casually in a regional area when permanent full-time work was available in the capital cities, most employee respondents stressed lifestyle choice. The influence of lifestyle and excess supply is also reflected in the lengthy tenure and low staff turnover of permanent employees. Furthermore, government policies, such as NSW State government initiatives to attract more people into nursing courses and encourage former nurses to return to practice (Sub-Regional Newspaper, 2000, p. 56), could serve to increase the potential supply of nurses. This was recognized by managers:

> The reason they're here is because they want to stay in [the area]. There's plenty of work in Sydney. However, we don't have a shortage of staff as such here. We have a theoretical shortage of permanent staff, but we have casuals available to work all shifts (Manager 33).

In this context, managers were acutely aware of the relative abundance of potential employees, enabling them to utilize casuals to work regular shifts. Managers in all of the hospitals were thus able to identify casuals that expressed a distinct willingness to work whatever shifts were available, across occupations, and use them in preference to other casuals who were not as compliant. Calling on the same casuals meant that the casual built up familiarity with ward practices and hence provided managers with the benefits of permanent employees with respect to loyalty and productivity. It also led to such employees receiving greater acceptance from permanent staff. However, the casual still did not receive job security in return. The need to have reliable and regular employees meant that casuals were effectively performing work that could be deemed as permanent, as seen with 33 per cent of casuals at Private Hospital with two or more years' service. Casuals in turn were aware of their employment insecurity and noted that management did not even have to dismiss them. An alternative to dismissal was simply to not offer shifts to casuals deemed to be unreliable or problematic.

The increase in fixed-term appointments, as used for probationary purposes, can partly be attributed to changes in clinical professions in the last 20 years, with in-house basic training being supplanted by university training. In part, this reflects increasing professionalization (and attendant lengthening of career ladders) within the allied health and nursing occupations in particular. However, the externalization of basic training can also be seen as a cost-cutting measure for government, with clinical students now having to pay for a degree education through a graduate tax applied under the Higher Education Contribution Scheme (HECS). This situation is exacerbated by the fact that casual employees had less access to funded training. Indeed, from the case studies it is apparent that a consequence of utilizing casuals is that the provision of training can become more externalized – in many cases falling on the employee concerned directly, if not essential to performing basic duties. The externalization of training poses a number of issues, both for the employee and the employer.

For the employer a key issue is continuity of care for the patient, which can be compromised if a different succession of casuals and agency workers are utilized. However, to the extent that the circumstances of the regional labour market enabled the use of regular casuals, this problem appears to have been alleviated. A secondary problem is whether casuals are accepted by the permanent workforce. Again, to the extent that they were regular casuals, this increased their familiarity with units and work practices. Where specialized knowledge was required (for example, in intensive care units), the employer could provide training to a casual when needed.

For the employee, a consideration is whether the likelihood of receiving less training would inhibit their career development. In nursing and allied health, the evidence presented suggested that casuals were attracted to the region for lifestyle purposes. If a permanent job was not obtained then they could obtain a job in Sydney – where permanent work was available. Similarly, those on fixed-term contracts also had the option to relocate if a permanent job was not available. This would suggest that career development is attainable for a casual or fixed-term clinical employee prepared to move between establishments ('horizontal job ladders'). In lower-skill occupations, the presence of involuntary casual and temporary work was more problematic as the manifest shortage of clinical employees at an Australia-wide level was not similarly evident in areas such as cleaning and catering. Thus, relocation to a metropolitan area was less of an option. This situation was recognized in the NSW public hospital sector with the negotiation of an award that meant temporary employees with more than 13 weeks continuous service were converted to permanent (a situation that already existed in private hospitals).

Thus, from this study, it is evident that the greater the degree of 'regularization' of employment, the greater the acceptance of a casual or fixed-term employee into the workplace. The desire for regular employees is most clearly apparent in the manifest distaste of hospital management to utilize agency workers – where agencies were used it was to perform recruitment. The fee an agency attracts also represents an added cost to budget-conscious managers. The occasional occurrence of tension between permanent and non-permanent employees suggests a need for clearly-defined grievance and dispute resolution procedures, both at a formal and informal level, in order to minimize tensions. Further, the higher commitment and patient knowledge displayed by permanent employees demonstrates the clear benefits of having regular, permanent employees. Indeed, where issues of flexibility as opposed to continuity of care is an issue, then it would be better to accommodate these trade-offs through an extended use of *permanent* part-time employment and flexi-time (where practicable).

Conclusion

This chapter has shown that the use casual and temporary employment has been a significant aspect of HRM practice in hospitals. Casual and fixed-term employment provided advantages to hospital management vis-à-vis cost reduction and flexibility. However, at the same time, hospital management desired to have regular employees, who could demonstrate familiarity with unit practices, and (for clinical positions particularly), maintain quality continuity of patient care. Where casual and fixed-term employees were perceived not to demonstrate the same idiosyncratic knowledge of unit procedures, there was scope for tension to arise. This chapter in turn has suggested two approaches to countering this problem (where it exists). One approach is to seek to regularize hospital employees where possible, through extending the benefits of standard employment to non-standard employees. In this schema, flexibility would be achieved through the use of practices such as flexi-time, permanent part-time employment, and annualized hours contracts (as indeed is practiced for managerial positions at Private Hospital). Alternatively, where casual and fixed-term (temporary) employment must be resorted to, recognition needs to be made of the need to reduce barriers between permanent and non-permanent employees – both through information sharing, and through ensuring that casuals and fixed-term employees have the same access to skills development as permanent employees.

Notes

1 Unfortunately, no data was available on the extent of agency use, or the number of employees recruited through agencies.
2 It should be noted that the figures for casuals include all casuals 'on the books', and not just those actually working. However, from payroll data and interviews with Hospital managers, it is apparent that casuals and permanent part-timers contribute a majority of the hours worked at the hospital.

References

Allan, C. (1996) *Labour Utilisation in Queensland Hospitals* Unpublished Ph.D. Thesis (Faculty of Commerce and Administration, Griffith University, Queensland, Australia).
Arrowsmith, J. and Mosse, P. (2000) 'Health Care Reform and the Working Time of Hospital Nurses in England and France' *European Journal of Industrial Relations*, 6(3), pp. 283–305.
Australian Bureau of Statistics (2000a) *The Labour Force*, Catalogue 6203.0.
Australian Bureau of Statistics (2000b) *Employee Earnings, Benefits and Trade Union Membership*, Catalogue 6310.0.
Australian Institute of Health and Welfare (1998) *Australia's Health 1998*, AIHW Cat. AUS 10 (Canberra: AIHW).
Bailey, J. and Hocking, J. (1997) 'Part-time Work for Nurses: A Case Study' *International Employment Relations Review*, 3(1), pp. 1–20.
Burgess, J. and Campbell, I. (1998) 'The Nature and Dimensions of Precarious Work in Australia' *Labour and Industry*, 8(3), pp. 5–22.
Burgess, J. and de Ruyter, A. (2000) 'Declining Job Quality in Australia: Another Hidden Cost of Unemployment' *The Economics and Labour Relations Review*, 11(2), pp. 246–69.

Burgess, J. and Strachan, G. (1999) 'The Expansion of Non-standard Employment in Australia and the Extension of Employers' Control' in A. Felstead and N. Jewson, (eds) *Global Trends in Flexible Labour* (London: Macmillan Business) pp. 121-40.

de Ruyter, A. (2002) *Labour Use Practices in the Regional NSW Acute Hospital Industry* Unpublished Ph. D. Thesis (Faculty of Business and Law, University of Newcastle, Newcastle, Australia)

Gough, R. and Fitzpatrick, M. (2000) 'Restructuring in a Major Public Hospital' *Proceedings of the 14th AIRAANZ Conference*, February 2–4, (Newcastle) pp. 154–59.

Hiscott, R. (1994) 'Changes in Employment Status: The Experience of Ontario Registered Nurses' *Canadian Journal of Nursing Research*, 26(2), pp. 43–60.

Kemp, J. (1994) 'Career Paths Revisited: The Experiences of Graduates in Nursing Who No Longer Work Full-time' *Journal of Advanced Nursing*, 20(2), pp. 377–81.

Lumley, C. (2001) 'Casualisation in Nursing: Friend or Foe?' Unpublished Master's Thesis (School of Public Health, La Trobe University).

Patrickson, M., and Maddern, J. (1996) 'Human Resource Management in Hospitals: A Contested Arena for Jurisdiction' *Australian Health Review*, 19(3), pp. 104–16.

Reeves, K. (1999) *Part-time Work and the Satisfaction of Organisational and Employee Needs: A Case Study in Public Hospital Nursing* Honours Thesis (School of Management, University of Newcastle, Newcastle, Australia).

Short, C. (1993) 'Part-time Work: Barriers to Integration into the Mainstream Full-time Workforce' *Paper presented to the Conference of Economists* (Perth: Murdoch University).

Standing, G. (1997) 'Globalization, Flexibility and Insecurity' *European Journal of Industrial Relations*, 3: 7–37.

Young, S. (2003) 'Outsourcing and Benchmarking in a Rural Public Hospital: Does Economic Theory Provide the Complete Answer?' *International Journal of Rural and Remote Health*, 3 {online} http://rrh.deakin.edu.au

Young, S. (2002) 'Outsourcing and Downsizing: Processes of Workplace Change in Public Health ' *The Economic and Labour Relations Review*, December, 13(2), pp. 244–69.

6
The Processes of Workplace Change for Nurses in NSW Public Hospitals

Nadine White and Mark Bray

Introduction

Over the last two decades, public hospitals in New South Wales have seen huge workplace changes that have been caused by two main imperatives: increasingly neo-liberal solutions to public sector management by governments of both political complexions, which have led to great pressure for increasing efficiency and reductions in costs; and health sector-specific cost increases associated with new medical technologies and procedures. The cumulative effect of these two imperatives has been transmitted through strict limitations on funding and new hospital budgeting regimes that have forced hospital managers to seek new and cheaper ways to deliver patient care (Bray and White, 2002).

Many of these changes, in New South Wales and beyond, have become the focus of research. To cite just some of the studies, Bloom (2000) presents a collection of papers on the broad financial, provision and regulatory restructuring of the sector that devotes some attention to the changing roles of clinicians and models of reform in primary care and hospital treatment. Braithwaite (1993a, 1993b, 1997) provides several accounts of the pressures in the sector and the consequent organizational restructuring and workplace changes they produce in hospitals. One conclusion that parallels other research about work intensification is that the emphasis on cost reduction and increased productivity – what he calls the 'cult' of 'more is good' – does not necessarily produce better outcomes for patients (Braithwaite, 1997). Barnett, Buchanan, Patrickson and Maddern (1996) and Leece (1999, 2000) address the role of the human resource function in the management of change within the health sector in South Australia and Britain.

At a more micro-level, Gough and Fitzpatrick (2000) explore the implications of change for nursing managers in Victoria and Boyce (1991, 2001) describes the widespread change in the organization of work of allied health professionals. The intensification of nurses' work in Queensland and New South Wales is highlighted by Allan (1998) and White and Bray (2003, 2004).

This chapter focuses particularly on nurses within New South Wales public hospitals and two aspects of the workplace change they experienced. Firstly, in terms of the *substance* of change, this chapter emphasizes changes in 'work practices', which were defined by Sutcliffe and Callus (1994, p. 207) as: '...the formal and informal work arrangements and rules that influence the way that jobs and tasks are performed' (see also Alexander and Lewer, 2004, p. 313). In particular, changes to work practices affect the type of work tasks that nurses perform and the number of work tasks they are expected to perform. A recent British analysis of work intensification by Beynon, Grimshaw, Rubery and Ward (2002) provides a valuable typology that will be used to describe the types of workplace change experienced by nurses in New South Wales public hospitals (see also White and Bray, 2003).

Secondly, and more importantly, the chapter will explore the *procedures* or *processes* of workplace change. In particular, who determines the formal and informal work arrangements and who makes the rules about jobs and work tasks? How are new rules introduced to produce new work practices? To what extent do these rules represent a negotiated compromise that enjoys the support of concerned parties as opposed to a decision unilaterally imposed by one of the parties? The framework that is used to address these questions of process draws on mainstream industrial relations scholars, such as Flanders (1969) and others, who broadly describe and analyze several different types of rule-making processes: *unilateral regulation*, in which one of the parties to the employment relationship imposes rules on the others; *joint regulation*, in which employers and employees (directly or through representatives) jointly author rules; *state regulation*, in which the state authors rules through the direct legal regulation of work; and *social regulation*, in which regulation flows from custom and practice rather than from the direct or conscious rule-making of any party.

These issues of substantive and procedural change at work will be explored through two case studies in the same division of a large metropolitan hospital, one of registered nurses and one of nursing unit managers (NUMs). The broad argument that emerges is that the most important substantive workplace changes affecting the work practices of nurses in the case study organizations during the late 1990s and early 2000s were introduced through unilateral processes: managerial decree. In other words, despite the operation of apparently strong state regulation, through the education and registration of nurses, and of apparently extensive joint regulation, through a powerful union representing nurses and a comprehensive award regulating terms and conditions of employment, nurses and their unions rarely participated in consultation, let alone negotiations, over important workplace changes. This conclusion is considered to have significant implications for the likely success of workplace change in achieving the goals of organizational efficiency and equity for nurses.

The regulatory context

In New South Wales, the work of nurses (both NUMs and registered nurses) has been, and continues to be, regulated by various mechanisms. On the one hand, there is state regulation through legislation, registration boards, and educational and professional institutions. On the other hand, there are various forms of industrial regulation, especially involving joint regulation through awards and enterprise agreements. Each will be discussed separately, but the individual mechanisms are intricately linked, forming a web of regulation. Despite this apparently comprehensive web of regulation, however, none of the mechanisms expressly regulates in any detailed way the work practices and especially the workloads of nurses. They mostly regulate who may perform the work of nurses rather than what work they do.

The first form of state regulation involves a myriad of legislation that regulates the work of nurses; the most significant in New South Wales being the *Nurses Act 1991*, whose long title states that the *Nurses Act* is: '...An Act to regulate the practice of nursing...'. The Act regulates by providing for the establishment of the New South Wales Nurses Registration Board (NRB), by defining the functions of the NRB and by requiring annual registration for authority to practice in New South Wales. Additionally, legislation such as the *Poisons and Therapeutic Goods Act 1996 (New South Wales)* also regulates the role of health professionals, including nurses, in the management and administration of drugs and therapeutic goods.

Secondly, the NRB regulates the work of nurses through the control and coordination of an annual registration process in New South Wales. However, the NRB, as the main regulatory body, does not expressly regulate 'what' a nurse does rather it regulates 'who' can be a nurse. It does so by establishing barriers to entry and formal mechanisms for deregistration or exit from the profession. Other than clinical and professional guidelines, such as Professional Conduct and Boundaries of Professional Practice, the NRB does not regulate the day-to-day operational work activities of a nurse.

Thirdly, accredited by the NRB, the work of nurses is regulated by education and professional institutions, predominantly through university undergraduate degree programs. These programs are charged with training nurses in the knowledge and skills they require to undertake the clinical tasks involved in nurses' work. Again, however, this regulates who may become a nurse (such as, those who have completed the training and demonstrated their competence) rather than what work nurses actually undertake during the course of their day-to-day working lives.

In addition to these forms of state regulation, there are various forms of joint regulation that impact on the work of nurses. In these processes, nurses are represented by the New South Wales Nurses' Association, a state-based union with impressive levels of membership of around 60–70 per cent, while on issues involving other unions the New South Wales Labour Council frequently becomes involved. 'Employer' representatives range from local managers at ward, division or hospital level through to the New South Wales Health Department (see Bray and White 2002, and White and Bray, 2003).

The dominant and most formal joint rule-making processes in New South Wales public hospitals produce awards, which are occupation-specific and state-wide in coverage; in the case of nurses, the relevant award is the *Public Hospital Nurses' (State) Award*. Technically, awards are a form of state regulation, in that they are the outcome of compulsory arbitration that imposes legally-binding minimum terms of employment. However, in reality, the boundary between awards and collective bargaining is ambiguous because most awards are actually the result of tribunal members ratifying agreements reached privately by collective bargaining between unions and employers.

What aspects of the working life of nurses does the award regulate? In the 2002 award and its predecessors, including the enterprise agreements during the mid-1990s, the focus is almost exclusively on conditions of employment, such as pay, hours of work, leave entitlements and specific allowances. The award identified job and wage classifications, but only in a perfunctory manner. There was no definition or statement of what activities a registered nurse undertook or was capable of doing within the public hospital workplace. The only definition of a 'registered nurse' did not state what nurses do during the course of their work, but rather defined who a nurse is. This came from *Clause 3 – Definitions* in the award, which stated that: 'Registered Nurse means a person registered by the Board as such'. Earlier in the section, Board is defined as meaning: '...the Nurses' Registration Board of New South Wales'.

There was only one specific clause in the award that makes reference, albeit by exception, to the work activities of nurses. *Clause 40 – Domestic Work* of the award clearly states that:

...nurses shall not be required to perform, as a matter of routine, the following duties: viz.: washing, sweeping, polishing, and/or dusting of floors, walls or windows of wards, corridors, annexes, bathrooms or verandahs or any duties which are generally performed by classifications other than nursing staff, but this provision shall not preclude the employment of nurses on any such duties in an isolation block where the performance of those duties involves disinfection.

In addition to this express clause, there was a variety of clauses that provide for payment or allowances for particular nursing activities. For example, Clause 22 of the award provided for payment, at both ordinary hours and overtime, for a nurse engaged in the official escort of patient.

Other than these statements of what was not the work of a nurse (for example, clause 40) and that nursing work may include escorting patients between facilities (for example clause 22), the award did not contain provisions determining the actual work tasks, skills and activities of a registered nurse. In particular, and this is vital for this chapter, there was no provision that regulated the type and number of tasks to be undertaken by nurses during their working day.

For NUMs, the award was slightly more detailed in that it provided a summary of responsibilities for each of the three levels of NUM, as detailed in Table 6.1. While more detailed than the definition of a registered nurse, this list of responsibilities was broad in its range and did not clearly state or identify the day-to-day operational tasks, skills or activities of a NUM. An outcome of this broad 'list' of responsibilities was that it provided hospital or health service management with the discretion to interpret and determine 'what' work a NUM was actually required to undertake within the workplace, so long as it fitted within the broad 'list' of responsibilities.

Table 6.1 The responsibilities of nursing unit managers

Nursing Unit Manager: means a registered nurse in charge of a ward or unit or group of wards or units in a hospital or health service and shall include:

Nursing Unit Manager Level 1, whose responsibilities shall include:

Coordination of Patient Services	Unit Management	Nursing Staff Management
• Liaison with all health care disciplines for the provision of services to meet patient needs • The orchestration of services to meet patient needs after discharge • Monitoring catering and transport services	• Implementation of hospital/health service policy • Dissemination of information to all personnel • Ensuring environmental safety • Monitoring the use of maintenance of equipment • Monitoring the supply and use of stock and supplies • Monitoring cleaning services	• Direction, co-ordination and supervision of nursing activities • Training, appraisal and counselling of nursing staff • Rostering and/or allocation of nursing staff • Development and/or implementation of new nursing practice according to patient need

Nursing Unit Manager Level 2, whose responsibilities in relation to patient service, ward or unit management and staff management are in excess of those of a Nursing Unit Manager Level 1.

Nursing Unit Manager Level 3, whose responsibilities in relation to patient service, ward or unit management and staff management are in excess of those of a Nursing Unit Manager Level 2.

Source: Adapted from Clause 3 of Public Hospital Nurses' (State) Award

The only other section within the award that related to the wage or job classification was *Clause 8–Salaries*, which referred to a salary table in Part B of the award, a table of actual wages paid. Clause 8, through the table, identified an eight-year incremental wage scale for registered nurses and the three-level grading system for NUMs. The remainder of the 80 pages and 52 clauses of the award were concerned with conditions of employment, entitlements, and procedural clauses. Eight clauses were dedicated to specific categories of leave, including annual, sick, long service, repatriation, military, personal carers', and parental leave. Thirteen clauses were procedural in nature relating to grading of positions, pilot projects, and general procedural clauses such as dispute resolution. The remainder, or 31 clauses, related to conditions of employment, ranging from accommodation and board provisions, car allowances, fares and expenses, higher grade duties, hours of work, overtime, penalty rates, provision of equipment such as communication devices, rosters, salaries, salary packaging, salary sacrifice, telephone allowances, and uniform and laundry allowances.

In other words, other than the list of responsibilities for NUMs and the Domestic Work clause, which defined work nurses and NUMs were not required to do, the award was silent on rules regarding workloads and work practices. The award did not address the identification, range or scope of clinical tasks, duties, responsibilities or work practices, nor did it address patient loads and/or staff-to-patient ratios.

Formal forms of regulation may, of course, be supplemented by more informal forms. For example, more decentralized and informal collective bargaining between union representatives at workplace level and local management (such as joint regulation) can result in informal verbal, or sometimes written, arrangements. Similarly, social regulation may be important; in other words, it is likely that there are many informal understandings shared by doctors, nurses and other hospital staff about what is nurses' work, how many patients they can reasonably be asked to care for and so on. However, these forms of regulation have not been systematically researched and they are likely to vary considerably from hospital to hospital, if not from ward to ward.

In summary, none of the formal instruments that regulate the work of nurses (which are associated with state regulation and joint regulation) actually addressed the types of tasks undertaken by nurses in the workplace and the number of those tasks on a day-to-day basis. In the absence of such regulation, in particular in the absence of regulation by awards and/or enterprise agreements, management had the *legal* right to introduce changes to these work tasks unilaterally. This simply reflected the general legal situation that applied to all employees: when issues are not specifically contained in awards, then they become matters of managerial prerogative (Creighton and Stewart, 2000). The extent to which management's exercise of this legal right has in practice been either limited by informal local joint regulation or moderated by management voluntarily consulting with employees may vary considerably from workplace to workplace.

The Cases and the research methods

The two case studies presented in this chapter examine changes in work practices and workloads of, first, NUMs and, second, registered nurses in the Division of Medicine at a large teaching hospital, which is part of a New South Wales Area Health Service (regional grouping). Contextual data for the Area Health Service were obtained from documentary and interview sources as part of a larger study over the period 1999 to 2002.

The Division of Medicine is the largest in the hospital, comprising a number of sub-specialties, which were established or consolidated and relocated to the Division upon commissioning of the hospital in 1991. At the time of the data collection in 2002, the Division consisted of 11 wards, each of which was managed by a NUM and staffed by registered and enrolled nurses and administrative staff (ward clerks).

Despite the limitations of the case study method, which are discussed later, these two case studies are particularly valuable in exploring the substance and processes of workplace change for several reasons. First, nurses represent a high proportion of total employees within public hospitals; for example, the Area Health Service workforce consists of approximately 42 per cent nursing employees (Annual Report, 1998–9). Second, nurses work under a centralized and apparently prescriptive award. Third, levels of unionization are unusually high both within the public hospital sector and compared to most other industries (Bray and White, 2002).

The account of the two cases presented in this chapter unfolds at two levels of analysis and involves several research methods. First, for both cases, the analysis of awards and the more centralized rules was mostly through documentary analysis, complemented by a small number of interviews with Health Department managers. Documents included awards, Industrial Relations Commission records and quantitative data from New South Wales Health Department.

Second, the local rules and work practices in the Division, again for both cases, were gathered and analyzed using qualitative methods; in particular, documents and semi-structured interviews. Documents included Annual Reports (of the Area Health Service and the hospital), formal job descriptions, budgets, staff profiles, activity data, applications for regrade of position and patient/client information pamphlets. Interviews were semi-structured, asking open-ended questions regarding the substance and process of workplace change. Interviewees were primarily NUMs and registered nurses in each of the case studies, although additional interviewees included senior managers (nursing and non-nursing).

In the NUM case study, the intention was to interview all ten NUMs (one NUM managed two wards) across all wards within the Division. Several NUMs, however, were not interviewed for various reasons, including work pressures. During the data collection phase in spring of 2002, six NUMs were interviewed. In the registered nurses case study, the intention was to interview all 32 registered nurses across one ward within the Division. Of the 32 invited to participate, ten registered nurses were interviewed over eight interview sessions in a one-month period in Spring 2002. Access to the nursing staff on the ward was granted on the condition that participants would be interviewed during the hand-over period between the morning and afternoon shifts. Approximately two-thirds of ward nursing staff and one-third of NUMs failed to respond to the invitation to participate or were not interviewed. This may have been due to lack of interest, or time, pressures of workload, or not receiving the information of the study or, as one nurse speculated, for fear of an adverse reaction from senior management, despite assurances that participation was confidential.

The substance of workplace change

Following the broader work of Beynon *et al.* (2002), the imperatives for changes to work practices and workloads experienced by nurses may be divided into three main categories: an increased focus on customer service and customer expectations; wider responsibilities; and an increasing presence of surveillance, regulation and management of nurse performance. While these categories are extremely useful in identifying workplace changes, they overlook an important fourth category of workplace change; namely, the volume of work or simply 'doing more of the same work' (this section draws heavily on White and Bray, 2003). Each of the above four categories will be addressed below, with evidence from the case study units.

Firstly, nurses and NUMs were being subjected to increasing pressures, beyond the professional tradition, to meet the expectations of their *customers* (patients or clients). Examples from the case study units include the introduction of quality assurance programs, focussed on patient access and transition, and increasing community representation on hospital boards and management committees. More importantly, there was increased monitoring of customer attitudes through patient satisfaction surveys and front-line management of complaints systems, both of which resulted in increased workload and stress for NUMs and registered nurses.

Secondly, over the 1990s the health sector experienced rationalization, decentralization and restructuring of services which resulted in NUMs broadening their functional and line management *responsibilities*. For NUMs, this change occurred especially in the areas of staff management and finance and budget activities. For nurses, the broadening occurred mainly in the areas of increasing accountability and documentation, and changes to clinical practice.

Thirdly, nurses and NUMs have experienced increasing *surveillance, regulation and performance* as a result of changes to management practices, such as the introduction of performance management and staff surveys, increasing reliance on output measures in the form of budget control and patient care planning information management systems, such as Excelcare. Furthermore, there was increasing pressure to improve safety within the workplace.

Fourthly, and finally, both NUMs and nurses have experienced work intensification through *greater work volumes*; in other words, increased work effort through doing more of the same work. State-wide and division data are presented in Tables 6.2 and 6.3. With respect to the former, state-wide data for 1998–9 indicate that admissions increased only marginally, bed occupancy rates increased

Table 6.2 Activity and performance data, NSW public hospitals, 1995/96–1998/99

	1995/6	1996/7	1997/8	1998/9
Admissions	1,253,755	1,242,232	1,265,318	1,267,957
Total Non Inpatient Occasions of Service	15,976,520	17,459,872	17,715,618	21,335,300
Bed occupancy rate (%)	83.0	82.8	83.8	84.8
Average Length of Stay of Acute Episodes	5.7	5.7	5.6	5.9

Source: NSW Public Hospital/Health Comparison Data Books

Table 6.3 Activity data, division of medicine, hospital, 2000–2001

	2000	2001	% Change
Admissions	19,031	22,437	18% increase
Separations	23,430	26,751	14% increase
Day Stays	18,136	21,197	17% increase

Source: Organisational Reports

progressively and that there was a minor increase in length of stay. Overall, this points to slight productivity increases for in-patients. Yet the same table also clearly demonstrates significant increases in non-inpatient numbers, suggesting that the acuity of in-patients is increasing. In other words, patients were kept in the wards only for the periods in which they were sickest and in which they required the most intensive care from nurses. This is supported by division data in Table 6.3, which presents disaggregated data from the division of medicine indicating an 18 per cent increase in admissions, a 14 per cent increase in 'separations' (for example, the completion of an episode of care through a discharge, transfer or death of a patient) and 17 per cent increase in day stays over just a two-year period to the end of 2001. There was no increase in staffing levels within the Division over the same period.

The process of change: overview

All of the substantive workplace changes discussed earlier were implemented without reference to formal regulatory mechanisms, in particular the existing award. Indeed, the award in operation at the time of data collection did not contain any clause or provision relating to any of the categories of workplace change discussed earlier. For example, the award did not contain provision for an increased customer focus through quality improvement, front-line complaints management systems or increasing reliance on patient satisfaction surveys. Nor did the award contain any reference to the widening of responsibilities for nurses or NUMs. The award did not include any mention or anticipate any increase in surveillance, regulation or performance through workplace changes such as budget performance and control, performance management systems, staff satisfaction surveys, increased safety awareness, use of information management systems (such as Excelcare) or other output measures. Finally, the award did not provide for more of the same work or staff-to-patient ratios.

Furthermore, the interviews reported later reveal that there were no collective negotiations either locally within the Division of Medicine or centrally at state level to enable these workplace changes to occur, either through the award or an alternative industrial instrument, such as an enterprise agreement. Some of the changes were recognized retrospectively in 1997 and compensated through what were termed 'work value' wage increases in the award for NUMs (White and Bray, 2003). However, these work value wage increases are evidence that workplace changes had already occurred rather than representing a mechanism by which changes were introduced.

The process of change: NUMs

This section confirms, through interviews with NUMs in the Division of Medicine, that the substantive workplace changes discussed above were introduced incrementally through the exercise of managerial prerogative. Indeed, when NUMs were questioned about how the changes to their work were implemented, what type of consultation occurred and how frequently consultation or negotiation occurred, interviewees invariably responded with raised eyebrows and quizzical looks, suggesting that they had not comprehended the question. When prompted, all too often the response was '...it just happened...', indicating that the NUMs were rarely involved in any explicit decision making, let alone negotiation or consultation over the changes.

There were a number of consistent themes from the interview data regarding the process of implementing the substantive changes. Firstly, it appeared that the changes to work practices and workloads experienced by NUMS were generally reactions to changes elsewhere within the health service based on budgetary decisions. These were often cost shifting of functions from centralized departments to the line manager that occurred without any consultation. For example, all NUMs interviewed discussed the widening of their responsibilities, particularly in relation to finance and budget, rostering (through software packages like Proact), payroll and human resources:

> ...structurally it is being driven from the top, definitely. Because we are doing the Proact (rosters) and payroll, they are reducing staff numbers in areas, pay office areas.... (M1: 4)

...It has been directed that you will do Proact. In fact, until two years ago I didn't even have a computer to do it on. I would go to another area and do it. It is only two years I have had this computer in my office... (M1: 4)

Secondly, all interviewees agreed that there had been no or little consultation regarding the changes:

...It was just done. It was instructed. A memo came out... (M2: 3)
...It is related through NUMs meetings or special meetings.... (M5: 5)

Thirdly, most were adamant that they had not been involved in the decision making, that they had at times argued against the decision after it was announced, and that they had sometimes even refused to accept the decision once it was made.

...Not a lot I would say, most of the ones have been out of our control or where we have said no, we have been overridden. We didn't want to take on payroll at all... (M3: 7)
...Well, we would fight and argue when we found out about it, but usually the top-level managers are making the decisions for us. And when we have fought and argued and said no we can't you know take on this role, even as a group, there was no, sometimes no consultation. This is just how it will be done area-wide and this is what you will do. And then a quick education program will come in and say this is the new version of Proact or this is how you are going to order for stores and that's how all of these things have evolved for the Nurse Manager to have to do.... (M3: 4)

In relation to formalizing some of these changes into a generic NUM job description, one very concerned interviewee stated that:

...It was given to us and we sent back a draft with amendments and it was sent back to us and then it was changed and put out as ratified without further consultation...(M5: 6)

But by the actions (or inaction) of NUMs, the changes had often been implemented without disruption or union involvement:

...I think through lack of our enthusiasm to get everyone together to actually grumble enough to say, '...how come we are taking on this other role, or this other department's role...'. Where most of the time it is thrown back in our faces that you are the front line manager, you are the person responsible. And we as a group haven't really pursued the union... (M3: 6)

The process of change: Registered nurses

Like the NUMs who were interviewed, the registered nurses interviewed were unable to clearly articulate how workplace changes had been implemented. More probing questions revealed that there had rarely, if ever, been any consultation regarding changes to work practices. Moreover, changes to workloads were a matter that was never discussed unless it was in the context of *'you can do better'* or the disbelief associated with the actual Excelcare units of care undertaken in the ward.

When questioned about whether they were consulted directly or whether their representatives were consulted about proposed changes to their work practices or workloads, the interviewees responded negatively:

...No. No. Not that I can recall... (N1: 2)
... I don't see ever... (N4: 4)
...To be honest I don't know whether they [the Association] have been consulted... (N1: 2)

The fact that staff members were not consulted over the proposed changes did not mean that there was no 'communication' regarding the change. For example, interviewees commented on how they found out about changes in the ward:

... I don't ever recall being asked. We are always educated: '...oh this is what is going to happen and this is how you do it...'. But I don't ever recall being asked if we want it to happen. That would be a novel idea, wouldn't it? (N1: 2)
...Usually ...either you get an inservice on it [if] it is a procedure. You usually get a memo and then they get an inservice on it showing you how to...on what has actually changed... (N7: 3)

Most of the interviewees were aware of the significance of the changes experienced and they felt confronted about their introduction, with several making comments like:

.... Oh no, no, we don't get consulted. It is very much '...this is the way we do things now...'. And we're asked to consider how we do it and we'll do all these surveys and you have got your problems we are always very accessible and do all these Excelcare with your care plans and they all provide evidence to increase our staffing load, but it never does. It is sort of evidence that has sort of gone into the big black void... (N2: 2)

...You just get confronted with it. You just get confronted with it and you are just left... they are expecting ...that you can deal with that, that you can do it... (N3: 2)

...We are confronted... We are not consulted at all. It's a case of don't say anything. Sink or swim. If you can't cope, why can't you cope (laughing)? (N5: 2)

...Like our NUM would come in now and say, 'blah, blah, blah has changed, or you are getting this patient from ICU who has all these requirements...' And you just have to cope as best you can. (N5: 3)

The perception of being confronted with change is consistent with the interview data from NUMs on the introduction of change: changes to work practice and workloads are occurring as a result of management direction and management initiatives in the workplace.

Conclusions and implications

The case studies reported in this chapter demonstrate that the operation of an industry-wide award regulating the work of a strongly unionized occupational group did not prevent or even moderate the introduction of substantial workplace change that greatly increased productivity in New South Wales public hospitals and intensified the work of nurses. At least in the case studies, these changes were introduced relatively easily and without resistance, and they were essentially determined unilaterally by managerial.

Clearly, there are significant limitations to the generality of this account because of the case study methodology adopted. In particular, there is no way of knowing how typical the cases are in terms of the scope of issues regulated by the award, the types of workplace change introduced or the many factors that explain the process and outcomes of change. Despite these qualifications, these findings would hardly surprise researchers or practitioners in the health sector. Nor would the imperatives behind the change be unfamiliar. Like their counterparts in other states of Australia and in other countries around the world, public hospitals in New South Wales have been squeezed between rising medical costs and cost-conscious governments, a pressure that has been manifest in tight budgets that have to be met.

The dominance of unilateralism as the main process for the introduction of workplace change, as opposed to alternative processes, has at least three possible implications. First, there is considerable literature suggesting that workplace change that is introduced through collective bargaining or consultation is more likely to be accepted by employees and to genuinely improve the efficiency of the organization. For example, a recent report by the International Labour Office on trends in workplace flexibility in 22 countries concluded that:

> In most cases, however, flexibility has meant less employment security, less income security, and a continuous adjustment to new, often uncomfortable working conditions... It is therefore clear that the introduction of flexibility can be smoothly implemented only if workers are associated with the process, and their views duly taken into account in selecting the forms of flexibility to be introduced and determining the ways in which they should be introduced (Ozaki, 1999, p. 148).

These sentiments are confirmed by a wide range of studies from overseas (Freeman and Medoff, 1984; Ichniowski, Kochan, Levine, Olson and Strauss, 1996; Guest and Peccei, 2001) and Australia (see, for example, Alexander and Green, 1993; Deery, Erwin and Iverson, 1999) that have found that management consultation with employees and/or management negotiation with unions over workplace change leads to better outcomes. In this context, the unilateralism observed in the case studies above augurs badly for the longer-term effectiveness and sustainability of the workplace changes.

Second, there is increasing literature that suggests work intensification, like that observed in the case studies, leads to employee stress that is manifest in many undesirable workplace behaviours, ranging from low morale and dissatisfaction to illness, occupational health and safety problems and high absenteeism and labour turnover (Burchell, Lapido and Wilkinson, 2002; Allan, 1998). Again, this suggests that the increasing demands on nurses (and other health care workers) revealed in this and many other studies may have deleterious unintended consequences not only for nurses, but also for healthcare delivery in public hospitals.

Third, as might be predicted from the previous two observations, the growth of work intensification amongst nurses and the unilateral process by which it has been introduced appear to have produced a reaction from nurses and the union that represents their interests.

During 2002, the New South Wales Nurses' Association mounted a campaign to increase the wages of nurses. The Association's previous practice of seeking monetary compensation for work intensification (called 'work value' in the New South Wales industrial relations system) led to an interim decision by the New South Wales Industrial Relations Commission in December 2002 granting a six per cent wage increase. However, in a new development, the Association also sought provisions in the award to regulate the workload of nurses. In December 2003, the Commission's final decision included a procedure by which nurses would be guaranteed 'reasonable workloads'. Under the new Clause 48 of the award, 'reasonable workload committees' would be established at workplace level in New South Wales public hospitals to deal with grievances in relation to workload, while a state-wide Reasonable Workloads Taskforce would be established to make recommendations on interim workload calculation tools and ideas for implementation and evaluation. This development, which parallels new regulatory measures in South Australia (see Willis, 2002) and Victoria (see Buchanan, Briggs, Considine and Heiler, 2002), suggests that the days of unilateral increases in the workload of nurses may be numbered.

References

Alexander, M. and Green, R. (1993) 'Workplace Productivity and Joint Consultation' *The Economics and Labour Relations of Australian Workplaces: Quantitative Approaches* (Sydney: Conference Proceedings, ACIRRT).

Alexander, R. and Lewer, J. (2004) *Understanding Australian Industrial Relations* (6th edn) (Melbourne: Thomson Learning).

Allan, C. (1998) 'The Elasticity of Endurance: Work Intensification and Workplace Flexibility in a Queensland Public Hospital' *New Zealand Journal of Industrial Relations*, 23(3), pp. 133–51.

Barnett, S., Buchanan, D., Patrickson, M., and Maddern, J. (1996) 'Negotiating the Evolution of the HR Function: Practical Advice from the Health Care Sector' *Human Resource Management Journal*, 6(4), pp. 18–37.

Beynon, H., Grimshaw, D., Rubery, J. and Ward, K. (2002) *Managing Employment Change: The New Realities of Work*, (Oxford: Oxford University Press).

Bloom, A. (ed.) (2000) *Health Reform in Australia and New Zealand* (Melbourne: Oxford University Press).

Boyce, R. (1991) 'Hospital Restructuring – the implications for allied health professionals' *Australian Health Review*, 14(2), pp. 147–154.

Boyce, R. (2001) 'Organisational Governance Structures in Allied Health Services: A Decade of Change' *Australian Health Review*, 24(1), pp. 22–36.

Braithwaite, J. (1993a) 'Identifying the Elements in the Australian Health Service Management Revolution' *Australian Journal of Public Administration*, 52(4), pp. 417–30.

Braithwaite, J. (1993b) 'Strategic Management and Organisational Structure: Transformational Processes at Work in Hospitals' *Australian Health Review*, 16(4), pp. 383–404.

Braithwaite, J. (1997) 'Competition, Productivity and the Cult of "More is Good" in the Australian Health Care Sector' *Australian Journal of Public Administration*, 56(1), pp. 37–44.

Bray, M. and White, N. (2002) 'A System under Pressure: Industrial Relations in NSW Public Hospitals' *New Zealand Journal of Industrial Relations*, 27(2), June, pp. 193–220.

Buchanan, J., Briggs, C., Considine, G. and Heiler, K. (2002) 'Unions and Work Intensification: Insights from the Australian Metal and Engineering, Mining and Nursing Sectors', *Paper Presented to Conference on Work Intensification* (Centre D'Etudes De L'Emploi, Paris) November.

Burchell, B., Ladipo, D. and Wilkinson, F. (eds) (2002) *Job Insecurity and Work Intensification* (London: Routledge).

Creighton, B. and Stewart, A. (2000) *Labour Law*, Federation Press (3rd edn), Sydney.

Deery, S., Erwin, P. and Iverson, R. (1999) 'Industrial Relations Climate, Attendance Behaviour and the Role of Trade Unions' *British Journal of Industrial Relations*, 37(4), pp. 581–97.

Flanders, A. (ed.) (1969) *Collective Bargaining* (Melbourne: Penguin Books).

Freeman, R. and Medoff, D. (1984) *What Do Unions Do?* (New York: Basic Books).

Gough, R. and Fitzpatrick, M. (2000) 'Restructuring in a Major Public Hospital' in J. Burgess and G. Strachan (eds) (2000) *Current Research in Industrial Relations: Proceedings of the 14th AIRAANZ Conference* (Newcastle, NSW) February.

Guest, D. and Peccei, R. (2001) 'Partnership at Work: Mutuality and Balance of Advantage' *British Journal of Industrial Relations*, 39(2), pp. 207–36.

Ichniowski, C., Kochan, T., Levine, D., Olson, C. and Strauss, G. (1996) 'What Works at Work: Overview and Assessment' *Industrial Relations*, 35(3), pp. 299–333.

Leece, P. (1999) 'On the Cutting Edge of Strategic Human Resource Management in Health Care' *Australia New Zealand Academy of Management Conference Paper*.

Leece, P. (2000) 'Strategic Change in the Health Sector: Is the HR Function a Help or a Hindrance?' *Australia New Zealand Academy of Management Conference Paper*.

Ozaki, M. (1999) *Negotiating Flexibility: The Role of the Social Partners and the State* (Geneva: International Labour Office).

Sutcliffe, P. and Callus, R. (1994) *Glossary of Australian Industrial Relations Terms* (ACCIRT and ACSM).

White, N. and Bray, M. (2003) 'The Changing Role of Nurse Unit Managers: A Case of Work Intensification?' *Labour and Industry*, 14(2), December, pp. 1–20.

White, N. and Bray, M. (2004) 'Awards, Managerial Prerogative and Workplace Change: Case Study Evidence from the Health Sector' *Paper Presented to 18th AIRAANZ Conference*, February (Queensland).

Willis, E. (2002) 'Enterprise Bargaining and Work Intensification: An Atypical Case Study from the South Australian Public Hospital Sector' *New Zealand Journal of Industrial Relations*, 27(2), June, pp. 221–32.

Organizational documents

Division of Medicine, Activity Reports
Area Health Service, Annual Report, 1998–99
NSW Health Department (1995/96–1998/99) *NSW Public Hospital – Health Comparison Books*

7
Work Intensification for Personal Service Attendants and Medical Scientists

Eileen Willis and Kerryn Weekes

Introduction

The processes used for achieving reform in the public healthcare sector in Australia have taken two directions. The initial strategy employed by governments was to introduce efficiency measures into the sector via policy directives that usually tied funding to productivity. These have been broadly defined elsewhere in this book as the strategies of New Public Management. The introduction of Casemix diagnosis related groups (DRGs) and the incentives built into the various Medicare Agreements are two examples of this approach. This strategy motivated many hospital managers to engage in workplace reform with financial assistance provided by both Labor and Liberal–National Federal Governments through such incentive programs as the National Hospital Demonstration Program. The second strategy has been industrial relations reform aimed at increasing workplace flexibility in order to increase productivity and efficiency gains. Both reform strategies have impacted on the working life of health professionals and occupational groups in the sector.

This chapter explores the impact of workplace change on the work intensification of personal service attendants (PSAs) in South Australia (SA) and medical scientists in Victoria.[1] Data for the two case studies is taken from research carried out by both authors. The case study of the personal service attendants comes from an ethnographic study conducted by Willis between 1998 and 2002 in a large public acute hospital called Westernvale.[2] The case study of the medical scientist is drawn from two studies conducted by Weekes (Weekes, Peterson and Stanton,

2001; Weekes, 2003). While PSAs and medical scientists are two distinct occupational groups with very different education, training, income and status attributions, their experiences of the reform processes are not all that dissimilar. This chapter argues that most occupational and professional groups across the country have experienced some form of work intensification – no occupational group has been quarantined – although the impact varies between professional groups and occupations. The chapter is divided into three sections. First we provide a framework for examining work intensification; in the second section the two case studies are presented; and finally in section three a brief commentary and analysis supports our argument that both these groups of workers have undergone significant work intensification.

One further caveat needs to be made about this chapter. In both states the 1990s reform of the public hospital sector was accompanied by an accelerated introduction of Casemix DRGs and a change from a Labor to a conservative state Liberal government. However, while these two factors are significant, they should not be read as separating Victoria and SA out from those states in Australia where Labor governments were in power at this time and where the fiscal situation was healthier. The differences are matters of degree, rather than direction, since the impetus for health and workplace reform had already begun under the Federal Labor Government with the 1989–91 National Health Strategy and in the mid 1980s with the various shifts in industrial relations, culminating in 1993 with the Commonwealth Industrial Relations Act which introduced Enterprise Bargaining (Morris, 1996).

The evidence of work intensification in the health sector in Australia

Any discussion of work intensification requires some understanding of its dimensions and what it entails. Green and McIntosh (2001, p. 56) suggest two varieties of work intensification. First, workers claim that they are working longer hours. They refer to this as *extensive work effort*. Secondly, workers argue that while at work, the tasks must be done at a faster pace; this is *intensive work effort*. We extend this latter point to incorporate shift work. Shift work is characterized by non-standard and unsocial hours of work. For many health professionals working in hospitals the second shift traditionally has a reduced number of staff because it is assumed that the work tapers off. Likewise weekends have fewer staff rostered on duty as there is an assumption that patients are not admitted or surgery not timetabled, except of an emergency nature.

While most workers make claim to working harder and longer, finding the evidence for these two forms of work intensification is another matter. White and Bray (2004) provide a brief overview of some of the key research in work intensification in the Australian healthcare sector reported on in the last decade. Two salient points can be drawn from their paper. The first is that the majority of authors they cite have published studies that focus on work intensification for nurses (Allan, 1998; Considine and Buchanan, 2002; Gough and Fitzpatrick, 2002; Willis, 2002). Only two studies deal with other groups; O'Donnell (1995) focuses on personal service attendants and Weekes, Petersen and Stanton (2001) explore medical scientists. While there is no doubt that much of the burden of reform in the healthcare sector has fallen to nurses, it is also true that those working alongside them; whether they be of a higher or lower status, are also making claims to work intensification. It is this very fact that reinforces the work intensity of each occupational group; everyone is stretched to the limit within the system, whether they are the paramedic having to bypass a packed Accident and Emergency Department or the medical scientist supporting the salaried medical officer.

The second factor highlighted by White and Bray (2004, p. 2) notes that the various studies published in Australia on work intensification in nursing lack a coherent theoretical or empirical approach. In providing a framework of analysis they draw on work by Beynon, Gromshaw, Rubery and Ward (2002) and Green (2004) to identify five processes contributing to work intensification. These are: the increasing dominance of the customer whose demands are analogous to an additional supervisor; job redesign, such as multiskilling and upskilling; and new methods of control that have arisen out of computer-based technology with its capacity for increased surveillance, along with the pervasive techniques of human resource management such as performance appraisal and regular audits (Beynon *et al.*, 2002).

The fourth and fifth factors suggested by Green (2004) are that workers are likely to claim their work has intensified where the power of their union has diminished and there is rising job insecurity. These processes can impact on one another. For example a weak union may precipitate the introduction of new technology, while the threat of redundancies softens workers up to accept job redesign (Green, 2004, p. 14). White and Bray (2004, p. 3) add a sixth factor to the list in support of work intensification. They suggest that in many instances it is possible to provide evidence of increased work volume. A seventh factor suggests that if one occupational group makes a claim to work intensification, this is likely to impact on the work of others in the team, especially where multidisciplinary team work is required. In this chapter these seven processes are applied to the claims for work intensification of two groups; the occupation of personal service attendants in SA and the profession of medical scientists in Victoria.

Case study one: Personal service attendants as a third level carer

In SA, PSAs are a newly created group emerging out of the occupations of nurse assistants, kitchen staff, cleaners, porters and orderlies. As an occupational group they are closely aligned to care attendants working in nursing homes but they perform fewer direct nursing tasks. Previously these occupational groups operated independently of one another with a tendency for men to be orderlies and porters and women to function as nursing assistants, cleaners and kitchen staff. Around 35–40 per cent of their time is spent in cleaning clinical areas such as patient rooms, toilets and showers as well as offices within generalist and labour wards, emergency departments and theatres. They also perform a range of tasks known as 'fetch and carry' such as transporting patients to and from tests, to home wards or to discharge areas. This takes up to 20 per cent of their time. Other duties such as distributing meals, moving beds and lockers around the ward and in some areas shaving patients prior to surgery make up the remainder of their job description.

This newly created occupational group cannot be examined outside the processes of health and workplace reform, including the transfer of nurse education to the tertiary sector and the subsequent loss of cheap, low-grade, student-nurse labour. While some hospitals in Australia, such as in Victoria and New South Wales, employed PSAs prior to 1995, in SA their introduction was a direct result of budget restraint and the need to create a more flexible and cheaper workforce able to perform a range of lower level tasks that were once part of nursing. Similar developments occurred in other Australian states at this time as it did also in the USA, Britain, Canada and Hong Kong (Brannon, 1996; Badovinac, Wilson and Woodhouse, 1999; Houson, 1996). Commenting on the USA situation, Brannon (1996) pointed to the fact that unlicensed assistive personnel (UAP) allowed new models of nursing care to be designed that left registered nurses (RNs) working with higher numbers of UAPs, but fewer registered nurses. Brannon also noted that their introduction created a further division of labour, while Badovinac *et al.* (1999) reported increased stress levels for RNs who had to manage their patient load with lower-skilled carers. Interestingly, consistent with Australian figures Badovinac *et al.* (1999) found that over 50 per cent of UAPs were 40 years of age or older, while 50 per cent of RNs on the wards were under the age of 35 pointing to status differences based on age and education that may contribute to tension between the two groups.

This tension was most evident in Britain where healthcare assistants (HCA) were introduced into public hospitals, or their numbers increased, following the 1980s National Health Service reforms. Their presence created considerable ambiguity in nursing circles where their introduction confounded the hopes of many registered nurses that the new Primary Nursing, where one nurse cares for the patient from admission to discharge, would facilitate a post-Fordist climate of task reunification, flexible specialization and job enrichment (Daykin and Clarke, 2000).[3] Daykin and Clarke (2000) reported that registered nurses' resistance to HCA arose from the fact that the promise of holistic care was abandoned. Nurses were relegated to high level technological care and administration – and upskilled – while the day to day lower level caring work involving patient interactions was performed by HCAs. As a consequence, for both RNs and HCAs their work became routinized and repetitive, although O'Donnell (1995), commenting on the employment of PSAs in hospitals in New South Wales, noted that they enjoyed their new multiskilled role and preferred to work as part of the nursing team, rather than under the direction of hospital managers and administrators. However, the PSAs in O'Donnell's study also reported high levels of stress because they worked in self-regulating, non-hierarchical teams where authority structures were unclear, but audit requirements were high and responsibility for performance was shared equally by all.

The introduction of PSAs into South Australian hospitals goes hand in hand with healthcare reform. In 1994–5, Casemix DRG funding was introduced into all hospitals, following the collapse of the State Bank and a change of government. The resounding win by the state Liberal Government was seen as a mandate to reduce the state debt through curtailing public expenditure. Consequently Casemix was introduced at the same time as the public health sector sustained a budget reduction of $30 million over the three-year period 1994–96. Fifteen million dollars of this was carried by the public hospital sector; or four per cent in real terms (Brooker, 1997).

Funding to individual hospitals was negotiated through service agreements, which in effect outlined for each hospital their share of the state debt and introduced the principle of contestability (selected government services had to be put out to tender) and the privatization of non-core activities. As a consequence of these real budget cuts to 1993–94 activity levels, hospitals were forced to either intensify labour, reduce staffing levels, redesign work processes and comply with the principle of contestability. Two areas for privatization were cleaning and the preparation of meals.

Many hospital managers and clinicians believed that to outsource the services of kitchen staff, cleaners, orderlies, porters and nursing assistants through a tendering process would be counter-productive to quality care. One way of preserving this workforce as 'core' was to allocate them to the wards with specific duties, rather than have their services managed centrally. The re-organization of hospitals into divisions, or the Johns Hopkins model of devolution, following the logic of Casemix DRGs facilitated this. A second gain to this proposal was that once attached to a ward, this newly created occupational group could respond immediately to nurse or doctor requests for test results to be collected or patients to be moved. Previously when nurses or doctors wanted these tasks done they had to contact centralized services and wait for orderlies to arrive; sometimes up to half an hour. Managers who were concerned about patient throughput could see the advantages of a multiskilled newly created workforce attached to specific wards who could respond 'just in time' to requests that facilitated patient throughput. Added to this they created a less expensive carer than enrolled nurses, and although the state branch of the Australian Nursing Federation (ANF) viewed the introduction of PSAs with some skepticism, it was easier to achieve ANF acceptance of their role than to get agreement for an increase in the ratio of Enrolled Nurses (ENs) to RNs which continues to be governed by Enterprise Bargaining.

Despite this, the introduction of PSAs to hospitals in SA was not achieved without considerable opposition from the Australian Liquor, Hospitality & Miscellaneous Worker's Union (LHMU); the union representing the various occupational groups. Prior to the Liberal government reform, a number of hospital managers had attempted to negotiate with the LHMU for the creation of a multiskilled occupational group. There was a strong feeling amongst hospital managerial staff that the union was resisting the need to comply with the 1980s Structural Efficiency decisions of the Australian Industrial Relations Commission to build a multiskilled and flexible workforce. At the local level managers found it difficult to bring the work of orderlies under the control of human resource departments. However, by 1994, given that many public hospitals in the state were forced to offer redundancy packages to these workers in order to meet budget targets, and the alternatives facing hospital managers was to put the services out to tender, the union was forced to acquiesce. A secondary motivating factor was the fact that many of the cleaners and kitchen staff believed the new occupational group would provide them with more interesting and meaningful work, although the male porters and orderlies were less sure. While the LHMU wished to resist the state liberal government reforms, and attempted to do so through invoking a state based 1994 Enterprise Bargaining clause which required management to consult with unions on workplace change, local union members realized that most of their members found the offer attractive. Given that the union challenge to the competitive tendering principle was overturned in the Supreme Court in March 1996 as not a violation of the 1994 Enterprise Bargaining (EB) agreement and the offer made to workers was financially attractive; all were appointed at a higher classification level, moving them from level one and two to three, the union withdrew its opposition. The newly created PSAs were given one weeks training; two weeks short of what was previously offered to cleaners.

The process of work intensification

There is no doubt that those PSAs who upskilled from previous occupations as cleaners or kitchen staff enjoy their work, however, they do report that their working day is more intense than previously. Evidence for this can be gauged by examining the introduced of PSAs in 1996 on to the wards of a major public acute hospital in SA, called Westernvale hospital. At Westernvale senior administration employed some workload measures to calculate the number of PSAs needed in each division, but as mentioned above their introduction was a cost cutting measure, as well as a productivity and efficiency strategy. Not all cleaners or orderlies transferred to the newly created positions, significant numbers took redundancy packages so that while PSAs were trained to perform the range of tasks once restricted to narrow occupational groups, the pool of staff was reduced. For example when PSAs were first introduced at Westernvale the number of service type staff was reduced by 30 per cent. This was a nine per cent reduction in the workforce and just under $1 million in salary savings.

The significance of this reduction in numbers can be gauged by examining Table 7.1, taken from the Westernvale annual reports for 1994 through to 2000. In 1994 the complement of hotel staff, the category assigned to PSAs, including orderlies was 314. By 2000, the number was reduced to 144 representing a 45 per cent reduction in staff numbers over the eight-year period, although presumably some of this work was outsourced to private companies employed to clean the more public areas in the hospital. At the same time the number of registered and enrolled nurses dropped from 922 in 1994 to 833 in 1995 and remained below 1994 figures until 2001 when the EB agreement between the ANF and the Department of Human Services brought nursing numbers back up above 1994–5 levels. Given that the table shows clearly that hospital occupancy increased, the number of same day procedures intensified and the length of stay remained relatively stable, the work of PSAs like that of nurses intensified. It is not surprising that by 1998 PSAs and nursing staff were reporting several difficulties with this new occupational group. The three major areas of dissatisfaction reported by PSAs themselves were; a reduction in cleaning standards, dissatisfaction with rosters and an increase in workplace injuries.

Table 7.1 Activity data and staffing numbers 1994–2000 Westernvale Hospital

Year	Occupancy %	Same day	Nursing staff	Hotel staff-PSAs	Patient LOS	Beds or bed days available
1994/1995	N/A	13,186	922	314	5.1	402
1995/1996	86.9	14,232	833	200	5.22	402
1996/1997	87.8	N/A	857	180	5.3	413
1997/1998	88.3	16,553	882	146	5.01	427
1998/1999	87.3	17,860	918	150	4.72	437
1999/2000	95.40	20,035	881	144	5.10	402

One of the major difficulties for PSAs is to complete all the cleaning, but at the same time respond 'just in time' to the requirements to have patients delivered to rehabilitation classes or medical tests. When PSAs leave their cleaning work to respond to a nurse request, on return to the ward they are forced to begin their cleaning work again, rather than take up where they left off, because cleaning agents must be freshly applied. Added to this, they must organize their work without disrupting medical rounds or treatment regimes performed by allied health staff and nurses. Nor can cleaning be performed during patient meal times. While PSAs at Westernvale work without direct supervision, in most public hospitals their cleaning work is audited on a three monthly basis by independent companies contracted by hospital management. Following each audit, wards are assigned a score which becomes public knowledge, but is also aggregated for each site visit and for the year, as well as benchmarked against other public hospitals around the country and state. The scores contribute to the hospitals' initiatives in maintaining accreditation. Accreditation is a major benchmark for hospital quality assurance and has become increasingly important over the last few years as the evidence of the risks associated with hospitalization becomes more public.

The second and third concerns raised by PSAs at Westernvale are interrelated. As early as October 1996 the LHMU conducted a mass meeting at the hospital following complaints from its members about working rosters. PSAs were used to rosters of 152 hours across a 28-day cycle with fixed days off each month. PSAs now worked a similar shift pattern to nurses of a seven-day rotation per month of either an early (7am to 3pm) or late (1pm to 9pm) shift without the benefit of fixed days off. The number rostered per ward is considerably fewer than nurses with usually only three on duty for the morning shift and two for the late shift. Like nurses they find the seven continuous days arduous, but unlike nurses, on average they are older, much of their work involves heavy manual handling tasks and their fewer numbers mean they cannot negotiate changes to their roster. By 1997 many nurse managers were finding it difficult to adhere to the agreement covering PSAs and were regularly altering their rosters. In May 1997 the Head of the Occupational Health Unit at Westernvale reported that the injury rate amongst PSAs was 4.3 per cent per year, compared with the overall hospital rate of 2.5 per cent for other staff. By mid 1998 this had risen to 6.6 per cent, while the rate for other professional and occupational groups remained stable at 2.6 per cent. By 1998 Workcover claims had risen by almost 50 per cent from 14 in 1995 to

27. The number of PSAs not reporting for work due to injuries resulted in a crisis on the wards, where senior nurses were unable to replace them, or did so by asking part-time staff to work full-time. This in turn led to lower standards in cleaning, low morale and exacerbated their susceptibility to injuries. In response to the problems highlighted above, Westernvale instigated a detailed task analysis of PSA duties and as a consequence appointed them more equitably across the wards, but did not increase their numbers.

Case study two: Medical scientists and work intensification in the state of Victoria

In Victoria medical scientists are a small group of healthcare professionals who perform valuable diagnostic and research functions integral to the running of acute public health services. Their activities are both highly specialized and very diverse. Most medical scientists employed in the acute healthcare sector are involved in 'state of the art' laboratory testing but others are employed in nutritional services (dietetics), respiratory and lung function testing, neurophysiology and in monitoring sleep disorders. Medical scientists also include clinical perfusionists who monitor heart-lung bypass machines during cardiac operations and audiologists (Weekes *et al.*, 2001).

In Victoria medical scientists comprise 71.4 per cent of the scientific staff in laboratories with nearly 29 per cent Australia-wide holding a higher degree (Australian Institute of Health and Welfare [AIHW], 1998). Specialization occurs in pathology laboratories where scientists have a professional focus on haematology, biochemistry, microbiology, anatomical pathology, cytogenetics and more recently molecular biology. Laboratory-based scientists mainly test specimens for diagnosis, screening and monitoring or they work in medical research in various universities or in departments attached to a public hospital (Gardner and McCoppin, 1994, p. 406). Of the 3548 medical scientists working in Victoria in 1996, 68 per cent were female (AIHW, 1998) and 54.4 per cent worked in the public sector (AIHW, 1998). Historically, their role has been subordinated to the medical profession in the division of labour in healthcare despite their arguments that they perform 90 per cent of the work in medical science (Gardner and McCoppin, 1994, p. 408).

In 1993, medical scientists developed a set of competencies designed to reflect the standard expected from a person at entry level into the profession (Whitfield, Bell and Groot Obbink, 1993) due to concerns that there would be vertical encroachment from lower grade medical technicians. Victoria is particularly vulnerable to this because of the high proportions of medical scientists employed in comparison to other states (Gardner and McCoppin, 1994, p. 414). Up until 2003 the ratio of scientists to technicians was controlled by the regulations imposed by the *Pathology Services Accreditation Act 1984*. The Victorian *Pathology Services Accreditation (General) Regulations 2001* specified that persons conducting tests must be directly supervised by a scientist on the premises in the larger laboratories at all times. This contrasts with the Commonwealth government accreditation (through the National Pathology Accreditation Advisory Council known as NPACC) which states that a supervising pathologist or senior scientist must usually be present during normal working hours and available for telephone (or other electronic mode) consultation at other times (Services, 2001). The *Pathology Services Accreditation Act* was revoked in 2003 bringing Victorian accreditation into line with other states.

Industrially, medical scientists in Victoria are represented by the Medical Scientists' Association Victoria (MSAV: Health Services Union of Australian (HSUA) No 4 Branch), an industrial organization covering science-based professionals which also provides professional indemnity insurance to members (Eichenbaum, 1999). The MSAV is a separate entity to the scientific professional bodies and also provides industrial representation for the Victorian Psychologists Association (VPA) (Bremner and Kelly, 2000, p. 7). Although professional and industrial representation is separate, medical scientists still have the dilemma of balancing professionalism against rising militancy similar to other groups such as the teachers and nurses (Bremner and Kelly, 2000).

In 1999 the Medical Scientists' Association of Victoria (MSAV) decided to measure the extent of workplace change by surveying members. This was performed in conjunction with the Australian Council of Trade Unions (ACTU) survey of trade union members and designed to directly compare with results from the ACTU *Working Time and Employment Security Survey* (1999). Significantly, the survey showed that medical scientists were experiencing more work intensification, less control over their work and were more stressed than workers in both the ACTU survey and the Australian Work and Industrial Relations Survey 1995 (AWIRS95) (Weekes *et al.*, 2001). This stress was argued to be a direct response to increasing workplace change and increased management control resulting in decreased work satisfaction (Weekes *et al.*, 2001). The results of this survey suggested that there was more significant change taking place in workplace activities and how work is done than is generally acknowledged by government or the media. The survey also suggested that there is limited knowledge of the negative affects of rapid change in the workplace and little involvement of the scientist in the change process (Weekes *et al.*, 2001).

In 2001, a qualitative study was performed using focus groups exploring medical scientists' perceptions on the causes, effects and problems created by change in the health care sector (Weekes, 2003). This further study found that in order to facilitate workplace reform, work processes in the laboratory had changed. There was increased shiftwork, multi-skilling and job broadening with fewer training and research opportunities. These changes resulted in work intensification as scientists struggled to maintain the quality of work produced (Weekes, 2003). The following discussion draws upon this study.

The processes behind workplace change

The history of change that produced work intensification for medical scientists pre-dates the shift to a state Liberal–National government and the introduction of Casemix DRGs. In 1989, two per cent of the staff in laboratories were medical doctors, but their salaries represented eight to ten per cent of total costs. As a consequence productivity gains and cost cutting targets needed to be achieved and since medical scientists were by far the largest group in pathology laboratories in Victoria at that time, their work became a prime target for rationalization. Little consideration was given to the impact this rationalization might have on the working conditions of medical scientists employed in this area. The National Health Strategy *Directions for Pathology* (Deeble and Lewis-Hughes, 1991) background paper heralded a series of reviews at the major laboratories throughout metropolitan Melbourne including a Ministerial Review recommending streamlining of pathology services by merging or contracting out several public pathology services to other public hospitals (Deloitte, Touche and Tohmatsu, 1993). Cost containment became an important issue for governments and the Kearney and Whitfield Review (1991) found that there was potential for rationalization of routine, highly automated services among the hospitals within the inner city area, in the interests of cost efficiency.

When the state Liberal–National government came to office in 1992 pathology was identified as a 'non-core' business enabling it to be outsourced or transformed into a business (fee-for-service arrangements) with the hospital being accountable for the financial performance of the unit but not funded to run it as part of the ordinary operations of the hospital (Duckett, 1995, p. 118). This led to the introduction of the 'level playing field' allowing public pathology services to compete with private sector pathology. The radical reduction in public funding for hospital pathologies forced many to reduce staffing levels through Voluntary Departure Packages (VDPs). By 1995 most country and regional pathology services were privatized (Bremner and Kelly, 2000, p. 9) and many skilled and experienced scientists left the public system because the VDPs were structured in such a way that were more attractive to those on higher salaries (Bremner and Kelly, 2000, p. 8). It also led to a radical shift in the nature of work performed by medical scientists, from a set of routine and highly specialist tests linked to diagnosis and research performed for public patients, to routine high volume tests ordered by doctors for their patients, either public or private. At the same time staffing profiles shifted with the replacement of managers drawn from the ranks of scientists to those with business backgrounds. The scientists were left to deal with the day-to-day activities; managers to financial issues (Weekes, 2003).

At the same time as these changes in the organization of health services and work were being introduced, the Liberal–National government instigated a series of industrial relations changes to create a 'more malleable and compliant' workforce (Teicher and von Gramberg, 1998, p. 62). In order to maintain existing conditions, the medical scientists sought to move from state to federal award industrial coverage (Bremner and Kelly, 2000, p. 4). This development moved the Medical Scientists' Association Victoria into the federal government arena. However, in 1996, the introduction of the *Workplace Relations Act* by the Liberal–National government made collective bargaining the dominant dispute settlement process and encouraged the development of enterprise bargaining (Fox 1998, p. 281). This altered the way disputes were settled, creating the possibility of increased industrial action (Fox, 1998, p. 283). This was clearly demonstrated during the 1997 enterprise bargaining process when an angry MSAV membership smarting after years of budget cuts, entered into its first state-wide strike, in fact the first wide scale industrial action by medical scientists in more than 10 years (Stanton, 2002, p. 113). Similarly in 2001 during the third enterprise bargaining round the union was forced again to recommend industrial action to its members (Kelly, 2001).

However, the processes of work intensification for medical scientists went well beyond industrial relations reform, tensions between their union and employers or the impact outsourcing and privatization had on the organization of work. The use of pathology has grown significantly over the last 25 years (Deeble and Lewis-Hughes,

1991), suggesting an increase in consumer demand. Now, however, pathology's focus is more on the doctor ordering a battery of routine tests, and less on the patient in need of specialist investigation. In the study medical scientists reported that balancing the demands of doctors in private against the needs of sick public patient was stressful. For those working in the public sector the increase in private demand, along with the reduction in staffing numbers had resulted in increased workload. Added to this, previous activities directed towards staff education, teaching and research were abandoned or diminished, as they require funding outside of that generated through the business component of the service. Continuing education for medical scientists was for the most part, done in their own time as there are few lulls in the flow of work. The outsourcing and privatization of pathology services has also had a profound effect on training and research. Fewer opportunities now exist for research or for on-the-job training, not just for scientists, but also for the medical specialisms of pathology and radiology (Royal College of Pathologists, date not known). The scientists argued that the lack of research has impacted on the quality of service as has the general processes of work intensification and job insecurity.

Radical changes in medical technology have also impacted on the way the work is organized for medical scientists. Over the last decade the need to contain costs, increase quality control and efficiency and the development of new assay techniques, automation, robotics and information technology has played a major part in changing the way medical scientists work (James, 1995). While much of this technology has enabled an increase in work volume, it has also created ambiguity around the issue of autonomy. In some instances the technology does the diagnosis, in others it merely performs the routine and mundane tasks. However, many medical scientists argued that the current emphasis on efficiency promulgated in the marketing of instrumentation in laboratories emphasizes workload issues and ease of use (Abbott Diagnostics, 1993). Quality and scientific interpretation are relegated into third and fourth place so that the work has become less professional and more Tayloristic in its execution.

Automation had also brought increased work to laboratory staff, especially where equipment is not compatible with existing technology. It has increased work demand by simplifying the processes enabling round the clock services resulting in increased amounts of shift work for scientists. This invariably means that working hours have extended into what was previously social time. Further to this, where previously large numbers of staff worked during business hours, now more staff work shifts outside business hours, with senior medical scientists required to be on-call 24-hours a day. The impact of shift work goes beyond enduring unsocial hours; scientists complain that they have fewer opportunities for professional contact with peers, which in turn reflects on their expertise. As a consequence there is considerable debate about whether the new technology had resulted in upskilling, deskilling or merely multitasking.

There is a personal cost to the medical scientists resulting from the radical changes that have impacted on the organization of work. The scientists in the study argued that they had no control over the change process and consequently felt powerless. Thus there was resistance, as they perceived that the change processes were damaging to their careers and job prospects as they had been deskilled. There was also increased job dissatisfaction due to the work intensification, the move to automation and the lack of control over their work. The participants were suffering from high stress levels and had observed that morale was low in the workplace. High stress levels resulting from deskilling can result in ill-health through alienation and the lack of control over the labour process (Peterson, 1999: 71–72). Several participants in the study had experienced ill health due to work related stress with one manager reporting he had suffered a classical case of 'executive burnout'. As scientists they had expected to be involved in the change process but argued that the type of changes that were occurring were not intellectually challenging and had ultimately led to deskilling. Change fatigue (Rance, 2002) had set in and most study participants felt exhausted.

Discussion and conclusion

This chapter has provided two case studies that examined the claim that the work of personal service attendants in one hospital in SA and medical scientists in Victoria has intensified as a result of changes in their work. These case studies can be examined in the light of the framework outlined in the introduction of this chapter. The case of the PSA's demonstrates both extensive and intensive work effort. Changes to the work of PSA's included radical job redesign to create a new occupational group, changes in duration and timing of their shifts and less flexibility in their working hours. Job redesign also significantly impacted on multiskilling and upskilling of tasks supporting another facet of Beynon et al.'s (2002) thesis. This in turn created a series of problems where PSAs found that a number of cleaning jobs needed to be re-commenced or schedules reorganized to fit the work demands of higher status professional groups. PSAs also feel the pressure of increased work surveillance through the pervasive human resource technique of the quarterly cleaning audits (Beynon *et al.*, 2002). There is also strong evidence of increased work volume, given the data on patient throughput and patient reduced length of stay outlined in Table 7.1.

In the past few years the PSAs in this study have also been subject to job insecurity through a number of redundancies, although there is insufficient evidence to suggest the union's power has diminished or that new technologies have impacted on their work (Green, 2004). What is clear is that as their numbers reduced so too did those of nursing staff. One of the key processes contributing to work intensification is the increased pressure placed on other groups of workers, when other occupational or professional groups in the team are under pressure. In this study, one of the most significant factors of work intensification for PSAs is related to work intensification experienced by the nurses. When the nurses are under pressure, much more of the mundane cleaning, patient retrieval and domestic work is left to PSAs. This increased work volume is exacerbated by the reduction in PSA numbers which in turn impacts on stress levels and as the evidence suggests increases the injury rate.

The case of the medical scientists in Victoria also provides evidence of work intensification. The introduction of shift work illustrates an extensive increase in hours worked at least in terms of the hours being non-standard in duration. Further, the shift from specialized diagnostic testing to high volume routine work, supported by new technology indicates an increase in intensive work effort. Job redesign demanded by new technology and automation also produced job broadening, but whether this has resulted in upskilling or just multi-tasking is a moot point. Many medical scientists regard the labour saving technologies as part of the process of de-skilling. Perhaps a more appropriate label is 'job broadening', regardless of it being multiskilling, upskilling or deskilling.

Few lulls in the daily routine that once allowed for a focus on education, training and research confirm the scientist's view that the nature of their work has changed. New methods of control have arisen as a result of the introduction of more computer-based technology and increased emphasis on quality control. The organization of work has also changed for medical scientists; the ratio of pathologists to scientists has shifted, managers are now more often non-medically trained and their focus is on profit, not science; and privatization (without the bolstering of government funding) has resulted in downsizing and a concentration on profit-making activities over service to the public sector and research. Significantly, medical technology has contributed to this shift in the labour process, with many routine tasks now performed by machines, but the high cost of this technology demanding 24-hour, round-the-clock service (Beynon et al., 2002). New forms of control have appeared as there is increasing dominance of the doctor rather than the patient as the customer creating stress for medical scientists. Privatization has resulted in a shift in emphasis away from offering a service to sick public patients to providing quick results for doctors, whether they have public or private patients. There is also evidence of increased work volume due to amalgamations, downsizing and aggregation of private laboratories, and the departure of many scientists. The introduction of new technology has increased expectations of the customer for a quicker turn around time for their results thus increasing the pace of work.

Medical scientists employed in pathology services appear to have strong links to their union and to readily engage in EB when it comes up for renewal; their allegiances have shifted ground from a strong sense of professionalism over unionization to a more middle ground. However, this does not mean that the union has increased its strength over this period of industrial dispute. Young (2002) writing of the same period notes that while union membership remained stable for medical scientists the shift to the private sector reduced its influence. This may well be because the shift to privatization has resulted in fewer opportunities for advancement and a narrower career path, along with less opportunity for professional and union activity.

There has been considerable increase in work intensification in the health sector. It has not been restricted to nurses or doctors, but is system wide and, as a consequence, is doubly intensified for health professionals and occupational groups given the high demand placed on them all to integrate their work in order to ensure efficient, health-promoting patient flow through the system. In this chapter we have focused on PSAs and medical scientists, but no doubt the processes of work intensification are also evident in the community and private sector. The negative implications of this work intensification on caring and service labour are outlined in other chapters in this book.

Notes

1 A version of this chapter which focuses on the Personal Service Attendants was presented by the first author at the AIRAANZ conference in Sydney in 2005.
2 Because of the need to maintain anonymity references are used sparingly in this case study.
3 Three models of nursing are practiced in Australian hospitals; team nursing where tasks are divided between staff according to experience and grade; comprehensive where a team of nurses perform all the tasks for a patient during their shift and primary nursing where one nurse performs all tasks for the client during the patient's episode of care.

References

Abbott Diagnostics (1993) 'Beckman SYNCHRON CX5CE to be Released' *Australian Journal of Medical Science*, 14, pp. 83–5.

Australian Council of Trade Unions [ACTU] (1999) *Employment Security and Working Hours – A National Survey of Current Workplace Issues* (ACTU) July.

Australian Institute of Health and Welfare [AIHW] (1998) *Health and Community Labour Force 1996* (Canberra: Australian Institute of Health and Welfare).

Allan, C. (1998) 'The Elasticity of Endurance: Work Intensification and Workplace Flexibility in a Queensland Public Hospital' *New Zealand Journal of Industrial Relations*, 23(3), pp. 133–51.

Badovinac, C., Wilson, S. and Woodhouse, D. (1999) 'The Use of Unlicensed Assistive Personnel and Selected Outcome Indications' *Nursing Economics*, 17(4), pp. 194–200.

Beynon, H., Gromshaw, D., Rubery, J. and Ward, K. (2002) *Managing Employment Change: The New Realities of Work* (Oxford: Oxford University Press).

Brannon, R. (1996) 'Restructuring Hospital Nursing: Reversing the Trend Toward a Professional Workforce' *International Journal of Health Services*, 26, pp. 643–54.

Bremner, J. and Kelly, R. (2000) 'The Medical Scientist's Association of Victoria: A Case Study of Professional Trade Unionism in the 1990's ' in *Unions 2000, Retrospect and Prospect Conference* (Melbourne: Monash University).

Brooker, J. (1997) *An Evaluation of Casemix Funding in South Australia 1994–95* (Adelaide: Casemix Development Program Commonwealth Department of Health and Family Services and the South Australian Health Commission).

Considine, G. and Buchanan, J. (2002) *The Hidden Costs of Understaffing. Analysis of Contemporary Nurses' Working Conditions in Victoria* (Sydney: Australian Centre for Industrial Relations Research and training [ACIRRT] University of Sydney).

Daykin, N. and Clarke, B. (2000) '"They'll Still get the Bodily Care" Discourses of Care and Relationships Between Nurses and Health Care Assistants in the NHS' *Sociology of Health and Illness*, 22, pp. 349–65.

Deeble, J. and Lewis-Hughes, P. (1991) *Directions for Pathology* (Canberra: Australian National University).

Deloitte, Touche and Tohmatsu (1993) *Ministerial Reference Group-Review of Pathology Services in the Parkville Area* (Melbourne: Deloitte, Touche and Tohmatsu).

Duckett, S. (1995) 'Hospital Payment Arrangements to Encourage Efficiency: The Case of Victoria, Australia' *Health Policy*, 34, pp. 113–34.

Eichenbaum, S. (1999) *Benefits of Union Membership* (Melbourne: Medical Scientists and Pharmacists Association).

Fox, C. (1998) 'Collective Bargaining and Essential Services: "The Australian Case"' *The Journal of Industrial Relations*, 40, pp. 277–303.

Gardner, H. and McCoppin, B. (1994) 'Struggle for Survival by Health Therapists, Nurses and Medical Scientists' in H. Gardner (ed.) *The Politics of Health* (Melbourne: Churchill Livingstone) pp. 371–428.

Gough, R. and Fitzpatrick, M. (2002) 'Reluctant Managers: Nurses Surviving Despite the Bottom Line', *Paper Presented to the Workforce Issues in the Health Sector Conference* (Newcastle).

Green, F. and McIntosh, S. (2001) 'The Intensification of Work in Europe' *Labour Economics*, 8, pp. 291–308.

Green, F. (2004) 'Why Has Work Effort Become More Intense?' *Industrial Relations*, 43, pp. 709–41.

Houson, C. (1996) 'Unlicensed Assistive Personnel: a Solution to Dwindling Health Care Resources or the Precursor to the Apocalypse of Registered Nursing? *Nursing Outlook*, 44, pp. 67–73.

James, J. (1995) *Human Resource Consequences of Technology – Driven Multi-Disciplined Laboratories in Australian Blood Transfusion Services* (Melbourne: Melbourne Business School University of Melbourne).

Kearney, B. and Whitfield, J. (1991) *Review of Pathology Services in Inner North and West Melbourne* (Melbourne: Health Department Victoria).

Kelly, R. (2001) *Annual Report* (Melbourne: The Medical Scientists Association of Victoria, Health Services Union of Australia No. 4 Branch and the Victorian Psychologists Association, 2001).

Morris, R. (1996) 'The Age of Workplace Reform in Australia' in D. Mortimer, P. Leece and R. Morris (eds) *Workplace Reform and Enterprise Bargaining* (Sydney: Harcourt Brace).

O'Donnell, M. (1995) 'Empowerment or Enslavement? Lean Production, Immigrant Women and Service Work in Public Hospitals' *Labour and Industry*, 6, pp. 73–94.

Peterson, C. (1999) *Stress at Work: A Sociological Perspective* (New York: Publishing Company).

Rance, C. (2002) 'Workers Suffer in Corporate Shuffles' in *The Age* (Melbourne) 23/3/2002, p. G1.

Royal College of Pathologists Australia (date unknown) '*Pathology Workforce in Australia: Fact Sheet*' http://www.rcpa.edu.au/ (Accessed 14/9/2004).

Services (2001) *Review of the Pathology Services Accreditation Act 1984* (Melbourne: Victorian Government Department of Human Services).

Stanton, P. (2002) *Changing Employment Relations in Public Hospitals 1992–1999* (Bundoora: School of Public Health, Faculty of Health Sciences, La Trobe University).

Teicher, J. and van Gramberg, B. (1998) 'Industrial Relations and Public Sector Reform' *Australian Journal of Public Administration*, 57, pp. 60–67.

Weekes, K., Peterson, C. and Stanton, P. (2001) 'Stress and the Workplace: The Medical Scientists' Experience' *Labour and Industry*, 11, pp. 95–120.

Weekes, K. (2003) *The Impact of Workplace Change on Medical Scientists in Victoria*, Masters of Health Sciences Thesis (Melbourne: La Trobe University, School of Public Health).

White, N. and Bray, M. (2004) 'The Changing Role of Nursing Unit Managers: a Case of Work Intensification *Labour and Industry*, 14(2), pp. 1–20.

Whitfield, J., Bell, W. and Groot Obbink, D. (1993) *Competency-based Standards for Medical Scientists* (Canberra: Australian Government Publishing Service).

Willis, E. (2002) 'Enterprise Bargaining and Work Intensification: An Atypical Case Study from the South Australian Public Hospital Sector' *New Zealand Journal of Industrial Relations*, 27(2) pp. 221–32.

Young, S. (2002) 'Outsourcing and Downsizing: Processes of Workplace Change in Public Health' *The Economic and Labour Relations Review*, 13(2), pp. 244–69.

8
Emotional Labour and Aged Care Work
Sue Stack

Introduction

This chapter considers the risks inherent in managing those performing emotional labour in environments that reflect the philosophies of managed care. Drawing on a South Australian case study in aged care, it illustrates the link between the demands of emotional labour and the contradictions imposed on managers attempting to simultaneously minimize costs while providing quality care and quality work environments. Health and aged care workers experience the weight of emotional labour in both their jobs and in the framework of their organizational settings, often in ways that challenge their health and well-being and that ultimately has an impact on organizational performance. A deeper understanding of the range of factors aggravating the emotional labour content of care work is a salient concern given the need to attract and retain workers to the health and aged care sectors. It alerts us to the broad dimensions of human resource management characteristic of this industry.

Background context to aged care work

With one of the highest rates of residential aged care in the world, Australia's 3000 residential aged care providers accommodate and support approximately 144,000 people who can no longer manage to live in their own homes. This occurs in residential aged care facilities where a mix of private, not-for-profit and government organizations provides low level (hostel) and high level (nursing home) care. Residential aged care is funded from a combination of fees and payments levied on those entering care (determined by the level of care required and based on an income test) and offset by government subsidies (Commonwealth expenditure on residential aged care in 2000–03 was $4.3 billion). Reforms flowing from the *Aged Care Act* (1997), the legislative framework under which care is provided, have generated significant changes to the environment within which care is delivered. (Commonwealth Department of Health and Ageing, 2002a; Aged and Community Services Australia, 2004).[1]

A case study carried out in South Australia drew attention to a dimension of these reforms that have not always clearly focused on the aspects of emotional labour that are inherent in effective aged care work and that can affect good outcomes in this and other areas of organizational performance. In an industry where labour accounts for around 80 per cent of costs (Duckett, 2000) a key and contentious feature of the reforms is the demand it places on providers themselves to balance cost effectiveness with quality care. This pressure and an underlying fear that cost efficiency now takes priority over care, has led to strong resistance to these reforms from health professionals in Australia (Braithwaite, 2001; Crew, Armstrong and Van Der Weyden, 2003).

Coinciding with the reforms have been changes to the aged care workforce. These include a decline in the size of that workforce (Australian Institute of Health and Welfare, 1999) with a significant number moving out of the aged care industry to find employment elsewhere as well as an increasing number of nurses who are registered to practice, choosing not to work as a nurse. There has also been a reduction in the number of specialist aged care nurses, with an 18 per cent reduction in the number of geriatric/gerontology clinicians with professional training (Healy and Richardson, 2003, p. 4).[2]

At the same time, there has been a rapid expansion of employment for personal care assistants (PCAs), those performing a range of personal tasks associated with the daily living activities that nursing home residents can no longer manage for themselves. These include help with personal hygiene – toileting, bathing, grooming, dressing, feeding and mobility. In a period of just five years (1993–99) the number of PCAs has more than doubled in nursing homes, and has come close to doing the same in hostels. The minimum qualification for PCAs to perform basic activities associated with low care needs is a Certificate III in Health and Community Studies, while for those providing services to the 74,000 elderly with complex or high care needs, a Certificate IV is considered appropriate. Theoretically, these are the minimum qualifications for PCAs yet, in reality, about 40 per cent of them have not studied beyond secondary school (Healy and Richardson, 2003, p. 13).

These trends of labour substitution represent one of the measures that providers take to contain service costs. However, the movement of highly qualified aged care workers such as nurses out of the nursing labour force and the difficulty of attracting and retaining sufficient people willing to undertake paid care work largely reflects the impact of other cost minimization techniques on what is essentially emotional labour.

The significance of the concept of emotional labour as integral to service work and the caring professions is well recognized (Hochschild, 1983; Scott, Aiken, Mechanic and Moravcsik, 1995; Davies, 1995; Steinberg and Figart, 1999). Like physical labour, it can feel difficult and can leave the worker tired and drained. Workers in aged care experience the weight of emotional labour from the job itself and from the organizational setting in which the work is performed; often in ways that challenge their health and well-being and that can ultimately impact on organizational performance. Understanding how changes to the aged care environment add organizational stressors to work that is already high in its emotional labour content is an important first step in attracting and retaining sufficient workers to meet the anticipated increase in demand for carers. What is it then that we know about the nature of emotional labour in aged care work?

Emotional labour

Emotional labour and the idea of regulating one's emotions are not new. Goffman's (1959) early work suggested that people play roles and attempt to create certain impressions in practically all social interactions. This act of displaying appropriate emotion or 'conforming with a display rule' rather than expressing inner feelings (Ashforth and Humphrey, 1993, p. 90) locates the idea in everyday life, while other definitions focus on the effort, planning and control needed to express 'organizationally desired' emotions during interpersonal transactions (Morris and Feldman, 1996, p. 987). Hochschild's concept of emotional labour helps us to understand the regulation of emotions at work. The concept of emotion work[3] referred to here is not limited to the unidimensional positive or negative display of emotions that Hochschild identified as being expected of employees in their relations with customers or other members of their own organization and of the sort found in service occupations such as flight attendants or debt collectors (Hochschild, 1983). A prominent issue in some of those cases is that of 'authenticity', the problem that the feelings an employee is expected to display are not those that the employee actually feels (Kunda and Maanen, 1999).

Different issues arise when the expression of organizationally desired emotions are consistent with the feelings experienced by employees, in ways that enhance emotional congruence and positively relate to their personal accomplishment. This congruence can be found among care workers, who are known to come to aged care work with a predisposition for enjoying the relational aspects of caring (Lescoe-Long, 2000, p. 73). It signals the positive implications of emotion work, confirming that the work *per se* is not necessarily negative but rather, it can be a source of reward, compensating for some of the stresses involved. Nevertheless, our understanding of the psychological wellbeing of those engaged in emotion work is limited if it fails to recognize that the positive feelings associated with job satisfaction are dependent on situational requirements not exceeding a person's abilities, needs and resources (Zapf, Vogt, Seifert, Mertini and Isic, 1999, p. 531).

The significance of situational variables is that it places emotional labour within a social context, highlighting policy frameworks and organizational environments as dimensions over and above the notion of an individual stress response, broadening our understanding of risks to occupational health and safety. The multidimensional construct proposed by Zapf *et al.* (1999) alerts us to two aspects of emotion work particularly relevant to aged care. They are, the 'sensitivity requirements' and 'interaction control' and each of these finds expression in two of Maslach's (2000) core components of the multidimensional theory of burnout: emotional exhaustion and reduced personal accomplishment.

The 'sensitivity requirement' (the necessity to be sensitive and to consider the emotions of another) is perhaps most clearly illustrated in many domestic settings, where we 'sense' the requirement to respond to partners or offspring for whom we experience some emotion, some feeling of compassion, sympathy or love. It is thus a component of caring in a domestic sense (Steinberg and Figart, 1999). We may also care for people when we promote or maintain their welfare, in ways that might not always involve those affections, but which will nevertheless require sensitivity to another.

Nursing home care work is one notable area where emotional labour is part of paid employment, but it also involves 'caring relationships'. In this context, a large body of literature has grown up about the nature of 'caring' in the nursing environment (Clifford, 1995 and references therein). For those nursing the elderly, caring is a fundamental component of their work for reasons that have to do with good clinical and psychosocial outcomes and sensitivity is integral to this. The sensitivity requirement is high because knowledge of the resident and/or their family is a prerequisite for appropriate responses on the part of the care worker. The greater the degree of sensitivity, the greater the likelihood that the bonds of trust and communication are fostered in ways that enable nurses and care workers to effectively diagnose, prescribe and gain compliance with prescribed regimens, in much the same way as it is integral to medical competence (Scott, Aiken, Mechanic and Moravcsik, 1995, p. 78).

Sensitivity is also paramount at the other end of the care continuum, where affective dimensions, including companionship and emotional support are involved (Aronson and Neysmith, 1996). In the aged care context, caring involves sensitively attending physically, mentally and emotionally to the needs of the resident. In other words, it is about 'caring for' (in the sense of 'caring about') as well as 'taking care of' the elderly. Thus, the empathy shown by the caregiver toward a resident and their family has a direct bearing on perceptions of service quality, notwithstanding the ethical and philosophical underpinnings of this requirement (Olsen, 1991; Provis and Stack, 2004). The affective responses to the elderly are a reality of working with people who may be ill or suffering and such responses are essentially human as much as they may be professional.

However, building relationships with residents and their families is something that takes time and requires considerable knowledge of the resident as a person. Organizationally, the degree to which work processes and workplace characteristics are themselves 'sensitive' to these requirements in turn influences service quality. In aged care, nurses and care workers exist in institutionalized settings that can diminish the likelihood of caring relationships developing between themselves and residents. Administratively and organizationally facilities that are built on hospital models of efficient, almost mechanized care can rob workers of an ability to get to know residents and respond to their individual needs. Aged care reforms that reflect the philosophies of managed care are one area where these difficulties are compounded.

Managed care

At its simplest, managed care is the term used to describe a health care delivery system that manages access, cost and quality of health care by monitoring how and in what manner services are provided. Originating in the United States during the 1980s, it arose at a time when insurance funds were passing back to employers, increases in health charges.[4] Employers responded by claiming that their international competitiveness was being compromised by the high cost of health insurance being paid by them on behalf of their employees. Against this background new organizations emerged that saw the potential to make large savings for employers by being more assertive in managing care and costs (Marcus, 2000).

These new, managed care organizations (MCOs) took a variety of forms but were, unlike the traditional indemnity-type insurance funds, mainly for-profit organizations. Spurred by the need to generate profits and provide returns to shareholders, MCOs made several innovations in order to reduce costs to employers and gain market share. Observing that 'if all care were of high quality and appropriate, and if resources were unlimited, managed care would be unnecessary', LaPuma, Schiedermayer and Seigler (1995, p. 643) alluded to the trade-off between quality and funding. Nevertheless, the promise of cost control and subsequent profits was seductive and a variety of managed care approaches have come to dominate the healthcare industry (Marcus, 2000).

In following the lead of Britain and New Zealand, the deregulation of aged care services in Australia represents a shift towards managed care, moving the provision of these services away from government and placing accountability for outcomes directly with individual providers (Barnett and Jacobs, 2000; Bach, 2002; Ham, 1997). It is witnessed by a reduction in federal government ownership of residential places from 11.6 per cent in 1996–7 to 9.4 per cent in 2000–1 (Aged and Community Services Australia, 2001). Aged care reforms have also discouraged the number of admissions to high care nursing homes, while encouraging the growth of low care hostel accommodation for the aged. At the same time, they have promoted the possibility that providers would be able to generate a 12 per cent return on investment (Aged and Community Services Australia, 2001). In moving from the direct provision of services, the government focuses instead on policies for health care financing, consistent with managed care and New Public Management philosophies. These are accompanied by a bewildering array of complex funding arrangements. At the most basic level, the elderly are assessed and approved eligible for care according to an eight-level scale where 'one' denotes the highest level of care (and the highest level of funding provided) and 'eight' denotes a lower level of care (and no government funding). Regardless of the funding mix, there exists the need to minimize costs if the profits are to be returned to the 27 per cent of private providers who own residential care places, while the 64 per cent of not-for-profit providers must similarly minimize costs if they are to remain viable.

A range of performance management systems supports the funding arrangements and increases in regulatory activity, with associated goals and targets reflecting policies directed toward increased efficiency and cost minimization. But these goals bring their own costs and the South Australian study, reflecting similarities with international studies, has highlighted a set of contradictions imposed on managers and workers attempting to provide quality care to the elderly under these regimes. In linking emotional labour to the requirements of managed care, the study provides particular insights into the burnout process among aged care workers, where feelings of inequity are experienced in their relationships with the recipients of their care and in their relationships with their organizations. The findings also illustrate one of the key and contentious features of managed care that requires care providers to be resource agents and assumes that they will be both patient advocates and MCO advocates, even when these roles seem to conflict.

Methodology

The study was an extension of a project that benchmarked absenteeism in the aged care sector and was designed to delve beneath the surface of the absentee rates to identify why staff stayed away from work (Stack, 2003). The earlier benchmarking exercise was itself consistent with trends associated with managed care requirements to report human resource outcomes and demonstrate continuous improvement in organizational performance. The extended project involved an in-depth case study of a not-for-profit aged care organization that employed some 300 care workers, under a variety of different employment arrangements, to provide 24-hour care for some 500 elderly people. Care was provided through two hostels, four nursing homes and 101 independent living units across five localities.

The study surveyed all care workers and their managers. Twenty-five per cent of respondents provided biographical data, reasons for absenteeism and levels of satisfaction with various aspects of work, descriptions of the most meaningful aspects of work performed and factors that undermined these. Care workers and their managers described their work experiences during follow-up interviews, while on-site observations added further insights into the nature of the work environment.

Study findings

Two key aspects of managed care linked to caring work and emotional labour raised concerns for workers. One of these was the impact of cost-minimization strategies and the other was role conflict. Among the findings that revealed links with specific forms of cost minimization, was labour substitution. Sixty-five per cent of study respondents were PCAs, while 25 per cent were registered nurses and 14 per cent, enrolled nurses. Further, the majority (70 per cent) of respondents were employed on a part-time basis, while 20 per cent were casual.

Respondents represented an ageing workforce, primarily women, and just over half the study respondents were the main income earners in their households, while 18 per cent had multiple employers. Their primary reason for absenteeism was personal sickness (cited by 58 per cent of respondents). In addition, 30 per cent nominated the need to care for family members, while 24 per cent also cited personal exhaustion as specific reasons for being absent from work. All interviewees described the work environment in which they cared for the elderly as characterized by labour intensive administrative processes that divert scarce resources from the provision of care to the processing of 'red tape'.

Discussion

It became clear that the managed care imperative of cost-minimization exacts it own toll. For employers, the duty of care to employees becomes more onerous the less skilled the workforce. There are added costs in terms of information, training and supervision to ensure workers are sufficiently well trained to safely perform their work.[5]

A broad appreciation of duty of care towards employees requires managers to acknowledge the interactive effects of the gendered nature of caring, the ageing of the workforce and the likelihood that workers may be performing both paid and unpaid emotional labour. We know that care workers come to aged care with considerable experience in this type of work, often having cared for their children or their parents and, in so doing, commodify skills gained through their lived experience. Many continue to have caring responsibilities outside their paid work (ABS, 1998),[6] yet changes in the workplace have reduced the number of hours available to spend on caring within the home and in communities (Hochschild, 1997; Pocock, 2003).

The concerns that workers in Pocock's (2003) study felt about 'being there' for the family or feeling 'out of control' 'being stretched or torn' are concerns that add to the emotional labour that they might perform at work. Unlike many of the participants in Hochschild's (1997) study who 'retreated' to the predictability and order of their work to escape from the emotionally high and increasingly chaotic demands of unpaid care work, aged care workers face these demands at work also. There is no suggestion here that either type of care work in its own right is directly responsible for the exhaustion that care workers feel. Rather, as international studies remind us, it is the conditions under which the work is performed that more strongly relates to strain and burnout (Maslach and Schaufeli, 1993; Hemingway and Smith, 1999; Seago, 2000).

In managed care environments, the paradox for workers attempting to balance their self-care needs with caring for others, by working casual or part-time, is that they find themselves exploited by a system that positively values the savings in labour cost, while the workers risk becoming the 'working poor'. In the study being reported on here, cost minimization already subjects care workers to low pay (even with the prospect of full-time, permanent work), uncertain terms and conditions of employment, poor training, little organizational support and a lack of collective representation.[7] Some resort to combining a variety of other jobs in order to survive (sometimes involving care work but not always) and, in doing so, further exacerbate the emotional overload that can lead to poor health outcomes for themselves, a diminished capacity to effectively care for others and workplace absenteeism.

The dilemma for service providers under managed care arrangements is that, while at arms length and purportedly liberated from government bureaucracy, they are nonetheless confronted with an actual increase in regulatory activity and performance management systems (The Aged Care Standards and Accreditation Agency Ltd, 2005). This has particular effects on those delivering aged care and, throughout the case study and at every level, carers expressed frustration with role conflicts brought about by the reforms.

These conflicts revolve around service providers' responsibilities to residents and the sometimes contrary demands that are made on them where they are held accountable for a range of administrative 'outcomes' seemingly unrelated to hands-on care, or meeting the deeper emotional needs of residents necessary to promote their quality of life. This is consistent with international studies that have shown that the subsequent role conflict cascading down to care workers is one of a range of organizational stressors leading to exaggerated levels of emotional exhaustion that can adversely affect quality of care (Zapf *et al.*, 2001).

Care workers in the South Australian study expressed their intense frustration with the requirement for increased recording and documenting of activities that encroach on the time available for residents' care, describing it as *'time that could be better spent caring for people'*, as cutting into *'actual care time'* and *'severely hampering ability to meet resident care needs'*. The tensions and pressures on staff of not having enough time to interact with residents and provide personal care are well documented as contributing to high attrition rates in nursing homes (Commonwealth Department of Health and Ageing, 2002a). This is further compounded by resultant staff shortages.

Likewise, managers experience conflict between their role as health professionals, their role as managers of care workers and their role as resource agents. As health professionals they recognize their role as advocate for the elderly and are conscious of the link between the privatization of aged care and the lower quality of that care (Braithwaite, 2001, p. 445). They know too that many nursing home residents are very ill or cognitively impaired, lacking the ability both to discern and to identify aspects of quality. Notions of 'choice' for these elderly are unrealistic when they are too sick to vote with their feet and have little choice but to remain where they are. Residents are often highly dependent people, unable or unwilling to speak out and, without active kin or guardianship support they lack sufficient representation of their interests to have an effective voice on matters of quality.

For managers, their own work environment compromises their role as resident advocate. They are subject to work intensification and organizational productivity imperatives requiring their greater attention to managing administrative processes and performing back-office work. This distances them from the resident-carer interface, increasingly inhibiting their ability to fully know about the needs of both workers and residents, undermining their ability to make well-informed, quality decisions about resource allocation within their sphere of influence.

The language of managed care distances staff from an individualized understanding of the concept of caring. While residential 'care' was once provided in 'old people's homes' we now provide 'services' to 'clients' in aged care 'facilities', a vernacular reinforcing systems and processes that coalesce to challenge the role of caring in a personal sense.

Managed care sidelines the strategic human dimensions of care in other ways that create conflict for managers. A quality focus that prizes technical systems, processes and the physical infrastructure was evidenced in the study organization, where managers were busy ensuring building redevelopment incorporated a specified number of en suite bathrooms for residents. However, they complained that nowhere among the many performance standards to which they were subject was there a specified minimum staff: resident ratio. As one manager observed it doesn't matter how many en suites we have if we haven't got the staff to help the residents use them.

Minimizing labour costs affects organizational capability in other ways. Not only is there the conflict for managers in the organization's reduced capacity to provide care for residents, it also diminishes their own professional status. Lacking pay parity with similar professionals and occupational groups in the health sector, managers in aged care environments feel marginalized, seeing themselves as *the poor cousins of the health professionals*. Commenting on similar affects on professionals in the UK National Health Service, Flanagan noted that these conditions undermine managers' ability to create positive organizational cultures because, 'when managers themselves feel under threat, undervalued and over-stressed, they are considered less likely to be mindful of the sensitivities of their staff' (Flanagan, 1997, p. 188). Evidence of this is the increase in reported incidents of bullying of staff by managers in aged care facilities (The Liquor, Hospitality & Miscellaneous Workers Union, 2004).

Managed care frameworks overlook two facts. First, they give rise to factors conspiring against sensitivity and supportive organizational cultures. Secondly, these factors are particularly important to the work environment for workers performing emotional labour. The reality for workers is that there will be nursing home residents incapable of expressing gratitude or returning positive feelings to care workers, who then require avenues for restoring balance and reciprocity to the caring relationship. In other words, care workers' emotional investment in residents needs to be balanced by the organizations for which they work, by alleviating workloads or providing some other form of social support. Essentially, this describes the dual-level, social exchange model of burnout.

Under this model, if emotional work is high, if there is little reciprocity at the interpersonal level, if the organization stressors are high and if the individuals believe that more could be done to reduce these stressors, then the emotional demands at the interpersonal level may not be seen as balanced at the organizational level (Schaufeli, Van Dierendonck and Van Gorp, 1996). Given these circumstances, emotional labour is being performed under aggravating conditions, a coincidence that relates to high levels of burnout. The irony is that the emotional dissonance and exhaustion for care workers that these conditions create, affects other performance outcomes that managed care would wish to see avoided, namely, the direct and indirect costs associated with absenteeism and high turnover (Commonwealth Department of Health and Ageing, 2002b).

Another performance indicator, 'quality' of care, can be affected in one of two ways. One way is for scarce resources and work intensification to simply result in carers neglecting residents. Burnout and exhaustion among care workers on the other hand has other more serious implications for how the elderly are treated. They may be at risk of carers adopting inappropriate but nonetheless well recognized coping mechanisms that lead them to distance themselves from residents, to develop attitudes of protective cynicism, to dehumanize them or treat them in demeaning ways (Scott *et al.*, 1995, p. 83). It is at this point that we witness the intersection of human resource management with risk management.[8]

Nevertheless, in managing risks to quality and risks to occupational health and safety, audit cultures characteristic of managed care focus more on technical systems of measuring and accounting for performance indicators, than they do on understanding the interactive effects of work with a high emotional labour content, the conditions under which it is performed and the individual characteristics of those performing it. Poignant reminders of how this may lead to inappropriate problem-definition and, hence, inappropriate solutions are found in the following examples.

In one very simple case a care worker in the study bemoaned the fact that she did not have ten minutes to help a nursing home resident start her knitting. She felt frustrated by this because to do so would have been an appropriate response to the resident's psychosocial care needs, enabling her to engage in a meaningfully activity for the remainder of the day, something the carer expected would contribute to her contentment and well-being. The carer further observed that this aspect of quality care often results in a more settled and responsive resident later in the day. The interactive effects described by the carer who wanted to engage in an act of human kindness that was part of effective care work is largely ignored by the tight scheduling of carers' time.

In another case, a managed care focus on lowering costs (through work-related insurance claims), while framed as an exercise in continuous improvement in working conditions for carers, illustrates the extent to which the focus was more on technical aspects of the problem than on the human element. Not only can residents fail to acknowledge and reciprocate the efforts of carers, they can also be resistant to care in ways that impact on workers' safety. In exploring the prevalence of residents being resistant to care as a cause of staff injury in residential aged care one insurance company study took as its point of reference the elderly person as the problem and explored ways to deal with 'the difficult resident' (Cody and Grealy, 2000).

Recommendations arising from that investigation suggested that management might approach the problem by minimizing the frequency of activities of daily living intervention whilst increasing the therapeutic interventions. If the therapeutic interventions included helping residents who wanted to start their knitting, or engage in other activities that might be conducive to a more contented resident at days end – one less resistant to care, this seems a worthwhile suggestion. However, the further suggestion that management investigate hygiene approaches other than the standard showering and sponging of residents (though what 'other' approaches there might be are hard to imagine) overlooks that aspect of hygiene that carers tell us is already both frustrating and emotionally demanding for them and demeaning for residents.

Carers in the South Australian study who were relatively new to aged care were 'shocked' that they were required to undertake hygiene routines 'on a production-line basis' having only 'fifteen minutes to wake, toilet, shower, dress and feed residents in the morning'. They spoke of the complexity of delivering these services to residents distinguished by their different individual physical and social needs, while being required to arrange the care around them as though they were inanimate objects.

From the birthplace of managed care, Gass (2004) studied residents in Hall 300, and provided poignant and heroic examples of carers attempting to perform these dual roles, observing that, although the business of performing intimate tasks for residents becomes quotidian enough, it is a never-ending battle between these basic demands and the filling of deep emotional holes in the 17.3 minutes per day each resident can ask of the carers time. Other studies have also highlighted the poverty of interaction resulting when there are too few resources in terms of available carers and the time they have to care (Edwards *et al.*, 2003). Residents can simply be left staring at the world for hours on end, unable to access something that may be of interest, while the busyness of managed care goes on around them.

Conclusion

Under managed care environments emotional labour is being harnessed to increase productivity and improve organizational performance in health and aged care settings, but a key theme to emerge from this study is that managed care promotes discrete outcomes in areas where interactive effects are not easily accounted for. While organizations seek to provide quality care, managed care regimes fail to capture the reality of workers' concrete circumstances that bear on their ability to effectively respond and provide that care.

In the case of care work performed in environments that are insensitive to the requirements of emotional labour, we find a conceptual overlap between task – or organization related – and interaction related predictors of exhaustion and burnout among an aged care workforce. The study findings highlight the practical implications of this overlap and an environment where health outcomes are defined in abstract and often narrow economic terms, where aspirations are expressed as goals concerning process (for example number of Workcover incidents and reduction in costs), rather than goals concerning the quality of human interaction: the essence of caring.

Clearly, aspects of the work are satisfying for those individuals struggling to provide effective care. The challenge is to address, in an integrated way, the range of factors aggravating the emotional labour content of care work that undermines job satisfaction and to provide workplace conditions that restore balance and reciprocity to the caring relationship. Only then can we achieve good performance outcomes in terms of attracting and retaining an aged care workforce and providing quality care.

Notes

1 For a comprehensive analysis of aged care policy in Australia see Kendig, H. and Duckett, S. 'Australian Directions in Aged Care: The Generation of Policies for Generations of Older People', Australian Health Policy Institute Commissioned Paper Series 2001/05, at www.usyd.edu.au/chs/ahpi/publications
2 Comparing Census 1996 and 2001, it is noted that the 83,833 employed persons in the aged care workforce (nursing homes and aged accommodation combined) represents a 14 per cent reduction in the size of the aged care workforce over that period (Healy and Richardson, 2003: 20)

3 In this chapter the terms 'emotion work' and 'emotional labour' are used interchangeably as appropriate to the discussion.
4 Unlike Australia, Canada and the United Kingdom, the United States does not have a universal publicly financed health scheme. While it does have two publicly funded schemes for the elderly and some of the poor (Medicare and Medicaid), the working population are either covered by private health insurance or are uninsured.
5 That these costs are not being provided for is reflected in the absenteeism study where less than half the respondents had received personal stress management training and just over half had received specific training in understanding dementia and dealing with aggressive behaviour, while accessing training was made more complicated by fragmented employment arrangements.
6 In 1998 women made up 70 per cent of the unpaid primary carers of the disabled and aged while 13 per cent of the total workforce had caring responsibilities for an older person or someone with a disability (ABS Cat. No. 4436.0, 1998).
7 Assistant Secretary, South Australian branch of the Liquor, Hospitality & Miscellaneous Workers Union Assistant Secretary, reports that union density among workers in residential aged care facilities in South Australia averages around 30 per cent although this varies significantly from site to site.
8 The employer's duty of care to employees under common law (Occupational Health, Safety and Welfare Act, 1986 [SA]) covers more than the work they are doing and workplace conditions, to include potential exposure to risk from the foreseeable conduct of third parties and some workers are at an increased risk of violence either because of where they work, or the type of work that they do. For aged care providers, the challenging and potentially violent behaviour likely to result from increasing numbers of elderly residents suffering dementia compels them to find ways of minimizing physical risks to carers.

References

Aged and Community Services Australia (2001) *Two Year Review of Aged Care Reform: An Industry Response* (Melbourne: Aged and Community Services Australia).

Aged and Community Services Australia (2004) *Fact Sheet 2: Residential Aged Care* http://www.agedcare.org.au/factsheets/factsheet2residentialagedcare.htm (Accessed 21st September, 2004).

Aged Care Act (1997) Office of Legislative Drafting and Publishing, Attorney-General's Department, Canberra.

Aronson, J. and Neysmith, S. M. (1996) 'You're Not Just In There To Do the Work' *Gender & Society* 19(1), pp. 59–77.

Ashforth, B. E. and Humphrey, R. H. (1993) 'Emotional Labour in the Service Roles: the Influence of Identity' *Academy of Management Review*, 18(1), pp. 88–115

Australian Bureau of Statistics (1998) *Caring in the Community* Australia, Cat. No. 4436.0 (Canberra: Australian Bureau of Statistics).

Australian Institute of Health and Welfare (1999) *Nursing Labour Force 1998*, Cat. No. HWL 14 (National Health Labour Force Series) (Canberra: Australian Institute of Health and Welfare).

Bach, S. (2002) 'HRM in the British Health Service', Keynote Address to *Workforce Issues in the Health Sector Conference*, 31/5/2002 (Newcastle: University of Newcastle).
Barnett, P. and Jacobs, K. (2000) 'Policy-making in a Restructured State: The Case of the 1991 Health Reform Policy in New Zealand' *Australian Journal of Public Administration*, 59(1), pp. 73–87.
Braithwaite, J. (2001) 'Regulating Nursing Homes. The Challenge of Regulating Care for Older People in Australia' *British Medical Journal*, 323, pp. 443–6.
Clifford, C. (1995) 'Caring: Fitting the Concept to Nursing' *Journal of Clinical Nursing*, 4(1), pp. 37–41.
Cody, S. J. and Grealy, J. (2000) *Investigation of the Prevalence of Resistance to Care as a Cause of Staff Injury in Residential Aged Care Facilities in South Australia* (Adelaide: Workcover Corporation).
Commonwealth Department of Health and Ageing (2002a) *Aged Care in Australia* (Canberra: Australian Government Printer).
Commonwealth Department of Health and Ageing (2002b) *Recruitment and Retention of Nurses in Residential Aged Care* Final Report (Canberra: Australian Government Printer).
Crew, M. Armstrong, R. M. and Van Der Weyden, M. B. (2003) 'Can Compassion Survive the 21st Century?' *Medical Journal of Australia*, 179(11/12), pp. 569–70.
Duckett, S. (2000) 'The Australian Health Workforce: Facts and Futures' *Australian Health Review*, 23(4), pp. 60–77.
Davies, C. (1995) 'Competence Versus Care? Gender and Caring Work Revisited' *Acta Sociologica*, 38(1), pp. 17–31.
Edwards, H., Gaskill, D., Sanders, F., Forter, E., Morrison, P., Fleming, R., McClure, S. and Chapman, H. (2003) 'Resident-staff Interactions: A Challenge for Quality Residential Aged Care' *Australasian Journal on Ageing*, 22(1), pp. 31–7.
Flanagan, H. (1997) 'What Chance a Caring Management Culture?' *Health Manpower Management*, 23(5), p. 188.
Gass T. (2004) *'Nobody's Home: Candid Reflections of a Nursing Home Aide' Culture and Politics of Health Care Work* (Ithaca: Cornell University Press).
Goffman, E. (1959) *The Presentation of Self in Everyday life* (New York: Doubleday Anchor).
Ham, C. (1997) *Health Care Reform: Learning from International Experience* (Buckingham: Open University Press).
Healy, J. and Richardson, S. (2003) *Who Cares for the Elders? What we Can and Can't Know from Existing Data* (Adelaide: National Institute of Labour Studies).
Hemingway, M. A. and Smith, C. S. (1999) 'Organizational Climate and Occupational Stressors as Predictors of Withdrawal Behaviours and Injuries' *Nurses' Journal of Occupational and Organizational Psychology*, September, 73(3), pp. 285–99.
Hochschild, A. R. (1997) *The Time Bind When Work Becomes Home and Home Becomes Work* (New York: Metropolitan Books Henry Holt and Company Inc).
Hochschild, A. R. (1983) *The Managed Heart* (Berkeley: University of California Press).
Kendig, H. and Duckett, S. (2001) 'Australian Directions in Aged Care: The Generation of Policies for Generations of Older People' Australian Health Policy Institute Commissioned Paper Series 2001/05, www.usyd.edu.au/chs/ahpi/publications (Accessed 21st September, 2004).

Kunda, G. and Van Maanen, J. (1999) 'Changing Scripts at Work: Managers and Professionals' *The Annals of The American Academy of Political and Social Science*, 561, pp. 64–80.

Lescoe-Long, M. (2000) 'Why They Leave' *Nursing Homes Long Term Care Management*, 49(1), pp. 70–5.

Liquor, Hospitality & Miscellaneous Workers Union (2004) *Personal Communication with Assistant Secretary, South Australian Branch*, September.

LaPuma, J., Schiedermayer D. and Seigler, M. (1995) 'Ethical Issues in Managed Care' Trends in Health Care, *Law & Ethics*, 10(1/2). Reprinted in L. P. Hartman (1998) (ed.) *Perspectives in Business Ethics* (Chicago: Irwin).

Marcus, D. (2000) 'Prospects for Managed Health Care in Australia,' Parliamentary Research Paper 25, Parliament of Australia. http://www.aph.gov.au/library/pubs/rp/1999-2000/2000rp25.htm (Accessed 21st September, 2004).

Maslach, C. (2000) 'A Multidimensional Theory of Burnout', in C. L. Cooper (ed.) *Theories of Organizational Stress* (Oxford: Oxford University Press).

Maslach, C. and Schaufeli, W. B. (1993) 'Historical and Conceptual Development of Burnout', in W. B. Schaufeli, C. Maslach and T. Marek (eds) *Professional Burnout: Recent Developments in Theory and Research* (Washington: Taylor and Francis).

Morris, J. A. and Feldman, D. C. (1996) 'The Dimensions, Antecedents and Consequences of Emotional Labor' *Academy of Management Journal*, 21, pp. 989–1010.

Occupational Health, Safety and Welfare Act, 1986. Parliament of South Australia.

Olsen, D. (1991) 'Empathy as an Ethical and Philosophical Basis for Caring' *Advances in Nursing Science*, 14, pp. 62–75.

Pocock, B. (2003) *The Work Life Collison* (Adelaide: Federation).

Provis, C. and Stack, S. (2004) 'Caring Work, Personal Obligation and Collective Responsibility' *Nursing Ethics*, 11(1), pp. 5–14.

Schaufeli, W. B., Van Dierendonck, D. and Van Gorp, K. (1996) 'Burnout and Reciprocity: Towards a Dual-level Social Exchange Model' *Work and Stress*, 10, pp. 225–37.

Scott, R. A., Aiken, L. H., Mechanic D., and Moravcsik, J. (1995) 'Organizational Aspects of Caring' *The Milbank Quarterly*, 73(1), pp. 77–95.

Seago, J. A. (2000) 'Registered Nurses, Unlicensed Assistive Personnel and Organizational Culture in Hospitals' *Journal of Nursing Administration*, 30(5), pp. 278–86.

Stack, S. (2003) 'Beyond Performance Indicators: A Case Study in Aged Care' *Australian Bulletin of Labour*, 28(2), pp. 143–61.

Steinberg, R. J. and Figart, D. M. (1999) 'Emotional Labor since the Managed Heart' *Annals of the American Academy of Political and Social Science*, 561(Jan), pp. 8–26.

The Aged Care Standards and Accreditation Agency Ltd (2005) *Accreditation Standards* http://www.accreditation.aust.com/accreditation/standards.html (Accessed 20th April 2005).

Zapf, D., Seifert, C., Schmutte, B., Mertini, H. and Holz, M. (2001) 'Emotional Work and Job Stressors and their Effects on Burnout' *Psychology and Health*, 16, pp. 527–45.

Zapf, D., Vogt, C., Seifert, C., Mertini, H. and Isic, A. (1999) 'Emotion Work as a Source of Stress. The concept and development of an instrument' *European Journal of Work and Organizational Psychology*, 8, pp. 371–400.

9
Flexibility at a Cost: Responding to a Skilled Labour Shortage

Keith Townsend and Cameron Allan[1]

Introduction

There is currently a major shortage of working nurses in Australia. It is expected that this shortage will worsen in the immediate future (AIHW, 2003; Buchanan and Considine, 2002; DEST, 2002). A recent government report indicates a shortfall of 31,000 nurses by 2006 (DEST, 2002). This skilled labour shortage is not confined to Australia and is an international problem (Loquist, 2002). Countries such as the UK and the USA have experienced long-term problems in nursing labour supply and have relied extensively on immigration to supplement local labour shortages (Davis and Nichols, 2002).

In Australia, one of the features with the nursing labour shortage, particularly for hospital nurses, is that many trained nurses are not working in nursing or not working as hospital nurses. One of the consequences of labour shortages is that the existing nursing workforce has to labour more extensively and intensively to compensate for the shortage of nurses (Buchanan and Considine, 2002). Nursing shortages can create a negative cycle where long working hours leads to work dissatisfaction for nurses and exit from the occupation or industry which in turn exacerbates the nursing shortage (Allan, 1998). A critical imperative for managers and policy makers, therefore, is to find ways to recruit and retain nurses to augment the labour supply and ease the workload of the existing nursing workforce.

This chapter examines this issue by exploring the strategies adopted by one hospital to deal with the problems of a nursing labour shortage and excessive workloads for their nursing staff. The organization, Sympathy Hospital, initially used agency labour to supplement the permanent workforce. However, due to problems associated with labour quality and cost, the organization devised a new policy of working-time flexibility as a means of attracting new recruits to the hospital. This chapter explores how this new work-time policy worked in practice and examines some of the problems that arose from its implementation.

The nursing shortage – problems and responses

The current shortage of skilled nursing labour will worsen before it improves (AIHW, 2003; Buchanan and Considine, 2002; DEST, 2002). Research has identified four factors which will contribute to continuing labour shortages (Armstrong, 2001; Fleming, Evans and Chutka, 2003; Loquist, 2002; Watson, 2001). First, the average age of the nursing population – currently 42 years – is increasing (AIHW, 2004). When the cohort of older nurses retires in the next decade or so, the problem of labour shortage will get considerably worse (Armstrong, 2001).

Second, there is a reduced level of graduates from nursing programmes in Australian universities (AIHW, 2004). From 1996 to 2001, the number of nursing graduates from higher education dropped by 19 per cent. While there has been an increase in the number of commencing undergraduates in 2001 and 2002, there are insufficient numbers of younger people entering nursing to replace those who are leaving the workforce (Armstrong, 2001).

Third, demand for health care services is increasing. Health expenditure has increased from 8.1 per cent in 1991/92 to 9.3 per cent in 2001–02 (AIHW, 2004). Economists (Guest and McDonald, 2000) estimate that due to the ageing of the Australian population, the demand for health services, and hence nurses, will increase markedly in coming decades.

Finally, and most importantly for the context of this case study, there is a significant number of nurses who choose not to work for various reasons. A recent New South Wales (NSW) study has found that up to a third of nurses who were registered to practice in that state were either not working or not working in nursing (Nursing and Health Services Research Consortium, 2000). The reasons why nurses are not working in nursing include work intensification (Buchanan and Considine, 2002; Victorian Government Department of Human Services, 2001), the real or perceived threat of violence in the workplace (Victorian Government Department of Human Services, 2001), declining intrinsic satisfaction with nursing work due to managerial preoccupation with cost control (Buchanan and Considine, 2002) and the inability to balance work/life issues (Queensland Nurses Union cited in Lumley, 2001).

Policy makers and managers have a range of strategic options for increasing the size of the active nursing workforce. One option is to increase the labour supply either by educating more nurses in Australia or through immigration. As noted above, the current nursing graduation rates from higher education are inadequate to meet current shortages. While there has been an increase in undergraduate entry to universities, it will take some time for these new graduates to enter the workforce.

An alternative solution to boost labour supply is to attract overseas nurses. Recruiting nurses trained overseas is a common practice in countries such as the UK and the USA (Davis and Nichols, 2002; Loquist, 2002; Randolph, 2003; Smith, 2003). The USA has recruited foreign-trained nurses since World War II, particularly from the Philippines (Davis and Nichols, 2002). In Australia, in terms of net migration, there are currently slightly more nurses arriving in Australia than departing each year (AIHW, 2004). This modest addition to the supply of nurses is unlikely to satisfy the current nursing shortage. While increased immigration may be part of a longer-term solution, attention should not be distracted from the factors causing nurses to leave nursing in the first instance (Armstrong, 2003).

A second option to increase nursing labour supply is to improve wages and conditions. A study by Buchanan and Considine (2002) found that significantly improved pay would go some way towards compensating nurses for the declining intrinsic satisfaction of nursing work. However, health care administrators are generally reluctant to adopt this option as nursing salaries comprise a significant component of health care and hospital expenditure. The pursuit of comparative wage justice is a strong normative influence on health unions and wage increases offered to one occupational group are likely to spark comparative wage claims from other heath workers to restore historical wage relativities (see for example, Allan and Barry, 1999).

A different strategy to deal with the shortage of nurses is to allow other categories of workers – such as enrolled nurses, assistants-in-nursing, personal care assistants and administrative or operational staff – to undertake work traditionally done by registered nurses (RNs). Through this labour substitution strategy, the demand for RNs would be lowered. This type of an adjustment process is essentially a longer-term solution and needs to be considered in the context of national nursing standards and regulations as laid out by the national Australian Nursing and Midwifery Council and the various states nursing councils. This type of adjustment is also confounded as there are demarcation disputes in some states between nursing and general unions over the boundaries between nursing and non-nursing work. Any shift away from the use of RNs needs to be considered with some care as some research indicates the quality of care is positively associated with a skill mix were there is a higher proportion of RNs (Shullanberger, 2000).

Perhaps the most obvious issue for dealing with labour shortages is devising strategies to retain the existing workforce and to attract nurses who are currently not working in nursing back into the labour force. Research indicates that one of key desires of nurses is the attainment of greater working time flexibility. A recent study (Nursing and Health Services Research Consortium, 2000) of registered and enrolled nurses not working in nursing found that more suitable working hours was the most important factor that would attract these people back to nursing (67 per cent). For these nurses, working time flexibility was far more important than better pay (30 per cent), support in education and training (26 per cent), improved working conditions (18 per cent) and changes to management and work processes (17 per cent).

The ability to avoid the collusion between their work and non-working lives is a major concern for employees (Pocock, 2003; Watson, Buchanan, Campbell and Briggs, 2003). This desire for a work/life balance is particularly pronounced in female-dominated occupations, such as nursing, as women continue to do the majority of unpaid work in the households of Australia (Morehead, 2003). Research (Lumley, 2001; Morehead, 2003) indicates that some nurses in some cases are choosing casual or agency employment as a means of gaining greater control over their work time.

In the following case study, we explore how one organization has responded to the nursing shortage through the provision of greater working time flexibility. We commence the chapter by outlining our research methods and some basic features of nursing employment in Queensland. We then provide a case study description of the introduction of working time flexibility at Sympathy Hospital. We conclude the chapter by examining some of the implications of our findings.

Methods

This chapter focuses on the management of labour shortage at a private hospital: Sympathy Hospital. This case study was part of a larger case study and survey project that examined the transformation of working time in Australia. The larger study involved 17 case studies of working time change in Queensland workplaces.[2] This chapter reports on the detailed case study conducted at Sympathy Hospital and includes some broader statistic evidence gathered from Sympathy and other case study sites.

We selected Sympathy hospital for study because we were aware that the organization was experimenting with work time change. At Sympathy Hospital, the data collection involved interviews with managers and key personnel and focus groups with employees. Interviews were conducted with the Director of Nursing (DON), Assistant Director of Nursing, and Care Centre Managers. Four focus groups were conducted with different cohorts of existing nursing staff, new recruits and trainees. To ensure the identity of participants remained confidential, no details about the staff position and date of interview are displayed in the following discussion.

We also administered a survey at Sympathy Hospital and at 14 other organizations as part of the larger study mentioned above. A random sample was drawn at each workplace. The total response from the 15 organization was 963 useable surveys giving a response rate 42 per cent. At Sympathy Hospital we received some 56 returns from nurses representing a return rate of 23 per cent. In this chapter we will use this comparative data to provide an interesting picture of the differences between the views and experiences of nurses and a wider sample of employees in other organizations.

Acute hospitals in Queensland

The provision of hospital services in Queensland is dominated by the public sector which accounts for approximately three-quarters of all activity and employment (Allan, 1996). The private sector, though, is still a major source of economic activity and employment. In 2001–2, there were 52 private acute hospitals in Queensland representing some 19 per cent of all private hospitals in Australia. In the same period, these hospitals provided some 5279 beds or approximately one-quarter of all private acute hospital beds in Australia. Approximately half of these facilities were operated on a for-profit basis and a half operating on a not-for-profit basis. There were almost 11,000 personnel employed in Queensland acute and psychiatric private hospitals in 2001–2 with a wages bill totalling $565 million. Total income generated by these hospitals was $1.1 billion (ABS, 2003, Tables, 4, 10, 11, 14).

Nurses comprise approximately two-thirds of all employed staff in private hospitals. Industrially and professionally, these nurses are represented by the Queensland Nurses' Union of Employees (QNU). Blue-collar staff employed for laundry work, cooking, cleaning, maintenance and gardening account for roughly a quarter of the hospital workforce. These workers are represented by the Australian Workers' Union (AWU). The clerical and administrative staff are covered by the Australian Services Union (ASU). Private hospitals generally employ a small number of maintenance staff, covered by various craft unions. Very few other health professionals such as doctors, physiotherapists, radiographers, pharmacists and other allied health staff are employed directly by private hospitals, particularly so in smaller establishments (Allan and Barry, 1999).

Sympathy hospital – recruitment at a cost

The Sympathy Hospital is a large 200 bed not-for-profit, inner-city, Brisbane hospital. The hospital offers a wide range of acute and medical services in specialities such as ear, nose and throat; gastroenterology and endoscopy; gynaecology; IVF; ophthalmology; oral and facio-maxillary surgery; orthopaedics; paediatric surgery; physical rehabilitation; thoracic surgery; urology; vascular surgery; and cardiology. It also has an accident and emergency unit, cardiac catheter laboratory, several intensive care units, an endoscopy clinic, and a rehabilitation unit. On a per annum basis, the hospital admits more that 10,000 patients and undertakes in excess of 10,000 operating theatre procedures. Gross financial turnover is in the tens of millions of dollars.

The hospital employs more than 700 staff. Nurses are the most numerous occupation comprising more than 50 per cent of the workforce. In recent years, the organization had a policy of ensuring that 25 per cent of labour hours were undertaken by casual or agency labour due to the variably in demand for hospital services. That is to say, each area of the hospital had a permanent staff allocation (calculated in terms of labour hours rather than personnel) of 75 per cent of projected load. These permanent staff could be any combination of full-time and part-time positions – depending on the needs of the department and the requirements of staff. Any additional staff required above this allocation were employed as casual or agency staff.

Changing government policies and labour shortages

In 2000, there was a dramatic surge in demand for hospital services due to Liberal–National federal government changes to hospital insurance arrangements. The federal government offered a 30 per cent rebate to join private health insurance (Hall, 2001). One result of these government changes to private insurance was a marked increase in private hospital occupancy rates throughout Brisbane from the middle of 2000. At Sympathy Hospital, occupancy rates approached 100 per cent and remained at that level throughout 2000 and 2001. This exceptionally high level of demand for hospital services resulted in a higher demand for labour. As per the existing staffing policy, the hospital increased the usage of casual and agency staff to accommodate the demand surge. In some areas, the use of casual and agency staff doubled.

This additional demand for labour, primarily nursing labour, caused a number of problems. The demand for labour could not be met from the casual labour pool. This pool consisted of a limited number of nurses who had a medium-term commitment to working at the hospital on an ongoing basis. For personal reasons though, they elected to be employed on a casual rather than a permanent basis to enable them to decline work when it suited them, such as for family, study or other commitments. Lumley's (2001; 2004) research shows that many nurses prefer to remain in the casual labour pool as it provides them flexibility to meet work life demands; that there was always an excess of work available; and it avoided the increased responsibility expected from permanent staff. The casual pool staff at Sympathy Hospital were generally experienced personnel and could easily be allocated to a number of different wards in the hospital. This pool of labour could not readily be expanded at short notice.

As a result, the additional demand for labour was met primarily though the use of agency labour. However, as research has shown (Allan, 2000) the use of agency labour can be associated with negative cost and quality implications. At Sympathy, agency labour was the least preferred form of labour as the hospital had little or no control over staff selection and hence quality. The effectiveness of agency labour was further compromised as agency staff were often not familiar with the wards they were assigned to or the patients they cared for. Consequently, the workload of permanent staff increased, as they often needed to cover for the shortcomings of agency staff for the shift duration. Even if the same agency staff were reallocated to the hospital again in the near further they could just as easily be allocated to another unfamiliar ward. Thus, the extensive usage of agency staff, while it eased the labour shortage, also created some problems for the hospital.

The effect of very high occupancy rates and the labour shortage were felt quite severely by the permanent nursing staff. As much research indicates (Allan, 1998; Buchanan and Considine, 2002; White and Bray, 2003; and Willis, 2002) work intensification for nurses is an escalating problem in the health sector. At Sympathy, the closer the hospital came to full operating capacity, the greater the strain on staff and resources as there was virtually no 'slack' in the system. As capacity increased, there were fewer opportunities, for instance, to borrow staff from other wards to cover for short-term absences or problems. The continued high levels of occupancy created a sustained, demanding work environment without the periodic seasonal lulls that normally characterized hospital activity. The demands placed on staff were also exacerbated due to the high level of usage of agency labour.

In some instances, relief staff were totally unavailable. As a result, existing staff and particularly the part-time staff would be asked to do extra shifts. In the worse cases, staff would work back-to-back shifts to cover the labour shortfall. Our interviews with staff indicated that while these work pressures were felt across all clinic units, job intensification was particularly pronounced in the Intensive Care Unit (ICU) and the operating theatre; areas where there had been long-term acute labour shortage.

To explore the issue of workload and work stress, we asked nurses a series of questions about how aspects of their work had changed over the previous two years. Table 9.1 reports this data. This table indicates that over the preceding two years, nurses felt that they were more tired at work and that there was more stress in their job. As might be expected, nurses also reported that, compared to two years prior, it took more time to recover from their work and they were more likely to want to take a day off. When compared to employees in other industries, the nurses experience greater work pressure. This is a growing issue in the health care sector (see for example, Weekes, Peterson and Stanton, 2001).

In addition to the quality aspects of agency labour, there were also cost implications. Agency labour was more expensive to use than casual labour as the labour-hire agency charged an additional 25 per cent fee for supplying the agency labour. With the marked expansion of labour agency usage, average labour costs increased significantly in Sympathy Hospital. The Hospital Board became concerned about the labour cost escalation in late 2000 and recommended hiring directly more casual and permanent staff so that agency labour costs could be reduced. The aim was to reduce agency usage to 10 per cent of labour

Table 9.1 Pressure at work compared to employees in other industries (percentage)

Have the following gone up or down over the past two years?		Gone up	Stayed the same	Gone down	Total
The stress you have in your job?	Nurses	59	36	5	100
	Others*	46	40	14	100
How tired you feel at work?	Nurses	52	39	9	100
	Others*	39	51	10	100
How long it takes to recover from work?	Nurses	51	44	5	100
	Others*	33	58	9	100
How often you feel like taking a day off?	Nurses	54	37	9	100
	Others*	44	46	10	100

* 'Others' indicates responses from other 14 organizations surveyed in our larger work-time project.
Source: Working Time Changes – Employee Survey
n = 838 (nurses 57)

hours. Consequently, the hospital began to advertise for nursing staff in a major metropolitan newspaper on several occasions in the latter part of 2000. To the bewilderment of hospital administrators, no suitable applicants responded to these job advertisements. This shortage of labour reflected the excess demand for labour across the entire Brisbane labour market due to the city-wide demand explosion for private hospital services. Nurse managers knew there was a global shortage of nurses, but it was unprecedented in the history of the hospital to be unable to attract a field of applicants for nursing positions.

Locating and recruiting 'great nurses'

In December 2000, nursing administrators began exploring options for attracting more permanent staff to the hospital. Nurse managers were well aware that as an inner-city hospital they were disadvantaged. Generally, to work at an inner-city hospital, staff had to travel greater distances (or at least longer time) to get to work and pay for parking. To this extent, hospital managers knew that the hospital was a less attractive workplace than many suburban hospitals. This problem was soon to become even more acute as a new private suburban hospital was scheduled to open in 2001. For many nurses, the opportunity to work in a well-resourced, new facility with the latest equipment was a very attractive option, especially if the facility was closer to their suburban homes than their current workplace. With this in mind, nursing administrators at Sympathy were well aware that although circumstances were difficult, it may very well become more difficult in the future when the new hospital commenced operation.

Nurse managers participated in brainstorming sessions and labour market research to identify if there were potential groups of nurses that were available and interested in working, but might be hesitant to return to the hospital sector. It was noted by the nurse managers that there were a large number of nurses who had moved out of hospital nursing into other areas such as general practitioner's surgeries and clinics or had dropped out of nursing altogether but had retained their registration. Some of these nurses were bored with their current jobs but were reluctant to return to hospital nursing due to their lack of recent hospital experience and the inflexibility of the hospital shift work system.

Nurse management recognized that many nurses, over the course of their lives, had difficulty coping with the continuous shift system in hospitals. Nurses are overwhelmingly female and many of them have families, sporting and education commitments or other interests that restrict their availability to work at various stages of their life. Accordingly, it was decided by management that the hospitals would have to be more flexible in meeting the working time preferences of nurses if they were to attract and retain new staff. It was also hoped that a more flexible approach by management to the needs of nurses would enable the hospital to attract experienced staff from other hospitals.

Nurse managers met with personnel from the hospital's Marketing Department to discuss recruitment problems and the need to develop an effective advertising campaign to attract applicants. It was decided that the advertising campaign should be more generic than was normally the case in job advertisements. Thus, job description details did not need to be included in the advertisement as there was a standard job description across the industry. Rather than being highly prescriptive, the new, simplified newspaper advertisements merely stated in very large type 'Great Nurses', and then interested job applicants were directed to phone the DON, 'Betty'. This advertising style was considered more akin to advertisements for other professional groups. In addition, the first name reference to the DON was also designed to imply that applicants would receive personal attention and consideration by senior management.

The Marketing Department also concluded that such generic advertising could also serve as general advertising for the hospital as well.

The theme of the 'Great Nurses' campaign signified that the hospital employed fantastic nurses. To further promote the message, advertisements were also taken out on large roadside billboards. A series of radio advertisements along the same lines, were also commissioned. This level of job advertising was unprecedented at the hospital. The hospital also started some targeted advertising to recruit particular types of nurses. First, special 'Great Nurses' advertisement were run for ICU nurses who were in critically short supply – the majority of staff in ICU were agency nurses. Secondly, the hospital also tried to attract nurses who would be prepared to work four-hour shifts. These were predominately nurses with family commitments who wanted to work in a hospital, but not on eight-hour shifts. The hospital could easily use nurses on four-hour shifts to assist during the several busy periods each day: meal times, bath times and daily admissions. Thirdly, the hospital also targeted nurses wanting permanent night duty. If permanent night duty staff could be found, it was thought that it would be easier to attract staff to work the remaining day and afternoon shifts.

The advertising campaign generated a surprisingly large number of inquiries from potential job applicants in late 2000. Senior nurses could not explain fully why this advertising campaign had been so much more successful than their other advertisements. Some part of the success was attributed to the nature of the slogan 'Great Nurses' that somehow seemed to attract interest and connect with nurses in a way that had not been experienced before. The hospital was inundated with expressions of interest.

After the advertisements were placed, all calls from potential applicants were fielded by either the DON or one of the two Assistant Directors of Nursing. In this way, the senior managers were able to make personal contact with potential applicants that demonstrated that the organization was genuinely interested in the needs of staff. Senior staff explored the caller's current circumstances and their personal needs for hospital employment. Managers investigated individual's specific requirements in terms of where and when they wanted to work and other issues such as training needs. For instance, a nurse may have stated that she wanted to work in the medical area for 18 hours a week, between Monday to Thursday with no night shifts.

Senior nurses recorded all the individual requests and then consulted with the managers of the various nursing units to establish if it was possible to accommodate the requests of the applicants. It was common for applicants to request to work little if any night duty or weekend work. Given the shortage of staff, unit managers were generally accommodating with applicants' requests. Where applicants had highly idiosyncratic requests – such as fixed hours on specific days – that could not be met by a single ward, then these staff were offered permanent employment but no guarantee of which ward they would be working in on any given day. The net result of the recruitment and selection process was that the organization acquired almost 80 new staff which equated to approximately 50 effective full-time positions.

In addition to offering tailored shifts, the hospital also introduced a number of financial incentives to attract new recruits. Nurses prepared to work four-hour shifts were offered free parking in the adjacent commercial park. This incentive was offered to offset the relative high costs of parking in comparison to the small salary earned in a four-hour shift. An incentive of $1000 was offered to recruits prepared to work permanent night duty for a minimum of two nights a week – subject to a qualifying period. An incentive of $5000 over two years was offered to ICU nurses. The value of this incentive reflected the relative shortage of such nurses in the labour market.

Consultation over recruiting policies

The senior management team and the board were in agreement on the need to increase the size of the permanent nursing workforce and reduce the use of agency labour. The senior nursing team and the DON in particular were largely responsible for conceiving, developing and implementing the specific recruitment initiatives. It was only a matter of a couple of weeks from when the DON initiated the 'Great Nurses' idea to recruits being employed. The senior nurses worked closely together with the Marketing Department to fashion the campaign. Nurse managers who were responsible for the individual wards, were advised of the upcoming campaign at their regular fortnightly nurse managers meeting. These middle level managers were instructed to advise their staff of the current initiatives. Unions played no role in the process as the matter was viewed by management to be one of managerial prerogative.

As will be discussed below, many staff were upset about the lack of consultation of the 'Great Nurses' campaign and the special treatment afforded to the new recruits. Interviews with senior managers indicated that lack of consultation and communication with base grade staff was a major contributor to staff discontent. Senior managers conceded that at the time, the primary aim was to attract new staff as quickly as possible and this haste mitigated against extensive consultation. Still, lack of communication was acknowledged by staff and management as a key contributor to staff discontent.

Nursing views

Focus groups with the new recruits indicated that they were highly satisfied with being able to select their own working time. The new staff were pleased that the organization was prepared to accommodate their personal preferences. Further, the new staff were generally glad to be returning to work in a major hospital, in a way that suited them. Many staff recruited to the hospital had been working in non-acute areas of nursing such as in doctor's surgeries, laser clinics and aged care facilities. Many of these nurses were experienced hospital nurses who felt that their skills were under-utilized in the non-acute sector. They were appreciative of the opportunity to get back into hospital work and do so in a way that allowed them to balance their work and family lives.

Some of these staff were concerned about whether it was going to be possible for them to work only their chosen hours in the longer-term. It was common practice for staff to be called upon to work extra shifts when patient numbers increased or staff were off sick before management engaged agency labour. The new recruits were very conscious that there was a strong sense of shared responsibility among nurses for the welfare of their colleagues and patients on their wards. These staff recognized that over time, managers would be bound to ask them – as they had asked of other staff – to work extra hours outside their preferred arrangements. As such, they were unsure if they would be able to retain their special shift requests in the longer-term. Indeed, some of these recruits indicated that if there was pressure placed upon them, they would consider leaving rather than succumb to pressure to change their working arrangements.

Existing staff – as opposed to the new recruits – had quite different views about the efficacy of the 'Great Nurses' programme. Equity was a major issue for these staff. Existing staff felt that they had proven their dedication and commitment to the hospital through many years of services. They felt they should be given priority over the new recruits. Existing staff found it particular annoying to have to work around the needs of the new arrivals, especially when the new nurses were more junior and less experienced staff. Existing staff were particularly frustrated as they had to train some of the new staff and carry them in the ward until they gained experienced to operate autonomously.

Existing personnel were also very upset at the provision of financial incentives for new recruits. It was seen as vastly unfair that one group of staff were receiving more favourable treatment than another. The ICU nurses in particular were irate that new recruits would receive a bonus of $5000 over two years for commencing work at the hospital, whereas existing staff were offered nothing. The ICU nurses formed a united front on the issue, approached management and demanded equal treatment; otherwise, they threatened to resign in protest. Management conceded to their demands and provided them with an equivalent bonus, paid in quarterly instalments. While this settled matters in the ICU, it fuelled the resentment of staff in the rest of the hospital as another example of inequitable treatment of staff by management.

The major issue for long serving staff was retention, not recruitment. Long serving Sympathy Nurses saw the recruitment programme as a short-term solution to the longer-term problem of turnover and retention. They felt that while the new programme had increased permanent staff levels – which most people agreed was a desirable outcome – this did not guarantee that staff would stay for long periods. Indeed, reflecting Lumley's research (2001; 2004) we asked several of the younger recruits of their medium term goals. All of them had plans to leave Sympathy hospital or to develop their careers in other ways. For example, some interviewees stated they wanted to gain a wider range of hospital experience, to leave the labour force to have a family or to travel overseas. Interviews with more mature new recruits suggested that many of these staff were content with current arrangements and would remain at the hospital in the foreseeable future.

Staff frustrations became evident in our survey results which indicated a low level of trust between the workforce and management (see Table 9.2). At Sympathy hospital, when asked if all groups of nurses were treated with equal fairness, some 47 per cent of employees disagreed, while only one-third of respondents agreed with this sentiment. Only 39 per cent of respondents agreed that management tried to co-operate with the workforce. Almost one-third of staff (31 per cent) reported that employees had enough say when problems arose with management. An overall indicator of the low level of trust between management and workers was that only ten per cent of staff agreed with the statement 'management can be trusted to tell things the way they are'. As can be seen in Table 9.2 the views of nurses were less favourable than the views of employees in other organizations in our study.

Such was the level of discontent among existing staff that a petition was taken up and signed by some 100 hospital personnel including nurses and other staff in late 2001. In essence, the letter to the DON explained that existing staff felt their contribution to the hospital was not valued as highly as that of the new recruits. They felt that the new recruits, were receiving special treatment because they could nominate their own shift preferences. Staff expressed their dissatisfaction at the unfairness of the financial incentives offered to the ICU staff and permanent night duty recruits. Staff were also upset because staff working four-hour shifts received free parking.

The DON responded to the petition with an open letter to all nursing staff. The DON explained that all staff were valued equally for their contribution; however, the DON stated that nurses were in short

Table 9.2 Employee perceptions of management and unions between Sympathy Hospital nurses and workers from other industries (percentage)

		Agree	Neither	Disagree	Total
All groups of employees here are treated with equal fairness.	Nurses	32	21	47	100
	Others*	44	17	39	100
Management tries to co-operate with employees.	Nurses	39	28	33	100
	Others*	61	18	21	100
Unions are effective in this workplace.	Nurses	14	34	52	100
	Others*	40	27	33	100
You would prefer if a union was more effective at this workplace.	Nurses	58	27	15	100
	Others*	32	38	30	100
Employees here have a say if a problem arises with management	Nurses	31	19	50	100
	Others*	56	14	30	100
Management can be trusted to tell things the way they are.	Nurses	10	18	72	100
	Others*	36	19	45	100

* 'Others' indicates responses from other 14 organizations surveyed in our larger work-time project.
Source: Working Time Changes – Employee Survey
n = 873 (nurses 57)

supply, nationally and internationally, and that the first priority of the hospital was to attract enough nurses to ease the excessive workloads of current personnel. To achieve this, some incentives had to be offered and external nurses had to be offered greater choice in terms of working time. But, she noted, incentives were open to all staff willing to work permanent night duty, in the ICU or four-hour shifts. Existing staff also had the same opportunity as new staff to negotiate a working time pattern that suited themselves and the hospital. Staff merely needed to make a request in writing and management would try where possible to accommodate staff needs. In addition, the DON visited three nursing units where staff feeling ran high. Through direct dialogue with staff, the DON was able to pacify staff to some extent and explain to them more fully the rationale for the current initiatives and the lack of options.

Certainly, the dissatisfaction among existing staff would have been much greater had it not been for the system of self-rostering used at the hospital. It had long been a practice for staff to select their own shifts. The exact operation of this system differed slightly between wards, but generally the unit manager would place a fortnightly blank roster on the notice board and staff would choose their own shifts. Staff who got to the roster early had a greater choice of shifts than later ones. The manager would allow staff with special requests for example, to select their preferences before other staff. Managers would advise staff that it was essential that the ward had a reasonable skill mix at all times (i.e., an adequate number of experienced staff on the ward) and for staff to select shifts accordingly. If, upon inspection, the manager felt that there were skill imbalances on any shift, then staff would be moved around to balance the skill mix on all shifts.

Under the self-rostering system, staff already had some control over their working time. As Morehead (2003, p. 96) notes, while nurses do not have much flexibility to take time off during the day or vary their starting and finishing times, they generally do have some control over how many hours they work and which shifts they work. Indeed Table 9.3 confirms this observation and shows that most staff at Sympathy had some control over their working time; particularly when compared to workers in other organizations. But self-rostering was quite different to the system of shift self-selection that was made available to the newly recruited staff. The new employees were given the opportunity to nominate exactly when and for how long they wanted to work. When these staff members were recruited, they were told by management that their working time preferences would be met. The hospital thus had a clear moral obligation to these staff to

Table 9.3 Control over working time for nurses at Sympathy Hospital compared to employees in other industries (percentage)

		A great Deal	Quite a lot	Some	None	Total
How much say do you have over the number of hours you work in a week?	Nurses	46	27	21	6	100
	Others*	14	17	34	35	100
How much say do you have over the shifts you will be working?	Nurses	25	44	31	0	100
	Others*	15	15	25	45	100

* 'Others' indicates responses from other 14 organizations surveyed in our larger work-time project.
Source: Working Time Changes – Employee Survey
n = 873 (nurses 57)

meet their work time preferences over and above the preferences of other staff. The existing staff received no such commitment. Rather, under the self-rostering system, the existing nurses were given the opportunity every fortnight to select their shifts for the coming period. Staff selected shifts knowing full well that they would be expected by management and their work colleagues to work a reasonable amount of night and afternoon shifts and weekends. The choices, therefore, were constrained by the need to balance their own preferences with the needs of the ward and their colleagues.

Clearly, the nurses at Sympathy Hospital have, when compared to other workers in a variety of industries, much greater control over many aspects of their working time. However, when management implemented policies without adequate consultation, and with special treatment for new recruits, there is a corresponding backlash from the existing employees.

Conclusion

This chapter has examined the problems of inadequate nursing labour supply and the efficacy of working time policies to attract satisfactory levels of skilled nurses. Due to the increased demand for private hospital service as a result of government changes to private health insurance, Sympathy Hospital experienced severe labour shortages. Initially, the hospital reacted by increasing the number of agency nurses usage. However, the hospital's administration realized that the reliance upon agency staff was having a detrimental effect on profitability, staff morale, turnover, and the provision of service.

Staff shortages also increased the workload of existing staff as they took on more work to cope with rising level of hospital utilization. While increased workloads represents a obvious short-term response to labour shortages, in the longer-term excessive workloads can lead to nurse dissatisfaction and higher rates of turnover (Victorian Government Department of Human Services, 2001). Alternative measures need to be considered.

The strategy adopted by Sympathy Hospital was to offer working-time flexibility to attract more staff. In this case study, the organization was not merely making some minor adjustment so that nurses would have a little extra 'room to move' in balancing their work and family lives (Morehead, 2003). Instead, the organization was quite explicit in their aim of offering new recruits the flexibility they wanted as a condition of engagement.

However, due to poor implementation and lack of consultation, the policy generated considerable opposition from existing staff. While staff recognized the need for new staff, they were also highly resentful that management had focused so strongly on recruitment without giving due attention to the issue of retention. Clearly, managerial initiatives that ignore workers' perennial concern for fair and equitable treatment at work are unlikely to be successful, even in the short term.

This case study indicates that the development of more employee-oriented, working-time policies is potentially a very important means of providing the largely female workforce with the flexibility to balance their work and non-working lives. Unless health organizations are able to offer nurses the types of flexibility they need to manage their work and families over the course of their career, then high attrition rates will lead to chronic problem of nursing shortages. While nurse retention is linked to broader issues – such as pay, workload, career progression and so on – working time is undoubtedly one of the major areas where there is a need for greater experimentation and innovation to improve the quality of working life for nurses.

Notes

1 We would like to thank the nurses who participated in our study. We would also like to acknowledge the assistance and support of our colleagues, Andrea Fox, Chris Houghton, David Peetz and Bob Russell. This project was funded by an Australian Research Council Linkage Grant.
2 The cases included a balance of female-dominated, male dominated and mixed gender workplaces with a mix of strongly, weakly and non-unionized workplaces. Sectors covered included: a printing company, a construction company, a health product manufacturer, mining companies, government agencies, a bank, a theme park, a retailer, a trade union, educational institu-

tions, and a truck repair company. The major findings of this project were published in *Working-Time Transformations and Effects* (2003).

References

ABS (Australia Bureau of Statistics) (2003) *Private Hospitals Australia*, Cat. No. 4390.0 (Canberra).
AIHW (Australian Institute of Health and Welfare) (2003) *Nursing Labour Force 2001*, AIHW Cat. No. HWL 26 (Canberra).
AIHW (Australian Institute of Health and Welfare) (2004) *Australia's Health 2004*, AIHW Cat. No. AUS 25 (Melbourne).
Allan, C. (2000) 'The Hidden Organisational Costs of Using Non-Standard Employment' *Personnel Review*, 29(2), pp. 188–206.
Allan, C. (1998) 'The Elasticity of Endurance: Work Intensification and Workplace Flexibility in the Queensland Public Hospital System' *New Zealand Journal of Industrial Relations*, 23(3), pp. 133–151
Allan, C. (1996) *Labour Utilisation in Queensland Hospital*, Unpublished PhD thesis (Faculty of Commerce and Administration, Griffith University).
Allan, C. and Barry, M. (1999) 'The Private Hospitals' Association of Queensland' in P. Sheldon and L. Thornthwaite (eds) *Catalysts and Captives: Employer Associations and Industrial Relations Change in Australia* (Sydney: Allen and Unwin) pp. 159–166.
Armstrong, F. (2001) 'Addressing Workforce Issues: Federal Election 2001' *Australian Nursing Journal*, 9(1), pp. 28–31.
Armstrong, F. (2003) 'Migration of Nurses: Find a Sustainable Solution' *Australian Nursing Journal*, 11(3), pp. 25–6.
Buchanan, J. and Considine, G. (2002) *'Stop Telling us to Cope!': NSW Nurses Explain Why they are leaving the Profession* (Sydney: ACCIRT, University of Sydney).
Davis, C. and Nichols, B. (2002) 'Foreign-Educated Nurses and the Changing U.S. Nursing Workforce' *Nursing Administration Quarterly*, 26(2), pp. 43–51.
DEST (Department of Education, Science and Training) (2002) *National Review of Nursing Education* (Canberra).
Fleming, K., Evans, J. and Chutka, R. (2003) 'Caregiver and Clinician Shortages in an Ageing Nation' *Mayo Clinic Proceedings*, 78(8), pp. 1026–41.
Guest, R. and McDonald I. (2000) 'Population Ageing and Projections of Government Social Outlays in Australia' *The Australian Economic Review*, 33(1), pp. 49–64.
Hall, J. (2001) *The Public View of Private Health Insurance* (Sydney :The Australian Health Policy Institute, University of Sydney).
Loquist, R. (2002) 'State Boards of Nursing Respond to the Nurse Shortage' *Nursing Administration Quarterly*, 26(4), pp. 33–9.
Lumley, C. (2001) 'Casualisation in Nursing: Friend or Foe?' Unpublished Master's Thesis (School of Public Health, La Trobe University).
Lumley, C. (2004) 'Casualisation Friend or Foe? A Case Study Investigation of Two Australian Hospitals' *New Zealand Employee Relations Journal*, 29(2), pp. 33–49.
Morehead, A. (2003) 'Managing Flexible Working Time Arrangements: Negotiations between Mothers and Managers in a Canberra Hospital' *Labour and Industry*, 14(1), pp. 91–106.

Nursing and Health Services Research Consortium (2000) *NSW Nursing Workforce Research Project* (Sydney: Nursing and Health Service Research Consortium).

Pocock, B. (2003) *The Work/Life Collision* (Annandale: Federation Press).

Queensland Nurses' Union (2004) 'The Nursing Perspective' *Work, Time and Life Conference*. http://www.qnu.org.au/worktimelife.htm.

Randolph, L. (2003) 'Why consider travel nurses?' *Nursing Management*, 34, pp. 4–5.

Shullanberger, G. (2000) 'Nurse Staffing Decisions: An Integrative Review of the Literature' *Nursing Economics*, 18(3), pp. 124–48.

Smith, A. (2003) 'Nurses under your Nose: The Chicago–Mexico Nurse Initiative' *Nursing Economics*, 21(4), pp. 176–87.

Victorian Government Department of Human Services (2001) *The Nurse Recruitment and Retention Committee Final Report* (Melbourne).

Watson, I., Buchanan, J., Campbell, I. and Briggs C. (2003) *Fragmented Futures: New Challenges in Working Life* (Sydney: The Federation Press).

Watson, J. (2001) 'Post-Hospital Nursing: Shortage, Shifts and Scripts' *Nursing Administration Quarterly*, 25(3), pp. 77–82.

Weekes, K., Peterson, C., and Stanton, P. (2001) 'Stress and the Workplace: The Medical Scientist's Experience' *Labour and Industry*, 11(3), pp. 95–120.

White, N. and Bray, M. (2003) 'The Changing Role of Nursing Unit Managers: A Case of Work Intensification?' *Labour and Industry*, 14(2), pp. 1–20.

Willis, E. (2002) 'Enterprise Bargaining and Work Intensification: An Atypical Case Study from the South Australian Public Hospital Sector' *New Zealand Journal of Industrial Relations*, 27(2), pp. 221–32.

Part III

Future Challenges in Healthcare Reform and Workplace Change

10
Inspiring Innovation
Sandra G. Leggat and Judith Dwyer

Introduction

> 'It's no wonder that innovation is so difficult for established firms. They employ highly capable people – and then set them to work within processes and business models that doom them to failure' (Christensen and Overdorf, 2000, p. 66).

The workplace reform that is the subject of this book has been justified on the basis of the need for higher productivity, cost control, modernization and greater accountability of healthcare providers to government, the community and the corporation. Productivity has indeed improved and government has had some impact in addressing costs. Many customs and practices have been modified, and outputs are now more tightly specified by governments for the public sector and by corporate owners in the private sector. However, the pressure on the Australian health system has only strengthened, with workforce shortages, budget deficits in public hospitals, turbulence in the profitability and ownership of private hospitals, and increasing concern about quality and safety in all sectors.

Management of the healthcare workforce for innovation is now a defining challenge. Throughout the world there is a perception that, while there have been significant reforms, healthcare systems have not been successful in incorporating acknowledged best practice. Hospitals in particular are seen as being big and slow moving, hungry, self-interested and unresponsive to the need to adapt. Recently it has been suggested that systemic factors have limited the ability of health service managers to encourage and exploit innovation (Dwyer and Leggat, 2002; Leggat and Dwyer, 2005; National

Institute for Clinical Studies, 2003; Braithwaite and Hindle, 1999; Ibrahim and Majoor, 2002).

In this chapter we look to the future and discuss how health sector organizations can succeed in innovation. We explore the general management literature and the literature specific to health services management and draw conclusions for inspiring innovation in the healthcare sector. We first consider the nature and role of innovation and assess the innovation track record of Australian healthcare organizations.

What is innovation?

Innovation is generally defined as the introduction of '... an idea, practice or object that is perceived as new' (Rogers, 1995, p. 11), or more pragmatically, 'innovation is about putting ideas to work' (Department of Industry Science and Resources, 2000, p. 9); and 'innovation is a synonym for the successful production, assimilation and exploitation of novelty in the economic and social spheres' (European Commission, 1995, p. 1). Innovation itself is not new and has characterized society since the transition from the stone age through the tool age to the current wave in information and communication technology. A review of innovation waves over time has concluded that large social and economic changes occur with each wave, including:

- an evolving 'best practice' form of organizations;
- changing supply and skill profile of the workforce;
- different product mixes; and
- infrastructure investment (Department of Industry Science and Resources, 2000).

These aspects that support and reinforce the necessary behavioural changes among workers and managers are required for successful innovation. There is good evidence that successful innovation cannot be achieved without corresponding changes at the individual, operational, organizational and industry levels, and that the management of change is a challenge in itself. It is important to note that, exciting as innovation is, it is a means towards goals like productivity, quality, effectiveness, competitive positioning and long-term growth, rather than an end in itself. Not everything new is worth having.

Innovation in Australia

Australian governments have not typically taken a strong role in encouraging innovation, with government intervention more focused on addressing market failure than pro-active innovation development strategies (Department of Industry Science and Resources, 2000). This has resulted in little coordinated effort, with the existing Australian innovation system described as:

- highly fragmented;
- producing sub-optimal research;
- having poor, or even non-existent linkages among public and private sector participants; and
- having little coordination of effort between government agencies (Department of Industry Science and Resources, 2000, p. 26).

In comparison with companies in other countries, Australian firms do not have a strong track record in successful innovation, and have shown a pattern of decreased innovation over recent years (Department of Industry Science and Resources, 2000). 'Australia's geographical isolation from the developed western economies has inhibited the development and adoption of new products and processes' (Innovation Summit Implementation Group, 2000, p. 5). Australia has historically had a comparatively high cost structure, which has resulted in a lower level of research and development expenditure. When businesses cannot match the operating results of other countries, there is little incentive to invest in research and development.

The problems of entrenched work practices and outdated skills in Australian workplaces were identified in the late 1980s, and the federal government moved to reform work practices and increase investment in training and development. Measures included the 'structural efficiency principle' in award restructuring (which aimed to enable more efficient job design and work practices through, for example, the removal of barriers created by traditional role demarcations), and a requirement to spend at least 1.5 per cent of payroll on training and development, with an emphasis on portable skills (Stone, 2002). While overall spending did increase, the Report of the Industry Task Force on Leadership and Management Skills published in 1995 (at the end of the period of the levy) suggested that Australian work practices and management skills were not attaining world's best practice (Karpin, 1995). The Task Force recommended upgrading vocational education, training and business support, best practice management development, and reform of management education. The background paper for the 2000 National Innovation Summit supported this view (Department of Industry Science and Resources, 2000).

Innovation in healthcare

The record of innovation in the Australian health sector can be assessed in relation to changes in the delivery of care and in the structure and management of the system. We are interested in innovation throughout the sector, but recognize that hospitals, as the most resource intensive component, are a major focus.

Innovation in care delivery

The drivers of change in healthcare over the last 20 years have been a powerful combination of improved technical capacity (to diagnose, treat and provide care); expanding demand particularly in relation to the 'new epidemic' of chronic life-style diseases; the resultant need to contain costs to sustainable levels; and the wave of global changes in public sector management which aimed to improve the efficiency and responsiveness of public services (Pollitt, 1995). In the public sector, the struggle to contain increasing demand and provide timely access for public patients to inpatient care, within the constraints of available resources, has dominated efforts to reform care delivery. The growing predominance of emergency admissions has further complicated hospital access problems. Over the last 15 years, hospitals have experienced a fundamental and continuing shift in their workload towards emergency admissions (Emergency Demand Coordination Group, 2002). The unplanned nature of these admissions, combined with high daily bed occupancy rates, have made it more likely that emergency patients will wait for a bed (Bagust, Place and Posnett, 1999) and elective patients will experience cancellations.

Hospitals have responded with a range of innovations directed to reducing the utilization of inpatient care, through reducing the rate of admission and/or lengths of stay. Methods for managing the level of demand for care have been the subject of several Australian government reports in recent years (NSW Health Council, 2000; Anderson, Bernath, Davies and Ludolf, 2001; Dwyer and Jackson, 2001; Patient Management Task Force, 2001; Banscott, 2003; Generational Health Review, 2002). Examples of demand management innovations by Australian hospitals include 'rapid response' services in emergency departments (Coopers and Lybrand, 1997), emergency department observation/short stay wards (Williams *et al.*, 2000), chest pain assessment units (Hider *et al.*, 1998), outpatient heart failure clinics (Gregoroff, McKelvie and Szabo, 2004) and post-discharge interventions such as assistance with management of medication (Stewart *et al.*, 1998) and hospital in the home (HITH) (Shanahan *et al.*, 2001). While initiatives like HITH are successful in reducing inpatient demand or days of stay, and generally have good patient outcomes and acceptance, the evidence on cost effectiveness is mixed (Bonevski *et al.*, 2002; Goddard, McDonagh and Smith, 1999; Hider *et al.*, 1998).

The single most significant innovation for improving throughput has been the shift to day admissions (day surgery and some medical day admissions such as for chemotherapy). Day-of-surgery admissions (DOSA), supported by the use of pre-admission clinics, have also made a significant impact. Improvements in discharge practice are widespread, supported by increased availability of community- and home-based support services (Health Services Research Unit, 2000). Yet, those who require admission to long-term care are still most likely to experience delayed discharge (Harris *et al.*, 1997; Department of Human Services Victoria, 2002).

The significant effort by the hospital sector to design, introduce and sustain these innovations has not resolved the problem. Some initiatives have demonstrated success in reducing average length of stay or the need for admission or readmission for the targeted patient groups. However, any gains have been swamped by continuing increases in demand, and evidence on the cost-effectiveness of the alternative services is equivocal (Goddard *et al.*, 1999). Goddard *et al.* (1999) also noted that even if alternative services were cost-effective, they may not be cost-reducing due to expansion of eligibility and/or coverage. Evidence from around the world suggests that hospitals continue to admit patients for whom less intensive care could be effective (DeCoster *et al.*, 1999; Hider *et al.*, 1998) because alternative forms of care are not available at the right time.

Consistent evidence regarding the drivers or enablers of innovation in the system of care is scarce. Clearly, the daily pressure experienced in emergency departments, on the inpatient wards and from adverse media coverage has driven interest in innovation for clinical staff, hospital management and central health authorities. Given the lack of evidence, it is difficult to predict the factors that facilitate innovation with any certainty, but it does seem clear that the availability of funding to support innovation has been critical.

Perhaps the largest single funded experiment in innovation in Australia has been the Coordinated Care Trials. Findings from the National Evaluation of the Coordinated Care Trials (Commonwealth of Australia, 1999; Department of Health and Aged Care, 2000) suggested that while the various forms of care management trialled in these pilots had many benefits, they did not uniformly reduce the use of inpatient care. Subsequent studies have also demonstrated that while patient satisfaction was high, the costs of care management outweighed any savings from reduced use of acute care (Perkins et al., 2001). However, evidence from other approaches to integrated care (Eng et al., 1997) indicates that real gains in terms of reduced demand are possible. Building on the basic concept of coordinated care, several healthcare providers and jurisdictions have begun funding and trialling 'disease management', which aims to better manage complex, ongoing conditions, in partnership with patients and their families/carers (see, for example, Emergency Demand Coordination Group, 2002).

A great deal of effort by state and territory governments has been devoted to assisting hospitals to address access difficulties (for example, Greater Metropolitan Services Implementation Group, 2001; NSW Health Council, 2000; Patient Management Task Force, 2001) with some success. Their methods have included targeted funding and a range of incentives and penalties for performance on key targets. The Australian government has contributed to this effort through the Best Practice in Health Program (National Health Strategy, 1993) and the National Demonstration Hospitals Program (Department of Health and Aged Care, 2001). The Best Practice in Health Program focused on reforming work practices to improve the processes of care (for example, through job redesign and work flow changes), and required funded agencies to work constructively with unions and professional associations. Competition for funding was strong, and for some recipients, the program provided their first experiences with reform of basic operating practices.

More recently, the National Demonstration Hospitals Program (NDHP) funded a large set of projects aimed at improving throughput, reducing utilization and supporting the dissemination of best practice. Four funding rounds addressed increasing the use of day surgery and day of surgery admission; the concept of integrated bed management; integration among hospitals and the primary and community service sectors; and improved hospital-based care for older Australians. NDHP enjoyed strong support and was seen by the participating public hospitals as a positive investment in their capacity to innovate and improve care (Department of Health and Aged Care, 2001). One of the important features of NDHP was its requirement for both clinical and managerial commitment and leadership. Initiatives which focus on use of timely data to engage and motivate clinicians to achieve better throughput and demand management have shown some success (Cameron, Scown and Campbell, 2002). The Clinical Support Systems Program, sponsored by the Australian government and auspiced by the Royal Australian College of Physicians, enjoyed remarkable support from clinicians and managers (Long et al., 2002). This Program aimed to demonstrate methods of translating new knowledge into workable models for healthcare delivery. It borrowed many characteristics from the NDHP, and explicitly required multidisciplinary involvement (including physicians) and both clinical and management leadership.

The enthusiasm with which funding for innovation has been taken up can perhaps be seen as evidence of the hunger for resources in the healthcare sector. It can also be seen as evidence of the underlying recognition that care processes, and the organizational structures and work practices which have evolved to support them, need to change in a fundamental way. In any case, it is clear that funding has been a vital enabling factor for innovation in this area.

Innovation in structure and management

Hospitals have historically been stable organizations, characterized by a strong commitment to professional autonomy for clinicians and a hierarchical formal structure. The same forces that have driven change in care delivery have caused significant change in both the structures and the management styles of healthcare organizations. Recent changes in structure and management in Australia can be read as the search for effective ways of increasing the accountability of healthcare providers and driving their performance on key indicators (such as reducing lengths of stay, reducing waits, reducing inpatient admissions and increasing the range and levels of care provided in the community). Measures such as Casemix funding and health service agreements have brought some real gains for healthcare, not least of which is the incentive for providers to maximize the use of funding for direct service delivery. There have also been efforts to improve the efficiency and effectiveness of support services (Young, 2002).

Industries are rarely static, with ongoing evolution changing the structure and mode of operations. In recent times in Australia the health sector has been oscillating between fragmentation and reconsolidation. This is true in most parts of the world, with, for example, more than 72 per cent of all hospitals in the United States belonging to a network or system (Bazzoli et al., 1999). The shift away from the stand-alone single-service type agency has also been profound in Australia. The Area Health Services in NSW, established in 1986, have been the most stable example, bringing responsibility for all state-funded healthcare for a region within one governance structure. Overall, there is a trend towards consolidation in both public and private sector health organizations. In the private sector there is increasing corporate ownership (as opposed to community and private ownership). In the public sector, the trend is towards direct management of public healthcare agencies at state health authority level, with regionalized sub-structures in most (Dwyer, 2004), and increasing use of networking or alliances among types of care providers.

The move away from stand-alone agencies is seen to have brought benefits for both staff and patients, such as improved standards of care, better career paths, economies of scale and more effective support services. On the other hand, local hospitals, mental health services and community health services need flexibility to innovate to best meet local health needs. Overzealous consolidation, while providing the advantages of centralization such as consistency in strategic and operational direction, foregoes the aspects of decentralization that are necessary for innovation (Bazzoli et al., 2001). In all industries in recent years the validity of a strategy that encapsulates all the elements of production within a single firm has been questioned, and focused concentration on identified core competencies is sometimes seen as more effective (Friedman and Goes, 2001).

It is not yet possible to assess the impact of different governance arrangements on innovation in Australian healthcare agencies. Healthcare systems in most parts of the world have been the subject of successive waves of reform in structuring, financing, accountability and the operating environment. However, there is little confidence that the goals of reform – generally expressed as improving the ability for the system to deliver equity, efficiency and quality – have been achieved.

Success in innovation is mixed

Participants in the bumpy ride of the healthcare sector in Australia during the 1990s have experienced an interesting paradox: while change is all about them, many intractable problems seem incapable of resolution. The 'best practice form of organization', referred to above as an important characteristic of successful waves of innovation, has not yet emerged; the workforce is seen as lacking needed skills; new products and services have often not brought the anticipated results, or have proven too hard to introduce; and it has been difficult to acquire the funds needed for investment in new infrastructure to support innovation. In comparison to other industries, healthcare systems throughout the world are seen to have been slow to change and to adopt the many new and improved methods, techniques and ideas that become available each year (Adamson and Adamson, 2001). Hospitals, like universities and large accounting and law firms, are characterized by a culture that welcomes technical or program innovation, and at the same time can be fiercely resistant to systemic change (Mintzberg, 1991). The culture of teaching hospitals in particular values new insights and technologies, and often rewards those who originate and implement them. On the other hand, innovations perceived as disruptive, which challenge established orthodoxies are often rejected, at least for a while (Christensen, Bohmer and Kenagy, 2000), and system change, when it challenges established work practices and professional roles, can be very difficult to achieve. The often quoted lament that '...the problem with hospitals...is that they are run by people who like them' and who therefore fail to see the need for change (US Commission for the Future quoted by M. Wooldridge, 1996), is one perspective on this tendency.

The diffuse power structure and competing interests in hospitals are factors that enable resistance to change (Glouberman and Mintzberg, 2001). Relationships between clinicians and managers retain much of their traditional character, with jealous guarding of the contested border between clinical autonomy and managerial prerogative. While there are some promising signs that the concept of clinical governance (which clarifies and reinforces the responsibility of the governance level of the organization for the standard of clinical care) is providing a new way of thinking about and responding to this problem, the development of effective shared decision-making between clinicians and managers is a major outstanding challenge.

While there has been significant change in the structure and management of the health sector the evidence of effectiveness is scant, and some of the changes, such as implementation of network structures in Victoria and Western Australia, have been revised or reversed too quickly for reliable judgements to be made. There is also a sense that most of the big questions are left unanswered (Lovelace, 2000). Despite a relatively clear understanding of the forces impacting on the health of the population and the nature of healthcare delivery, there has been relatively little successful translation of the collective global knowledge of best practice into the practices of the Australian health sector. 'More recently, advances in practice and technology have been impressive, but the sector is exhibiting signs of systems failure, despite the skills and efforts of the individuals who work within it' (Braithwaite and Hindle, 1999, p. 292). Ferlie and Shortell (2001) suggested that the relative lack of success of change in healthcare organizations relates to the fact the system embraces narrow, single-level technical and programmatic change, while resisting more innovative, comprehensive, multilevel approaches. There is also evidence that successive waves of policy and structural reform, driven by the need for cost containment and without a well-articulated vision or feasible goals, have increased the resistance of healthcare staff to change (Van Eyk, Baum and Houghton, 2001). In addition, the focus on cost constraint, with regular budget reductions is also likely to have reduced the enthusiasm for change throughout the sector. 'Health policy and employment strategies based on cost reduction and competition can undermine innovation and creativity....' (Stanton, 2002, p. 96).

This is a fairly negative assessment, which led us to question the factors that have made innovation in healthcare so difficult. We explored the large literature related to innovation in healthcare and other industries. Within healthcare the majority of the studies were related to the American healthcare system, the findings of which are not always transferable to the Australian situation. Recently, there has also been an increased focus on healthcare innovation in the United Kingdom, and some empirical evidence is emerging. The following sections draw heavily on the limited applicable studies in healthcare and the experience of other industries that can be reasonably applied to healthcare.

We identified some general principles. Effective change in the health system needs to be based on concerted action at four levels: the individual, the group or team, the organization, and the larger system or environment (Ferlie and Shortell, 2001). Successful innovators within the American healthcare system have recognized that every employee, every patient, every supplier, every donor, and even every competitor has a role to play in facilitating innovation (Homsy, Totten and Orlikoff, 2004). Most significantly, we found that the evidence points to a focus on the role of the health workforce, and therefore on effective human resource management. In the following section, we review the requirements for successful innovation.

Innovation in the health workforce

Peter Drucker once said that innovation will be the core competency of the next century (Drucker, 1992). How then might the capacity of the health sector workforce to achieve real innovation and change be enhanced? Although innovation cannot be forced, governments and industry participants can create an environment that supports and encourages innovation through enabling elements. Based on our analysis of innovation in Australian healthcare, we conclude that innovative capacity can be enhanced through alignment of three strategies: a consistent financial, policy and governance framework; combined with a supporting human resources strategy that enables and rewards innovation; and an education and training approach that equips the workforce with the skills to innovate. We focus in this section on the human resource strategies for innovation, but suggest that the innovative potential of the sector could also be improved through reforms at health system level (a focused policy, funding and governance framework) and in the universities (the education of health professionals).

Inspiring the individual

Empirical evidence suggests that there are people management practices that are effective in inspiring individuals to innovate. The most important appears to be leadership throughout the organization that facilitates psychological safety – the belief among staff that interpersonal risk taking is safe (Edmondson, Bohmer and Pisano, 2001; Edmondson, 1999). Psychological safety was originally defined by Kahn as an employee's 'sense of being able to show and employ one's self without fear of negative consequences to self-image, status or career' (Kahn, 1990, p. 708). In psychologically safe workplaces staff (and in hospitals this includes visiting medical practitioners) believe that questioning established practices and contributing ideas for innovation are an accepted part of their work. Psychological safety, that enables staff to challenge current practice, and sometimes, to challenge the authority that maintains current practice, has been shown to correlate directly with increased levels of creativity and innovation (Sutton, 2001). For example, the UK National Health Service (NHS) modernization process required innovative leaders at all levels in the NHS 'who are not afraid to be "off-the-wall", to inspire and to stand above their own local cultures' (Maddock, 2002, p. 38).

The link between psychological safety and innovation has been well demonstrated (Edmondson *et al.*, 2001; Edmondson, 1999; Baer and

Frese, 2003). Thompson Health in the US provides an example of the success of psychological safety in facilitating innovation. This organization increased the level of innovation by enabling all employees to implement, without supervisory approval, small-scale change that improved their work processes (Homsy et al., 2004). Analysis of the modernization agenda in the UK NHS suggested that the necessary innovation would only occur with a change from a paradigm with leaders only at the top, to a new paradigm that included transforming leadership expectations of more junior staff (Maddock, 2002).

Yet in the Australian healthcare sector the current strategy of empowerment of health sector employees has been described as only rhetoric for top-down management (Lloyd, Braithwaite and Southon, 1999). Bruce Barraclough, Chair of the Australian Council for Safety and Quality in Healthcare, argued that hospital management needed to change to ensure frontline clinicians and nurses had the opportunity to influence management decisions (Barraclough, 2001), more evidence that the sector has yet to achieve best practice in inspiring individual innovation. Experience from the UK suggested that many senior healthcare managers were promoted on the basis of financial and operational skills, rather than the necessary people management skills (Maddock, 2002), and greater attention to people management skills was required for the future. While there is frequent talk about the need for innovation in the sector, existing human resource processes reinforce the traditional practices of the healthcare workforce.

Although there are few studies from healthcare, studies in other industries have identified factors that increase the likelihood of innovation. Initiatives such as mentoring, job rotation, collaboration with universities, conferences and 'share fairs', and award and recognition programs have been effective (Thite, 2004). In particular, personalized recognition systems drawing on intrinsic rewards assisted in creating the conditions for innovation (Judge, Fryxell and Dooley, 1997). Intrinsic rewards relate to the built-in feedback that arises from seeing the results of a meaningful task which has been well done, as opposed to abstract feedback – 'you have done a good job' – at the end of the year. Studies have suggested that intrinsic motivation is a key driver of individual innovation and that extrinsic rewards and evaluations may in fact adversely impact on innovative behaviour (Ahmed, 1998; Barron and Harrington, 1981). The existence of strong intrinsic motivation in this area also underlines the importance of selecting employees for creativity and innovation (Delaney and Huselid, 1996).

Again, linked to intrinsic motivation, life-long, self-directed learning has been shown to be an important facilitator of individual innovation, with the suggestion that managers need to evolve from 'organizers of training' to 'facilitators of learning' (Thite, 2004; Pfeffer and Sutton, 1999) as employees take responsibility for their own information needs (Drucker, 1992). Continuing education is acknowledged as a necessity for health professionals, but tight budgets over the last decade have seen healthcare organizations reduce their investment in study leave and staff training and development.

In summary, although there is evidence for selecting staff who demonstrate characteristics associated with innovation (Sutton, 2001; Delaney and Huselid, 1996), individuals can be inspired to innovate through leadership that provides a psychologically safe environment for questioning and creativity. This can be achieved through human resource management practices that develop leaders throughout the organization and assist these leaders to promote psychological safety; as well as implementing job design and recognition and reward mechanisms that target intrinsic motivation for innovation.

An underlying theme in many innovations in care delivery is the redefinition of roles and relationships among the professions for more effective care and better use of scarce resources. Some of the hardest challenges faced by reformers arise when traditional roles and work practices of health professionals need to change. The traditional training and socialization of the health professions tends to emphasize individual skills, autonomy, accountability and achievement. Recent work on improving the quality of care has consistently identified this individual focus as a barrier to system improvement (Institute of Medicine, 2001), and argued that innovation depended on a system focus, and the development of working styles which supported the complex team-based care required in health services. The existing 'professional prerogatives and separate roles' (Institute of Medicine, 2001, p. 83) need to be replaced by cooperation, mutual respect and teamwork. Unfortunately, the education and training systems have not been suitably adapted to provide health professionals with the requisite skills for innovation in the new environment and in the short term employers must take on this role.

Inspiring the team

Healthcare delivery is a team process and organizational and team leadership needs to focus on ensuring team performance in innovation. Cross-sectional research and case studies suggest that openness and participation in teams (in which members have developed sufficient trust and psychological safety to constructively question behaviours and discuss mistakes openly) are strongly positively associated with clinical and organizational innovation. This was found in different parts of the world in studies of acute care (National Coalition on Health Care and Institute for Healthcare Improvement, 2002), implementation of new clinical procedures in an operating theatre (Edmondson *et al.*, 2001), in successful adoption of clinical guidelines (Merlani *et al.*, 2001), and within a nursing home (Yeatts and Seward, 2000). In all cases, the team leadership was instrumental in either facilitating or discouraging the necessary participation and psychological safety.

In innovative teams, the traditional reliance on hierarchy is replaced with participative safety that encourages team members to make suggestions, to try things that might not work and admit mistakes (Anderson and West, 1998; Pech, 2001; Sutton, 2001). Tolerance for mistakes is a key component of the learning process in these settings (Martins and Terblanche, 2003; Sutton, 2001). However, there are several seemingly intractable barriers to the creation of effective participative teams in hospitals.

The relationships between doctors, nurses and other health professionals and between the various levels of health professionals have typically been authoritarian in nature. In comparing medicine and aviation, Sexton and colleagues found that significantly more doctors (as compared with pilots) supported the hierarchical model of practice, believing that junior team members should not question decisions made by senior doctors (Sexton, Thomas and Helmreich, 2000). Nursing teams operated with a hierarchical mechanistic structure with a strong focus on task that undermined participation (Cott, 1997). This hierarchy does not facilitate non-punitive leadership, participation, trust and psychological safety. Instead of fostering effective participation and trust, hospitals consistently display poor communication between team members, which has been shown to cause medical errors (Wachter, 2004; Vincent, Taylor-Adams and Stanhope, 1998). For example, the division of the clinical operating units by clinical and administrative 'silos' was identified as a factor that limited quality patient care in New South Wales (Macarthur Expert Clinical Review Team, 2003). In recognition of the importance of teamwork in healthcare, the NHS has recently increased the focus on ensuring human resource management (HRM) and organizational systems reward and promote effective teamwork (Arthur, Wall and Halligan, 2003).

Cross-functional team membership and diversity (Martins and Terblanche, 2003) has also been shown to facilitate team innovation. That is, teams which can tolerate diversity in the skill and personal mix are more successful as innovators. Cross-functional teams are necessary for operational innovation in healthcare, as important innovations involve end-to-end processes that cross departmental boundaries (Hammer, 2004). Hyland and colleagues suggested that the palliative care teams they studied were successful at innovation for their patients as the teams contained both background knowledge and diversity of views (Hyland, Davison and Sloan, 2003).

In summary, the research tells us that innovative teams use diverse interdisciplinary membership and demonstrate participative safety. Structuring teams for innovation requires human resources management practices that promote questioning, admitting and learning from mistakes, and facilitate experimentation with new ways of working together for better patient care.

Inspiring the organization

The literature suggested that there were complex interactive relationships among factors that influenced innovation within an organization – relationships that have not been confirmed or clearly specified (Matthews, 2002; National Institute for Clinical Studies, 2003; Fleuren, Wiefferink and Paulussen, 2004). Yet it is becoming increasingly clear that organizational innovation can be facilitated through the creation of conditions that encourage individual and team innovation (Matthews, 2002), with consistent trends identified in most industries. It starts with a compelling vision (Young, 2000; Weiner, Shortell and Alexander, 1997), through which leaders articulate and enact support for innovation within the organization (Anderson and West, 1998). In most cases, demonstrating support for innovation requires organizations to change outdated structures for new ways of sharing information and educating staff (Homsy et al., 2004).

The evidence is also mounting that progressive HRM, in particular employee selection, participation and empowerment, goal setting and feedback, and learning and training (Delaney and Huselid, 1996; Borrill et al., 2002; West et al., 2002) have a strong relationship with improved innovation. It is these aspects of strategic human resource management (SHRM) that influence the psychological and participative safety and intrinsic motivation required for individual and team innovation. With progressive HRM individual and team innovation can be promoted throughout the organization through provision of appropriate employment security (Pfeffer and Veiga, 1999), facilitating learning experiences (Thite, 2004), and transferring control of career agendas to workers (Kanter, 1997).

Australian healthcare leadership still relies too much on hierarchical authority as the preferred method of managerial and clinical accountability. There is little evidence that the existing leadership divide between managers and clinicians has been bridged, and effective multidisciplinary teamwork is still the exception rather than the rule. The continued focus on training health professionals (and sometimes managers) in isolation, with the traditional emphasis on hierarchy and on individual skills, autonomy, accountability and achievement is not helpful to the goal of innovation in the changing world of healthcare. Existing employee performance management systems undermine the transition to participative teamwork and have difficulty incorporating the systems perspective required for quality and safety improvements (Soltani, 2003). Enhanced innovation will only be possible in the Australian healthcare sector when workplace reform facilitates the resolution of these long standing barriers.

Steps to innovation

At the beginning of this chapter we cited the major changes that accompanied successful waves of innovation including, new organizational forms; a changing workforce; new products; and investment in infrastructure (Department of Industry Science and Resources, 2000). We have noted that although structural change, with accompanying infrastructure investment, has been prominent, the 'best practice' form of healthcare organizations is yet to emerge. There is a sense of uncertainty about how to improve the design of systems to achieve the required integrated care to address the 'new epidemic' of chronic diseases in an ageing population. Instead of ensuring 'form follows function' health sector reforms in Australia appeared to have focused on the form and hoped that the functions would follow appropriately. Our review of innovation performance suggests that the focus of healthcare reform should be directed to ensuring effective teams; that is, to focus on team development for safe, high quality care delivery and design the workforce, organizations and systems to support this teamwork.

In many ways the workplace reforms we have seen in the health sector in Australia have not had an appreciable impact on developing a workforce that can adapt, or more importantly, lead the required wave of innovation. Health system reforms, possibly because they have tended to be politically motivated (Stoelwinder and Viney, 2000) and conceived in isolation from human resources management (Bach, 2003), have not fully addressed the important issues. The status quo is often reinforced through defensive people management policies and procedures (Argyris, 1986). An emerging theme among those who watch the healthcare sector in Australia is the recognition that many of the factors, policies and procedures that shaped health organizations are no longer relevant and need to be re-examined (Braithwaite and Hindle, 1999; Hillman, 1999; Menadue, 2003). While unions and professional associations have played a role in advancing the agenda of health sector reform, they have also tended to cling to established custom and practice in the roles and responsibilities of their members. In order for organizations to leverage knowledge faster and better, organizational policies and procedures related to people management must reflect a new social contract (Kanter, 1997). Unions and employees should be looking for new motivational tools.

There is limited evidence that, after a period of considerable reform, the workforce is any better matched to the needs of the healthcare production process, with continuation of the entrenched hierarchical roles and responsibilities that obstruct psychological and participative safety. These roles continue to be reinforced through isolated training and development of the health team members. While different service models have been a feature of the recent waves of change, it seems that further innovation is required. Yet there is little evidence that the necessary human resource management practices are in place to guide the workforce changes required for innovation. The inflexible award-based compensation and working conditions that characterize the Australian healthcare system (Braithwaite, 1997) are in many ways incompatible with the human resource management practices required for creativity and innovation (Bazzoli et al., 2001).

We conclude that while there has been a great effort to innovate, and many changes in practice, there is a sense that the big problems have not been solved, and that the system is still trammeled by hierarchical thinking and a focus on control rather than innovation. Workplace reforms have delivered some of the necessary conditions for effective innovation, by modifying many established practices and roles. But these conditions have not been fully exploited and further workplace reform needs to be linked to desired innovation outcomes through SHRM practice.

References

Adamson, G. J. and Adamson, L. U. (2001) 'The Chief (Experience) Officer: A New Light in Health Care' *Health Forum Journal*, 79, pp. 429–57.

Ahmed, P. K. (1998) 'Culture and Climate for Innovation' *European Journal of Innovation Management*, 1, pp. 30–43.

Anderson, J., Bernath, V., Davies, J. and Ludolf, S. (2001) *Literature Review on Integrated Bed and Patient Management* (Melbourne: Centre for Clinical Effectiveness and Southern Health).

Anderson, N. R. and West, M. A. (1998) 'Measuring Climate for Work Group Innovation: Development and Validation of the Team Climate Inventory' *Journal of Organizational Behavior*, 19, pp. 235–58.

Argyris, C. (1986) 'Reinforcing Organizational Defensive Routines: An Unintended Human Resources Activity' *Human Resource Management*, 25, pp. 541–55.

Arthur, H., Wall, D. and Halligan, A. (2003) 'Team Resource Management: A Programme for Troubled Teams' *Clinical Governance: An International Journal*, 8, pp. 86–91.

Bach, S. (2003) Human Resources and New Approaches to Public Sector Management: Improving Human Resources Management Capacity in P. Ferrinho and M. Dal Poz (eds) *Towards a Global Health Workforce Strategy Studies in Health Service Organisation and Practice*, Vol. 21 (ITG Press Antwerp).

Baer, M. and Frese, M. (2003) 'Innovation is not Enough: Climates for Initiatives and Psychological Safety, Process Innovations and Firm Performance' *Journal of Organizational Behavior*, 24, pp. 45–68.

Bagust, A., Place, M. and Posnett, J. W. (1999) 'Dynamics of Bed Use in Accommodating Emergency Admissions: Stochastic Simulation Model' *British Medical Journal*, 319, pp. 155–8.

Banscott, H. C. (2003) *Report of the Review of the Northern Territory Department of Health and Community Services* (Darwin: Department of Health and Community Services).

Barraclough, B. (2001) 'Safety and Quality in Australian Healthcare: Making Progress' *Medical Journal of Australia*, 174, pp. 616–7.

Barron, F. B. and Harrington, D. M. (1981) 'Creativity, Intelligence and Personality' *Annual Review of Psychology*, 32, pp. 439–76.

Bazzoli, G. J., Shortell, S. M., Ciliberto, F. M., Kralovec, P. D. and Dubbs, N. (2001) 'Tracking the Changing Provider Landscape: Implications for Health Policy and Practice' *Health Affairs*, 188, pp. 1–8.

Bazzoli, G. J., Sortell, S. M., Dubbs, N., Chan, C. and Kralovec, P. (1999) 'A Taxonomy of Health Networks and Systems: Bringing Order Out of Chaos' *Health Services Research*, 33, pp. 1683–1717.

Bonevski, B., Doran, C., Bailey, C. and Lowe, J. (2002) 'Description of an Early Discharge Post-Acute Care Program: Length of Hospital Stay, Patient and Carer Needs and Cost' *Australian Health Review*, 25, pp. 78–86.

Borrill, C., Carletta, J., Carter, A. J., Dawson, J. F., Garrod, S., Rees, A., Richards, A., Shapiro, D. and West, M. (2002) *The Effectiveness of Health Care Teams in the National Health Service* (London: Aston University University of Glasgow University of Leeds).

Braithwaite, J. (1997) 'The 21st-Century Hospital' *Medical Journal of Australia*, 166, p. 6.

Braithwaite, J. and Hindle, D. (1999) 'Research and the Acute Care Hospital of the Future' *Medical Journal of Australia*, 170, pp. 292–3.

Cameron, P., Scown, P. and Campbell, D. (2002) 'Managing Access Block' *Australian Health Review*, 25, pp. 59–68.

Christensen, C. M., Bohmer, R. and Kenagy, J. (2000) 'Will Disruptive Innovations Cure Health Care?' *Harvard Business Review*, 78, pp. 102–12.

Christensen, C. M. and Overdorf, M. (2000) 'Meeting the Challenge of Disruptive Change' *Harvard Business Review*, 78, pp. 66–77.

Commonwealth of Australia (1999) *The Australian Coordinated Care Trials: Interim National Evaluation Summary* (Canberra: Department of Health and Aged Care).

Coopers and Lybrand (1997) *Evaluation of the Emergency to Homecare Outreach Service (ETHOS) Final Report* (Adelaide: Flinders Medical Centre).

Cott, C. (1997) 'We Decide, You Carry it Out: A Social Network Analysis of Multidisciplinary Long-Term Care Teams' *Social Science and Medicine*, 45, pp. 1411–21.

DeCoster, C., Peterson, S., Carriere, K. C. and Kasian, P. (1999) 'Assessing the Extent to which Hospitals are Used for Acute Care Purposes' *Medical Care*, 37, pp. 151–66.

Delaney, J. T. and Huselid, M. A. (1996) 'The Impact of Human Resource Management Practices on Perceptions of Organizational Performance' *Academy of Management Journal*, 39, pp. 949–69.

Department of Health and Aged Care (2000) *The Australian Coordinated Care Trials: Interim Technical National Evaluation Report* (Canberra: Commonwealth of Australia).

Department of Health and Aged Care (2001) *National Demonstration Hospitals Program Phase 3: Health Service Research Reports* (Canberra: Department of Health and Aged Care).

Department of Human Services (Victoria) (2002) *Hospital Highlights Report: December Quarter 2001* (Melbourne: Department of Human Services).

Department of Industry Science and Resources (2000) *Shaping Australia's Future. Innovation – Framework Paper* (Canberra).

Drucker, P. (1992) *Managing for the Future* (London: Butterworth-Heinemann).

Dwyer, J. (2004) 'Regionalization: Are Even the Flaws Quintessentially Canadian?' *Healthcare Papers*, 5, pp. 81–7.

Dwyer, J. and Jackson, T. (2001) *Literature Review: Integrated Bed and Patient Management* (Melbourne: Patient Management Task Force, Department of Human Services).

Dwyer, J. and Leggat, S. G. (2002) 'Innovation in Hospital Care', *Australian Health Review*, 25, pp. 19–31.

Edmondson, A. (1999) 'Psychological Safety and Learning Behavior in Work Teams' *Administrative Science Quarterly*, 44, pp. 350–3.

Edmondson, A. C., Bohmer, R. and Pisano, G. P. (2001) 'Disrupted Routines: Team Learning and New Technology Implementation in Hospitals' *Administrative Science Quarterly*, 46, pp. 685–716.

Emergency Demand Coordination Group (2002) *Hospital Admission Risk Program (HARP) Background Paper* (Melbourne: Department of Human Services).

Eng, C., Pedulla, J., Eleazer, G. P., McCann, R. and Fox, N. (1997) 'Program of All-Inclusive Care for the Elderly (PACE): An Innovative Model of Integrated

Geriatric Care and Financing' *Journal of the American Geriatrics Society*, 45, pp. 223–32.
European Commission (1995) *Green Paper on Innovation* (European Commission).
Ferlie, E. B. and Shortell, S. M. (2001) 'Improving the Quality of Health Care in the United Kingdom and the United States: A Framework for Change' *The Milbank Quarterly*, 79, pp. 281–315.
Fleuren, M., Wiefferink, K. and Paulussen, T. (2004) 'Determinants of Innovation within Health Care Organizations: Literature Review and Delphi Study' *International Journal for Quality in Health Care*, 16.
Friedman, L. and Goes, J. (2001) 'Why Integrated Health Networks have Failed' *Frontiers of Health Services Management*, 17, pp. 3–55.
Generational Health Review (2002) *Discussion Paper* (Adelaide: Government of South Australia).
Glouberman, S. and Mintzberg, H. (2001) 'Managing the Care of Health and the Cure of Disease – Part 1: Differentiation' *Health Care Management Review*, pp. 56–69.
Goddard, M. M., McDonagh, M. and Smith, D. (1999) *Acute Hospital Care: Final Report* (York Centre for Health Economics).
Greater Metropolitan Services Implementation Group (2001) *Report of the GMSIG* (Sydney: NSW Department of Health).
Gregoroff, S. J., McKelvie, R. S. and Szabo, S. (2004) 'The Impact of an Outpatient Heart Failure Clinic on Hospital Costs and Admissions' *Leadership in Health Services* 17, pp. 1–11.
Hammer, M. (2004) 'Deep Change. How Operational Innovation Can Transform your Company' *Harvard Business Review*, 82, pp. 85–93.
Harris, J. H., Finucane, P. M., Healy, D. C. and Bakarich, A. C. (1997) 'Use of Inpatient Hospital Services by People Aged 90–99 years', *Medical Journal of Australia*, 167, pp. 417–20.
Health Services Research Unit (2000) *Performance Indicators for Effective Discharge* (Monash University, Melbourne: Department of Human Services).
Hider, P., Kirk, R., Bidwell, S., Weir, R., Cook, L. and Tolan, C. (1998) *Acute Medical Admissions: A Critical Appraisal of the Literature, NZHTA Report 6* (Christchurch: New Zealand Health Technology Assessment).
Hillman, K. (1999) 'The Changing Role of Acute-Care Hospitals' *Medical Journal of Australia*, 170, pp. 325–8.
Homsy, V. T., Totten, M. K. and Orlikoff, J. E. (2004) 'Innovation: From Theory to Practice' *Trustee*, 57, p. 15.
Hyland, P. W., Davison, G. and Sloan, T. R. (2003) 'Linking Team Competencies to Organisational Capacities in Health Care' *Journal of Health Organization and Management*, 17, pp. 150–63.
Ibrahim, J. and Majoor, J. (2002) 'Corruption in the Health Care System: The Circumstantial Evidence' *Australian Health Review*, 25, pp. 20–6.
Innovation Summit Implementation Group (2000) *Elements of a National Innovation System – International Ratings, ISIG Information Paper IV* (Canberra: Commonwealth of Australia).
Institute of Medicine (2001) *Crossing the Quality Chasm. A New Health System for the 21st Century* (Washington: National Academy Press).
Judge, W. Q., Fryxell, G. E. and Dooley, R. S. (1997) 'The New Task of R&D Management: Creating Goal-Directed Communities for Innovation' *California Management Review*, 39, pp. 72–85.

Kahn, W. A. (1990) 'Psychological Conditions of Personal Engagement and Disengagement at Work' *Academy of Management Journal*, 33, pp. 692–724.

Kanter, R. M. (1997) Restoring People to the Heart of the Organization of the Future in F. Hasselbein (ed.) *The Organization of the Future* (San Francisco, CA: Jossey-Bass).

Karpin, D. (1995) *Enterprising Nation: Renewing Australia's Managers to Meet the Challenges of the Asia-Pacific Century – A Report of the Industry Task Force on Leadership and Management Skills* (Canberra: Commonwealth of Australia).

Leggat, S. G. and Dwyer, J. (2005) 'Hospital Performance in Quality and Safety: Is it the Culture?' *Hospital Quarterly*, 8(2), pp. 60–6.

Lloyd, P., Braithwaite, J. and Southon, G. (1999) 'Empowerment and the Performance of Health Services' *Journal of Management in Medicine*, 13, pp. 83–94.

Long, P. W., Larkins, R. G., Patterson, C. G. and Hyde, J. J. (2002) *Getting Evidence into Practice: Facilitating Best Practice –Transferring the Lessons of the Clinical Support Systems Program* (Sydney: Royal Australasian College of Physicians).

Lovelace, C. (2000) 'Foreward' in A. Bloom (ed.) *Health Reform in Australia and New Zealand* (Melbourne: Oxford).

Macarthur Expert Clinical Review Team (2003) *Recommendations to the Minister for Health* (Sydney: Macarthur Health Service).

Maddock, S. (2002) 'Making Modernisation Work' *International Journal of Public Sector Management*, 15, pp. 13–43.

Martins, E. C. and Terblanche, F. (2003) 'Building Organisational Culture that Stimulates Creativity and Innovation' *European Journal of Innovation Management*, 6, pp. 64–74.

Matthews, J. (2002) 'Innovation in Australian Small and Medium Enterprises: Contributions from Strategic Human Resource Management' *Asia Pacific Journal of Human Relations*, 40, pp. 193–204.

Menadue, J. (2003) 'Healthcare Reform: Possible Ways Forward' *Medical Journal of Australia*, 176, pp. 267–9.

Merlani, P., Garnerin, P., Diby, M., Ferring, M. and Ricou, B. (2001) 'Linking Guideline to Regular Feedback to Increase Appropriate Requests for Clinical Tests: Blood Gas Analysis in Intensive Care' *British Medical Journal*, 323, pp. 620–4.

Mintzberg, H. (1991) 'The Professional Organisation' in *The Strategy Process: Concepts, Contexts, Cases* (2nd edn) (New Jersey: Prentice Hall).

National Coalition on Health Care and Institute for Healthcare Improvement (2002) *Accelerating Change Today A.C.T. for America's Health* (Robert Wood Johnson Foundation).

National Health Strategy (1993) *Health that Works: Workplace Reform and Best Practice in the Australian Health Industry* (Canberra: National Health Strategy).

National Institute for Clinical Studies (2003) *Factors Supporting High Performance in Health Care Organisations* (Health Management Group, La Trobe University, Melbourne: NICS).

NSW Health Council (2000) *Report of the NSW Health Council – A Better Health System for NSW* (Sydney: NSW Government).

Patient Management Task Force (2001) *Serving the Needs of the Patient: Better Patient Management in Melbourne's Public Hospitals* (Melbourne: Department of Human Services).

Pech, R. J. (2001) 'Termites, group behavior, and the loss of innovation: conformity rules' *Journal of Managerial Psychology*, 16, pp. 559-74.
Perkins, D., Owen, A., Cromwell, D., Adamson, L., Eagar, K., Quinsey, K. and Green, J. (2001) 'The Illawarra Coordinated Care Trial: Better Outcomes with Existing Resources?' *Australian Health Review*, 24, pp. 161-71.
Pfeffer, J. and Sutton, R. I. (1999) 'Knowing "what" to do is not Enough' *California Management Review*, 42, pp. 83-108.
Pfeffer, J. and Veiga, F. (1999) 'Putting People First for Organizational Success' *Academy of Management Executive*, 13, pp. 37-48.
Pollitt, C. (1995) 'Justification by Works or by Faith?: Evaluating the New Public Management' *Evaluation*, 1, pp. 133-54.
Rogers, E. M. (1995) *Diffusion of Innovations* (New York: Free Press).
Sexton, J. M. B., Thomas, E. J. and Helmreich, R. L. (2000) 'Error, Stress, and Teamwork in Medicine and Aviation: Cross Sectional Surveys' *British Medical Journal*, 320, pp. 745-49.
Shanahan, M., Hass, M. ,Viney, R. and Cameron, I. (2001) 'To HITH or not to HITH: Making a Decision about Establishing Hospital in the Home' *Australian Health Review*, 24, pp. 179-86.
Soltani, E. (2003) 'Towards a TQM-Driven HR Performance Evaluation: An Empirical Study' *Employee Relations*, 25, pp. 347-70.
Stanton, P. (2002) 'Managing the Healthcare Workforce: Cost Reduction or Innovation' *Australian Health Review*, 25, pp. 92-7.
Stewart, S., Pearson, S., Luke, C. G. and Horowitz, J. D. (1998) 'Effects of Home-Based Intervention on Unplanned Readmissions and Out-of-Hospital Deaths' *Journal of the American Geriatrics Society*, 46, pp. 174-80.
Stoelwinder, J. and Viney, R. A. (2000) 'Tale of Two States: New South Wales and Victoria' in A. Bloom (ed.) *Health Reform in Australia and New Zealand* (Melbourne: Oxford).
Stone, R. J. (2002) *Human Resource Managemen* (4th edn) (Brisbane: Wiley and Sons).
Sutton, R. I. (2001) 'The Weird Rules of Creativity' *Harvard Business Review*, 79, p. 94.
Thite, M. (2004) 'Strategic Positioning of HRM in Knowledge-Based Organizations' *The Learning Organization*, 11, pp. 28-44.
US Commission for the Future (1996) quoted by M. Wooldridge.
Van Eyk, H., Baum, F. and Houghton, G. (2001) 'Coping with Health Care Reform' *Australian Health Review*, 24, pp. 202-6.
Vincent, C., Taylor-Adams, S. and Stanhope, N. (1998) 'Framework for Analysing Risk and Safety in Clinical Medicine' *British Medical Journal*, 316, pp. 1154-7.
Wachter, R. (2004) 'Encourage Case-Based Discussions of Medical Errors' *AHA News*, February, 14.
Weiner, B. J., Shortell, S. M. and Alexander, J. (1997) 'Promoting Clinical Involvement in Hospital Quality Improvement Efforts: The Effects of Top Management, Board and Physician Leadership' *Health Services Research*, 32, pp. 491-510.
West, M. A., Borrill, C., Dawson, J. F., Scully, J., Carter, M., Anelay, S., Patterson, M. G. and Waring, J. (2002) 'The Link between the Management of Employees and Patient Mortality in Acute Hospitals' *International Journal of Human Resource Management*, 13, pp. 1299-1310.

Williams, A. G., Jelinek, G. A., Rogers, I. R., Wenban, J. A. and Jacobs, I. G. (2000) 'The Effect on Hospital Admission Profiles of Establishing an Emergency Department Observation Ward' *Medical Journal of Australia,* 173, pp. 411–4.

Yeatts, D. E. and Seward, R. R. (2000) 'Reducing Turnover and Improving Health Care in Nursing Homes: The Potential Effects of Self-Managed Work Teams' *The Gerontologist,* 40, pp. 358–63.

Young, G. J. (2000) 'Managing Organizational Transformations: Lessons from the Veterans Health Administration' *California Management Review,* 43, pp. 66–83.

Young, S. (2002) 'Outsourcing and Downsizing: Processes of Workplace Change in Public Health' *The Economic and Labour Relations Review,* 13, pp. 244–69.

11
Developing a Strategic Approach to People Management in Healthcare

Tim Bartram, Pauline Stanton and Raymond Harbridge

Introduction

Over the past twenty years there has been an international focus by governments on achieving efficient and effective health services through health sector reform. Yet until recently little attention has been given to people management approaches in healthcare (Saltman, Figueras and Sakellarides, 1998), or the impact of government policies and environmental change on the management of the workforce at the organizational level (Bach, 2003). This lack of focus on people management is surprising considering that the industry is labour intensive, highly educated and accounts for a large proportion of total costs. Instead the health labour force has been seen as a target for cost savings and government policies have often focused on costs and efficiency (Thornley, 1998) rather than innovation and human capability building (Bach, 2000; Stanton, 2002a).

In this chapter we argue that Strategic Human Resource Management (SHRM) might offer new opportunities to improve the management of people within the public health sector. Although this chapter sets out to explore the promise of SHRM specifically within the Victorian public health sector, we also draw implications for research and practice within the Australian and international contexts. First, we investigate the concept of SHRM and its potential benefits for the public health sector. Secondly, based on a series of interviews with key actors within the Victorian public heath sector, we explore the views and experiences of employers and managers, trade union officials and state government officials concerning SHRM. Thirdly, based on a benchmarking survey of public health facilities in Victoria we analyze the adoption of SHRM from the perspectives of chief executive officers

(CEOs), human resource directors (HRDs) and general functional managers (GFMs). Furthermore, we also explore their views as to positive aspects of the HRM function in healthcare organizations, barriers to practicing HRM and areas for improvement. Finally we discuss the implications of our findings and make some suggestions for further action.

Strategic human resource management: what, why and how

The last two decades have witnessed an enormous growth in academic and practitioner interest in SHRM. SHRM advocates the mutual interdependence and congruence of key organizational variables including; structure, strategy, people, management style, human resource systems and functions (such as recruitment, selection, and performance appraisal, training and development, induction and reward management), procedures and culture (Boxall and Purcell, 2003; Legge, 1995). In essence, SHRM suggests that the HRM functions should consistently influence employee and management behaviour so as to enable and achieve the strategic plans of the organization. Numerous contemporary commentators have advocated and illustrated the importance of HRM and strategic congruence (Schuler, 1992; Walton, 1985; Wright and McMahan, 1992) arguing that there should be an alignment or congruence between each HRM function and strategic planning.

There is also a growing body of research that explores the critical role of human resource management in improving organizational outcomes with some evidence of a measurable and positive impact on organizational performance (Delaney and Huselid, 1996; Huselid, Jackson and Schuler, 1997). Therefore designing and implementing a set of internally consistent policies and practices that ensure a firm's human capital contributes to the achievement of its business objectives – via compensation systems, team-based job designs, flexible workforces, quality improvement practices, and employee empowerment is a major feature of SHRM (Wright and McMahon, 1992; Lado and Wilson, 1994; Huselid *et al.*, 1997). In theory SHRM practices provide great promise for people-rich organizations and industries (Bartram and Cregan, 2001; McDuffie, 1995; Jackson, Schuler and Carlos Rivero, 1989). A more proactive approach to people management has much to offer the health sector and in a context of fiscal pressures, successful not-for-profit organizations are said to need innovatory service methods with pro-active, multi-skilled workers (Boxall and Purcell, 2003).

SHRM and its potential for the healthcare sector

A labour intensive, highly motivated, highly skilled professional workforce as in the health sector should be an ideal context for the successful implementation of human resource management practices. However, the empirical literature suggests otherwise in a number of ways. First of all the people side of management has often been ignored in the pursuit of health reform both internationally (Saltman *et al.*, 1998; Bach, 2000) and in Australia (Stanton, Bartram and Harbridge, 2004). Secondly, the health sector is largely government funded and often organized around a public service model focusing on process and good practice rather than organizational outcomes. The experience of HRM in the public sector has not been encouraging. For example, a report from the OECD suggests that the public sector is still 'highly centralized, rule bound and inflexible' in its HRM practice (Bach, 2000). Thirdly, despite the contention from Kessler and Purcell (1996) that government reforms had given organizations such as hospitals more strategic choice at the organizational level, recent evidence suggests otherwise. Bach (2000) in the UK argued that hospital employers were constrained in their actions not only because they were subject to the whims of government policy but also because they sit within a wider framework of powerful stakeholders. Stanton (2002b) found a similar situation in Victoria and that even though Victorian hospitals had more independence than many of their interstate counterparts they still had to work within a wider centralized employment relations framework.

Barnett, Buchanan, Patrickson and Maddern (1996), in a comparative study from the United Kingdom (UK) and South Australia (SA) on the experience of HRM in hospitals, expressed optimism from the UK findings but pessimism from the South Australian experience. In the British case study they found that the HRM department had some success in shaping local factors (for example occupational health and safety). However, in South Australia, Barnett *et al.*, (1996) argued that the centralized industrial relations framework limited the HRM function. They also noted that there often existed contested ownership within the senior management structures with some hospital managers not willing to allow a strategic role for the HRM department. Patrickson and Maddern (1996) found that HRM in South Australian hospitals largely carried out a regulatory 'personnel' function as 'the keeper of the rules'.

Recent studies have highlighted the need for innovation, particularly in the area of HRM, viewing the workforce as an asset not just a cost.

Innovation can be enhanced through better people management practices and can directly support other goals such as providing a quality and safe service (Dwyer and Leggat, 2002; Stanton, 2002b). Likewise, case studies of high-performing organizations have consistently pointed to effective people management as a critical factor in the success of those organizations. The high performance management literature links people management strategies to performance. One of the issues here is getting support and recognition of this in the healthcare sector. Also a major problem in the healthcare sector is the contentious nature of the measurement of performance. Performance is often seen in terms of activity such as increased throughput, but increased throughput can undermine the quality of service delivery and hence patient satisfaction (Duckett, 1995).

Two notable studies have attempted to link people-management practices to improved patient mortality in acute hospitals. A study of the 'Magnet' hospitals in the USA focused on hospitals that attracted and retained good nurses through their people-management practices. The study examined the relationship between good nursing care and mortality rates and found that hospitals that were 'magnet' hospitals had lower patient morality rates (Aitkin, 1994). West *et al.* (2002) in the UK also focused on patient mortality but included a range of people-management practices including appraisal, teamwork and training. Again the researchers found a link between these specific practices and lower patient mortality.

There has been no comparable study in Australia. However, Australian state governments as the major funders and providers of public hospitals are increasingly concerned with the quality and effectiveness of service provision. There is increasing awareness amongst the key stakeholders that an emphasis on people management might offer some direction in this area.

People management practices in the Victorian public health sector

Since 1992 there have been two distinct government policy directions in the Victorian public healthcare sector that have had substantial impact on people management within the sector. The Liberal–National government (1992–9) focused on a cost reduction approach towards funding arrangements, leading to a culture of 'doing more with less', and a decentralized 'arm's length' or 'steering not rowing' approach to the management of health organizations. Policies included; the introduction of Casemix funding, severe budget cuts, the encouragement of outsourcing and enterprise bargaining and the reorganization of the metropolitan hospitals into networks managed by a commercially focused board of management. Stanton's (2002b) study into employment relations in the Liberal–National years in public hospitals found that much of the promised autonomy did not eventuate and health organizations were still controlled by government directions. There was also inadequate long-term human resource planning within the health sector and no proactive support for investment in local HRM during this period (Stanton, 2002b).

In contrast, the Labor government (1999–current) has invested more heavily in the health care sector, but has relied more openly on greater centralization particularly in areas such as industrial relations. The Labor government inherited a public health industry that was in poor shape financially because of years of budget cuts. Its response was to put more money into the sector, to re-emphasize planning including establishing a Workforce Planning Branch, to put a greater focus on quality not just efficiency and on collaboration rather than competition (Stanton, 2002a). The government also reorganized the metropolitan healthcare networks reorientating their primary focus to one of good patient care. However, it has again left human resource management to the organizations.

Methodology

The data in this study is drawn from four major sources. The first source is a study carried out by one of the researchers into employment relations in the public health sector during the years of the Liberal–National government (Stanton, 2002b). The study involved a collection of key documentation and included a series of semi-structured key informant interviews carried out between 1999 and 2000 with a purposive sample of eight senior employers and human resource directors, seven trade union officials from all the major unions and two officials from the Victorian Department of Human Services. The documentation included data from the Australian Bureau of Statistics, the Department of Employment, Workplace Relations and Small Business, the Industrial Registry and both state and federal government reports.

The second source of data is an in-depth case study of a large regional hospital (over 2000 employees), carried out by another of the researchers (Bartram, 2002), in which a number of key informants were interviewed, including the CEO, the executive HRM director, a HR manager, one functional general manager, three shop stewards and a trade union branch secretary. Interviews were carried out between August 2000 and March 2002. The archival data consisted of annual reports and the current enterprise bargaining agreement. The third source of data is a current action research study. The first part of this study also included a collection of background documentation including annual reports, government documents and quality management frameworks and another series of key informant interviews which were carried out in 2002–3. A series of semi-structured interviews were conducted with one CEO, four executive HRM directors from rural, regional and metropolitan health services, three government officials from the Victorian DHS, and six trade union officials of three major health unions. The interviews were transcribed and analyzed using a coding framework to identify themes, categories and patterns in the data. This was an iterative process that involved reorganizing and refining the data against an analytical framework developed from the literature review. From this process concepts emerged and were formulated into a logical and systematic narrative.

The second part of the action research study and fourth source of data, involved a survey of public healthcare facilities in Victoria, including metropolitan health services which are the large city-based teaching hospitals, the large regional base hospitals, smaller non-teaching district and bush hospitals and community health services (130 organizations) between December 2003–April 2004. Five hundred and thirty six questionnaires were distributed to the CEO, human resource director and two general functional managers (often Directors of Nursing or Medical Directors) per organization. A total of 184 questionnaires (34 per cent response rate overall) were returned including 64 from CEOs, 35 from HRDs and 85 from GFMs (almost 50 per cent response from CEOs and an estimated 90 per cent response rate from HRDs as all organizations do not have a designated HRD).

There were two survey instruments, one directed at the HRD and the second to the CEO and general functional managers of the organization. The HRDs survey comprised of questions relating to strategic HRM, questions relating to the full range of HRM functions including recruitment and retention and a comprehensive set of HRM outcomes such as industrial relations outcomes, recruitment and selection and turnover outcomes. The CEO and GFM survey contained the same SHRM questions, a less comprehensive set of the same group of HRM functions plus questions pertaining to the organizational outcomes monitored by their organization.

Perspectives from employers and managers, government officials and trade unions: the key informant interviews

The Liberal–National government did not see HRM as being the business of government. To a certain extent this 'arms length' approach to management provided some opportunities for local initiative, however, the focus on cost control heavily constrained the development of SHRM. Employers were critical that there was no money available to invest, of the lack of overall planning and of the government's approach to industrial relations. The Liberal–National government had encouraged enterprise bargaining in theory yet in practice had constrained independent initiative through its funding policies.

In contrast, employers welcomed the fact that the Labor government has invested heavily in the system but expressed concern that its initiatives particularly in industrial relations have been centralized and hence have provided another kind of constraint for the development of local SHRM. An example of this is the nurse: patient ratio of four patients to one nurse, which was introduced as part of the arbitrated Nurses' Award in 2000. Employers saw this policy as constraining labour utilization at the local level and were critical of such developments. Most employers agreed with a centralized role for wages and conditions but wanted to have some flexibility at the local level for labour utilization issues. They argued that a 'one size fits all' centralized approach does not allow for local peculiarities.

All employers and managers interviewed for this study remarked on the potential of SHRM to rejuvenate and improve organizational performance and most of them identified improved practices. However, they all described the lack of active support from government to help their practice. Employers and managers argued that given the fiscal pressures in the healthcare sector, re-organization and greater investment in SHRM is pivotal but successive governments have not appreciated this point and in fact existing structures and processes have undermined local investment. Employers also commented on the political nature of the healthcare sector, and government's knee jerk response to issues like hospital waiting lists and problems with ambulance bypass. Employers believed such issues will always receive priority funding over HRM initiatives, which in the eyes of the public would be 'spending money on more managers and administrators'.

Employers also recognized the complex web of well-established institutional arrangements within the public health sector and the potential conflict between central and local decision making. No employer wanted government to play a more 'hands on' role. Instead, many of the HRDs interviewed suggested that the government could play a more visionary role with respect to health sector innovation than they do at present. This could include a more enabling role, setting general policy parameters and encouraging local SHRM initiatives by supporting them with appropriate funding.

Managers also recognized that HRM within the workplace should not just play a regulatory function and that genuine strategic human resource change means changing culture, improving communication, empowering staff and getting the right structures in place that can enable staff development. In order to play a key part in this cultural change, HR directors argued that they should have 'a seat at the table' giving them power within the organization as a part of the executive decision-making team.

Overall, employers held the view that greater decentralization of the HRM function to the workplace level would be an important advance. This decentralization necessarily requires greater resourcing of the HRM function and management development. Employers held the view that the role of government in workplace management should be to identify system-wide issues and difficulties, and provide leadership and resources to minimize these problems.

There was a clear difference of views expressed by officials from the two different periods of government. Department of Human Service officials under the Liberal–National government did not see HRM as their concern. However, one official did comment on the lack of human resource planning, believing that hospitals were limited in their ability to influence future labour markets, and stated that the government's lack of attention in this area was leading to massive labour supply problems, not only in nursing but also in areas such as pharmacy and radiography.

Under the Labor government the officials are more proactive. The DHS now actively collects data on a range of issues not considered vital by the previous government, including the numbers of staff employed, labour turnover, and sickness and absenteeism figures. The Workforce Planning branch also investigates workforce issues for different professional groups and streams of care, and invites applications from the field for funding of innovative pilots around recruitment and retention.

Government officials from the Labor government also stressed a bigger focus on partnerships, in particular building relationships between employers and unions in the area of industrial relations.

They did not apologize for the government's more centralized approach to industrial relations, although one official did stress the importance of developing closer relationships with the HRDs whom he argued understand the realities of the industrial situation 'on the ground'. He also stressed the difference between the systemic issues and the local organizational issues and the DHS role in each. He argued that the DHS can encourage collaboration with organizations around particular policy initiatives that are systemic, and need systemic solutions such as nurse recruitment, but argued that many HRM issues such as staff retention need local solutions. In many ways this view was similar to that of the employers who saw government as the enabler, setting the broad agenda and funding pilot studies of industry-wide issues.

Although the trade union officials interviewed were supportive of HRM in theory, they were also the most forceful in support of centralization, particularly in terms of industrial relations and the bargaining process. From the interviews with trade union officials it was clear that they would not give this greater centralization away without a fight. All of the health sector trade unions had resisted decentralization of wages and conditions through enterprise bargaining during the Liberal–National years (Stanton, 2002b). In the 2004 enterprise bargaining round, under the Labor government, the Australian Nursing Federation fought a strong campaign to protect the nurse: patient ratios won in 2000. Their success in this struggle was largely due to the fact that they could mobilize the support of their members and the public over issues of patient care.

One trade union official was critical of the lack of information that the government had about the sector, arguing that wage increases were not always fully funded because the government could not adequately cost them, leading to hospitals cutting corners in the implementation of wage agreements. In her view this led to an irritant in the system as members had to battle individually for their entitlements, thus undermining staff commitment and creating staff dissatisfaction with their organization.

Overall, trade union officials interviewed held positive views towards the promise of HRM within the Victorian public health sector. In addition, they held the view that the HRM function should be better funded. Despite the positive views of HRM by the trade unions, it was evident that they emphasized the implementation of collectivist and humanistic HRM policies, which may not always be congruous with that of management. In a similar vein, trade unions were also critical of any management or government attempts to decentralize the collective bargaining process.

It is clear from the interviews that context is important, and that context is directly influenced by government through its funding policies and priorities. However, it was also clear was that many claims were made by each of the actors about the practice of HRM in the sector with very little supportive evidence. Without such evidence these claims become little more than unsubstantiated views. The next stage of the project was to explore the character of HRM in the public health sector via a systemic survey.

Survey of the Victorian public health sector: Barriers and challenges to the practice of SHRM

We only focus here on one aspect of the survey data, the practice of Strategic Human Resource Management. The survey questionnaire contained both qualitative scales and quantitative questions designed to understand the current use of, and barriers towards the practice of SHRM, and the Strategic HRM Index (Huselid, 1995) was used to capture the use of SHRM (please see Appendix 1 for a description of the Strategic HRM Index). We also explore qualitative responses to three questions from the total sample: 'What aspects of HRM does your organization do well?', 'What are the current barriers to practicing HRM in your organization?' and 'Which areas of HRM could be improved in your organization?'.

Three separate one-way ANOVA tests were conducted to ascertain the extent of differences in perceptions of the practice of SHRM across the healthcare groupings (i.e. metropolitan hospitals, base hospitals, district hospitals and community health services) from the perspectives of the three groups of managers, CEOs, HRDs and GFMs. Tables 1, 2 and 3 provide a summary of results of the one-way ANOVAs. Table 11.1 provides responses obtained from chief executive officers (CEOs); Table 11.2 provides those from general functional managers (GFMs); and Table 11.3 presents the responses from human resource directors (HRDs). The means of each SHRM variable are provided for each hospital grouping.

Whilst there were some differences between the means of SHRM variables across the four different healthcare groupings for the CEOs responses, these differences were not statistically significant. CEOs across all four groups held the view that their organizations were practicing SHRM – that is integrating human resource management functions with organizational goals.

Table 11.1 ANOVA of strategic human resource management for CEOs

Variable	Mean Metropolitan	Mean Base	Mean District	Mean Community health	SD	F	Aggregate Mean
SHRM 1	4.38	3.86	3.71	3.90	0.934	1.050	3.88
SHRM 2	3.75	4.00	3.68	3.95	0.924	0.453	3.81
SHRM 3	4.00	3.57	3.54	3.86	1.019	0.667	3.70
SHRM 4	3.13	3.00	2.96	2.67	1.223	0.374	2.89
SHRM 5	4.50	4.14	4.18	4.29	0.642	0.594	4.25
SHRM 6	3.75	3.43	3.21	3.33	1.057	0.537	3.34
SHRM 7	3.75	3.00	3.43	3.43	0.887	0.888	3.42
SHRM 8	3.25	3.71	4.04	3.52	0.996	1.874	3.73
SHRM 9	3.50	3.29	3.11	2.86	0.938	1.047	3.09
SHRM 10	3.75	4.00	4.11	3.81	0.722	0.918	3.95
SHRM 11	4.00	3.71	3.68	3.81	0.831	0.332	3.77
SHRM 12	3.75	3.00	3.39	3.48	0.832	1.059	3.42
SHRM 13	3.88	3.57	3.89	3.86	0.801	0.300	3.84

n = 64
df = 63
* $p < 0.05$
** $p < 0.01$

The HRDs shared similar views concerning the practice of SHRM across the four groups, however, the HRDs were less positive about its practice than CEOs in Metropolitan Health Services and more positive than CEOs in the other groups. There was also a statistically significant difference between the groups with regards to SHRM7 'this organization matches the characteristics of managers to the strategic plan of the organization'. Whilst the means of SHRM7 for metropolitan health services, district hospitals and community health services are all greater than 3, HR directors in base hospitals reported lower mean scores.

In contrast, responses collected from general functional managers across the four groups tell a somewhat complex story relative to the CEOs and HRDs. There are a number of significant differences between the means of the items across the four groups. Statistical differences were found among six items – SHRM1, SHRM7, SHRM8,

Table 11.2 ANOVA of strategic human resource management for general managers

Variable	Mean Metropolitan	Mean Base	Mean District	Mean Community health	SD	F	Aggregate Mean
SHRM 1	3.25	3.33	3.86	3.92	0.811	1.050 *	3.72
SHRM 2	3.50	3.50	3.77	3.88	0.836	0.927	3.73
SHRM 3	4.00	3.50	3.57	3.35	0.994	1.208	3.55
SHRM 4	2.92	3.25	3.03	3.12	0.961	0.276	3.07
SHRM 5	4.17	4.17	4.03	3.92	0.794	0.385	4.04
SHRM 6	2.83	3.00	3.20	3.19	1.051	0.449	3.12
SHRM 7	2.75	2.58	3.29	3.54	0.866	5.228 **	3.19
SHRM 8	3.00	3.00	3.60	3.77	0.868	4.028 **	3.48
SHRM 9	2.25	2.33	2.83	3.15	0.891	4.469 **	2.78
SHRM 10	3.58	3.42	3.46	3.54	0.946	0.096	3.49
SHRM 11	3.50	2.83	3.43	3.88	0.946	3.833 *	3.49
SHRM 12	2.83	3.08	3.20	3.77	0.939	3.854 *	3.31
SHRM 13	2.83	3.50	3.43	3.88	0.946	3.833 *	3.49

n = 85
df = 63
* p < 0.05
** p < 0.01

SHRM9, SHRM11, SHRM12, and SHRM13. In relation to SHRM1, 'human resources strategies are effectively integrated with the organization's strategy', metropolitan and base hospitals reported the lowest means, 3.25 and 3.33 respectively. In relation to the question, 'this organization matches characteristics of managers to the strategic plan of the organization' (SHRM7), metropolitan and base hospitals both displayed mean scores of less than 3 (2.75 and 2.58 respectively). The metropolitan and base hospitals further reported lower means relative to district and community health services concerning 'this organization identifies managerial characteristics necessary to run the organization in the long term'. Community health services reported the highest mean of 3.15 concerning the statement, 'this organization modifies the compensation systems to encourage managers to achieve long term strategic objectives'. Base hospitals reported the lowest mean for the statement (2.83), 'this

Table 11.3 ANOVA of strategic human resource management for human resource directors

Variable	Mean Metropolitan	Mean Base	Mean District	Mean Community health	SD	F	Aggregate Mean
SHRM 1	3.89	4.40	4.00	3.86	0.767	1.050	4.00
SHRM 2	3.67	4.00	4.00	4.29	0.857	0.680	3.97
SHRM 3	3.67	4.80	3.57	4.00	1.115	1.728	3.86
SHRM 4	2.78	3.60	2.71	2.86	1.022	0.978	2.89
SHRM 5	4.22	3.80	4.21	3.86	0.919	0.440	4.09
SHRM 6	3.44	2.60	3.43	2.57	1.216	1.326	3.14
SHRM 7	3.11	2.20	3.50	3.00	0.832	3.820 *	3.11
SHRM 8	3.78	4.00	3.86	3.29	0.886	0.831	3.74
SHRM 9	2.11	2.20	2.57	2.57	1.006	0.494	2.40
SHRM 10	3.89	3.40	3.79	3.86	0.942	0.306	3.77
SHRM 11	3.89	3.00	3.86	3.43	0.838	1.815	3.66
SHRM 12	3.11	2.60	3.43	3.00	1.004	0.908	3.14
SHRM 13	3.56	3.60	3.93	3.43	0.900	0.586	3.69

n = 35
df = 63
* $p < 0.05$
** $p < 0.01$

organization evaluates key personnel based on their potential for carrying out strategic goals', SHRM11. Finally, in terms of SHRM12 'job analyses are based on what the job may entail in the future' and SHRM13, 'development programs are designed to support strategic changes', metropolitan hospitals reported the lowest means, 2.83 and 2.83 respectively. In other words, GFMs across the whole of the public health sector were less positive about the use of strategic HRM than either CEOs or HRDs. However, general managers did think that HRM would become more important in their organizations in the future and general managers in metropolitan health services thought that HR personnel have a key influence in setting HR strategy in their hospitals.

Given the organizational size, availability of resources and geographical differences it was expected that the larger the health services, the more likely we were to find the practice of SHRM. This proposition is in line with contemporary scholarly research that suggests that SHRM is more likely to be practised in larger organizations, with greater financial resources, as well as specialized human resource managers (Bartram, 2005; Guest, 1995). However, we found that the larger the organization the greater the divergence of perceptions concerning the practice of SHRM between the CEOs, HRDs and GFMs. These results support Bartram and Cregan's (2001) research which found that different levels of management may have very different perspectives on working in organizations (e.g. use of strategic HRM).

Qualitative Data Analysis

Tables 11.4, 11.5 and 11.6 show the frequencies for the responses to the open-ended questions in the survey. Responses have been aggregated. Respondents were asked three open-ended questions concerning the aspects of HRM that their organization does well, barriers to practicing HRM and which areas of HRM could be improved. Ninety-five respondents completed this section of the questionnaire.

Twenty-eight per cent of respondents perceived that their organization performed well in the area of participation and empowerment. Nineteen per cent agreed that human resource development was also practiced well.

Table 11.4 Aspects of HRM that your organization does particularly well at

HRM Function	Number of Respondents	%
Participation and empowerment ^^	28	29%
Human resource development %	19	20%
Recruitment and selection *	13	14%
Leadership and management #	13	14%
Employment relations **	10	11%
Performance management and appraisals ^	8	8%
OH&S	4	4%

Please note that the above functions also include the following categories:
* induction
^ remuneration; reward and recognition
# management of culture; change management; staff supervision; policy; leadership and management development; collaboration between staff and management
** grievance handling; consultation with unions
^^ access to information; staff support; workforce wellness; Employee Assistance Program; staff satisfaction surveys; Equal Employment Opportunity; flexible working conditions; communication; teamwork
% training and development; youth employment; credentialing; improved skill mix; mentoring; human resource planning; HR specialist staff; HR information systems

The most significant barriers to practising HRM within the public health care facilities, from the perspective of the aggregated sample, were (in sequential order) inadequate funding (28 per cent), inadequate HR specialist staff (23 per cent), which was particularly true for the district hospitals, and limited resources (23 per cent).

Respondents further identified areas of HRM that could be improved. The main function that respondents noted that could be improved was human resource development. Fifty-five of the 148 responses (37 per cent) identified areas such as training and development; mentoring and management development and improvement in specialist HRM training as areas that could be further improved in their organization.

Table 11.5 Barriers to practicing HRM in your organization

Barrier	Number of Respondents	%
Inadequate funding	32	28%
Inadequate HR specialist staff	26	23%
Limited resources	26	23%
Skill base of management staff	13	11%
Lack of commitment to HR	9	8%
Time constraints	8	7%

Table 11.6 Which areas of HRM could be improved?

HRM Function	Number of Respondents	%
Human resource development %	55	37%
Strategic approach	25	17%
Participation and empowerment ^^	22	15%
Recruitment and selection *	19	13%
Performance management and appraisals ^	18	12%
Almost all	9	6%

Please note that the above functions also include the following categories:
* induction
^ remuneration; reward and recognition
^^ access to information; staff support; workforce wellness; Employee Assistance Program; staff satisfaction surveys; Equal Employment Opportunity; flexible working conditions; communication; teamwork
% training and development; youth employment; credentialing; improved skill mix; mentoring; human resource planning; HR specialist staff; HR information systems

This was also reflected in the quantitative data in which variables concerning management development scored poorly. This next important area of improvement noted was practising a more strategic approach to human resource management in the organization (17 per cent).

Future directions for people management within the Victorian public health sector

Bringing together all of the data collected so far presents a complex picture. First, the collection of narratives from the three main players supports the view that HRM practices and strategies are inextricably linked to the surrounding organizational environment. Our results also support the conclusions of Bach (1998), suggesting that the reform of management practices in the health sector is a long-term and challenging endeavour due to the structural constraints impinging on management practice. It is obvious that the development of new managerial approaches need to be identified and developed jointly with the major players within the health sector that can meet the needs of all of these stakeholders. At the level of the organization it is clear that CEOs and HRDs are concerned with SHRM practice. However, the responses from the GFMs suggest that in reality such practices are not so visible. It appears that, particularly in the metropolitan and base hospitals, general functional managers do not share many of the same strategic HRM experiences at the operational level of the organization. This may be for a number of reasons. Given the large scale of these organizations some managers may not be privy to many of the SHRM plans and strategies developed at the apex of the organization. Moreover, many of the HRM plans and strategies may not be fully operationalized at the lower levels of the metropolitan and base hospitals. In contrast, given the smaller size of the district hospitals and community health centres, those managers that develop SHRM plans and policies may also implement them on the ground. Also, the discrepancies in responses from the General Functional Managers with those of their CEOs and HRDs might be a related to a lack of their specialist human resource management knowledge. However, the results also suggest that despite the optimism of the CEOs and HRDs, SHRM is either not taking place, or is limited, as the general functional managers such as Directors of Nursing and Medical Directors are obviously not engaged with the process. This does not suggest a great deal of alignment and congruence of management practices nor of internally consistent policies and practices. In fact it appears that the general functional managers in the large organizations largely see HRM happening somewhere else.

Secondly, the relationship between the central and the local level in terms of people management needs a more strategic response from government than there appears to be at present. The key informants suggested that at government level, people management has largely focused on industrial relations. Industrial relations has clearly become more centralized under the Labor government. Unions and most employers welcome some aspects of centralization, particularly of wages and terms of employment as these issues affect the public healthcare system. More specifically however, some employers advocated a 'hybrid' of decentralization and centralization of approaches to healthcare management. Human resource practitioners and employers view the centralization of wages and conditions of employment, and the decentralization of HRM practices and policies that reflect the idiosyncrasies of individual hospitals, as ways of enabling local management to focus resources on labour issues that are relevant for their workplaces.

On the ground the picture becomes more complex. Wages in the health industry are inextricably associated with conditions of employment, career structures, labour utilization and other issues. The Labor government's return to centralization has not helped this situation allowing even less flexibility at the local level and undermining the employers' scope to manage the HRM issues. Since hospitals within the Victorian public health system are heterogeneous entities, government policy needs to reflect this heterogeneity and the voice and experience of a range of employers needs to be heard. We found that the different divisions had different issues and dilemmas. This fits with the fact that some of the employers we interviewed suggested that the current government approach does not currently understand and reflect the diverse HR related issues at hospitals.

The employers believed that currently there is little policy direction and a lack of leadership from the Labor government concerning HR issues. They suggest that the government should play a more visionary role than they do at present. For example the Liberal–National government took the view that people management was not its problem – that was the problem of the hospitals. This allowed some local autonomy but health organizations were constrained by the government's focus on costs. In contrast, the Labor government has put more money into the sector but allowed a return to more rigid central rules and procedures that apply a 'one size fits all' approach that undermines local autonomy. The continued centralization of wages and working conditions could be a way of 'freeing-up' management and trade unions so that they could concentrate on local people HRM issues but only if some flexibility at local level is encouraged and championed. There must be a clearer identification of the relationship between the role of government and the role of hospital management and an acknowledgement that government policy directly impacts on local practice.

Thirdly, the role of HRM within the organization needs to be addressed. Employers are very aware of the human resource challenges facing them if they are to improve organizational performance and outcomes for patients. The results of our open-ended questions reveal that inadequate funding, lack of specialized human resource staff, inadequate management development and a lack of commitment to human resource management are regarded as the most significant barriers to the practice of HRM in the Victorian public healthcare facilities. In order to do all of these things the HRM function needs to have decision-making authority at the highest level within the organization. Some hospital managers voiced some degree of dissatisfaction with the current management structures. This may involve developing and harnessing managerial skill in order to maximize the success of cultural change. Building partnership and trust between the employer, trade union and employees is essential to the effective management of hospitals. In the highly unionized health sector a key component of effective management is the ability to manage the trade union/management relationship. Until the facilitating and enabling role of HRM is improved and express links made between HRM and patient outcomes HR will continue to be seen as an administrative function vulnerable to financial restraint in difficult times.

Fourthly, all of the key players, government officials, union officials and employers interviewed expressed that a major impediment to developing and harnessing the potential of human resources within the health sector was the lack of resources. Again, this was also echoed in the results of our open-ended questions. Approximately 51 per cent of respondents suggested that 'inadequate funding' and 'limited resources' were seen as the major impediment to the practice of strategic HRM in the Victorian public health sector. There was also a view held by some HR directors that directing government funds to an area that could be seen to spending more money on managers would be very unpopular with the electorate. A fundamental aspect of developing the promise of HRM is to ensure that it is properly resourced. Trade unions officials, employers and managers interviewed all agreed that HRM is valuable and does urgently warrant the greater government funding and investment from senior hospital management. Both parties argue that devoting greater resources to HRM may foster conditions for the development and support of a talented, highly skilled and innovative healthcare workforce. Employers and HR directors welcomed the Labor Government increases in funding of the health sector.

Conclusion

Despite qualitative and quantitative results indicating that there is some knowledge and adoption of SHRM, particularly at the strategic apex of the organization, the practice of SHRM does suffer from a number of barriers and challenges. In the larger organizations the general functional managers who are the people charged with the everyday practice of people management either were not aware of SHRM or did not think it took place. This is a concern and raises issues of management development and the improvement of integrated systems and processes in those organizations. A number of other areas were also identified for further improvement. Further understanding the relationships between the government, trade unions and management and better managing central-local tensions are paramount. Continual research of the relationship between layers of management concerning the practice of SHRM within public health facilities is also vital. Greater dialogue between trade unions, management and the government concerning system-wide concerns and resourcing are also important steps to improving HRM. The public healthcare system is an integral and valuable institution within our community. As academics and practitioners it is valuable, not only to better understand the role of people management practices in the effective provision of healthcare, but to challenge ineffective practices, structures, roles and relationships.

References

Aiken, L., Smith, H., and Lake, E. T. (1994) 'Lower Medicare Mortality among a Set of Hospitals Known for Good Nursing Care' *Medical Care*, 32, pp. 771–87.

Bach, S. (1998) 'NHS Pay Determination and Work Reorganization: Employment Relations Reform in NHS Trusts' *Employee Relations*, 20(6), pp. 565–76.

Bach, S. (2000) 'Health Sector Reform and Human Resource Management: Britain in Comparative Perspective' *International Journal of Human Resource Management*, 11(5), pp. 925–42.

Bach, S. (2003) 'Human Resources and New Approaches to Public Sector Management: Improving Human Resources Management Capacity' in W. Van Lerberghe, G. Kegals and V. De Brouwere *Towards a Global Health Workforce Strategy, Studies in Health Services Organization and Policy*, 21, pp. 105–46.

Barnett, S., Buchanan, D., Patrickson, M. and Maddern, J. (1996) 'Negotiating the Evolution of the HR Function: Practical Advice from the Health Care Sector' *Human Resource Management Journal*, 6(4), pp. 18–37.

Bartram, T. (2002) 'Human Resource Management in a Unionized Setting: A Casestudy of an Australian Health Service' in H. Forbes-Mewett and G. Griffin (National Key Centre in Industrial Relations, Monash University) pp. 27–42.

Bartram, T. (2005) 'Small Firms, Big Ideas: The Adoption of Human Resource Management in Australian Small Firms', *Asia Pacific Journal of Human Resources*, 43(1), (forthcoming).

Bartram, T. and Cregan, C. (2001) 'Human Resource Management in a Union Setting: Configurations and Systems', *Paper presented at Academy of Management Annual Meeting*, Washington, D. C.

Boxall, P. and Purcell, J. (2003) *Strategy and Human Resource Management* (Basingstoke: Palgrave Macmillan).

Delaney, J. T. and Huselid, M. (1996) 'The Impact of Human Resource Management Practices on Perceptions of Organizational Performance' *Academy of Management Journal*, 39, pp. 949–69.

Duckett, S. (1995) 'Hospital Payment Arrangements to Encourage Efficiency: The Case of Victoria, Australia' *Health Policy*, 34, pp. 113–34.

Dwyer, J. and Leggat, S. G. (2002) 'Innovation in Australian Hospitals' *Australian Health Review*, 25(5), pp. 18–31.

Guest, D. E. (1995) 'Human Resource Management, Trade Unions and Industrial Relations' in J. Storey (ed.) *Human Resource Management: A Critical Text* (London: Routledge).

Huselid, M. (1995) 'The Impact of Human Resource Management Practices on Turnover, Productivity and Corporate Financial Performance' *Academy of Management Journal*, 38(3), pp. 635–72.

Huselid, M. A., Jackson, S. E. and Schuler, R. S. (1997) 'Technical and Strategic Human Resource Management Effectiveness as Determinants of Firm Performance' *Academy of Management Journal*, 40(1), pp. 171–88.

Jackson, S. E., Schuler, R. S. and Carlos Rivero, J. (1989) 'Organizational Characteristics as Predictors of Personnel Practices' *Personnel Psychology*, 42, pp. 727–85.

Kessler, I. and Purcell, J. (1996) 'Strategic Choice and New Forms of Employment Relations in the Public Service Sector: Developing an Analytical Framework' *The International Journal of Human Resource Management*, 7(1), pp. 206–29.

Lado, A. A. and Wilson, M. C. (1994) 'Human Resource Systems and Sustained Competitive Advantage: A Competency-Based Perspective' *Academy of Mangement Review*, 19(4), pp. 699–727.

Legge, K. (1995) *Human Resource Management: Rhetoric and Realities* (London: Macmillan Business).

McDuffie, J. P. (1995)' Human Resource Bundles and Manufacturing Performance: Flexible Productions Systems in the World Auto Industry' *Industrial and Labor Relations Review*, 48(2), pp. 197–221.

Patrickson, M. and Maddern, J. (1996) 'Human Resource Management in Hospitals: A Contested Arena for Jurisdiction' *Australian Health Review*, 19(3), pp. 104–16.

Saltman, R., Figueras, J. and Sakellarides, C. (eds) (1998) *Critical Challenges for Health Care Reform in Europe, State of Health* (Buckingham: Open University Press).

Schuler, R. (1992) 'Strategic Human Resource Management: Linking People with the Strategic Business Needs of the Business' *Organizational Dynamics*, 21(1) pp. 18–32.

Stanton, P. (2002a) 'Managing the Healthcare Workforce: Cost Reduction or Innovation' *Australian Health Review*, 25(4), pp. 92–8.

Stanton, P. (2002b) *Employment Relations in Victoria Public Hospitals: 1992–1999* Unpublished PhD thesis (School of Public Health, La Trobe University).

Stanton, P., Bartram, T. and Harbridge, R. (2004) 'People Management Practices in the Public Health Sector: Development from Victoria, Australia' *Journal of European Industrial Training*, 28, pp. 310–328.

Thornley, C. (1998) 'Contesting Local Pay: The Decentralization of Collective Bargaining in the NHS' *British Journal of Industrial Relations*, 36(3), pp. 413–34.

Walton, R. E. (1985) 'From Control to Commitment in the Workplace' *Harvard Business Review*, 63(2), pp. 77–84.

West, M., Borrill, C., Dawson, J., Scully, J., Carter, M., Anelay, S., Patterson, M. and Waring, J. (2002) 'The Link Between the Management of Employees and Patient Mortality in Acute Hospitals' *International Journal of Human Resource Management*, 13(8), pp. 1299–1310.

Wright, P. M. and McMahan, G. C. (1992) 'Theoretical Perspectives for Strategic Human Resource Management' *Journal of Management*, 18, pp. 295–320.

APPENDIX 1   Definitions of variables

Variable	Definition
SHRM 1	Human resource strategies are effectively integrated with this organisation's strategy
SHRM 2	Human resource practices are integrated to be consistent with each other
SHRM 3	Human resource personnel are a key influence in setting HR strategy
SHRM 4	Human resource strategy is distinct from the business strategy
SHRM 5	Human resource management strategy will become a more important influence on this organisation's strategy in the future
SHRM 6	Human resource strategy has an insufficient input-influence on this organisation's general strategy
SHRM 7	This organisation matches the characteristics of managers to the strategic plan of the organisation
SHRM 8	This organisation identifies managerial characteristics necessary to run the firm in the long term
SHRM 9	This organisation modifies the compensation systems to encourage managers to achieve long term strategic objectives
SHRM 10	This organisation changes staffing patterns to help implement business or corporate strategies
SHRM 11	This organisation evaluates key personnel based on their potential for carrying out strategic goals
SHRM 12	Job analyses are based on what the job may entail in the future
SHRM 13	Development programs are designed to support strategic changes

12
Clinical Governance: Complexities and Promises

Rick Iedema, Jeffrey Braithwaite, Christine Jorm, Peter Nugus and Anna Whelan

Introduction

This chapter considers the scope of clinical governance by tracing its origins to the National Health Service in the United Kingdom, and by outlining its heterogeneous impacts on health sector employment relations in Australia. The concept of clinical governance originated in the United Kingdom (UK) in 1997 in The New NHS report, which describes it as an instrument that aims 'to assure and improve clinical standards at the local level' (Gray, 2004; UK Department of Health, 1997). Its formal definition is often derived from a later article:

> ... a framework through which NHS organizations are accountable for continually improving the quality of their services and safeguarding high standards of care by creating an environment in which excellence in clinical care will flourish (Donaldson and Gray, 1998, p. S38)

Classed by several commentators as an extension of the New Public Management discourse that had begun to reconfigure UK public administration in the 1980s (Dent, 1998; Flynn, 2002; Walsh, 1995), clinical governance served as a rallying cry in the UK for those who felt that the prevailing 'cost containment' philosophy was narrow in conception and counter-productive in execution (Nicholls *et al.*, 2000), and that emphasis needed to shift towards a mode of control of clinical work that was more effective than existing controls. Some commentators (like Dent and Flynn) have linked the concern with clinical governance to the somewhat more sinister sounding notion of 'governmentality'

(Brown and Crawford, 2003; Foucault, 1976) as a means of connecting recent policy developments with emergent, more dispersed and more far-reaching kinds of state control (Deleuze, 1995)[1] that aim to act on clinicians' 'soul' (Iedema, 2003; Rose, 1999). We return to this critical analysis later.

As in the UK, the initial intent of health sector reform in Australia in the 1980s was to promote methods whose main concern was resource usage measured through 'output-oriented and financially-driven approaches to service funding and management' (Degeling et al., 2000). Around the same time, traditional approaches to risk management were found wanting for containing the problems and errors that we have now come to recognize as (latently) inherent in healthcare systems and practices. More recently, UK, USA and local reports have begun to call expert clinical autonomy in health into question following revelations about sub-standard clinical work (Douglas, 2002; Kennedy, 2001; Kohn et al., 1999; Runciman and Moller, 2001; Vecchi, 2003; Walker, 2004b; Wilson et al., 1999; Wilson et al., 1995). The concern with quality of care that these enquiries and reports produced meant that cost containment and risk management approaches have begun to be revised and complemented by 'more integrated, evidence-based and outcome-focused approaches to clinical service provision' (Degeling et al., 2000).

In Australia, the Harvard Medical Malpractice Study (Brennan et al., 1991) and the Quality in Australian Healthcare Study (Wilson et al., 1995)[2] are often cited as having provided impetus and legitimacy for policy makers and health managers to start asking questions about the efficacy of technical approaches to re-structuring healthcare (Blandford and Smythe, 2002). Using clinical governance as their conceptual means, policy makers and health managers started targeting those dimensions of the clinical work that were previously considered to be too expert-dependent, personal and ephemeral to be susceptible to targeted management, monitoring and intervention (Donabedian, 1981; Flynn, 2002). Through clinical governance, those working in health policy and health management aimed to integrate and co-configure earlier quality and safety practices that had remained fragmented, local and at times idiosyncratic, such as medical auditing, constructing clinical guidelines, devising and applying performance indicators, engaging consumers and practising evidence-based medicine. These concerns were locally consolidated with the establishment of The Australian Council for Quality and Safety in Health Care ('ACQSHC') and the National Institute of Clinical Studies ('NICS') following the Australian Health Ministers' meeting in 2000, creating new 'cross-boundary' sites where the struggle over the control of healthcare work was to be waged.

Clinical governance as a guiding concept has sometimes taken a back seat in recent discussions and documents compared to notions like quality and safety, but the spirit of radical change that informed original calls for clinical governance certainly appears to live on in these more recent directions and initiatives. In attempting to tease out some of these complexities, this chapter will consider how 'clinical governance' enabled policy makers, health managers and clinicians to rally around concerns that had previously been considered the exclusive domain of autonomous expert medical professionals. The chapter sets out the variety of associated initiatives and concerns that are captured under the rubric of clinical governance to address perceived healthcare shortcomings. We note that, given this multiplicity of initiatives and concerns, it is not surprising that some see clinical governance as collaborative improvement and as a new work method (Gray, 2004), and that for others, clinical governance embodies a formal structural arrangement that seeks inspectorial oversight in order to institute audits of clinicians' work (Charlton, 2001; Roland *et al.*, 2001). In Australia, these tensions are evident from the ways that the concept is deployed in the policy, professional and academic literatures and from the ways that specific initiatives embody a mix of orientations and understandings. The chapter finishes with an analysis of recent developments in New South Wales and of how a recent enquiry there into healthcare practices is providing momentum towards strengthening healthcare-funder monitoring of and prosecutorial power over clinicians; in short, a momentum towards the 'inspectorialization' of healthcare funder-provider relationships.

Clinical governance: Genealogy and scope

As noted above, the idea of clinical governance is a British one, and it is therefore appropriate to examine the term's historical antecedents in the National Health Service (NHS). In doing so, we can discern many themes which, drawn together, highlight the evolution of thinking leading to clinical governance as a set of management principles and ideals (Braithwaite, 1999; Braithwaite *et al.*, 2004; Braithwaite and Westbrook, 2004).

Following a number of related reports (for example, The 'Cogwheel' reports, 1967/72/74), the Griffiths enquiry in 1983 was influential in concentrating the attention of policy makers on devising strategies, resource management initiatives and clinical directorates that were decidedly managerialist in orientation (Griffiths Report, 1983). The Griffiths Report argued that general local management was the way forward for the NHS. By improving management at the area and hospital level (intended to replace the tripartite, consensus team-management system of a director of medical services, director of nursing services and director of administrative services), it was envisaged that earlier problems of policy implementation and adherence would be remedied. Yet, the local NHS agencies, 'each with accumulated culture, history and tradition, and unique demographic and epidemiological characteristics' could not be forced to yield 'to a central political will. The dilemma is at the heart of central-local relations in the health service' (Stoten, 1985, p. 235). Even the centralization-decentralization debate itself that occupied NHS policy makers played itself out against a backdrop of local practitioner indifference.

On the other hand, there were remarkable levels of innovation and willingness to embrace local initiatives. Thus it became evident that the key political force was not exhortation by central policymakers, but immediacy and relevance of stakeholder concerns and interests, even if these were not infrequently dominated by clinical interests rooted in clinical status, technology and professional values. The partisan and powerful nature of local concerns was recognized by Packwood et al. (1991), who scrutinized and evaluated the resource management initiative within the NHS between 1986 and 1991. This initiative was concerned to provide clinicians and managers in six hospitals with more effective tools to manage resources under their control. There were four aspects to this resource management initiative: strategies to improve quality of care; the involvement of clinicians in operational management; better provision of information to improve the use of resources; and improved control of resources through better resource management and allocation. Packwood et al. (1991) argued that in this context the emergence of clinical directorates as the means to realize the initiative was both logical and functional: the entry of clinicians into resource management necessitated some form of organizational structure that could facilitate this new clinician-management engagement, while at the same time ensuring local concerns gained a channel for their articulation.

In describing the tensions that these new arrangements nevertheless caused, Packwood et al. (1991) commented on the intention to 'subordinate ... clinical freedom through tighter control of costs and activities and the imposition of a managerial hierarchy' (Packwood et al., 1991, p. 160). This problem was seen to centre on the importance attributed by clinicians to their clinical autonomy, and their rejection of budget-oriented control. One important issue that emerged was that while the head of a clinical directorate could be charged with being accountable for the performance of the directorate by upper management, the directorate's clinicians did not necessarily feel they needed to share that burden of accountability, creating a disjunction between how the work was done (local concerns) and how it was managed (central concerns).

Before the introduction of the clinical directorate, clinicians were of course never entirely disengaged from the management of the hospitals in which they worked. Clinicians traditionally occupied positions from which they have lobbied hospital managers and board members, negotiated their positions, sought and acquired resources, advocated their view to management, encouraged or discouraged other organizational players and generally exerted influence. These kinds of engagement are very different, however, from the ones promoted in the UK government reports cited earlier, according to which clinicians should be encouraged to take up formal management positions within the hospital hierarchy through their participation in clinical directorates, and adopt strategies for managing resources, people, processes and outcomes. The clinical directorate, then, became the principal site and focus of struggles between formal and traditional approaches to management on the one hand, and clinical approaches to and expectations of management on the other.

Until the end of the 1980s there were multiple skirmishes between stakeholders trying to settle the question about the extent to which clinicians should be managed or incorporated into management (Braithwaite, 1999). This culminated in a shift during the 1990s both in the UK and in Australia in recognition of the problem that traditional ways of managing budgets, controlling processes, targeting risks and maintaining quality and safety failed to translate public expectations about standards of care into acceptable clinical practices, let alone improvements. But while the impetus towards new ways of involving clinicians in management was given legal proportions in the UK following local enquiries, it was yet to remain rather more discursive and voluntary in Australia.

Dove-tailing with the commercial sector and its concern with 'corporate governance' (Daily et al., 2003), then, the vacuum between clinical management and organizational management attracted not only a range of new technical and structural mechanisms (TQM, clinical directorates, information technologies), but now also ideas targeting the moral-ethical dimensions of how healthcare is organized, and foregrounding the outcomes for patient that healthcare organizations are able to 'produce'. This shift from a traditionally managerial to a technical-moral framework for encapsulating healthcare reform was particularly evident from the kinds of questions that began to be asked. Thus, previously favoured methods and approaches for framing healthcare reform came to be called into question, including:

- the efficacy of Casemix budget management approaches aiming to cap budgets;
- the effects of internal market approaches favouring contracting among clinical directorates as independent budget units;
- the effectiveness of risk management as an occasional and management-centred assessment of and response to extant risk;
- the success of resource management approaches seeking to enrol clinicians into management to tighten links between clinical and resource dimensions of care;
- the consequences of organizational restructuring into clinical directorates and matrix structures for the quality and safety dimensions of care;
- the implications of the emergence of a non-delegable duty of care of an organization to its patients;
- the impact of changing societal perspectives of and expectations about professional work; and
- the influence of rising levels of medical-clinical indemnity insurance and pay-outs.

In response to these questions, new managerial, scientific and policy endeavours emerged to bolster the clinical-managerial relationship in healthcare (Dent, 1998; Dent and Whitehead, 2002). Bypassing traditional vocabularies, this relationship is recast as being constituted in 'governance'. The term's current popularity may derive from the fact that 'governance' was first used in medieval-religious contexts (in the 14th Century) to denote personal and communal standards and methods of discipline, predating the arrival of 'government' and 'management' (both 16th Century) by more than a century (Weekley, 1967). This etymology serves to not only highlight the pre-nation-state and pre-bureaucratic connotations inherent in 'governance', but also lend force to its claim of harbouring a radically new amalgam of moral-disciplinary meanings.

Two discursive positions on clinical governance: Inspection and collaboration

This enhanced emphasis on the disciplinary and moral dimensions of healthcare relationships is more than evident from the current health policy and health management discourses. Thus, on the one hand, emphasis is placed on disciplinary devices that afford inspection: data generation, gathering and storage; data analysis including variance review and comparative performance monitoring and accreditation; more extensive and informated modes of personnel and organizational performance management; integration of clinical work data with resource expenditure data; targeted guideline and protocol production and dissemination, and increasing inter-weaving of global research evidence into everyday practice. On the other hand, we read about moralizing devices through which to enhance collaboration: open disclosure, no blame, just culture, leadership, quality and safety, teams, collaboratives, consumer involvement and patient centredness.

Figure 12.1, below captures these two categories of concepts that we regard to be associated with clinical governance. The dotted circles towards the left in Figure 12.1, contain concepts whose emphasis is on collaboration; the thick-lined circles towards the right contain concepts that are inspectorial in orientation.

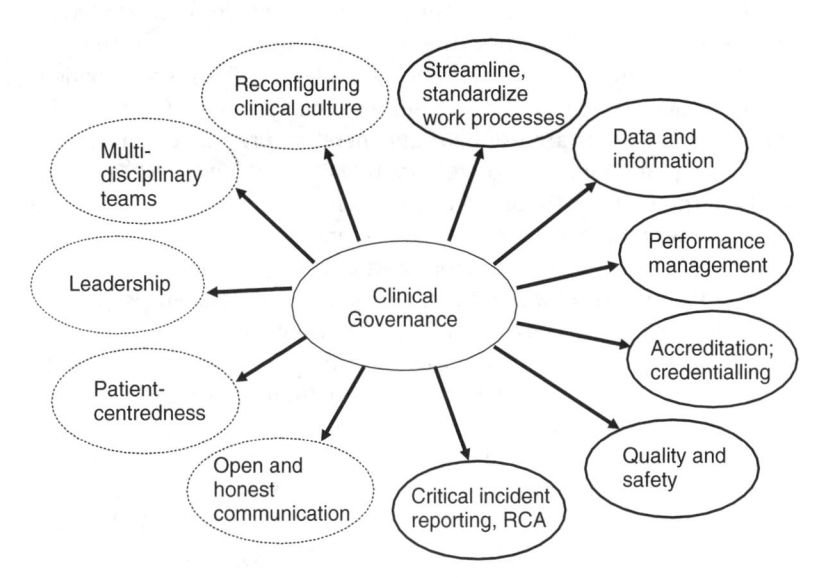

Figure 12.1 Collaborative and inspectorial concepts associated with clinical governance

As Figure 12.1, underscores, clinical governance embodies a dual strategy: it aims to make clinicians more visible by inviting them to be team members, leaders, practice improvers and collaborators, while, at the same time, it aims to make their presence visible and calculable by casting it into numerical, statistical and other technical meta-discourses (Iedema, 2003).

This dual strategy of encouraging organizational-managerial participation by clinicians and of requiring documentary transparency into their work notwithstanding, it would be unwise to invest too much confidence in the ability of this strategy to bring about change (Charlton, 2001). The inevitable distance that separates the representations and discourses that are taken to realize clinical governance from the conducts that constitute everyday clinical work clearly produces an enhanced opportunity for front-line clinicians to 'game' not just their documentation but also their participation (Iedema and Degeling, 2001). Before exploring the implications of this duality further, let us consider each of the five collaborative concepts and the six inspectorial concepts in somewhat greater detail.

Clinical governance as a collaborative mechanism

First, the rising number of references to reconfiguring clinical culture(s) appear to mark a concern to widen the sphere of organizational, managerial and policy influence and involvement from bureaucratic administration to encompass the way professionals enact (inter)personal relationships and perform their self-identity. This is also evident from the fact that 'culture' is becoming gradually accepted as a descriptor for 'how things are done around here' to provide contrast with 'how things are done over there' (Braithwaite et al., in press). Inherent in the term 'culture' therefore is the intent to objectify and relativize the practices and identities of groups of practitioners for those practitioners themselves, as if to afford and encourage a new modality of reflexivity through new and more personalized relationships at work. Objectifying and relativizing the ways of doing, being and saying displayed by a group of people means putting limits on their ability to regard who they are and what they do as natural, necessary and therefore unchangeable. As a descriptive concept, then, culture focuses attention on how one group's practices differ from those of others, on how 'aligned' or collaborative they are (Senge, 1990), and on how their professional sub-cultural identifications put limits on hospital reform and the achievement of clinical governance (Degeling et al., 1998). In that sense, the concept 'clinical culture' as it is now used in local health policy, health management and medical literatures seeks to re-cast the clinical-professional and sub-cultural 'stand-off' that often characterizes how professionals communicate and interact (Degeling *et al.*, 2003; Jorm and Kam, 2004) into not just a more reflexive idiom, but also a more interpersonally cooperative and mutually supportive one (Iedema, 2003).

A second way in which the collaborative ethos behind clinical governance is advocated is by 'celebrating' teams (Firth-Cozens, 1998). Team work is now lauded as the means par excellence through which to obviate concentration of control of increasingly complex kinds of work into single and often inaccessible points of bureaucratized managerial authority. The arguments offered centre on teams affording communication, knowledge and learning surpassing the abilities of individual practitioners (Bate, 2000; Bate and Robert, 2003; Shortell *et al.*, 1994); engendering mutually supportive and committed work relationships (Borrill *et al.*, 2000; Ducanis and Golin, 1979; Harris *et al.*, 2002); and offering immediate and flexible resolution of work problems in the absence of interference from or delay by management (Firth-Cozens, 1998; Mickan and Rodger, 2000; US Institute of Medicine, 2001). The political, moral and practical challenges that each of these 'affordances' presents however, remain more often than not backgrounded in both the policy literature (for example, Western Australian Department of Health, 2003) and the professional-academic literature (Mickan and Rodger, 2000). In this regard, a particular obstacle remains the divergence between management, medicine and nursing (Degeling *et al.*, 2003), rendering acceptance of multi-disciplinary team work a considerable challenge.

A third focus of collaborative emphasis, leadership in health is being credited with focusing professional 'followers on the future to achieve commitment to an agreed vision' (Nicholls *et al.*, 2000, p. 177). Commentators draw not infrequently on the broader management literature to distinguish 'transactional' from 'transformational' kinds of leadership (Spurgeon and Latham, 2003). Thus, transformational leadership positions leaders as people who have visions that lead to change, can empower people, are excellent communicators, inspire trust in others, help individuals feel capable, have energy and are action-oriented (Spurgeon and Latham, 2003, p. 56). The transformational dimension of leadership is what has been picked up in local policy documentation, with special emphasis placed on leaders' energy and vision inspiring employees not merely to engage in continuous improvement of their work, but to develop self-targeted programs of life-long learning and personal learning plans (Queensland Department of Health, 2003). The intensity of personalization in how work relationships are to be enacted is clear from the emphasis in this clinical leadership literature on the ongoing reflexion on and re-invention of self-identity.

Fourthly, the recent emphasis on patient-centredness targets collaboration between clinicians by centring attention on their collaboration with patients. Patient-centredness is not specific to clinical governance, in that questions were raised many years ago about the acceptability of clinical care practices for patients. This focus on patients' concerns led to the formation of the Medical Consumers Association in the 1970s and the subsequent influence of the local consumer movement in the 1980s as a result of systematic government funding. Duckett comments on the number of Australian government organizations that were set up in the 1990s to provide a voice for consumers' interests, such as the Consumers Health Forum, the Victorian Health Issues Centre (Duckett, 2000, p. 231), and the Health Care Complaints Commission in New South Wales. These developments have helped put on the educational, research and policy agendas different facets of clinician-patient communication such as informed consent, family conferencing, guardianship, appropriately negotiating bad news, and so on.

An example of how collaborative and inspectorial influences can be in tension, however, is the way that patient-centredness is giving rise to a technical enterprise focusing on the measurement and comparison of functional health status, patient satisfaction, health outcomes and quality of life indicators. Here, the interpersonal dimension of paying attention to patients' needs (Benner, 1994) runs the risk of becoming overshadowed by objectifying measurements with which particular routines or efficiencies are legitimated. By the same token, the inspectorial potential inherent in modern technologies can also work to challenge routines and efficiencies, in that it is common now for patients to seek out medical and health process and outcomes information and request health organizations to provide it. The complex outcomes of these trends is that several states in Australia have health information web sites whose contents range from advice about exercise and nutrition, details about what is likely to happen when treated in an Emergency Department, to specific hospitals' and doctors' waiting times and records of success. All this shows that the actual scope and meaning of patient-centredness remains highly contested (Armstrong, 1994). However, it is precisely the potential of patient-centredness to augment professional-lay person involvement that renders it well-suited to join the panoply of conducts deemed to realize the collaborative face of governance (Gray, 2004, p. 5).

Fifthly, clinical governance is associated with the call for open communication among clinicians as well as among clinicians and patients. Such openness is contingent on an environment of mutual respect and what has more recently been termed 'just culture' (Ruchlin et al., 2004). Together with the potential displacement of legal responsibility for errors from the individual clinician to the healthcare provider organization (Blandford and Smythe, 2002), 'just culture' aims to ensure clinicians not just can but will learn from their practices without fear of undue legal, organizational or professional reprisal, and share information with patients to enhance mutual understanding.

A related notion that has recently made entrance into the policy literature to emphasize the moral and collaborative duality undergirding professional conduct is 'Open Disclosure'. Open Disclosure has recently been developed by the Australian Council for Safety and Quality in Health Care into a 'national standard' (Australian Council for Safety and Quality in Health Care, 2004). In addition to interprofessional sharing of both positive and negative data and information, Open Disclosure encompasses openness with patients and their families that is realized as informed consent, acknowledgement of patients' expectations and expressions of regret in the case of adverse events (Safety and Quality Council, 2003). Unfortunately, in practice, Open Disclosure raises as many questions as it answers; for example, at work clinicians are instructed not to admit liability, while it is equally the norm that patients should be notified of clinical events that affect them but of which they would otherwise remain ignorant. Here, the pragmatic or 'profane' imperatives driving hospital administration and health bureaucracy potentially contravene the 'sacred' moral and collaborative hortations underpinning Open Disclosure as 'an initiative aimed at enhancing communication at the point of care and, ultimately, leading to safer healthcare' (Australian Council for Safety and Quality in Health Care, 2004).

Clinical governance as an inspectorial mechanism

In contrast to these five collaborative concepts, clinical governance has also turned people's attention to the need to reconfigure the nature of the relationship between staff and the organization and infuse it with higher levels of managerial monitoring and technical assessment with the aim to facilitate and anchor disciplinary processes. It is here that a new range of analytical mechanisms is drawn on to give effect to this inspectorialism. The solutions proposed include work process standardization; data/information generation, access and review; performance measurement and management; accreditation and credentialling; critical incident reporting and monitoring, root cause analysis, and quality, safety and risk minimization. We will again briefly elaborate on each of these.

First, work process standardization can be seen to occur at a number of organizational levels. It occurs as an effect of medical research, of course, particularly when specific kinds of treatments are subjected to analytical scrutiny and procedural prescription or change. Already mentioned above, initiatives by central and departmental bodies cast aspects of practice in the form of guidelines and protocols that are then disseminated and promoted (by Health Departments and the Colleges).[3] The third kind of work process standardization is in the actual workplace where teams negotiate about how to map, review and improve the work they do (Iedema, 2003). Considered empirically, Australian healthcare institutions manifest a multiplicity of approaches ranging from general regularization and integration of service structures, to more targeted and therefore narrowly focused service and treatment design. Generally however, healthcare organizations display a relative absence of work process control (Degeling *et al.*, 2000). Degeling and colleagues' research into the 'organization of hospital care and its effects' showed that none of the three 'high volume' conditions targeted in the seven participating hospitals were fully subjected to work process standardization. This research was nevertheless able to point to a statistically relevant link between consumer satisfaction, efficiency, effectiveness, and work process standardization (Degeling *et al.*, 2000, p. 90).

Secondly, the level of expectation invested in data/information generation, access and review is evident from the considerable resources that are being allocated nationally to informating clinical work in a number of ways (National Electronic Decision Support Taskforce, 2002; National Health Information Management Advisory Council, 2001) and to 'health informatics' more specifically. Increasing amounts of resources are allocated to not only gathering state-wide data in huge inventories, but also to digitizing clinical information processes, including drug prescribing and test ordering (National Health Information Management Advisory Council, 2001). Another development concerns leveraging up the use of research evidence in the execution of the everyday clinical work by means of computerized systems provided as part of the Clinical Information Access Project or

'CIAP' (Gosling et al., 2003). While sophisticated health informatics models are being developed in Australia (Coiera, 2003), the actual impacts of (introducing) these computerized forms of communication access and information storage devices into existing healthcare systems and organizations is only beginning to be researched (Westbrook et al., 2004), which indicates that there is no clarity about their ability to deliver on expectations as well as their actual impact on everyday clinical work.

Thirdly, performance standards, performance measurement and performance management are also increasingly on the agenda in the health industry, in policy documentation, job contracts and position advertisements, as well as everyday practice (Irvine, 1997). In addition, and linking it to data and information generation and access (Corden and Luxmoore, 2000), performance variation is now not only measured and compared globally, nationally, and at state level, but also at the level of individual organizations, individual units and even individual clinicians. As part of this latter development, the Institute for Health Improvement has recommended that there be strengthened monitoring of everyday practice, including regulation, incentives and periodic examinations of doctors' and nurses' practices, including their re-licencing (Irvine, 1999).

Fourthly, the above ties in with the enhanced role envisaged for accreditation and credentialing of organizations as to how they reward safe practices and identify and deal with sub-standard practices (Australian Council for Safety and Quality in Health Care, 2000). The Australian Council of Health Care Standards (ACHS) has, since the 1980s, focused on hospital institutions; the Quality Improvement Council (QIC) that has been in charge of community and primary care settings; the Home and Community Care (HACC) for HACC-funded agencies, and Australian General Practice Accreditation Limited (AGPAL) operating as part of the Royal Australian College of General Practitioners (RACGP) for general practice accreditation.

The Australian Council of Health Care Standards (ACHS) has been particularly active in the area of producing not merely static organizational indicators and one-off surveys, but also self-assessment and self-improvement programs consisting of standards, guidelines and tools that target and set indicators for the details of the clinical and managerial work. In that sense, ACHS accreditation aims to:

> ... guide organizations seeking accreditation through a four-year program of self-assessment service, organization-wide survey and

periodic review conducted by industry peers to meet ACHS standards (Australian Council on Healthcare Standards, 2003).

Fifthly, as part of the effort to target quality, safety and risk minimization, ACHS's organizational and practice improvement program referred to as 'EQuIP' (Evaluation of Quality Improvement Program) was first published in 1997 and a number of versions have since appeared to refine and further develop its performance standards, guidelines and tools. A program deployed Australia-wide, EQuIP harbours a framework for realizing quality healthcare services, tools to monitor performance and achievements, periodic peer reviews, and plans for continuous improvement, all of which are structured such as to culminate in ACHS accreditation. At the heart of the ACHS accreditation program and the indicator assessment system of EQuIP is the desire to bring self-initiated work process improvement and external control into the ambit of organizational accreditation (The Australian Council on Healthcare Standards, 1996), in effect constraining clinical autonomy. Equally, balancing data and information generation and access with peer review and self-initiated change, ACHS's and EQuIP's focus on organizational, team and individual learning puts it at the forefront of approaches that attempt to give precedence to peer collaboration as the means through which to realize external inspection.

Sixthly, another technical-analytical strategy that has emerged as a way of monitoring clinical practice and tightening clinical-managerial relationships to ensure appropriate standards of quality is one that is referred to as critical incident reporting (Runciman *et al.*, 1993). Critical incident reporting enables the review of problematic practices by targeting adverse events whose outcomes do not incur legal procedures, such as 'near misses'. Integral to critical incident monitoring is the delicate taxonomization of errors, separating human errors from systems errors, and calibrating levels and degrees of seriousness of error (Beckmann *et al.*, 1996). In Australia, Runciman and colleagues have forged ahead with formalizing the critical incident monitoring process and with refining critical incident data analysis through the Adverse Incident Monitoring Scheme (AIMS), a new version of which has recently been released (the Advanced Incident Monitoring Scheme).

While the AIMS initiative is an important one, important questions about the execution and implementation of critical incident reporting remain. For example, it often remains unclear what exactly constitutes a critical incident (Hoff *et al.*, 2004) and how one is to be classified on the error intentionality scale (Runciman et al., 2000). There are also pragmatic issues such as at what level of health administration should incident reports be reported and analyzed. Significant from a monitoring and assessment perspective is the fact that national level reports summarizing critical incident occurrences may give a good overview but tend to have limited practical relevance for clinicians. By contrast, intermediate state level reports such as the ones produced by New South Wales and Victoria about incidents that have a high Severity Assessment Code ('SAC') may hold more promise.[4]

An important facet of this drive towards learning from errors is 'root cause analysis' ('RCA'). RCA is a mechanism for identifying systems causes, underlying errors and adverse events, and it seeks to make explicit all the actual, technical as well as human causes leading up to an undesirable event. The application of this manufacturing-industrial technique to healthcare work was pioneered by the US Veterans Health Administration ('VA') and is now required by The US Joint Commission of Accreditation of Healthcare organizations. In the VA system, staff are obliged to participate in RCAs, but this is not the case in Australia. On the other hand, questions have been raised about across-the-board applications of RCA. Richard Smith, editor of the British Medical Journal (Australian Broadcasting Corporation, 2004), for example, recently critiqued the way RCA's technical bias tends to rule the experiential and emotional or 'teleo-affective' (Schatzki, 2002) dimensions of making mistakes out of court. Smith argues that RCA not only ignores the phenomenological impact of errors on clinicians, but that the bureaucratic mechanisms targeting serious adverse or sentinel events can also lead to time-consuming internal investigations, in addition to (as in New South Wales) external reviews, coronial inquiries, and Health Care Complaints Commission scrutiny.

What the preceding overview bears out is that the policy, organizational and professional literatures are pluri-vocal not only about the intent and purpose of clinical governance, but also about its modes of implementation. The most obvious distinction lies between those who emphasize that clinical governance constitutes the means for tightening managerial-clinical accountability and discipline through inspectorialism, and those who see the self-organizing facets of clinical governance as central for achieving appropriate collaboration (Flynn, 2002; Roland et al., 2001). In the section that follows, we trace some recent developments in New South Wales as a way of illustrating how specific events appear to (at the time of writing) be pushing the balance in favour of increased inspectorialization, with clear consequences for the levels of control experienced by clinicians over the substance and direction of their work.

The inspectorialization of clinical governance in New South Wales

Compared to the largely voluntary uptake and mostly pluri-vocal manifestation of clinical governance that is evident in Australia, the uptake and manifestation in the UK are rather more targeted and efficiency-focused: '[t]he approach of the UK government is heavily top-down, with detailed processes and guidelines being determined at national level' (Roland *et al.*, 2001, p. 196). For example, and paralleling the hierarchic, surveillance-oriented intent of the NHS more broadly, the approach taken by the UK Centre for Health Improvement (CHI) monitors organizational and practice standards within a 'performance framework' by doing reviews of services; engages in a 'trouble-shooting role' in case sub-standard care is uncovered; and allocates assessments to organizations that have considerable resource and oversight consequences. The contradictions between this inspectorial oversight by bodies such as CHI and the current emphasis across the NHS on teamwork, leadership and 'bottom-up' modernization (Firth-Cozens, 1998) translate into tensions and confusions for clinical practitioners (Flynn, 2004).

A similar increase in external inspection of clinical practices may be seen to have followed on from recent adverse clinical events in Australia. Events at King Edward Memorial Hospital in Perth (Douglas, 2002) and at Camden and Campbelltown Hospitals in Sydney (Adrian, 2003; Walker, 2004b), in particular, have produced much media scrutiny, political anxiety and legal activity. A recent information paper issued by the NSW Health Department, titled 'Providing the best healthcare', follows on from a series of investigations into and changes to the ways that healthcare is being monitored in the state of New South Wales. These include a Special Commission of Inquiry into allegations of unacceptable mortality events at Campbelltown and Camden Hospitals; an Inquiry by the Legislative Council into inefficient health complaints handling by the Health Care Complaints Commission (HCCC); and a Review of the Health Care Complaints Act 1993 by the Cabinet Office; as well as a review of the Medical Practice Act to improve patient safety in cooperation with the NSW Medical Board. Collectively, these developments, the recommendations coming out of previous enquiries (Vecchi, 2003), the 2004 NSW Technical Paper, and the Walker interim and final reports produced as part of the Special Commission of Inquiry into Camden and Campbelltown

Hospitals appear to lay the ground work for a change of tune in how healthcare work is monitored and managed.

Most recent among these, the Walker reports describe the HCCC's handling of complaints as a 'sorry situation' and its misclassification of cases as 'indefensible' (Walker, 2004b; Walker, 2004a). Challenging the 'no blame' rhetoric that came on the back of calls for 'system improvements', Walker recommends that a more personalized targeting of substandard performers is required, and that the Health Care Complaints Act needs to be amended to institute HCCC's enhanced powers accordingly. NSW Parliament responded to these recommendations with great speed, and introduced on 31 March 2004 the *Health Care Complaints Amendment (Special Commission of Inquiry) Bill* 2004 ('the amending act') which was passed by both houses while still awaiting assent. One commentator notes that '[w]hile [the amendment] will certainly assist in achieving the purposes identified by Mr. Walker, there are significant concerns that it may go too far in eliminating the rights of practitioners' (Wade, 2004).

For its part, the NSW Health Information Paper also turns up the volume of inspectorialism by proposing the following institutional changes. First, the role of the NSW Clinical Excellence Commission (CEC), until recently carrying the somewhat less inquisitorial sounding name Institute of Clinical Excellence (ICE), is to be expanded. Previously an agency charged with providing practice improvement training and initiating, among other things, 'Breakthrough Collaboratives', CEC's role is to extend to 'assisting and supporting health services', 'advising on the development of clinical frameworks' and 'cooperating with health services ... [on developing] best practice', to include two additional functions:

- to provide a system-wide monitoring and audit function. The Commission will ensure an appropriate standard of quality and safety is met across the health system, by regularly assessing all health services on their performance in this area; and
- to provide an expert clinical support team to health services on an 'as needed' basis to assist individual health services with reviewing and improving their own systems and practices where a need is identified. (NSW Health Department, 2004).

The Clinical Excellence Commission's 'more active role' will centre on 'identifying, assessing and improving systemic shortcomings in patient care practices' (NSW Health Department, 2004), and '[i]mprovement of the system cannot possibly require removal of the possibility of disciplinary sanction for those who fall badly below the standards of conduct' (Walker, 2004a, p. 26). Second, the inspectorial reach of the Health Care Complaints Commission is to be broadened, with a closer and more complementary relationship between the CEC and the HCCC. In a more recent 'technical paper' following The Enquiry's final report (Walker, 2004b), the new HCCC role is framed in still much sterner terms. This document envisages that the HCCC will 'undertake a preliminary inquiry on each complaint', 'investigate complaints with a view to prosecution before the relevant health professional disciplinary tribunal', and 'maintain a watchdog role' (New South Wales Health Department, 2004).

What the effects of this inspectorialization will be on practitioner relationships and on practitioner-management relationships is highly uncertain at this point. Moreover, what the implications will be for initiatives that were mounted on a more collaborative basis to improving healthcare practices, such as the Australian Council of Health Care Standards' EQuIP and clinician-surveyor framework, also remains uncertain. Anecdotally, we know that the recent inquiries have led to higher levels of defensiveness, suspicion and even complaints and mutual charges among clinical staff. This tentatively suggests that inspectorialization runs the risk of creating 'on-the-ground' responses that are the obverse of the transparency and accountability that policy makers and managers seek to achieve, in effect exacerbating rather than mitigating the stale-mate that prevails among the various professional sub-cultures in health.

Conclusion

This chapter has provided an outline of the historical genesis of clinical governance and of its main components and their uptake in Australia. The chapter emphasized that the discourses around clinical governance are largely of two kinds: one collaborative and oriented towards self-management; the other inspectorial and disciplinary. Both these interpretations of clinical governance were further specified in terms of the concepts and initiatives that can be seen to realize collaboration and inspection. The chapter concluded with a discussion of some recent (in 2004) developments in New South Wales and pointed to what appears to be a strengthening of inspectorial powers and a tightening of clinical-legal requirements bearing on clinicians.

Overall, this chapter concludes on an uncertain note. It is not clear how the trend outlined will contribute to balancing the clinical governance profile of current healthcare provision and monitoring, given this is desirable (Timmermans and Berg, 2003). Our argument has been that the preferred road map would be to enable and allow clinical practitioners to define and refine discourses that make sense to them and that they see as useful for recording, reporting and reviewing their own work. We acknowledge that such collaborative and local production and review of data are contingent on two things. First, this depends upon clinicians being willing to negotiate the broad outlines and sequencings of their care with each other, and dialogue with others working elsewhere doing related kinds of service work. While clinical-medical research has always been part of such inter-organizational, national and international dialogues, its concerns have generally not spanned more than one discipline or specialty, have not focused on multi-disciplinary service aspects, and have not taken into account the overall effects and errors inherent in established clinical-medical practices in ways promoted under clinical governance.

Secondly, collaboration is contingent upon politicians, policymakers and management trusting and being able to work with the variability of locally produced discourses specific to practitioners' modes of care. If, as envisaged in the previous paragraph, the relationships among clinical professionals become more dialogic and more oriented towards mapping, reviewing and reconfiguring their work, then the relationships between these professionals and other stakeholders are clearly not going to be left unaffected. On the contrary, the very enactment of multi-disciplinary dialogue puts into play discourses that are radically different from the numerically-oriented reports that currently form the mainstay of managerial decision making. If we acknowledge the variable success of formalized and top-down kinds of performance management, monitoring and reporting (Townley *et al.*, 2003), and if we agree that more flexible conceptions and enactments of work are therefore both inevitable and more desirable, we must also accept that realizing a more dialogic mode of working cannot occur without loosening the dependence of managerial decision making on formal, abstract and distanced data. Inevitably, then, politicians, policymakers and managers will have to reconstitute themselves around discourses that are less oriented to their own statistical measurement preferences and more to clinical diagnostics and dialogical sensemaking (Iedema *et al.*, 2005a).

Our work has begun to delve into some of these complexities and possibilities. For instance, we have described how hard it is for clinician-managers to sit astride multiple stakeholders' ways of framing the problems and yet shape solutions and outcomes (Iedema et al., 2004). Analysis of clinician-managerial roles and conducts shows how multivocal and pluralist are the professions, and how challenging it is to manage care processes and sub-cultural compositions (Braithwaite and Westbrook, 2004; Braithwaite and Westbrook, in press). Admittedly, too, we have speculated about the limits that appear to be inherent in the organization of healthcare work with regard to the potential to develop cross-professional 'heedfulness' (Iedema et al., 2005b; Weick and Roberts, 1993).

On a more constructive front, and in recognition of the importance of both the collaborative and inspectorial aspects of health organizational change, we have begun to trial new modes of cross-disciplinary participation in the healthcare workplace, encouraging professionals to speak about their work to peers as well as others who play a role in the systems of care that they are part of in ways that make explicit and make it possible to (re)design those systems of care (Iedema, 2003). This methodology seeks to enhance cross-disciplinary participation by eliciting locally meaningful discourse or 'knowledging' from clinicians who are part to the work (Iedema et al., 2005a). While satisfying the requirement to monitor clinical practice, this 'knowledging' answers in the first place the need for staff to enact self-(in)forming kinds of relationships and practices, unencumbered by agendas that divert from improving patient care. All in all, our present program of research aims to assess the complexities of clinical practice and the extent to which its re-organization might afford clinical governance in any of the senses explored in this chapter.

We acknowledge that the challenges to realizing the different facets of clinical governance remain considerable. To achieve a more dialogic relationship between clinicians and an accepting attitude on the part of management towards the effects and products of locally-devised dialogues, we need to change not merely clinical and managerial cultures, but also bureaucratic, political and public mindsets with regard to what are acceptable care decisions and what constitutes reasonable healthcare for the resources available. While the time may appear to be ripe, in the minds of some, for greater emphasis on legal powers to prosecute erring clinicians, we run the risk of forgetting about not just the centrality of current systems of care but also about the tacit and embodied knowledges that buttress what individuals are ultimately able to do.

We also forget at our peril that for all the cross-cutting emphases on inspection, collaboration, empowerment, culture, data, performance, incident reporting and all the other ideas and approaches captured under the banner of 'clinical governance' and often hived off into distant committees (Degeling *et al.*, 2004), what patients want in the end are well organized services, provided by skilled professionals linked together for common purpose, delivered with care and compassion. Now if clinical governance can help that quest, it is a cause worth taking up to realize a health system of which we can all be proud.

Notes

1 Deleuze notes the transition in modern industrialized states from what Foucault called disciplinary society (enacted through identifiable, discrete institutions) towards control dispersed and spread across social-institutional life: 'We're in the midst of a general breakdown of all sites of confinement – prisons, hospitals, factories, schools, the family ... Control societies are taking over from disciplinary societies. "Control" is the name [with which] to characterize the new monster [of] free-floating controls that are taking over from the old disciplines at work within the time scales of closed systems' (Deleuze 1995: 178).
2 The Wilson study argued that 16.6 per cent of admissions was associated with adverse events (of which 8.3 per cent were judged to be preventable). The Runciman and Moller report (2001) put the adverse event rate somewhat lower, at 10 per cent.
3 The way in which dissemination and promotion are done, however, is much less consonant with the principles of clinical governance than might be expected. For example, the NSW Department of Health has recently added a Guidelines section to its widely used 'Clinical Information Access Program' information portal (CIAP). While stress has been placed on the need to assess guidelines using an appraisal methodology (such as that of the 'AGREE collaboration'), more than four hundred guidelines have been placed on the site without rating or assessment being performed.
4 For its part, New South Wales is currently planning to implement Runciman's AIMS as part of a state-wide computerized incident monitoring system. These efforts notwithstanding, there is little research evidence to support the view that centralized collection will positively affect the impact of critical incident reporting. While collating incident report data at levels above the hospital unit may serve to remove identifiability and mitigate the likelihood of confrontation, this practice also down-grades the usefulness of such data for clinicians working in specific sites. Centralized kinds of reporting about equipment failures and technical complications may be beneficial, but since most critical incidents relate to communication, local rather than distal modes of collection and analysis would seem more appropriate within the framework of clinical governance. Not surprisingly, the focus and level of this kind of monitoring remain highly contested issues.

References

Adrian, A. (2003) 'Investigation Report Campbelltown and Camden Hospitals MacArthur Area Health Service' (Sydney: Health Care Complaints Commission).

Armstrong, D. (1994) 'Bodies of Knowledge/Knowledge of Bodies.' in C. Jones and R. Porter (eds) *Reassessing Foucault: Power, Medicine and the Body* (London: Routledge) pp. 17–27.

Australian Broadcasting Corporation (2004) The Law Report: Medical Mistakes (Sydney Australia: ABC).

Australian Council for Safety and Quality in Health Care (2000) 'Safety First' (Canberra: ACSQHC).

Australian Council for Safety and Quality in Health Care (2004) Open Disclosure Education and Organisational Support Package (Sydney: Australian Council for Safety and Quality in Health Care).

Australian Council on Healthcare Standards (2003) The ACHS Evaluation and Quality Improvement Program (Sydney: Australian Council on Healthcare Standards).

Bate, P. (2000) 'Changing the Culture of a Hospital: From Hierarchy to Network Community' *Public Administration Review*, 78(3), pp. 485–512.

Bate, P. and Robert, G. (2003) 'Knowledge Management and Communities of Practice' in S. Dopson and A. L. Mark (eds) *Leading Health Care Organizations* (Basingstoke and New York: Palgrave Macmillan) pp. 81–99.

Beckmann, U., Baldwin, I., Hart, G. K. and Runciman, W. B. (1996) 'The Australian Incident Monitoring Study in Intensive Care: AIMS-ICU – An Analysis of the First Year of Reporting' *Anaesthetic Intensive Care*, 24(3), pp. 320–29.

Benner, P. (1994) 'The Role of Articulation in Understanding Practice and Experience as Sources of Knowledge in Clinical Nursing' in J. Tully (ed.) *Philosophy in an Age of Pluralism: The Philosophy of Charles Taylor in Question* (Cambridge: Cambridge University Press) pp. 136–55.

Blandford, J. and Smythe, T. (2002) 'From Risk Management to Clinical Governance' in M. Harris (ed.) *Managing Health Services: Concepts and Practice* (Sydney: MacLennan and Petty, pp. 378–401.

Borrill, C. S., Carletta, J., Carter, A. J., Dawson, J. F., Garrod, S., Rees, R., Richards, A., Shapiro, D. and West, M. A. (2000) *The Effectiveness Of Health Care Teams In The National Health Service* (Aston Centre For Health Service Organisation Research, University of Aston; Human Communications Research Centre, Universities of Glasgow and Edinburgh; Psychological Therapies Research Centre, University of Leeds).

Braithwaite, J. (1999) 'Incorporating Medical Clinicians into Management: An Examination of Clinical Directorates' Unpublished PhD Thesis (Sydney: Faculty of Medicine, University of New South Wales).

Braithwaite, J., Finnegan, T. P., Graham, E. M., Degeling, P. J., Hindle, D. and Westbrook, M. T. (2004) 'How Important are Quality and Safety for Clinician Managers? Evidence from Triangulated Studies' *Clinical Governance*, 9(1), pp. 34–41.

Braithwaite, J. and Westbrook, M. T. (2004) 'A Survey of Staff Attitudes and Comparative Managerial and Non-Managerial Views in a Clinical Directorate', *Health Services Management Research*, 17, pp. 141–66.

Braithwaite, J., Westbrook, M., Iedema, R., Mallock, N., Forsyth, R. and Zhang, K. (in press) 'A Tale of Two Hospitals: Clinical Service Structures as an Expression of Different Organisational Cultures' *Social Science and Medicine*.

Braithwaite, J. and Westbrook, M. T. (in press) 'Rethinking Clinical Organisational Structures: An Attitude Survey of Doctors, Nurses and Allied Heath Staff in Clinical Directorates' *Journal of Health Services Research and Policy*.

Brennan, T. A., Leape, L. L., Laird, M. M., Hebert, L., Localio, A. R., Lawthers, A. G., Nan, M., Newhouse, J. P., Weiler, P. C. and Hiatt, H. H. (1991) 'Incidence of Adverse Events and Negligence in Hospitalized Patients: Results of the Harvard Medical Practice Study' *New England Journal of Medicine*, 324, pp. 370–76.

Brown, B. and Crawford, P. (2003) 'The Clinical Governance of the Soul: "Deep Management" and the Self-Regulating Subject in Integrated Community Mental Teams' *Social Science and Medicine*, 56, pp. 67–81.

Charlton, B. G. (2001) 'Quality Assurance as a Managerial Technology: Clinical Governance and the Managerial Regulation of NHS Medical Practice' in A. Miles, et al., *Clinical Governance: Encouraging Excellence or Imposing Control?* (London: Aesculaepius Medical Press) pp. 73–86.

Coiera, E. (2003) *Guide to Health Informatics* (London: Edward Arnold).

Corden, S., and Luxmoore, J. (2000) 'Managing Performance for Better Results' in A. Bloom (ed.) *Health Reform in Australia and New Zealand* (Sydney: Oxford University Press) pp. 293–306.

Daily, C. M., Dalton, D. R., and Canella, A. A. (2003) 'Corporate Governance: Decades of Dialogue and Data', *The Academy of Management Review*, 28(3), pp. 371–82.

Degeling, P., Kennedy, J. and Hill, M. (1998) 'Do Professional Sub-Cultures set the Limits of Hospital Reform?' *Clinician in Management*, 7(2), pp. 89–98.

Degeling, P., Sorensen, R., Maxwell, S., Aisbett, C., Zhang, K. and Coyle, B. (2000) 'The Organization of Hospital Care and its Effects' (Sydney: Centre for Clinical Governance Research, The University of New South Wales).

Degeling, P., Maxwell, S., Kennedy, J. and Coyle, B. (2003) 'Medicine, Management and Modernisation: A "Dance Macabre"?' *British Medical Journal*, 326, pp. 649–52.

Degeling, P., Maxwell, S., and Iedema, R. (2004) 'Restructuring Clinical Governance to Maximize its Development Potential' in A. Gray and S. Harrison (eds) *Governing Medicine: Theory and Practice* (Maidenhead: Open University Press), pp. 163–79.

Deleuze, G. (1995) *Negotiations* (New York: Columbia University Press).

Dent, M. (1998) 'Hospitals and New Ways of Organising Medical Work in Europe: Standardisation of Medicine in the Public Sector and the Future of Medical Autonomy' in C. Warhurst and P. Thompson (eds) Workplaces of the Future (Basingstoke: Macmillan) pp. 204–24.

Dent, M. and Whitehead, S. (2002) *Managing Professional Identities: Knowledge Performativity and the New Professional* (London: Routledge).

Donabedian, A. (1981) 'Criteria, Norms and Standards of Quality: What do they Mean?' *American Journal of Public Health*, 71(4), pp. 409–12.

Donaldson, L. J. and Gray, J. A. M. (1998) 'Clinical Governance: A Quality Duty for Health Organizations' *Quality in Health Care*, 7 (Suppl), pp. S37–S44.

Douglas, N. (2002) *Inquiry into Obstetric and Gynaecological Services at King Edward Memorial Hospital 1990–2000* (Perth: Minter-Ellison Lawyers).

Ducanis, A. J. and Golin, A. C. (1979) *The Interdisciplinary Health Care Team* (Germantown, Maryland: Aspen Systems Corporation).

Duckett, S. J. (2000) *The Australian Health Care System* (Melbourne: Oxford University Press).

Firth-Cozens, J. (1998) 'Celebrating Teamwork' *Quality in Health Care*, 7 (Suppl), pp. S3–S7.

Flynn, R. (2002) 'Clinical Governance and Governmentality' *Health, Risk and Society*, 4(2), pp. 155–73.

Flynn, R. (2004) 'Soft bureaucracy', Governmentality and Clinical Governance: Theoretical approaches to Emergent Policy, *Governing Medicine: Theory and Practice* (Maidenhead: Open University Press) pp. 11–26.

Foucault, M. (1976) 'Governmentality' *Instrumentation & Control Systems*, 6, pp. 5–21.

Gosling, A. S., Westbrook, J. I. and Braithwaite, J. (2003) 'Clinical Team Functioning and IT Innovation: A Study of the Diffusion of a Point-Of-Care Online Evidence System' *Journal of the American Medical Informatics Association*, 10, pp. 246–53.

Gray, A. (2004) 'Governing Medicine: An introduction' in A. Gray and S. Harrison (eds) *Governing Medicine: Theory and Practice* (Maidenhead: Open University Press) pp. 1–7.

Griffiths Report (1983) *NHS Management Enquiry* (London: HMSO).

Harris, M., Harris, R. D. and Lynne Johnstone, P. (2002) 'Working with Health Teams' in M. Harris and associates (eds). Managing Health Services: Concepts and Practice (Sydney, Philadelphia & London: MacLennan+Petty) pp. 123–44.

Hoff, T., Jameson, L., Hannan, E. and Flink, E. (2004) 'A Review of the Literature Examining Linkages between Organisational Factors, Medical Errors and Patient Safety' *Medical Care Research and Review*, 16(1), pp. 3–37.

Iedema, R., and Degeling, P. (2001) 'Quality of Care: Clinical Governance and Pathways' *Australian Health Review*, 24(3), pp. 12–15.

Iedema, R. (2003) *Discourses of Post-Bureaucratic Organization* (Amsterdam/Philadelphia: John Benjamins).

Iedema, R., Degeling, P., Braithwaite, J. and White, L. (2004) '"It's an Interesting Conversation I'm Hearing": The Doctor as Manager' *Organization Studies*, 25(1), pp. 15–34.

Iedema, R., Meyerkort, S. and White, L. (2005a) 'Emergent Modes of Work and Communities of Practice', *Health Services Management Research*, 18, pp. 13–24.

Iedema, R., Sorensen, R., Braithwaite, J., Flabouris, A. and Turnbull, E. (in 2005b) 'The Teleo-Affective Limits of End-Of-Life Care in the Intensive Care Unit', *Social Science and Medicine*, 60(4), pp. 845–57.

Irvine, D. (1997) 'The Performance of Doctors (1/2): Professionalism and Self-Regulation in a Changing World' *Bristish Medical Journal*, 314, pp. 1540/1631.

Irvine, D. (1999) 'The Performance of Doctors: The New Professionalism' *Lancet*, 353, pp. 1174–77.

Jorm, C. M. and Kam, P. C. A. (2004) 'Does the Culture of Medical Specialty Colleges and Professional Organizations Limit Adoption of a Patient Safety and Quality Agenda and the Implementation of Clinical Governance? Lessons from Camelot' *Journal of Health Services Research and Policy*, 9(4), pp. 248–51.

Kennedy, I. (2001) *The Bristol Royal Infirmary Inquiry* (London: Department of Health).

Kohn, L. T., Corrigan, J. M. and Donaldson, M. S. (1999) To Err is Human: Building A Safer Health System (Washington D. C.: National Academy Press).

Mickan, S. and Rodger, S. (2000) 'Characteristics of Effective Teams: A Literature Review' *Australian Health Review*, 23(3), pp. 201–8.

National Electronic Decision Support Taskforce (2002) *Electronic Decision Support for Australia's Health Sector* (Canberra: Commonwealth Department of Health and Ageing).

National Health Information Management Advisory Council (2001) *Health Online – A National Information Action Plan* (Canberra: Commonwealth Government of Australia).

New South Wales Health Department (2004) *The NSW Patient Safety Program: Technical Paper* (Sydney: NSW Health).

Nicholls, S., Cullen, R., O'Neill, S. and Halligan, A. (2000) 'Clinical Governance: Its Origins and Foundations' *Clinical Performance and Quality Health Care*, 8(3), pp. 172–8.

NSW Health Department (2004) *Providing the Best Health Care* (North-Sydney: NSW Health Department).

Packwood, T., Keen, J. and Buxton, M. (1991) Hospitals in Transition: The Resource Management Experiment (Oxford: Oxford University Press).

Queensland Department of Health (2003) 'Queensland Health: Leadership Development Framework' (Brisbane: Queensland Department of Health).

Roland, M., Campbell, S. and Wilkin, D. (2001) 'Clinical Governance: A Convincing Strategy for Quality Improvement?' *Journal of Management in Medicine*, 15(3), pp. 188–201.

Rose, N. (1999) *Powers of Freedom: Reframing Political Thought* (Cambridge: Cambridge University Press).

Ruchlin, H. S., Dubbs, N. L. and Callahan, M. A. (2004) 'The Role of Leadership in Instilling a Culture of Safety: Lessons from the Literature' *Journal of Health Care Management*, 49(1), pp. 47–58.

Runciman, W. B., Webb, R. K., Lee, R. and Holland, R. (1993) 'The Australian Incident Monitoring Study: System Failure – An Analysis of 2000 Incident Reports' *Anaesthetic Intensive Care*, 21(5), pp. 684–95.

Runciman, W. B., Webb, R. K., Helps, S. C., Thomas, E. J., Sexton, E. J., Studdert, D. M., and Brennan, T. A. (2000) 'A Comparison of Iatrogenic Injury Studies in Australia and the USA II: Reviewer Behaviour and Quality of Care' *International Journal for Quality in Health Care*, 12(5), pp. 379–88.

Runciman, W. B. and Moller, J. (2001) 'Iatrogenic Injury in Australia' (Canberra: Australian Patient Safety Foundation).

Safety and Quality Council (2003) *Open Disclosure Standard: A National Standard for Open Communication in Public and Private Hospitals following an Adverse Event in Health Care* (Canberra: Commonwealth of Australia).

Schatzki, T. (2002) *The Site of the Social* (University Park, Penn.: The Pennsylvania State University Press).

Senge, P. M. (1990) *The Fifth Discipline: The Art and Practice of the Learning Organisation* (Sydney: Random House).

Shortell, S. M., Zimmerman, J. E., Rousseau, D. M., Gillies, R. R., Wagner, D. P., Draper, E. A., Knaus, W. A. and Duffy, J. (1994) 'The Performance of Intensive Care Units: Does Good Management make a Difference?' *Medical Care*, 32(5), pp. 508–25.

Spurgeon, P. and Latham, L. (2003) 'Pursuing Clinical Governance through Effective Leadership.' in S. Doipson and A. L. Mark (eds) *Leading Health Care Organizations* (Basingstoke: Palgrave Macmillan) pp. 51–62.

Stoten, B. (1985) 'Health' in S. Ranson, G. Jones and K. Walsh (eds) *Between Centre and Locality: The Politics of Public Policy* (London: George Allen and Unwin).

The Australian Council on Healthcare Standards (1996) *The EQuIP Guide* (Sydney: The Australian Council on Healthcare Standards).

The 'Cogwheel' Reports (1967/1972/1974) *Reports of the Joint Working Party on the Organisation of Medical Work in Hospital* (London: HMSO).

Timmermans, S. and Berg, M. (2003) *The Gold Standard: The Challenge of Evidence-Based Medicine and Standardization in Health Care* (Philadelphia: Temple University Press).

Townley, B., Cooper, D. J. and Oakes, L. (2003) 'Performance Measures and the Rationalization of Organizations' *Organization Studies*, 24(7), pp. 1045–71.

U. K. Department of Health (1997) *The New NHS: Modern, Dependable* (London: The Stationary Office).

US Institute of Medicine (2001) *Crossing the Quality Chasm: A New Health System for the 21st Century* (Washington: National Academy Press).

Vecchi, L. (2003) *Summary of Health Service Reviews: Patient Safety and Clinical Governance* (Melbourne: Peter MacCallum Cancer Centre).

Wade, M. (2004) *Commentary on the Bret Walker Interim Report of the Special Commission of Inquiry into the Death at Camden and Campbelltown Hospitals in Sydney* (Sydney: Findlaw.com).

Walker, B. (2004a) *Interim Report of the Special Commission of Inquiry into Deaths at Camden and Campbelltown Hospitals (31 March)* (Sydney: Special Commission of Inquiry into Camden and Campbelltown Hospitals).

Walker, B. (2004b) *Final Report of the Special Commission of Inquiry into Deaths at Camden and Campbelltown Hospitals (31 July 2004)* (Sydney: Special Commission of Inquiry into Camden and Campbelltown Hospitals).

Walsh, K. (1995) *Public Services and Market Mechanisms: Competition, Contracting and the New Public Management* (Basingstoke: Macmillan).

Weekley, E. (1967) *An Etymological Dictionary of Modern English* (New York: Dover Publications).

Weick, K., and Roberts, K. H. (1993) 'Collective Mind in Organizations: Heedful Interrelating on Flight Decks' *Administrative Science Quarterly*, 38, pp. 357–81.

Westbrook, J., Braithwaite, J., Iedema, R. and Coiera, E. (2004) 'Evaluating the Impact of Information Communication Technologies on Complex Organizational Systems: A Multi-Disciplinary, Multi-Method Framework' poster presented at MedInfo 2004, San Franscisco, submission date 15 Sep 2003.

Western Australian Department of Health (2003) *Clinical Governance Guidelines* (Perth: Western Australian Department of Health).

Wilson, R., Runciman, W. B., Gibberd, R. W., Harrison, B., Newby, L. and Hamilton, J. (1995) 'The Quality in Australian Health Care Study' *The Medical Journal of Australia*, 163(9), pp. 458–71.

Wilson, R., Harrison, B. T., Gibberd, R. W. and Hamilton, J. D. (1999) 'An Analysis of the Causes of Adverse Events from the Quality in Australian Health Care Study' *The Medical Journal of Australia*, 170(9), pp. 411–15.

13
E-health Services: Is the Future of Australia's Health Service Work in Offshore Outsourcing?

Jan Sinclair-Jones

Introduction

This chapter outlines findings from interviews conducted between 1999 and 2004 with the chief executive officers (CEOs) and directors of operations of offshore outsourcing organizations supplying health sector related work in Bangalore, India. These case studies consider established instances of relocation of health sector related work from the USA to India and are considered in the context of two associated developments: the shift towards introduction, or increased levels, of outsourcing of health sector service work in the United States of America (USA) and their relocation internationally, in the form of tele-mediated work.[1] The chapter attempts to identify some of the connections between the trends to commodification and outsourcing and offshoring of health sector services which are becoming increasingly well established in the USA and in doing so raises issues of relevance to similar areas of the health sector workforce in Australia.[2]

As Young (2000) notes, the reasons why organizations choose to outsource productive and business functions are various and complex and range across a spectrum from basic cost-cutting to the nuances of labour market flexibility. The outcomes are such, however, that in its annual review of Australia's top 500 public companies, *Business Review Weekly* (Thomson, 2004) identified the 'impressive result' in profits posted in the first half of 2004 as less a result of increased revenues than of cost-cutting in relation to labour costs and costs of supplies and went on to identify outsourcing of 'non-core but important' functions as the most popular model in achieving such cuts.

This trend towards outsourcing is significant on a global scale. The benefits to capital of 'flexible production' were powerfully identified in the secondary sector throughout the 1980s and 1990s as a strong connection was established between: the industrial ability to downsize, relocate, outsource, streamline (just in time) production; the breathtaking advances of micro-electronics and communications technologies; and the deregulation and expansion of the global economy (Harvey, 1990; James, Veit and Wright, 1997; Felstead and Jewson, 1999). As industrial corporations became familiar with the dynamic capacities of seemingly exponential change in communications technologies they identified and applied this potential to achieving the same benefits in the other parts of their organizations, or in other economic sectors. Throughout the 1980s and 1990s in Britain, the USA, Australia and elsewhere, populist arguments for the reduction of 'big government' as well as increased pressure towards the privatization of the public sector contributed towards growing attractiveness of outsourcing as a solution to 'burgeoning' costs in the public sector (see Leys, 2001). The trend towards outsourcing, as well as privatization of tertiary sector public activities, occurred within a context of both an ideological acceptance of these strategies as rational solutions to cost curtailment, and massive growth in technological capacity.

This discussion provides some illustrations of the ways in which the initial outsourcing of particular services in the USA's health sector has been facilitated by advances in information and communications technologies (ICTs) and, more particularly, how these changes have enabled the partial offshoring of some of these forms of work. The case studies relate to medical transcription, medical coding and bill processing, as well as the high-end service of radiological consultation and interpretation. Whilst, with the exception of radiology, these kinds of services are not exactly replicated in the Australia health sector, there are similarities to forms of Australian health sector work and health insurance organization that make them relevant in a discussion of the impact of outsourcing upon future patterns of work in the sector. There has been some examination of the impact of outsourcing upon some sections of the Australian health sector workforce and workplace change (see for example, Young, 2002), but outsourcing of business processes in the health sector is such a recent Australian phenomenon that little, if any, research has been conducted to date. This is then, a cautionary tale which illustrates potential developments in Australia and identifies the necessity for vigilance and research by those interested in the structure of the Australian health sector workforce.

The Indian IT industry

The ways in which ICT developments have enabled relocation of service sector work, (particularly call centre work) across the globe are widely recognized. Governments and politicians in the USA, Britain and Australia, are now confronted with popular and trade union concerns about the relocation of call centre and other Information Technology (IT) services.[3]
Throughout the 1990s India became recognized as the prime source of highly skilled IT specialist labour. In the initial stages this was mostly in the form of Indian software engineers hired by American and European companies as visiting workers (body shopping) (see Lohr, 2004); subsequently transnational corporations and Indian companies, such as Wipro and Infosys, invested in establishing facilities in the sub-continent itself (Patibandla and Petersen, 2002). Whilst software and software services exports are still the prime IT export earner of the Indian economy, job growth has occurred in associated areas, particularly in the IT enabled services-business process outsourcing (ITES-BPO) industry.[4] Commentators have recently begun to identify health services as an area of strong growth in Indian ITES-BPO services (NASSCOM, 2004c; Singh, 2003; Subramanyan, 2003a).

The medical transcription industry

In the late 1990s, medical transcription drew attention as the prime potential area of growth in BPO health services. Medical transcription is the process of transcribing medical records and details of every patient encounter with a doctor. With the application of word processing technology these records are converted by the medical transcriptionist into digital format and become part of a patient's medical record (see the Bureau of Labor Statistics (BLS, 2004d) for a more detailed account of this form of work). The medical transcription industry is a significant industry in the USA – reportedly worth about $15 billion per annum (Risen, 2004, p. 10). Estimates of employment vary, but the BLS (2004a; b) estimates around 100,800 transcriptionists with a predicted growth rate between 2002–12 of about 22 per cent. In part, the growth in demand for medical transcription in the USA has been driven by the insurance industry as it has sought to reduce the incidence of inaccurate or fraudulent litigation. Employment arrangements in the medical transcription industry are varied (in-house and home-based employees, subcontractors, self employed and independent contractors), but it is marked by a significant degree of outsourcing to both small and large service providers (BLS, 2004a; HayGroup, 1999). Medical transcriptionists in the USA are generally post-secondary trained and have frequently gained certification through the American Association for Medical Transcription (AAMT). However, certification is not an essential criterion for employment.

The extent to which medical transcription occurs as a standard form of patient record keeping in Australia is unclear. Searches by the author have failed to identify any reference to it as formal practice by Australian hospitals or medical practices. Medical professionals do use electronic technologies, such as micro-recorders, to record consultations, diagnostic reports and referrals, for example, and these generally seem to be transcribed by direct employees. However, one informant in the case studies reported doing transcription for an Australian hospital and there are Australian BPO provider websites claiming to provide transcription services to Australian hospitals, clinics, medical private practices and orthodontists (see for example, Pacific Outsourcing Solutions and Syberscribe Pty Ltd.) Again, there is a need for research into these services to establish the tendencies and extent of such outsourcing in Australia.

Medical transcription in India

The examples of a few successful Indian medical transcription companies in the 1990s led to great anticipation amongst small Indian operators that opportunities to tap into the USA's industry were limitless. Although by the early 2000s many of these organizations had faltered for a variety of quality and management-related issues, other companies moved from strength to strength. The success of companies such as Healthscribe India, a subsidiary of the USA transcription provider Healthscribe, has illustrated the ways in which offshore relocation can be extraordinarily successful.

Established as an outsource medical transcription service provider in the USA in the early 1990s, Healthscribe took advantage of the new IT capacity to digitize doctors' recordings of patient encounters. This digitization enabled electronic transfer of voice files with the result that medical transcription could be performed at any distance from its point of generation. Rather than being reliant on pools of labour in large expensive cost of living cities, Healthscribe used this flexibility to send the files to workers in a range of locations, thus taking advantage of cheaper domestic regional labour sources. This capacity to shift work regionally only briefly preceded its relocation offshore and in 1994 the organization established Healthscribe India in Bangalore, employing a small number of university graduates, and using specially designed training programmes trained them as transcriptionists (Sinclair-Jones, 2000).

Estimates of the number of medical transcriptionists employed by BPO providers in India are loose, a 1999 study by McKinsey estimated about 6000 workers (India Infoline, 2004), but one case study informant suggests that it would currently be at least 25,000. If we accept the lower estimate, this represents about six per cent of the estimated current levels of medical transcriptionists (100,800) employed in the USA (see above). The strong predicted growth in the employment of medical transcriptionists in the USA (22 per cent from 2002–12) suggests that the establishment of offshore providers is not anticipated to contribute to absolute job losses. However, the BLS (2004a) does acknowledge that this job growth will be supplemented by offshore provision.

Indian medical transcription providers cite a number of factors as contributing to their success; for example, shortage of labour supply in the USA, abundant highly skilled labour in India, time delay advantages, cheaper infrastructure and so on. However, it is undoubtedly the case that the prime advantage to medical transcription providers in India is the wage differential between the Indian worker and their USA counterparts – it is generally estimated to be a differential of about one to eight.[5] The extent to which this cost saving is passed back to the customer varies–one informant stated that the rate in the USA is about 15 cents per line whilst work done from India is generally charged at about six cents per line. Organizations with operations in both countries reportedly charge the higher rate for all the work regardless of the location of the service provider. Nevertheless, even where Indian suppliers charge the lowest rate, the significantly lower labour costs ensure high rates of profit.

A more recent significant development in the relationship between the USA health sector and its offshore provision is related to the transcription process. Medical coding and billing is the next stage of administration of insurance payments and healthcare organizations' receipts.

Medical coding and billing

The particular pattern of health provision in the USA has given rise to expansion in another form of health service administrative work – that of bill coding and processing. According to Singh (2003), profitability across much of the USA healthcare sector has been severely troubled over the past decade. In particular, the insurance industry reportedly had only a two per cent average profit margin in 2002 and 'profitability of U.S. hospitals fell from 6.1 per cent six years ago to 2.8 per cent in 2002' (Singh, 2003).

It is estimated that approximately 85 per cent of the population of the USA has some form of medical insurance.[6] After treatment of an insured patient the healthcare professional or hospital generally bills the insurer directly. Until the early 1990s 'insurance companies ... reimbursed all expenses as detailed by doctors' but the crisis of profitability saw the insurance companies tie payment directly to only those procedures which could be accurately 'verified by [standardised] coding' of both the diagnosis and treatment (Singh, 2003). In this way insurance companies have developed the ability to ensure that bills relate to appropriate forms of treatment and procedures for the diagnosis made, thus reducing the amount of disputation and apparent 'fraud due to overstating of expenses' (Singh, 2003).

Large healthcare organizations and hospitals employ medical coders and billers to maintain records and prepare accounts for distribution to insurers and patients. It does seem that the new stringency associated with the coding, as well as with coding guidelines for the electronic transfer of patient records set out under the Health Insurance Portability and Accountability Act (HIPAA) 1996 legislation,[7] has given rise to an expansion of the need for medical coders and billers.[8] In 2002 USA employment in the entire category of medical records and health information technicians was estimated to be about 123,000 with a predicted growth rate of about 52 per cent from 2002–12 (BLS, 2004c). Whilst accurate estimates of the size of the USA market for such services are not available, some actors in the industry estimate it to be at least $50 billion (Subramanyam, 2003a).

Since compulsory compliance with HIPAA guidelines in 2003, the associated increased complexity seems to have become a strong marketing advantage for outsourcing agencies (see for example, Doctor's shopper, 2004). Hospitals have tended to adopt a mixture of operating systems over the years and HIPAA compliance has meant that managing information across these systems has become hugely complex (Singh, 2003). The growing complexity has attracted many doctors and hospitals to move towards reliance upon outsource providers to complete this task, thus transforming an in-house administrative procedure into a service commodity. Developments in Information

Communications Technologies have facilitated the process of electronic transfer of coding sheets and patient records. In some cases the outsource provider supplies the chain of services from transcription, through coding to bill issuing, processing and receipting, in others the coding and processing alone may be done. Once outsourced, the possibility of the work being further relocated offshore is magnified. Individual medical practices and hospital administrators may not have the time, interest or expertise to directly seek out offshore outsource providers, however, the benefits to domestic outsource providers in establishing links with a further chain of production overseas can be significant.

Labour supply issues in the USA may also be a significant compulsion to initial outsourcing. The high rates of predicted job growth noted above suggest that demand for such workers is strong and turnover may be high. As with transcriptionists, training is post-secondary. Most employers seek workers with American Health Information Management Association (AHIMA) certification, but it is not mandatory (BLS, 2004d; Danni, 2004). One Indian supplier of these services noted that:

> ... we've just started a group of 30 doctor practices in Mississippi. ...The only reason they're coming to us, [via the USA based outsourcing agency]- not cost reduction–is because they are fed up with trying to recruit people and the long recruitment process, training and losing them. They're just fed up with it. So they basically said. 'You handle it, we don't want to know anymore.' And it's nothing to do with cost reduction.

Outsourcing has not been a long standing phenomenon in the Australian health insurance industry but is beginning to gain momentum. In 1999 the IT&T infrastructure services of the Health Insurance Commission (HIC) and the Department of Aged and Health Care were jointly outsourced to IBM Global Services Australia (IBM GSA) for a contract value of more than $350 million over five years with a predicted saving to the public purse of $54 million. One of the outcomes was that Medibank Private Limited also negotiated an outsourcing contract with IBM GSA for data processing services previously provided by the HIC. The announcement referred to 'strict privacy, security and confidentiality arrangements, including the application of the *Privacy Act*' and emphasised the government's determination 'to use outsourcing to promote the growth and development of the

Australian IT&T industries ...' (Department of Finance, 1999). In recent years the Australian private health insurance industry has been subject to strong criticism for its inefficiencies in terms of administration costs, outdated IT processes and over-reliance upon manual claims processing (Cant, 2002; Industry Commission 1997; National Office of the Information Economy, 2001 pp. 32–3). In September 2002 one of Australia's medium sized private health insurance funds, Grand United Friendly Society, announced a joint venture with a South African business process and IT consulting and outsourcing company. The media release announcing this new venture, HealthSource Australia, declared that it had been established as a 'complete back office processing solution' outsourcing organization to offer '...high-volume claim processing for multiple funds' (HealthSource, 2002).[9] Given government pressures to improve efficiencies in order to reduce costs and limit cost of premiums it is quite probable that outsourcing will become a strong option in the industry.

Medical billing and coding in India

In the cases of two Indian organizations already established in this business in Bangalore, both are providing services to USA outsourcing agencies. In early 2004 each of these organizations' involvement in this process was very recent: one had been established 18 months earlier specifically to access this sector of the USA market and the other, a large medical service and hospital chain, expanded into the field in late 2003. At least two other organizations in India have been working in the area for at least eight years and a number of other companies, including Healthscribe India, are expanding in to the field (Singh, 2003; Subramanyam, 2003b).

In the first case the organization had been established to provide transcription and coding services by an English businessman with long-standing experience as CEO of a large Indian medical transcription organization. For this businessman the recognition that bill coding, and ultimately processing, generates a higher return than transcription was critical: he stated that the organization earns four to five times more an hour on coding than on transcribing. The second organization is part of an existing Indian medical services and hospital chain which has expanded into the coding and processing arena. In early 2004 this organization was employing 40 coders and processors but was planning expansion to 120–130 within the next two months. A third organization, Healthscribe India, discussed above, was planning to expand its operations into coding and billing in order to take advantage of offering an integrated service (see also, Subramanyam, 2003a).

As with medical transcription, lower labour costs in India undoubtedly contribute to the profitability of medical coding and billing suppliers in India: according to one informant, coders in India earn around 288,000 rps (approx. US $7200) per annum compared to a range of between $33,000 to $41,500 in the USA.[10] However, the form of remuneration for these services presents suppliers with wider opportunities for marketing their services to USA clients as well as expanding profit margins.

One informant pointed out that where a supplier provides coding and bill processing services their charges are frequently based upon a proportion of receipts rather than on quantity of service provided: if billings can be increased both the customer and supplier benefit. He noted that coding and billing processes in many organizations are poorly developed and inefficient and stated that for his organization, which markets through an outsourcing agent in the USA, its major marketing strength has been to convince healthcare organizations that they can actually increase the amounts billed and received, thus ensuring increases in revenue. Bill coding becomes a value adding service. Given that insurance companies will only pay for procedures coded, this organization markets its services by offering a greater intensity of billing than their competitors by ensuring that for every event of treatment the full set of procedures are charged. For example, where a doctor omits to record the use of necessary analgesia for a minor procedure the coding company identifies the omission, follows up with the doctor and ensures that it is billed. This informant noted the example of his company's first client (a 300 bed hospital in the USA), that at the start of the contract in 2003 had $14 million of un-coded billings which by early 2004 had been reduced to $1.7 million (that is, $12.3 million increase in potential revenue). He saw this as the particularly significant advantage of Indian outsource companies in that the sub-continent not only has an abundance of highly skilled English speaking labour able to be trained as coders, but it also has the edge on development of IT expertise and procedures which can streamline these processes and overcome the fragmented systems currently in operation. He went on to argue that the IT expertise in India offers a huge potential for marrying the ability to develop new creative processes with labour supply as a particular combination of competitive advantage.

Another informant argued that in both the cases of transcription and bill coding and processing, the actual costs relative to other areas of running costs, such as health professionals' salaries, diagnostics and so on, were not significant enough to drive individual administrators to seek lower costs through outsourcing. However, given the trend towards consolidation and concentration of ownership of hospitals and healthcare providers, these line items begin to represent large expenditures and are significant to draw the attention of chief financial officers (CFOs) seeking to cut costs. In these cases, where an outsource provider can pass on to the client part of the benefits of reduced costs associated with offshoring, the reduction becomes significant and is a marketing advantage.

This informant went on to suggest that, in the case of coding, the benefits to clients were more than merely reduced service costs. He pointed out that insurance companies take some time to pay – 30 to 60 to 90 days. For small healthcare organizations the issue of outstanding billings relates predominantly to funds turnaround and cash flows but in the large corporate healthcare organization outstanding billings are significant in relation to overall profitability. Here, turnaround time between transcription, coding and billing and receipting involves large sums of money. The informant argued that by offshoring the coding and processing the advantage of time difference between the USA and India means that time between service and billing can be reduced, especially if the processes are streamlined such that one company does all three. By reducing this time, even by 24-hours, healthcare organizations can feasibly receive payments a day earlier – a day's interest on such sums of money are really significant in the eyes of a CFO.

A third informant acknowledged advantages of cheap labour supply and time differences, but emphasized the benefits of work practice and 'work ethic' amongst Indian employees. He noted that in his organization employees worked a six day week; were willing to work longer hours when required in order to meet deadlines or uneven flows of work; and were willing to work night shifts. He also identified the advantage of his organization's provision of both coding and bill processing through to receipts. The informant argued that the processes in his organization were set up in ways which ensured that outstanding billings were monitored much more closely than in comparative organizations in the USA: as soon as a bill is outstanding, processing staff in this organization phone the insurance company in the USA to follow up the account. In this way, the turnaround time and receipt of monies can be kept to a much tighter timeframe which is relevant in terms of organizations with large accounts for whom delays in receipts have a significant revenue implication.

Thus, according to these service providers, whilst cost reduction is a marketing edge, and the massive difference in labour costs makes the investment in the service in India attractive to the organization providing the service, it is not the only driving force of shifting the work offshore. Increased revenues make the service attractive to the USA outsourcing agent and their clients.

Teleradiology

The application of new ICTs to clinical medical and health services has been far more contentious than in the arena of health information services. Whilst there have been significant innovations in recent years in the use of ICTs to develop telehealth services, particularly to remote areas, there has been limited extension of such telemedicine services into the commercial arena. Interestingly radiology services were some of the first services to be outsourced to private providers as non core services in some sectors of Australian hospital services in the 1990s, however these services were still provided on-site (see Young, 2002). Doctors have tended to vigorously resist the suggestion that competent medical consultation and diagnosis can be performed at a distance from the patient and have argued that on-line consultations are fraught with problems.[11] Nevertheless, developments in digital technologies have laid the foundations of possibility for the commercialization of some remote procedures. Teleradiology is perhaps the most advanced of these. In large hospitals in particular, digital technologies are increasingly the form in which radiological and ultrasound diagnostics are captured, interpreted, recorded and stored. In this way a radiologist can be located in-house, or, as has become increasingly the case in the USA, located in an outsourced radiology group practice.

The technology has enabled outsourcing to radiology groups as a means of complementing hospital-based services. This occurs, for example, in the case of small hospitals that do not require the full time services of a radiologist. Similarly, large hospital emergency departments in the USA have moved towards employing radiology groups to provide night services on call. Radiology group practices roster members to be on call at night or weekends and each member has a broadband connection at home from which they can read scans and transmit reports. In some groups it became more efficient for one radiologist in the group to be rostered on all night and cover a number of hospitals and then take a day off. By the late 1990s, this more productive way of operating gave rise to the practice of 'nighthawk delivery services' in which some radiology groups specialize in specific night and weekend services. In these practices it is common for individual radiologists to be employed simply as night workers, usually working seven nights on and then seven nights off, for a full-time salary.

Initially the distance between hospital and such service providers grew only to take advantage of the time difference across the USA, where, for example, a radiologist on the west coast could work a staggered shift providing a service to hospitals on the east coast. This development drew attention to the possibility of radiologists on the other side of the world working during the day and providing nighthawk services to hospitals in the USA. Sydney based Nighthawk Radiology Services, established in 2001, is purported to be the first of such organizations. Since then other services have been established in at least Israel (Luce, Merchant and Roberts, 2003) and most recently, Bangalore, India.

The structural limits to large-scale international relocation of such operations are however, rather more complex than the relocation of transcription, coding and bill processing. Companies providing the latter from India have developed on site Health Insurance Portability and Accountability Act (HIPAA) compliant training programmes for all their operatives, but there are no issues of licensing and registration. However, practice restrictions for doctors are far more stringent. In order for a radiologist to be able to provide a service to a hospital or radiology group in the USA they must have three levels of qualification: first, they must be a registered radiologist in the USA; secondly, they must be licensed by the state in which the hospital is located; and thirdly, they must be credentialed by the hospital to which they are providing the service. In effect, such restrictions ensure that only doctors who have gained registration in the USA can work for such services.

Teleradiology in India

In this case study, an Indian radiologist, trained in New Delhi then specialized and worked at Yale. For family reasons he returned to live in India and spent some time commuting between the USA and India before deciding to settle permanently in Bangalore. In the process of transferring from Yale and establishing his consultancy and practice at a state of the art hospital in Bangalore this informant convinced colleagues at Yale to trial teleradiology. This involved the informant in Bangalore providing readings, in parallel with a colleague at Yale – the informant working during the day and his American colleague during the night. The trial, of 100 scans over a period of one month, found no significant discrepancy between the interpretations, with a slightly better turnaround time result for the specialist in India (Kalyanpur, Weinberg, Neklesa, Brink and Forman, 2003). The informant has since established his own successful nighthawk service (see Pollack, 2003). In February 2004 he had one partner in Bangalore, and was looking for another. They provide a service to about 30 hospitals in the USA, reading about 100 scans a day with a turnaround time of less than 40 minutes.

This case of international emergency teleradiology differs from the above examples of transcription and bill coding and processing in that it has not been primarily established with the direct intention of commercial expansion and extension of the market and service. Rather, the personal interests of the individuals performing the work have drawn this relocation. Indeed the radiologists involved must still carry the extremely high costs of medical liability insurance in the USA. They do, of course, gain some personal cost of living advantage from being located in Bangalore and they do need to use this advantage in order to market their services. The informant pointed out that he must charge marginally less than USA-based radiology groups in order to draw the business offshore. He argued that the real benefit to hospitals lies in outsourcing generally as hospitals can 'avoid a whole bunch of ancillary payments – you know, social security, Medicare, health insurance, pension, none of those things is there…'.

The informant argued strongly that, as a medical service, the issues of quality and risks of malpractice are so great that it is not viable for such a service to expand into a large commercial operation.

> There's a huge malpractice risk, you know you're basically providing a medical service, you mess up and you've got a lawsuit on your hands a million dollar lawsuit is not a joke. There's a different issue if a transcribed report goes out half an hour late or has a little typo in it – here a patient's life is on the line and so this whole model of scaling it up and making it into a 500 radiologist thing is just not feasible, practical, or safe.

However, it does seem that some form of commercial emergency radiology services is possible, even if rather smaller or more limited than envisaged above. Nighthawk Radiology Services, the Sydney based organization, currently lists 21 radiologists on its web page (Nighthawk Radiology Services, 2004). In another example, Pollack (2003) outlines the case of an arrangement between Massachusetts General Hospital and the Indian company Wipro Ltd in which 12 Indian based and trained radiologists 'receive scans electronically and provide interpretations to Wipro-employed licensed radiologists in the USA, who in turn consult with the client radiologist'.[12] Given that USA radiologists earn around $250,000 per annum and Wipro pays its Indian radiologists between $30,000 and $100,000 per annum it is able to provide its services for about half the cost of an organization operating wholly within the USA.

The reasons for outsourcing of radiology services from the USA seem to be strongly associated with labour supply at a time when demand for its services are expanding both in quantity and temporally (see Pollack, 2003). The informant identified a number of reasons for this shortage in supply.

> ... one is that the technology has developed very fast, evolved very fast so that the scanners have become much faster and more efficient and so the same scan that it would take half an hour to do in the past can now be done in less than three minutes ...so the number of scans being done has gone up like this ... [he indicated an exponential rise]. We estimate an increase of 40 per cent per year over a three year period from 98 to 2000 so it's huge. On top of that the population in the USA is also getting older and people are having more medical problems. People are having more scans than they used to. The utilization has also increased because that's one thing about radiologists is we go around doing all this research which shows we can diagnose this for you, we can diagnose that for you. Next thing you know you are woken up three or four times a night to make the same diagnosis, because two years ago it wasn't even happening, because you couldn't do it with radiology.

Thus, the accelerated capacities of the technology have increased the absolute number of scans for which the expensive machinery can be used, advances in diagnostic medical science have increased the number of scans required in any one diagnosis and the diagnostic pressures of an ageing population have increased demand for radiology services.

Conclusion

In each of these cases of offshore relocation of health sector work, the relocation to date has been enabled by the establishment of a service in India that has been successfully marketed to customers in the USA. In the cases of medical transcription and coding and billing services from India the service is purchased by an intermediary (an established transcription or billing agency). In the case of teleradiology, services are supplied directly to the hospitals using the service. The consistent factor in all of these cases is the increasing tendency of USA healthcare organizations to outsource these services. This capacity to outsource has unequivocally been facilitated by ICT developments that enable rapid transfer of information across any range of distance.

The imperatives to initial outsourcing are obviously complex. It does seem that in the cases of medical transcription, and coding and billing, the pressures from the health insurance industry and associated legislation, have increased the demand for such services at the same time as healthcare organizations have been suffering a crisis of profitability. Furthermore, institutional and legal requirements have contributed to a greater complexity in the performance of these services. The attraction of outsourcing such administratively 'time hungry' service functions to a specialist agency must be strong, even for administrators of fairly small organizations.

All of the informants referred to labour supply issues in the USA as contributing to the attraction of outsourcing. Difficulties of recruitment and shortage of labour supply contribute to the incentive for outsourcers to send work to India where there is an abundant supply of skilled English speaking labour. The vast differences in the cost of labour contribute to the viability of the operations but are not the only factor. Further marketing attributes which enhance value added appear to be real advantages in the highly competitive world of outsourcing.

Throughout all of the studies discussed here, the initial outsourcing in the source country is the primary occurrence and the space in to which offshore providers can move. Once a service is commodified and outsourced to a specialist agency, the service becomes that agency's core business and cutting costs of production directly affects its profits – the incentive to further outsource offshore becomes irresistible.

These cases illustrate the ways in which shifts to commodification of these services through outsourcing have provided spaces for the innovation of offshore relocation. The examples of work being both outsourced and sent offshore do not represent relocation of work from a static job market, but rather appear to be relocation of some of the expansion in the sector. In other words, employment growth in these sectors in the USA is not happening at the same rate as expansion of job opportunities overall; indeed it may be that growth is occurring disproportionately faster in the offshore destination.

These case studies have relevance for work in the Australian health sector. At the same time as labour economists project above average employment growth in the areas of health services, the slippage of at least some of this expansion into the international labour market should be acknowledged. In particular, the shift noted above, towards outsourcing of claims processing and other non-core processes in the health insurance industry, make such work enormously vulnerable to processes of de-skilling as well as relocation. This is not to say that particular destination countries will able to secure these jobs in the long term. The ease with which such work is relocated enables it to move to whichever destination is most viable at the time, especially as long as it is exchanged as a commodity and is dominated by 'middle' agent relationships where the risk is borne by the offshore supplier rather than the customer or agent in the source country. In both source and destination countries, once commodified and outsourced, secure employment becomes ever more precarious.

Notes

1. The term telemediated work refers to work in which relocation is enabled by the application of information and communications technologies.
2. I acknowledge that the term 'off-shoring', although popularly used to refer to such relocation in Australia the US and the UK, is regionally specific. For countries on the other continents of the globe international relocation is a more appropriate term. In the interests of clarity and given its accuracy in these cases, I use off-shoring as my preferred term.
3. See for example, "US lawmakers gang up against BPO to India", *The Economic Times Online*, 13 January 2004, http://economictimes.indiatimes.com, Prasun Sonwalkar, "UK authorities prepare to counter India's call centre challenge", *Hindustan Times*, 11 January 2004, http://www.hindustantimes.com/online, "Calls for government cooperation in offshoring solution", *The Contact Daily*, 15 January 2004, http://www.callcentres.net.
4. NASSCOM (National Association of Software and Service Companies) of India estimates that in 2003–4 employment in exports of ITES-BPO services, will approach a quarter of a million workers. Whilst US currently dominates the global spend in this market at 59% with Europe at 22%, the Asia Pacific region is the next largest market (see NASSCOM, 2004 a and b).
5. This ratio has been consistently quoted during interviews with different informants. The BLS (2004b) gives an median hourly rate of $13.26 which compared to informants quoted monthly earnings for an Indian operative of approx. 10–12,000rps per month is about a factor of 8.
6. The cover is usually provided through employee benefits from private insurers of through government programmes such as Medicaid and Medicare– see Centres for Medicare and Medicaid Services (2004a)
7. The Health Insurance Portability and Accountability Act of 1996 includes provision for establishment of 'national standards for electronic health care transactions and national identifiers for providers, health plans, and

employers. It also addresses the security and privacy of health data.' Centres for Medicare and Medicaid Services (2004b). See also US Dep't of Health & Human Services (2004).
8 See BLS (2004d) and R. Danni (2004) for descriptions of this occupation.
9 In May 2003, HealthSource announced the appointment of the former federal health minister, Michael Wooldridge, as its Chairman (Connors, 2003).
10 The BLS (2004d) cites median annual earnings in 2002 for medical records and health technicians as $23,890 – this category includes a broader range of work than coding and may account for the difference in estimates.
11 See for example Patty (2000), Stock (2000) and Minogue (2001).
12 Pollack (2003) explains that because of registration restrictions it can only provide a service 'converting two-dimensional images from scans into three-dimensional pictures that are more understandable to surgeons; that job is usually done by technicians in the USA.

References

Bureau of Labor Statistics, U.S. Department of Labor (2004a) 'Medical Transcriptionists' *Occupational Outlook Handbook, 2004–05 Edition*, http://www.bls.gov/oco/ (Accessed 10 May 2004).
Bureau of Labor Statistics, U.S. Department of Labor (2004b) 'May 2003 National Occupational Employment and Wage Estimates – Healthcare Support Occupations' *Occupational Employment Statistics* http://www.bls.gov/ (Accessed 11 May 2004).
Bureau of Labor Statistics, U.S. Department of Labor (2004c) 'Health Services' *Career Guide to Industries, 2004–05 Edition* http://www.bis.gov/oco/ (Accessed 10 May 2004).
Bureau Of Labor Statistics, U.S. Department Of Labor (2004d) 'Medical Records and Health Information Technicians' *Occupational Outlook Handbook, 2004–05 Edition* http://www.bls.gov/oco/ (Accessed 11 May 2004).
Cant, S. (2002) 'Sick Systems Plague the Health Funds' *The Age* (June 4), p. 7.
Centers for Medicare and Medicaid Services (2004a) http://www.cms.hhs.gov/medicaid/ and *Welcome to Medicaid* and *Medicare Information Resource* http://www.cms.hhs.gov/medicare/ (Accessed 17 May 2004).
Centers for Medicare and Medicaid Services (2004b) *The Health Insurance Portability and Accountability Act of 1996 (HIPAA)* http://www.cms.hhs.gov/ (Accessed 17 May 2004).
Connors, E. (2003) 'Wooldridge Joins Health Services Group' *Australian Financial Review* (29 May), p. 21.
The Contact Daily (2004) 'Calls For Government Cooperation in Offshoring Solution', (15 January) http://www.callcentres.net.
Danni, R. (2004) 'Medical Billing ad Coding Profession' http://www.thealli-need.com.
Department of Finance (1999) 'IT&T Boost for Health Agencies', Joint Media Release By Minister For Finance And Administration And Minister For Communications, Information Technology And The Arts (23 September) http://www.finance.gov.au/scripts/media.asp?table=MFA&Id=85.
Doctor's Shopper (2004) 'Bill of Health Services, Inc. – Outsourcing lets you Concentrate on your Patients' http://doctorsshopper.com/ (Accessed 7 May 2004).

The Economic Times Online (2004) 'US Lawmakers Gang up against BPO to India' (13 January) http://economictimes.indiatimes.com/.

Felstead, A. and Jewson, N. (eds) (1999) *Global Trends in Flexible Labour* (Houndsmill: Macmillan).

HayGroup (1999) *Compensation for Medical Transcriptionists* Report Prepared for the American Association Of Medical Transcriptionists (Modesto Ca.)

Harvey, D. (1990) *The Condition of Postmodernity* (Oxford: Basil Blackwell).

HealthSource (2002) 'New BPO Company will help Health Insurance Funds cut Costs' (30 September) http//www.Healthsource.com.au/.

India Infoline (2004) 'Introduction to I.T.Enabled Services' http://www.indian-infoline.com/.

Industry Commission (1997) *Private Health Insurance* Report No. 57 (Canberra: AGPS).

James, P., Veit, W. F. and Wright, S. (eds) (1997) *Work of the Future: Global Perspectives* (St Leonards: Allen & Unwin).

Kalyanpur, A., Weinberg, J., Neklesa, J., Brink, J. A. and Forman, H. P. (2003) 'Emergency Radiology Coverage: Technical and Clinical Feasibility of an International Teleradiology Model' *Emergency Radiology*, 10, pp. 115–8.

Leys, C. (2001) *Market Driven Politics: Neoliberal Democracy and the Public Interest*, (New York: Verso).

Lohr, S. (2004) 'High-End Technology Work – Not Immune to Outsourcing' *New York Times* (June 16) p. C2.

Luce, E., Merchant, K. and Roberts, D. (2003) 'Service Industries go Global' *The Financial Times* (20 August) p. 15.

Minogue, K. (2001) 'Doctor.Com – On-Line Medicos – The Pros and Cons' *The Daily Telegraph* (16 April) p. 94.

NASSCOM (2004a) 'Resource Centre: Indian IT Industry' http://www.nasscom.org/ (Accessed 6 May).

NASSCOM (2004b) 'IT Software and Services Market' http://www.nasscom.org/ (Accessed 8 July 2004).

NASSCOM (2004c) 'Indian Software and Service Exports' http://www.nasscom.org/ (Accessed 8 July 2004).

National Office of the Information Economy (2001) *National E-Commerce Scoping Study: Insurance@Risk* (Canberra).

Nighthawk Radiology Services (2004) 'Meet our Team of Experienced Radiologists' http://www.nighthawkrad.net/radiologists.htm (Accessed 18 May 2004).

Pacific Outsourcing Solutions http://www.pacificsolutions.com.au.

Patibandla, M. and Petersen, B. (2002) 'Role of Transnational Corporations in the Case of a High-Tech Industry: The Case of India's Software Industry' *World Development*, 30(9), pp. 1561–77.

Patty, A. (2000) 'Australia: Logging on for Free Visit to the Doctor' *Daily Telegraph*, (21 March) p. 14.

Pollack, A. (2003) 'Who's Reading Your X-Ray' *The New York Times* (16 November) p. 31.

Risen, C. (2004) 'Missed Target' *The New Republic* (2 February) p. 12.

Sinclair-Jones, J. (2000) 'E-Medicine and E-Work: The New International Division of Medical Labour?' *Annual Review of Health Social Sciences*, 10(1), pp. 19–30.

Singh, S. (2003) 'Cracking a Matrix' *Businessworld*, (15 September) http://www.businessworldindia.com/.

Sonwalkar, P. (2004) 'UK Authorities prepare to counter India's Call Centre Challenge' *Hindustan Times* (11 January) http://www.hindustantimes.com/.

Stock, S. (2000) 'AMA says Net Medicine puts Patients and Doctors at Risk' *The Australian* (15 May), p. 5.

Subramanyam, R. (2003a) 'Healthcare Sector finds BPO Pill a Heady Mix' *The Economic Times* (28 July) http://economictimes.indiatimes.com.

Subramanyam, R. (2003b) 'Healthcare BPO gets a Pep Pill' *The Economic Times* (24 July) http://economictimes.indiatimes.com.

Syberscribe (2004) http://www.syberscribe.com.

Thomson, J. (2004) 'Low Fat, High Profits' *Business Review Weekly* (29 April), pp. 50–1.

US Dep't of Health and Human Services (2004) *Office for Civil Rights – HIPAA* At http://www.hhs.gov/ocr/

Young, S. (2000) 'Outsourcing: Lessons from the Literature' *Labour and Industry*, 10(3), pp. 97–117.

Young, S. (2002) 'Outsourcing and Downsizing: Processes of Workplace Change in Public Health' *The Economic and Labour Relations Review*, 13(2), pp. 245–69.

14
Conclusion: Reflections on Past Healthcare Reform and Future Directions

Suzanne Young, Eileen Willis and Pauline Stanton

Introduction

The twelve chapters of this book highlight the massive changes that have occurred in the Australian healthcare sector since the early 1990s and their impact on the employment relationships of healthcare workers. In common with many other countries these changes have had a number of drivers, mostly linked to concerns over rising healthcare costs. Dramatic increases in information and changes in technology have led to increased demand and rising costs of both capital and medical services. At the same time consumers have higher expectations of access to the latest and the best techniques, and the ageing population has exerted pressure on service delivery and raised fears of unsustainable future costs. As Chapter 1 demonstrated, Australian state and federal governments have responded to these developments by placing an increased emphasis on attaining improvements in efficiency, productivity and effectiveness of healthcare delivery. They have done this largely through the introduction of neo-liberal policies with a focus on cost saving and a belief in the benefits of New Public Management. In the healthcare sector at the organizational level, decision making is strongly influenced by government policy. The government not only provides the majority of funding but also determines how it will be spent through its funding policies. Thus the actions of government impact directly on the employment relationships of those employed in these organizations. Also, as Chapter 2 demonstrates health employees are organized into a complex mix of professional and occupational groups that have their own histories, cultures and goals. All are key stakeholders in the system. These groups can act as a barrier to reform or as a conduit for more effective service delivery.

The responses of employers to change have differed within individual health organizations, different sections of the industry and different states. Similarly, health professionals, occupational groups and trade unions have also resisted or reacted differently to these changes. These responses have been highlighted in the case studies in Part Two of this book. However, the case studies still leave many questions unanswered. While we know that productivity in the Australian healthcare sector has increased since the early 1990s we do not know at what cost. The case studies suggest increased work intensification, demoralization and labour shortages in vital professional areas. They also demonstrate different impacts and responses from employers and workers in rural and metropolitan areas and between different occupational groups. The overall picture emerging is of a complex industry dominated by powerful groups and stakeholders often with different and competing interests.

Part Three of the book represents a search for new answers to old questions. These answers move away from a focus on efficiency and productivity and direct industrial relations changes, and instead explore more innovative ways of engaging staff through improved human resource management and leadership strategies involving communication, teamwork, and building of trust and commitment. In this view the focus is less on cost saving and more on a collaborative strategy enhancing quality and effectiveness of service delivery, although efficiency is a key idea underpinning evidence-based medicine and team work. However as many of the authors concede, such goals, no matter how worthy, are difficult to achieve in an industry dominated by professional rivalries, the vagaries of government and the high expectations of consumers.

In this final chapter first, we review various issues emerging out of the book as a whole, second, we identify outcomes that the contributors have highlighted, and finally we outline the emerging issues that we believe provide rich opportunities for future research in a challenging and dynamic industry.

Emerging themes

The healthcare industry is a labour intensive industry and one of the key challenges of the reform process is to change the way that healthcare work is carried out. One of the main strategies for dealing with this has been through industrial reform, specifically the introduction of enterprise bargaining, which has been adopted by Australian governments throughout the 1990s – the idea that workers will exchange their work practices for more money through local bargaining arrangements. However, as shown in Bray, Stanton, White and Willis in Chapter 3 it can be argued that despite a great deal of activity in most states public health sector enterprise agreements and industrial awards are still largely centrally determined and occupationally based. Factors contributing to this state of affairs include the reliance on government funding, the power of the trade unions and the political nature of the healthcare sector. This does not mean that workplace change has not taken place – it has – there is a great deal of evidence of increased productivity, flexibility and change in work practices. In many areas such as medical science and catering and cleaning, less staff are doing more work. There have also been attempts to break down demarcation barriers between the professions through the use of multidisciplinary 'care plans' and critical pathways. However, these changes have largely taken place outside of the enterprise bargaining process, in particular through outsourcing and privatization, budget cuts and the introduction of new forms of funding. Chapters by Young, Bray and White, and Willis and Weekes have demonstrated in practice how these changes have been introduced and how they have often strengthened managerial prerogative and control at the local level, whilst reducing the power of workers and associated unions.

However, the employee response to these developments cannot be under estimated albeit occurring more centrally. Trade unions have responded by using the enterprise bargaining process to claw back some of the gains made by employers in other areas. The Australian Nursing Federation (ANF) has also managed to utilize the enterprise bargaining process to build union membership and to extend the scope of bargaining. The union has sought to capitalize on the reform process by pushing the professional agenda; for example in the move towards Nurse Practitioners. Both nursing and medicine have benefited from strong unionization, but their central role in the delivery of healthcare is what gives the union leverage. While nurses represent the largest section of healthcare workers, doctors are the most powerful as they control the production process.

The impact on other health professions such as allied health workers is not so clear. There are certainly labour shortages for some professions such as pharmacists and radiographers, particularly in rural areas, which give them a certain amount of strength. In some states such as

Victoria an increase in union militancy has kept wages and conditions on a par with nurses, however, that has not been the case in South Australia where they have fallen behind, if not in financial remuneration, certainly in conditions of service. Perhaps the section of the health workforce that has been hit the hardest are those who provide the largely ancillary roles of cleaning, catering and portering. These groups, who do not provide a clinical service and are often seen to be expendable by employers, have been most affected by budget cuts. Overall, as the case studies suggest, while there has been significant reform over the last decade, the traditional division of labour in healthcare remains firmly intact.

It is also clear from the case studies that employers have utilized different strategies in metropolitan and rural locations. Duckett in Chapter 2 claims that there are different labour market conditions between metropolitan, rural and remote practices, in terms of the professions and remuneration as well as a higher ratio of general practitioners to patients in capital cities compared with rural and remote areas. In terms of managerial practices, in Chapter 4, Young notes that the nature of the rural labour market was important in managers' decisions about what services to outsource with problems in rural areas of recruiting and retaining specialist staff and the geographical distances making it difficult to bring in expertise at short notice. Inpatients at rural health organizations typically suffered from illnesses with less complexity and those patients with more complex illnesses were transferred to metropolitan health organizations. This meant that in some rural areas the complexity of tests in radiology, pathology and surgery were less thus making different demands on the skill level of employees. De Ruyter in Chapter 5 gives examples of an excess of nursing labour supply over demand in regional areas thus rendering it impossible for casual workers to obtain permanent work, which is opposite to the situation in metropolitan hospitals where supply is less than demand. It is interesting then that Bartram *et al.* conclude that in metropolitan and base hospitals (as opposed to district hospitals and community health centres) general functional managers such as directors of nursing and medical directors are not as concerned with, nor see the practical application of strategic human resource management as chief executive officers and human resource directors. For functional managers, human resource management is largely limited to a focus on recruitment and selection and training rather than linking people management practices to business outcomes. This suggests that within the larger organizations the human resource function is largely distant from key practitioners.

Another emerging issue from the case studies which has been largely ignored in the implementation of New Public Management practices is the use of a mix of emotional labour and technical process in the provision of care. A number of authors illustrate the importance of the caring role and of problems generated if the focus is purely on technical efficiency and profits. It is not simply that health workers now find themselves working longer hours, un-social shifts or more intensely. The complaint of these workers goes to the very heart of professional work. The 'product' of care workers – be they doctors, nurses or personal carers – is the healing or comforting self; any reform process that reduces the time for interaction or imposes a sequencing regimes on the delivery of care, impacts on the deep structures of the professional self – as healer. Until politicians and workforce planners realize this point, retention strategies, particularly for nurses, will continue to fail.

Interestingly, it has been the trade unions that have become aware that it is consumers who are the beneficiaries of good quality healthcare and the victims of poor service delivery. The ANF have used this in recent industrial campaigns and have appealed directly to the public promoting the union as defender of public services and good quality care. The union's strategy has involved closing beds rather than taking strike action, arguing that it has done this for patient safety thus stealing the high moral ground from the employers and winning the public to its side.

The feminized nature of the workforce has also had an effect on the types of strategies used and is an important factor in workforce planning, labour supply and demand for labour flexibility. For instance, contributors comment on the impact of feminization on workforce flexibility and the reduction in permanent full-time work, whether supply or demand driven, and the effect of the increased numbers of women graduating as medical practitioners. The on-going shortage of nurses continues to elude most workforce planners, and the feminization of medicine, particularly general practice has increased the costs of state supported medical education as the federal government moves to overcome this by funding three more medical schools in Australia at a time when the university sector is also under considerable financial strain.

Outcomes

Outcomes from the aforementioned approaches have been varied. First, selected chapters raise work intensification as a problem for nurses, which can be linked to the nursing profession's 'caring work ethic'. By and large, it is clear that right across the healthcare sector and across a variety of professions, the strategy of cost minimization has placed huge demands on the workforce, with intensification of work and role conflict between their administration and caring roles. Secondly, professional labour shortages has been commented upon by contributors, especially noteworthy in rural areas, and the case studies point to a number of strategies that have been used to address labour force shortages. The use of outsourcing of pathology and radiology, especially in rural areas, is discussed by Young. Duckett comments that the internationalization of pathology and radiology through e-medicine will impact on labour force requirements in the future. And Sinclair-Jones gives an extensive case study of the potential of off-shore outsourcing of radiology and medical transcription in solving the problems of recruitment and labour shortages. As she notes, this solution shifts the risk but leads also to precarious forms of employment on the home front. Thirdly, contributors raise flexibility of the workforce as an outcome. This is evident particularly in the nursing area with the use of agency workers and in non-clinical areas as an outcome of outsourcing. Linked to this, fourthly, is job broadening with contributors alluding to it as upskilling, deskilling or multitasking. Whatever name it is referred to, generally the sector has witnessed a change in the very nature of service work with many workers unable to balance the need for higher levels of technical or managerial work with the demands of caring. Fifthly, contributors comment on problems of loyalty, morale and commitment. Finally, due to problems of time or resources, or the temporary nature of employment, there has been a lack of education and professional development for healthcare workers, especially registered nurses in their need to upskill either in the use of new technology or to become nurse practitioners.

New strategies and directions

The importance of identifying new strategies and possible future directions is the underlying theme of Part Three. Various authors highlight possible individual strategies for emerging problems such as the role of 'nurse practitioner' as a method of addressing the shortage of medical practitioners in rural areas; in other states the idea of the generic health worker has been mooted. However, there are some larger underlying issues here. For example Dwyer and Leggat suggest that team work and participation in decision making, greater consultation and collaboration are innovative ways forward in attempting to decrease the power imbalance between the medical profession and others, and creating better practices that focus on quality care. However, this is sometimes harder to achieve in practice. Doctors and nurses often support hierarchical models of practice (maintaining power structures) which do not necessarily foster communication, participation or trust. Also increased managerial prerogative has often led to a lack of consultation and an increased focus on risk management, which is associated with surveillance and control, through both evidence-based medicine and the use of electronic technologies. Such approaches can lead to mistrust and suspicion and are not so easy to turn around. Despite these caveats it is possible that the new focus on quality and the search for best practice at the local level might prove to be a common goal for all players. However, as the chapters in this section illustrate this shift is not without its tensions. There remains a confluence of conflict of interests between the state, human resource managers, unions and health professionals.

Directions for future research

The contributors highlight a further set of lessons and sobering points that could be considered and used as a basis for further research. For example, problems of power imbalance between clinicians and managers will continue to impede change and innovation in the healthcare sector. Indeed, it is evident from the case studies that changes to processes only occurred when medical practitioners were involved, with the division of labour between medical and other workers still clearly defined. The strategies used have not challenged the existing power relationships and medical dominance remains intact. Hence structural and power impediments to change need to be overcome. A greater understanding of the roles and the relationships of clinicians and managers and the structures and processes that surround them is essential if change and innovation is to occur. For example the future of nurse practitioners goes well beyond solving the tensions between medicine and nursing to demand on-going commitment by the state to a reorganization of funding.

Deficient management skills, the lack of managerial inspiration and the need for management development are evident. Outsourcing, clinical governance, strategic human resource management, improved people management practices, education and professional development have been discussed as solutions. Governance problems in the Victorian health sector have also been highlighted recently in the popular press which points to a pressing need for further research into governance models. More systematic research needs to done in these areas.

Different approaches are evident between metropolitan and rural areas and decision makers and planners need to take the different needs and characteristics into account. There is a great deal of rhetoric from governments on this issue but again little systematic research undertaken.

The desire for a high performance work organization needs to concentrate on service delivery and the nature of the work. The success of team-based solutions depends on an understanding of the nature of the work and the way people work together in healthcare. We need to know what is working well and why. The focus on acute clinical and medical practice has lead to a dearth of resources for other areas, such as the community sector or changes to managerial practice. Yet it is often these sectors that are working in more innovative and dynamic ways, offering interesting solutions to the large more medically-orientated tertiary institutions.

The increasing focus on quality, which is evidence-based, has not necessarily highlighted the importance of the relationship between the carer and patient nor has it completely taken into account the patients' personal-care needs. The value of non-professional workers such as personal service assistants and cleaners has often been disregarded. However, their work is necessary as higher skill level workers spend more time on paper work and documentation.

The link between gender and the emotional nature of care is important in this sector and researchers need to take this into account. In this regard, retention strategies, broadening out from recruitment strategies, are needed to ensure that there is an adequate supply of labour. The research on strategic human resource practices within the industry is in its infancy however, this is an area that has much to offer the sector. Indeed, all contributors highlight the importance of 'people' in this sector and although increased and innovative use of technology is common, it is clear that it cannot be used without 'emotional' assistance. Linking this with strategic direction is an important dimension.

The mix of public and private sectors in the industry is also a particular feature of the Australian system that separates it out from other health systems such as the UK and USA. The public and private sectors operate alongside each other in the provision of services, structural arrangements and funding sources. The processes of the New Public

Management have seen an increase in privatization with a blurring of the lines between the two sectors. Little systematic work has been done in Australia to support the argument that privatization of public services results in reduced costs. While it may have resulted in reduced government expenditure, although even this is a moot point, the evidence from the USA would suggest that privatization leads to higher costs if GDP figures are used as a measure. In effect many of the current reforms are merely a means of shifting costs from the federal system to the state or the state to the consumer. Consumers may be one of the drivers of reform, but they are not necessarily winners. And even more importantly the link between privatization and improved quality is problematic.

In conclusion, decision makers in the healthcare sector have grappled with the pressure to increase competition and managerialism alongside a desire for increased collaboration, but problems have occurred due to the existence of powerful stakeholders and a division of labour impeding innovation and change. The current focus of reform has shifted from the 1990s that saw a marriage between New Public Management and industrial relations reform, to one that now focuses on strategic human resource management. For Australia there is a potential that the Free Trade Agreement with the United States of American will expand off-shore work and increase the deregulation of the professions and the healthcare sector leading to increased union activity. Such a move would require government regulatory and industrial intervention. Despite this trend, as the Federal Liberal–National government goes to its third term with a majority in both houses, a renewed industrial relations assault may eventuate consistent with these broader global trends. Whatever the future direction of healthcare in Australia it is clear that service is no longer seen simply in terms of a public good, part of the worker's social wage. Healthcare is now a commodity caught between the welfare state and market forces. Service provision is not optimized when subject to the vagaries of the market, with flaws in equality of access, price signals, and accessibility to, and understanding of, information. The work of health professionals stands poised between these two forces.

Index

Absenteeism   146, 176–7, 181, 184 n.5, 239
Accreditation   158, 160, 259, 264, 265–6
Acute Hospitals   191–2
Adverse (or Advanced) Incident Monitoring Scheme (AIMS)   266–7, 273 n.4
Aged Care Act (1997)   171
Agency labour   114, 115, 118, 128, 187, 190, 193, 194–5, 303
Agency theory   93
AGREE (Appraisal of Guidelines for Research & Evaluation)   273 n.3
Allied health   4, 16–17, 31, 33, 51–4, 55–6, 81, 83, 158, 299, 300
American Association for Medical Transcription (AAMT)   282
American Health Information Management Association (AHIMA)   285
Area Health Boards   78
Area Health Services   65, 68, 69, 70, 116, 118, 138, 216
Assistants-in-nursing   153, 155, 189
Attraction and retention   6, 38, 41, 42, 49, 98, 116, 126, 156, 162, 165, 170, 172, 187, 189, 190, 195–6, 197, 198, 200, 202, 204, 235, 237, 240, 302, 305
Audiology   16, 52, 159
Audit   152, 154, 158, 165, 181, 255, 269
Australian Council for Quality and Safety in Health Care (ACQSHC)   254, 263
Australian Council of Health Care Standards (ACHS)   265–6, 270
Australian Council of Trade Unions (ACTU)   24, 160
Australian General Practice Accreditation Limited (AGPAL)   265

Australian Health Care Agreements   13, 14, 21, 77–8, 150
Australian Health Workforce Advisory Committee (AHWAC)   34
Australian Health Workforce Officials Committee (AHWOC)   33–4
Australian Liquor, Hospitality & Miscellaneous Worker's Union (LHMU)   79, 83, 155–6, 158
Australian Institute of Health and Welfare (AIHW)   51
Australian Industrial Relations Commission (AIRC)   2, 24, 25, 75, 76
Australian Medical Association (AMA)   16, 26, 71, 72, 75
Australian Medical Workforce Advisory Committee (AMWAC)   34
Australian Nursing and Midwifery Council   189–90
Australian Nursing Federation (ANF)   16, 26, 71, 72, 76, 77, 78, 80–1, 82, 83, 85, 155, 157, 240, 300, 302
Australian Services' Union (ASU)   192
Australian Workers' Union (AWU)   192
Awards   66–8, 70, 74, 134–5, 300
'occupationally-streamed' awards   66, 69

Bargaining   63–4, 87
see also Enterprise bargaining
Agent   63
Cover   64, 84
Level   63
Scope   63, 84–5
Status   63
Base hospitals   237, 241, 243–4, 247, 301
Bed occupancy rates   140–1, 157, 193, 194, 212

308 *Index*

Benchmarking   21–2, 91, 92, 95, 101, 102, 158, 176
Best Practice in Health Program   214
Best practices   21, 209, 211, 217–18, 220, 224
Bracks Labor government   72, 76–7, 86
Brown Liberal government   79
Budget cuts   154–5, 235, 300
Budget-oriented control   257
Burnout   173, 176, 178, 180–1, 183
Business Process Outsourcing (BPO)   281, 282, 283, 294 n.4

Cain/Kirner Labor government   71
Camden/Campbelltown Hospital   268–9
Caring   171, 172, 173–4, 176–9, 180, 183
Car parking services   91, 92, 102, 104, 106
Carr Labor government   86
Casemix   21–2, 26, 53, 73, 75, 80, 150, 151, 154, 155, 161, 215, 235, 258
   see also Diagnosis related groups (DRGs)
Casual employment   5–6, 114, 115, 116, 126–7, 128–9, 190, 193
   Private hospital   122–3, 124–6
   Public hospital   117–19, 120–2
Centralization (decentralization)   5, 64, 68–9, 76–7, 84, 106, 235–6, 240, 248
Cleaners   17, 31, 79, 83, 125, 153, 155, 156, 305
Cleaning services   91, 92, 102, 153, 155, 157, 158, 159, 165, 192, 300, 301
Clinical autonomy   217, 254, 257, 266
Clinical culture   260–1
Clinical directorates   256–7, 258
Clinical Excellence Commission (CEC)   269–70
Clinical governance   7–8, 217, 253–5, 260, 270–3, 304
   Genealogy and scope   255–8

Clinical Information Access Program (CIAP)   264–5, 273 n.3
Clinical management   257–8, 266
Clinical services   91, 92, 98, 108
Clinical Support Systems Program   7, 215
Clinical workforce   44, 46
Collaboratives   259, 260–3, 272
Collective agreements   65, 66, 74
Collective bargaining   63, 84, 134, 146, 162, 241
Commonwealth Court of Conciliation and Arbitration   24
Commonwealth Industrial Relations Act (1993)   151
Commodification   279, 293
Community and Public Service Union (CPSU)   78, 81
Community health services   18, 216, 237, 241, 242, 243
Compensation systems   233, 243–4
Competitive tendering   23, 79, 92, 94, 114, 156
Comprehensive nursing   167 n.3
Conditions award   66
Consolidation of health services   209, 288
Consumer involvement   259
Consumers   8–9, 34, 43, 262, 298, 299, 302, 306
Consumers Health Forum   262
Contestability   155
Coordinated Care Trials   7, 214
Core competencies   93, 96, 216
Core services   92, 108
Corporate governance   257
Corporate Strategic Theory   93
Corporatization of General Practice   3, 15
Cost containment   19, 161, 172, 218, 253, 254
Cost minimization strategies   172, 176, 177, 178, 303
Cost-shifting   15, 142–3
Credentialing   264, 265, 290
Critical incident reporting   266–7
Cross-functional teams   223
Cultural change   7, 239, 249
Customers   139–40, 152, 166

Data generation 259
Data/information access 264
Data/information generation 264
Data/information review 264
Day-of-surgery admissions (DOSA) 213, 214
Demand management 212–13, 215
Dentists 16, 17, 31, 51, 52
Department of Administrative Services (DAIS) 78, 82
Department of Human Services (DHS) 70, 72–3, 75, 78, 79, 80, 82, 239
Diagnosis related groups (DRGs) 21, 22–3, 150, 151, 154, 155, 161
  see also Casemix
Dieticians 16
District hospitals 241, 242, 246, 247, 301
Doctors 16, 18–19, 42, 300, 304
Domestic work clause 135, 137
Downsizing 5, 95, 102, 106, 108, 166
Duty of care 177, 184 n.8

e-health 50–1
Emotional labour 170, 172–4, 177, 178, 180–1, 183, 302
Emotional work 172–3, 180
Employee empowerment 220, 223, 233, 246
Employee Relations Act (1992) 74
Engineering services 91, 92, 97, 98, 99, 102, 103
Enrolled nurses 16, 81, 155, 177, 189, 190
Enterprise bargaining (EB) 4, 5, 24–5, 25–6, 68–70, 74–5, 76, 79–80, 83–4, 105, 151, 155, 156, 162, 235, 240, 300
Escorting patients 135, 153, 158
Evaluation of Quality Improvement Program (EQuIP) 266, 270
Evidence-based medicine (EBM) 7, 254, 299, 304, 305
Excelcare 140, 141, 144, 145
Extensive work effort 151

Family and community service leave 66–7
Federal/state relations 4, 15–16

Female specialist workforce 44, 46
Feminization of workforce 5, 17–18, 46, 115, 302
Financial incentives 15, 198, 200, 201, 202
Fixed term employment 114, 119, 126, 127, 128–9
Flexible Firm theory 93
Flexible workforce 155, 233
Food services 96, 97, 98, 99, 100, 102, 104–5, 108
Foreign trained nurses 189
Foreign trained professionals 37

Gardens and grounds 96, 97, 102, 103, 104, 106, 108
General Practice 17, 302
General Practitioners 46–7, 301
Generational Health Review 78
Generic advertising 196–7, 198
Governance 258
Graduates of professional programs 35, 37
  Intake limitations 48–9
Great nurses 195–8
Guy Hospital model 22

Health care assistants (HCAs) 154
Health Care Complaints Amendment (Special Commission of Inquiry) Bill 269
Health Care Complaints Commission (HCCC) 262, 268, 269, 270
Healthcare reform 1, 5, 13, 26–7, 216, 224–5, 258, 298–9
  British and American research on 2–3
Health and Community Services Staffs Association (HCSSA) 71, 75
Health and Community Services Union (HCSU) 71, 75
Health and Research Employees Association (HAREA) 65, 66, 69, 120
Health Employees Conditions of Employment (State) Award 66
Health Employees Pharmacists (State) Award 66

Health Industrial Relations Strategic Advisory Committee (HIRSAC) 68–9, 70
health informatics 264–5
Health Insurance Commission (HIC) 285
Health insurance industry 285–6, 293, 294
Health Insurance Portability and Accountability Act (HIPAA) (1966) 284, 290, 294 n.7
Healthism 3
Health Managers (State) Award 66
Health Officers Association 66
Health Professionals Association (HPA) 75, 76
Healthscribe India 282–3, 286–7
Health Service Agreements 73, 215
Health Service Union of Australia (HSUA) 17, 71, 75, 99, 106
Hierarchy 19, 100, 215, 222, 224, 304
High Performance organizations 235, 305
Home and Community Care (HACC) program 265
Hospital Administrative Officers Association 72
Hospital in the home (HITH) 213
Hotel services 71, 72
Human kindness 181
Human resource management (HRM) 7, 131, 152, 221, 222, 223, 233, 238, 249, 299, 301
Human resource planning 76, 236, 239
Hygiene 171, 182

Incentive funding 21
India 8, 279, 281, 282–3, 286–9, 290–2, 293
Individual innovation 219–21
Industrial and Employee Relations Act 79
Industrial relations portfolio 82
Industrial relations reform 1, 2, 3, 4, 5, 74, 150, 162, 306
information and communications technologies (ICTs) 280, 281, 284–5, 289

Infosys 281
Innovation 209–12, 219, 224–5, 234–5, 304, 305, 306
Innovation in care delivery 212–15, 221–2
Innovation in structure and management 215–16
Inspectorialization 255, 259, 263–70, 272
Institute of Clinical Excellence (ICE) 269
Intensive work effort 151, 164, 165
interactive effects 177, 181, 183
International Labour Office 146
Intrinsic motivation 220, 223

Job redesign 152, 164, 165, 214
Johns Hopkins model 22, 155
Joint regulation 132, 134, 137, 138
Just culture 259, 263
Just in time 155, 158, 280

Kennett Liberal–National government 71–2, 73–6, 77, 79, 86–7, 91, 92, 101
King Edward Memorial Hospital 268
Knowledging 272

Labor Government 4, 21, 24, 48, 81–2, 83, 150, 151, 236, 238, 239–40, 248
Labour intensive 3, 19, 177, 232, 234, 299
Labour Market theories 93
Labour shortage 38–9, 190–1, 194, 195, 203–4, 299, 300, 303
Labour substitution 23–4, 42–3, 49, 55, 171–2, 177, 189–90
Labour utilization 19, 238, 248
Leadership 53, 219, 221, 222, 224, 239, 261–2
Legal right 137–8
Legislation 4, 24, 25
Liberal–National Government 4, 5, 15, 21, 25, 49, 67, 100, 150, 162, 192–3, 235–6, 238, 239, 248, 306
Licensing 290
Local bargaining units 68

Magnet hospitals 235
Maintenance services 5, 96, 97, 98, 99, 108, 114, 119, 192
Managed care 174–6, 177, 178, 179–80, 181–3
Managed care organizations (MCOs) 175
Management development 246, 250
Managerialism
  see New Public Management
Managerial prerogative 63, 86, 138, 142, 304
Marketing department 196, 198
Market-testing 91, 92, 95, 105
Medicaid 184 n.4, 294 n.6
Medical-clinical indemnity insurance 85, 160, 258
Medical coding and billing 280, 283–5, 286–9, 293
Medical practitioners 18, 31, 44, 49, 52, 67, 302, 303, 304
Medical professions 17, 65
Medical scientists 6, 81, 150–1, 152, 159–61, 165–6
  Processes of workplace change 161–4
Medical Scientists' Association of Victoria (MSAV) 71, 160, 162
Medical Specialties 16, 50, 138
Medical technology 8, 18, 163, 166
Medical transcription 8, 280, 281–3, 293, 303
Medicare 13, 16, 25, 26, 48, 184 n.4, 294 n.6
Medicare Agreements
  see Australian Health Care Agreements
Medicare benefits schedule 37, 52–3
Medicare Plus 52
Medicare provider numbers 46, 49, 81
Metropolitan hospitals 101, 120, 236, 241, 243, 244, 247, 301
Metropolitan Network Boards 73, 75
Multi-disciplinary care plans 53, 54, 300
Multi-disciplinary teams 22, 153, 224

Multi-skilling 125, 152, 154, 155, 161, 164, 165, 303

National Commission of Audit (NCA) 20
National Competition Policy (NCP) 5, 20–1, 91–2
National Demonstration Hospitals Program (NDHP) 7, 150, 214–15
National Health Strategy 19, 21, 151, 161
National Institute of Clinical Studies (NICS) 254
National Pathology Accreditation Advisory Council (NPACC) 160
Neo-Liberal 3, 20, 91, 94, 131, 298
New Public Management (NPM) 2, 4, 5, 19–20, 21, 26–7, 91, 112, 150, 175, 253, 298, 302, 305–6
New South Wales 3, 42, 64–70, 86, 131, 133–4, 145, 153, 154, 188, 216, 268–70
New South Wales Health Department 64–5, 68, 134, 138
New South Wales Labour Council 134
New South Wales Nurses' Association 65, 87, 134, 147
New South Wales Nurses Registration Board (NRB) 133–4
NSW Nurses' (State) Award 66
No blame 269
Non-clinical services 91, 92, 99–100
Non-clinical staff 66
Non-standard employment 112–16, 128–9
Nurse-patient ratios 77, 84–5, 238, 240
Nurse practitioners 5, 42–3, 82, 300, 303, 304
Nurse recruitment strategies 195–9
Nurses 16, 31, 49, 80–1, 82–3, 140, 152, 158, 165, 194, 196, 300, 302, 304
Nurses Act (1991) 133
Nursing education 189
Nursing graduates 188
Nursing homes 176, 179

Nursing shortages   41, 116, 187, 188–91,198
Nursing unit managers (NUMs)   6, 132, 135–6, 137, 138, 139, 140
  Process of workplace change   142–4
Nursing workforce   40–4, 187, 189, 301
  see also Casual employment

Occupational health and safety   114, 146, 157, 158–9, 173, 182, 184 n.8
Occupational Health, Safety and Welfare Act (1986)   184 n.8
Offshoring   279, 280, 282–3, 285, 288, 289, 292–3, 294 n.2, 303
Open disclosure   263
Organizational capability   180
Organizational cultures   180
Organizational innovation   222, 223–4
Organizational outcomes   7, 233, 234, 237
Organizational performance   170, 171, 172, 176, 183, 259
Organizational restructuring   55, 131, 251
Outsourcing   5, 8, 23, 91, 92, 161, 162, 163, 235, 279–80, 285–6, 293–4, 300, 303, 304
  Case studies   96–107
  Effects   94–5
  Reasons   93–4, 107–9

Paramedics   16, 17
Participative safety   222, 223, 225
Part-time employment   17, 83, 115, 120, 121, 129, 194
Pathology   5, 50, 91, 92, 96–7, 98, 99, 100, 102, 105, 159, 160, 161–2, 162–3, 303
Pathology Services Accreditation Act (1984)   160
Pathology Services Accreditation (General) Regulations (2001)   160
Patient-centredness   262–3
Pattern bargaining   69, 83
Performance framework   268

Performance indicators   98, 100, 181, 254
Performance management   140, 176
Performance measurement and management   181, 235, 265
Personal care assistants (PCAs)   171, 177, 189
Personal service attendants (PSAs)   6, 23, 24, 150–1, 152, 153–6, 164–5, 305
  Process of work intensification   156–9
Pharmacy   91, 92, 102, 104, 105
Physiotherapists   14, 16, 31, 50, 51, 52, 78, 192
Podiatrists   14, 16, 49, 51, 52
Poisons and Therapeutic Goods Act (1996)   133
Political theories   93
Post-Fordist   154
Poverty of interaction   182–3
Power imbalance   52, 304
Primary nursing   154, 167 n.3
Private health insurance rebate   15, 193
Private sector   15, 73, 81, 83, 112, 191–2, 305
Privicare   115–16
ProAct   142–3
Processes/Procedures of workplace change   132, 141–5
Psychological safety   219–20, 221, 222, 223
Public Choice theory   93
Public Hospital Nurses' (State) Award   134–5, 137, 141–2
Public hospitals funding   14–15, 72
Public Hospitals Medical Officers (State) Award   66
Public hospital workforce   65, 79
Public sector employment   86
Public Sector Management Act (1993)   78, 81
Public Service Association   66
Purchaser-provider   74

Quality (and safety)   1, 94, 97, 99, 101, 103, 108, 170, 171, 181, 183, 190, 235, 255, 266, 304, 305
Quality improvement   82, 141, 233

Quality Improvement Council (QIC) 265
Queensland 132, 190, 191–2
Queensland Nurses' Union of Employees (QNU) 192

Radiology 5, 50, 91, 92, 96, 97, 98–9, 100, 163, 303
  see also Teleradiology
Reasonable workload committees 147
Reasonable Workload Taskforce 147
Registered nurses 16, 41–3, 81, 135, 137, 144–5, 153–4, 177, 189–90, 196
Regulation 131, 133–8, 141
Residential aged care 170–2, 174
Resource management initiative 256
Retention
  see Attraction and retention
Risk management 27, 181, 254, 258, 304
Risk minimization 264, 266
Root cause analysis (RCA) 267
Rosters 66, 102, 118, 137, 157, 158
Royal Australian College of General Practitioners (RACGP) 7, 265
Royal Australian College of Nursing (RACN) 16
Royal Australian College of Physicians 7, 215
Rural labour market 97–8, 301
Rural workforce 5–6

Salaried medical officers 16, 18, 19, 78, 79, 152
Self-rostering 202, 203
Senate 4, 40, 41
Sensemaking 271
Sensitivity 173, 174, 180
Service agreements 155, 215
Severity Assessment Code (SAC) 267
Shift work 83, 126–7, 151–2, 158, 161, 163–4, 165, 196
  see also Self-rostering
  Back-to-back shift 194
  Shift self-selection 197–8, 201, 202–3
Skill mix 42, 190, 202
  see also Labour substitution

Social regulation 132, 137
South Australia 5, 22, 63, 77–84, 85, 86, 87, 147, 150, 154–5, 156, 164, 170, 171, 179, 184 n.7, 234
South Australian Health Commission 78
South Australian Salaried Medical Officers Association (SASMOA) 78
Speech pathologists 16, 51
Staff-patient ratios 137, 142
Stakeholders 256, 257, 271, 272, 298–9
State governments 85, 86, 101
State regulation 132, 133–4
Strategic Human Resource Management (SHRM) 223, 225, 232–3, 238–41, 250, 304, 305, 306
  Barriers and challenges 242–6
  For healthcare sector 234–6
  Index 241
Strategic human dimensions 180
Strategic planning 233
Stress 140, 146, 154, 160, 164, 165, 173, 194
Structural Efficiency Principle 24, 155, 211
Substantial change 132–3, 139–41, 145
Supply management 91, 102, 103, 104, 105, 106
Support workforce 31, 33, 119, 120
Surveillance 7, 139, 140, 141, 152, 165, 268, 304

Task reunification 154
Taylorism 163
Team-based job design 233
Team innovation 221–3
Team nursing 167 n.3
Teams 261, 264
Telemediated work 279, 294 n.1
Teleradiology 280, 289–92, 293
Temporary employment 117–18, 119–20, 123
Training and development 114, 116, 124–5, 127–8, 163, 177, 221, 304
Transaction Cost theory 93, 98, 103, 109

Turnover 86, 126, 146, 181, 200, 203, 204, 237, 239, 285

Unilateral regulation 67, 132, 137, 146
Unions 26, 65–6, 71, 74, 78–9, 83, 85, 87, 152, 240–1, 248, 299, 302
Union membership 64, 65, 71, 85
Union density 26, 71, 78, 85, 184 n.7
United Kingdom Centre for Health Improvement (CHI) 268
United Kingdom National Health Service (NHS) 18, 154, 180, 219, 220, 253, 255–6, 268
United States Joint Commission of Accreditation of Healthcare organizations 267
United States Veterans Health Administration 267
Universities 40, 43–4
Unlicensed assistive personnel (UAP) 153–4
Up-skilling 152, 154, 156, 164, 165, 303

Victoria 3, 5, 21, 22, 63, 70–7, 86–7, 91, 92, 101, 150, 153, 159, 160, 164, 165, 217, 235–6, 247
Victorian Healthcare Association 71
Victorian Health Issues Centre 262
Victorian Hospitals Association (VHA) 72, 73
Victorian Hospitals Industrial Association (VHIA) 74
Victorian Industrial Relations Commission (VIRC) 72, 74
Victorian Psychologists Association (VPA) 160
Violence in the workplace 184 n.8, 188

Vision 101, 218, 223, 261
Visiting medical officers (VMOs) 18, 78, 115
Voluntary Departure Packages (VDPs) 162

Wages 24, 31, 137, 189
see also Bargaining
Web of regulation 133
Wipro Ltd 281, 292
Workcover 158–9, 183
Work environments 170, 177, 179, 180, 194
Workforce 4, 16–19, 30–3, 44–7, 54
Workforce flexibility 5, 93, 94, 303
Workforce planning 33–5, 47–51, 56, 302
Workforce redesign 55
Workforce segmentation 38, 50
Workforce supply 49–50, 301
 Factors affecting 35–8
Working conditions 19, 25, 65, 86, 107, 146, 161, 182, 190, 225, 248
Working time flexibility 188, 190, 191, 196, 202–3, 204
Work intensification 6, 131, 132, 146–7, 150–3, 164–6, 188, 194, 299, 302
Work/life balance 189, 190, 194, 204
Workloads 6, 133, 137, 140–1, 147, 153, 163, 187, 194, 204
Workplace Relations Act (1996) 25, 75, 162
Work practices 132, 137, 211, 300
Work process standardization 264
Work time 50–1, 121, 188, 190, 191
Work value 87, 142, 147